the L-Shaped Party:

THE LIBERAL PARTY OF CANADA 1958-1980

McGraw-Hill Ryerson Series in Canadian Politics
General Editor — Paul W. Fox

POLITICS: Canada, 4th Ed.   Paul W. Fox
CANADIAN FOREIGN POLICY   D.C. Thomson & R.F. Swanson
THE CONSTITUTIONAL PROCESS IN CANADA, 2nd Ed. R.I. Cheffins &
R.N. Tucker

NATIONALISM IN CANADA   P. Russell
POLITICAL PARTIES AND IDEOLOGIES IN CANADA W. Christian &
C. Campbell
CANADA: A SOCIO-POLITICAL REPORT   R. Manzer
PRESSURE GROUP BEHAVIOUR IN CANADIAN POLITICS   A. Paul Pross

POLITICAL PARTIES IN CANADA   C. Winn & J.C. McMenemy
GOVERNMENT IN CANADA   T.A. Hockin
CANADIAN POLITICS: AN INTRODUCTION TO SYSTEMATIC ANALYSIS
J. Jenson & B.W. Tomlin
LOCAL GOVERNMENT IN CANADA   C.R. Tindal & S. Nobes Tindal
PUBLIC POLICY AND PROVINCIAL POLITICS   M. Chandler & W. Chandler
POLITICAL CHOICE IN CANADA (Abridged Edition)   Harold D. Clarke,
Jane Jenson, Lawrence LeDuc, Jon H. Pammett
CANADIAN FOREIGN POLICY: Contemporary Issues and Themes
Michael Tucker
CANADA IN QUESTION: Federalism in the Eighties, 3rd Ed.   D.V. Smiley
THE L-SHAPED PARTY: The Liberal Party of Canada 1958-1980
Joseph Wearing

FORTHCOMING

POLITICS AND MEDIA IN CANADA   Arthur Siegel

the L-Shaped Party:
THE LIBERAL PARTY OF CANADA 1958-1980

JOSEPH WEARING, D.PHIL.
Professor of Political Studies
Trent University

McGraw-Hill Ryerson Limited

Toronto   Montreal   New York   St. Louis   San Francisco
Auckland   Bogotá   Guatemala   Hamburg   Johannesburg
Lisbon   London   Madrid   Mexico   New Delhi   Panama
Paris   San Juan   São Paulo   Singapore   Sydney   Tokyo

The L-Shaped Party: The Liberal Party of Canada 1958-1980

ISBN 0-07-077869-8

1 2 3 4 5 6 7 8 9 0   HR   0 9 8 7 6 5 4 3 2 1

Printed and bound in Canada

Care has been taken to trace ownership of copyright material contained in this text. The publishers will gladly take any information that will enable them to rectify any reference or credit in subsequent editions.

Canadian Cataloguing in Publication Data

Wearing, Joseph.
   The L-shaped party

(McGraw-Hill Ryerson series in Canadian politics)
Includes index.
ISBN 0-07-077869-8

1. Liberal Party (Canada) - History.   2. Canada - Politics and government - 1957-1963.*   3. Canada - Politics and government - 1963-   *   I. Title.

JL197.L5W42   324.27106   C81-094132-5

To Sue, Peter, Alison and Timothy.

CONTENTS

FOREWORD xi
PREFACE xiii

1. THE LIBERAL PARTY, PRESENT AND PAST   1
   The Philosophical and Historical Traditions   3
   The Organizational Beginnings   6
   The National Liberal Federation   8
   Political Organization and the Federation   9
   Conservative Party Organization before 1957   13

2. DEFEAT AND REVIVAL (1957-63)   16
   The Kingston Conference and the National Rally   19
   Reassessment of the National Liberal Federation   20
   Organizational Revival   22
   Planning for the 1962 Election   30
   Election Strategy 1962   33
   1963 Campaign   40
   Conclusion   44

3. THE "NEW POLITICS" IN POWER (1963-68)   46
   Committees   49
   Patronage and the "New Politics"   51
   Financing the Party   58
   The 1965 Election   64
   The End of the Davey-Gordon Era   68
   The 1966 National Meeting   73
   The 1968 Leadership Convention   76

4. THE LIBERAL PARTY IN THE PROVINCES   81
   Newfoundland   87
   Maritime Provinces   89
   Quebec   96
      Old guards and new guards   96
      A model machine   105
   Ontario   108
      Funding the Party in Ontario   113
      *Party democracy — policy conventions and riding
         nominations*   115
   The Western Provinces   119
      The Davey strategy for revival   121
      Decline in the provinces: indigenous factors   124
      Provincial decline: exogenous factors   131
      The failure of federal leadership   135
      The future   138

5. CHARISMA AND PARTICIPATION (1968-71)   141
The National Office   144
Liaison — Advisory Groups, Political Cabinet, Prime Minister's
   Office   148
Political Cabinet   154
Prime Minister's Office   155
Participation and the 1970 Policy Convention   157
   Conclusion   172
Finances — The Attempt to Make the Federation Financially
   Responsible   173
Monitoring the Traditional Methods   180
Broadening the Base of Financial Contributions   183

6. SETBACK AND REASSESSMENT (1972-78)   187
The Trudeau Elections   190
Majority Government and Election Organization   192
The Fallout from the 1972 Election   199
The 1974 Election   202
Aftermath of the 1974 Election   204
Policy Conventions of the Seventies   206
National Office   214
   Women's and Youth Commissions   216
   Communications   219
National Executive   220
Finances and Fund Raising   224

7. POSTSCRIPT: REFORM PRE-EMPTED (1979-80) CONCLUSION   235
1979 Election   237
Rebuilding Begun   240
1980 Election   242
The Future   247
Conclusion   250

INTERVIEWS   253
INDEX   255

CHARTS, DIAGRAMS AND TABLES

Chart I   Relationship between turnout and the Liberal Swing in Ontario (1958-62)   38

Chart II   Liberal Results in Seats and Votes for Federal and Provincial Elections by Province (1956-80)   82-86

Diagram I   Liberal Party of Canada: Executive Office (1968)   146

Diagram II   Liberal Party of Canada (1970-79)   158

Chart III   Liberal Standings in the Gallup Poll (1968-80)   188-189

Table I   Contributions to LPC by Canada's Top 100 Companies (1978)   227-231

Table II   Contributions to LPC by Class of Contributor (1978)   233

FOREWORD

The publication of *The L-Shaped Party* by Professor Joseph Wearing marks a step forward in a new direction by the McGraw-Hill Ryerson Series in Canadian Politics. Although several of the previous seventeen books published in the Series have dealt with certain aspects of Canadian political parties, this study of the Liberal party is the first monograph in the Series to be devoted entirely to a single party.

For that reason alone it is a welcome addition to the Series. As observers have noted often, one of the most startling and unfortunate gaps in Canadian political literature has been the deficiency of studies of the Liberal Party of Canada. It is regrettable that so little has been written about a party that has dominated the federal scene by forming the government of the country during nearly two-thirds of Canada's existence. That lacuna has been partially filled by the recent publications on the Liberal party by Reginald Whitaker and Christina Newman. However, the former book dealt with the party from only 1930 to 1958 and concentrated on the subjects of organization and finance. While the latter monograph is more general, Professor Wearing's book picks up the history of the party at the point at which Professor Whitaker's study concluded and carries it forward to 1980.

The L-Shaped Party has more to recommend it than mere uniqueness. Although it deals for the most part with the federal Liberal party, it devotes a lengthy chapter to a description and analysis of the history and problems of each of the provincial parties. The explanatory text is embellished with a handy set of graphs depicting the fortunes of the Liberals in each of the ten provinces. There are also diagrams which portray the organizational structure of the federal Liberal party and its standings in recent Gallup polls. Two interesting tables list the financial contributions to the party by large corporations and other donors.

It is the theme of the book, however, which distinguishes it. Professor Wearing has focussed on the running battle between the parliamentary party and the extra-parliamentary National Liberal Federation. He documents very explicitly the see-saw struggle between the oligarchic inner faction, usually represented by the government of the day, and the populist elements in the democratic structure of the party. In doing so, he is concerned, of course, with a fundamental problem in modern mass democracy: the difficulty of maintaining a party which is responsible and responsive to its grass-roots members when the hierarchy in the party governs the country and must answer to Parliament and the electorate. In tracing the history of the Liberal Party of Canada from 1958 to 1980, the author shows how difficult it is to solve this problem.

Professor Wearing's analysis is engrossing, enlightening, and stimulating. He has not only searched the documentary sources carefully but he has interviewed many of the principal participants. He also does not hesitate to state his own strong opinions.

The result is a revealing and lively book which can be read with profit and pleasure by students, scholars, and laymen.

Paul W. Fox
General Editor

Erindale College,
University of Toronto,
October 1, 1980.

PREFACE

This is a book about that political organization known as the Liberal Party of Canada, beginning with the party at the nadir of its fortunes in the late 1950s, when the party organization created by King had virtually crumbled. A revival, which owed much to initiatives coming from the volunteer or extra-parliamentary wing of the party, saw the rise of a new elite who sought to make the party more centralized, but also more democratic, more open and more programmatic. They also believed that, by relying on the involvement and commitment of idealistically motivated volunteers, the party could be freed of its traditional dependence on government patronage and big business finance.

The reform movement at first appeared able to survive the challenge posed by the return to power in 1963, but the dominance of the parliamentary wing (the caucus, cabinet and the leader) became increasingly evident, particularly in the 1970s. With the Liberal government's defeat in 1979, the extra-parliamentary wing again sparked a new reform movement within the party. The astonishing turn of events in December 1979 and the subsequent victory in February 1980 ironically present the party organization with one of its most serious challenges to date.

For me, the task of trying to tell that story has been not a little daunting—how much more appealing to write about the more compact third parties in Canada! The Liberal party at times seems incredibly complex, at other times exasperatingly amorphous. Fortunately the number of Liberals who were anxious to help me and who believed that the party's story should be told as fully and as accurately as possible, far outnumbered those few who were anxious to give away as little as possible. The most valuable primary source material consisted of the correspondence, minutes and memoranda which the party's national office has generously deposited in the Public Archives of Canada. These papers, which cover the period up to 1973, are contained in well over a thousand volumes.

Since this book examines the organizing and financing of the Liberal party, it is in some ways a sequel to the very fine study of the party from 1930 to 1958 by Reginald Whitaker.[1] Like him, I have attempted mainly to describe how the party operates since this sort of factual information about the party has constituted a serious gap in Canadian political writing, as T.H.B. Symons noted in his Report to the Commission on Canadian Studies.[2]

[1] *The Government Party: Organizing and Financing the Liberal Party of Canada 1930-58.*

[2] *To Know Ourselves,* I and II, p. 70.

I believe the reader has the right to know that I am, among other things, a Liberal who has participated modestly in party activities over the last twelve years or so. It may not be any less difficult to be objective about another party than it is about one's own. Indeed, complete objectivity is probably neither possible nor desirable. It should be apparent that I am not an apologist for everything which the party has stood for in the period covered by this book. I admire idealism and regret cynicism, both of which have featured prominently in the party's history. The reader will have to judge whether I have given due regard to both. In one respect, I freely confess to a bias. I believe that the Liberal party, with all its faults and foibles, has made an important contribution to Canadian politics and that the party must periodically renew itself if it is to be a positive force in the politics of Canada's future. Those who believe that the Liberal party is perfect and needs no renewal or that it is beneath contempt and deserves to be eradicated—and either view has its adherents—will perhaps not want to read any further.

In the research which I did for this book, I received extremely able assistance from Corinne Wallace, Tony Keenleyside, Michael Jenkin and Christine McKennirey. I received research grants from the Canada Council and the Trent University Research Committee.

I am grateful to the Liberal party's various national directors, Torrance Wylie, Blair Williams, Gerry Robinson and Gordon Ashworth, who responded readily to what must have seemed like an endless series of requests. The staffs of the Public Archives of Canada, especially Dr. Margaret Mattson, the Parliamentary Library and the Bata Library of Trent University were also very helpful and courteous.

I want particularly to thank Barry MacDougall and Paul Fox who read the entire manuscript and made many helpful comments. My colleagues Denis Smith, David Kettler and Elwood Jones commented on various sections. Several Liberals checked parts of the manuscript for errors of fact: Gordon Ashworth, Gordon Dryden, Jean Fortier, Senator John Godfrey, Paul Klie, Blair Williams and Torrance Wylie. I alone can take credit for the errors and imperfections which remain.

Susan White, Dianne Thompson and Deborah Whyte typed the manuscript with care and amazing speed. My family showed understanding and impatience in just the right proportions, as did Elaine Maxymyshyn who was an editor with McGraw-Hill Ryerson, while the manuscript was being written. Peter Matthews edited the manuscript with exemplary skill and care.

Finally, I want to give special thanks to Tom Holmes of Harvard for providing an invaluable spark when the manuscript was in its final, but seemingly interminable stages.

Joseph Wearing
Trent University, March 1980.

ABBREVIATIONS AND SOURCES

Public Archives of Canada

Liberal Party of Canada Papers (LPC)
Progressive Conservative Party of Canada Papers (PC)
Charles Murphy Papers
Brooke Claxton Papers

The John Godfrey Papers are in the possession of Senator Godfrey.

Canadian Annual Review (after 1971, *Canadian Annual Review of Politics and Public Affairs) (CAR)*

Canadian Journal of Political Science (CJPS)

CHAPTER 1. THE LIBERAL PARTY, PRESENT AND PAST

On Monday, 4 June 1979, Pierre Trudeau drove up to Government House, casually taking his sports car through a few turns around the flower bed in front of the main entrance. With his accustomed insouciance, he was about to undergo something that normally fills Liberal hearts with disbelief and dread—the loss of power. Jack Pickersgill, a minister in two previous Liberal cabinets, betrayed a hint of his prejudice about such matters when he said that living under a Conservative government is like having a childhood disease: everyone has to experience it once, but never wants to do it again! So, as Pierre Trudeau went through the formalities of tendering his government's resignation to the Governor General, Edward Schreyer (whom Trudeau had recommended as vice-regal representative just a few months before), Liberals steeled themselves for another bout of Conservative government.

Although the electoral defeat of 22 May had made resignation virtually inevitable, it was by no means a crushing repudiation of the Liberal party. With 4% more of the popular vote than the Conservative party and 40% of the seats, the Liberals had a much larger parliamentary contingent than they had had after the routs of 1917 and 1958. But there were some distinctly ominous signs. Half of the Liberal MPs now came from one province, Quebec.

Less dramatic, but probably more significant in the long run, has been the steady diminution of Liberal strength at the provincial level which has been going on for some years: the loss of power in New Brunswick in 1970; Saskatchewan in 1971; Newfoundland the following year; Quebec in 1976; Nova Scotia in 1978; Prince Edward Island just a few months before the 1979 election. Even worse, in the four western provinces—where powerful Liberal premiers such as British Columbia's T.D. Pattullo, Saskatchewan's Jimmy Gardiner and Ross Thatcher, and Manitoba's Douglas Campbell, once held sway—there was only a single Liberal MLA.

The centre of the political spectrum is a notoriously difficult position to occupy strategically. In no Western democracy has a liberal party, which defines itself as being ideologically centrist and which faces major op-

1

ponents on both the Right and the Left, been able to survive as a major, governing party. The middle ground simply becomes untenable. Competition between parties of the Left and of the Right polarizes moderate opinion, particularly in jurisdictions that use the British electoral system of one-vote, single-member constituencies. Such an electoral system is fraught with danger, because a party can win a majority or sustain big losses within a spread of just fifteen percentage points of the popular vote. Standing in contrast is the principal alternative, proportional representation, which does not magnify gains or losses.

Some would argue that the Canadian Liberal party is not threatened by this sort of left-right polarization because all three major parties attempt to occupy the same central position. However, in three of the western provinces (i.e., except for Alberta), where the political spectrum is more relevant as a point of popular reference than it is in eastern Canada, polarization appears to have taken place already. The question is whether this trend will spread to the six central and eastern provinces, where the Liberal party forms the official opposition. It could be only a matter of time before a swing of the pendulum places these parties on the government benches again. Ontario and Quebec, because of their size, are the crucial provinces, although Liberal strength there could be deceptive. In Ontario, the Liberals are the official opposition by only the slenderest of margins and have slipped to third party status three times since 1943. The position of the Liberal party in Quebec, both federally and provincially, is perhaps stronger than anywhere else in the country—so strong, that it risks becoming identified in the rest of the country as a Quebec party. On the other hand, the political climate in Quebec has been so volatile over the last decade that one would be rash to predict the continuation of this Liberal strength into the foreseeable future.

At least twice before, the Liberals had been reduced to holding power in just one province after having suffered a crushing defeat in a federal election. After the 1930 election, they held only Quebec and, two years after losing in 1957, there was a Liberal government in just one provincial capital, St. John's, Newfoundland. In both instances, alarmed Liberals made prodigious efforts to rebuild the party. Deprived of the power and perquisites of office, the party had to fall back upon itself, on those outside Parliament and the provincial legislatures, on new generations of Liberals, and on liberal-minded Canadians who might be politically unaffiliated, but open to Liberal blandishments. In 1959, as in 1930, the party quickly rose above the nadir it had reached. By the time the Liberals won the federal election of 1935, they had regained power in every province but Alberta and had entered a coalition in Manitoba. Within a decade of losing power in Ottawa in 1957, they had returned to power there and in five provincial capitals.

The party's remarkable return to power in 1980 did not follow this pattern of rebuilding through the efforts of the extra-parliamentary wing at the provincial level. Has the traditional pattern now become obsolete or is the strength of the federal party in reality an illusion because it lacks firm foundations? By looking at how the Liberal organization has fared over the years since 1958, this book will attempt to answer those questions and show how the party has risen to past challenges or avoided them. Liberals, in common with the general Canadian public, have very little appreciation of even the party's most recent history. But in that story lie the lessons for the future.[1]

THE PHILOSOPHICAL AND HISTORICAL TRADITIONS

The ideological origins of the Liberal party of Canada lie within the corpus of nineteenth-century British liberalism, but the party's principles have also been very much shaped by Canadian circumstances and its own response to the problems that have arisen throughout the last hundred and fifty years of Canadian history. Its philosophical ideals are largely drawn from the heterogeneous collection of principles that make up the British liberal tradition, as one can readily see in perusing the political views of Canadian Liberal party leaders. In early nineteenth-century Canada, Robert Baldwin, arguing for the rights of an elected legislature against the presumptions of the Crown's representative and his Canadian advisers, found inspiration in the Whigs' belief in the suprem-

---

[1] The Liberal party has not had attention lavished on it by scholarly writers such as one might have expected. In the last few years, a start has been made on filling the lacuna. The most notable is Reginald Whitaker, *The Government Party: Organizing and Financing the Liberal Party of Canada 1930-58.* David E. Smith's *Prairie Liberalism: The Liberal Party in Saskatchewan 1905-71* is an excellent study of the party in one province. J.W. Pickersgill has very much a Liberal perspective in *The Liberal Party.*

There are several theses: P.H. Heppe, "The Liberal Party of Canada." Ph.D., Wisconsin, 1957; P. Regenstreif, "The Liberal Party of Canada: A Political Analysis." Ph.D., Cornell, 1963; J.W. Lederle, "The National Organization of the Liberal and Conservative Parties in Canada." Ph.D., Michigan, 1942; E.E. Harrill, "The Structure of Organization and Power in Canadian Political Parties: A Study in Party Financing." Ph.D., North Carolina, 1958; Brian M. McFadzen, "The Liberal Party and MacLaren Advertising Co., Ltd., 1957-65." M.A., Queen's, 1971.

A number of biographies provide valuable insights into the organization of the party, especially R. MacG. Dawson, *William Lyon Mackenzie King, 1874-1923;* H.B. Neatby, *William Lyon Mackenzie King: The Lonely Heights, 1924-1932* and *William Lyon Mackenzie King: The Prism of Unity, 1932-1939;* J.W. Pickersgill & D.F. Forster, *The Mackenzie King Record,* 4 vols.; J.L. Granatstein, *Canada's War: The Politics of the Mackenzie King Government, 1939-1945;* John English & J.O. Stubbs, eds., *Mackenzie King: Widening the Debate;* Denis Smith, *Gentle Patriot: A Political Biography of Walter Gordon;* Robert Bothwell, *Pearson: His Life and World;* George Radwanski, *Trudeau;* Walter Stewart, *Shrug: Trudeau in Power;* Anthony Westell, *Paradox: Trudeau as Prime Minister.* There are three notable autobiographies: Lester B. Pearson, *Mike: The Memoirs of the Right Honourable Lester B. Pearson,* 3 vols.; Judy LaMarsh, *Memoirs of a Bird in a Gilded Cage;* Walter L. Gordon, *A Political Memoir.*

acy of Parliament. George Brown's vigilance over Tory plans to aid the churches and to grant special school rights to Roman Catholics was likewise a typically whiggish response. Edward Blake, excoriating John A. Macdonald's government for its extravagance in building the Canadian Pacific Railway (let alone the whole question of state intervention in the domain of private enterprise) was in the best tradition of Gladstonian public frugality. The anticlericalism of the early nineteenth-century French Canadian *Rouges* came from continental European liberalism, though the ideas of British liberalism became more prominent in French Canada at the time of Wilfrid Laurier, who sought to avoid having religious differences as the basis of party politics. His liberalism was in the manner of John Stuart Mill and Gladstone: combining a belief in reform, progress, individual rights, parliamentary democracy and the perfectibility of human nature. The two election platforms in which he proposed free trade with the United States were quintessential nineteenth-century liberalism.

Mackenzie King's views reflected the new positive liberalism of T.H. Greene and L.T. Hobhouse in seeing the necessity for state intervention as a means of enhancing the individual liberty of society's weaker members. But King was not one to let his political ideals lead him into precipitate action. Apart from old-age pensions, his commitment to social security did not produce much legislation for over fifteen years until his wartime government accepted the Marsh Report—a Canadian equivalent of the social welfare plan devised by a British Liberal, Lord Beveridge, for postwar Britain. More recently, Pearson, with his extension of social welfare and his commitment to international as well as national conciliation, and Trudeau, with his return to an emphasis on individual rights (both legal and linguistic), have kept the Canadian Liberal party well within the mainstream of British liberalism—even when the latter has been reduced to little more than a rivulet.[2]

That is not to say that Canadian liberalism has always been faithful to these principles nor has it been free of the opportunism and moral flaccidity to which parties in power are especially prone. As two writers on Canadian ideologies have said, "practical politics tend to be not un-ideological, but ideologically fuzzy." Indeed, according to one study of the party, the conflicting strands of Mackenzie King's liberalism verged on hypocrisy as his government played its "by now familiar role as the defender of the people against the big interests and the defender of the big interests against the people".[3]

[2] W. Christian & C. Campbell, *Political Parties and Ideologies in Canada: liberals, conservatives, socialists, nationalists.* Frank H. Underhill, *In Search of Canadian Liberalism.* M. Hamelin, ed., *The Political Ideas of the Prime Ministers of Canada.*

[3] Christian & Campbell, p. 41. Whitaker, p. 141.

It would perhaps be more generous to say that the foremost Canadian Liberal leaders, whatever their philosophical underpinnings, have been pragmatists above all. Furthermore, the experience of practical politics has added some distinctively Canadian themes to Canadian liberalism, themes which—though distinctive—have not always been mutually consistent. In the pre-Confederation legislatures of the Canadas, Nova Scotia and New Brunswick, responsible government was the first big local issue to divide Tories and Reformers. After the cause was won, however, there was a party realignment, largely based on the religious controversies of the day, which put the Reform or Clear Grit opposition on the side of giving no state aid to religious denominations. Following Confederation, the Liberals in Ottawa were at best a loose amalgam of pro-Confederate Scotch Presbyterians (farmers from southwestern Ontario and businessmen from Toronto), anti-Confederate, anti-clerical Quebeckers, and other anti-Confederates of varying hues from Nova Scotia and New Brunswick. As the years passed, other strands were added to the Liberal party. From Ontario, came Oliver Mowat, the durable nineteenth-century premier and the first defender of provincial rights against centralizing Conservative governments in Ottawa. He allied himself with another Liberal premier, the nationalist Honoré Mercier from Quebec. When the Liberals, finally under Laurier, ended the long period of Conservative rule in Ottawa, they had become staunch defenders of French Canadian interests and provincial autonomy, although these two goals came into conflict when provincial governments in Manitoba and Ontario severely curtailed the use of French as a language of instruction in the schools.

The Ontario farmers who settled in southwestern Manitoba took their Scotch Presbyterian brand of liberalism with them and, in the other three western provinces, the lure of federal patronage permitted Liberal loyalties to take hold, at least to begin with. The Progressive revolt after the First World War was much influenced by American agrarian populism. It ended permanently the two-party system in Canada, even though the Progressives did not set out to create just another political party like the two older ones. Many of them took independent political action simply as a means of giving farmers a voice in Ottawa and of putting pressure on the Liberal party to recommit itself to the principles of free trade and the reform of government institutions. Others, like the United Farmers of Alberta, had more radical goals which the Liberal party could not be expected to endorse. And while most moderate Progressives gradually returned to the Liberal fold, the radicals became a nucleus of the socialist CCF party.

Electoral success (or the lack of it) also had its effect on what the Canadian Liberal party stood for. In the nineteenth century, the Liberal party, mostly in opposition in Ottawa and mostly in government in the provinces, was a staunch defender of provincial rights. In the twentieth century, the situation has been reversed: the Liberal party has almost monopolized power in Ottawa and provincial Liberal governments have increasingly become a rarity. During the latter period, when the federal Liberal party held power in Ottawa, it was not reluctant—at least until recently—to exercise federal powers vigorously. It won recognition of Canadian autonomy within the British Empire, mobilized the nation during the Second World War, introduced the social welfare legislation of the postwar period, and took responsibility for managing the Canadian economy on the Keynesian formula. When Newfoundland joined Confederation in 1949, the Liberal party had become the spokesman for the federal power and the wheel had turned full circle. Unlike the Maritime anti-Confederates of eighty years before who became Liberals, Newfoundland anti-Confederates became Progressive Conservatives and the Confederates, led by Joey Smallwood, became Liberals. (There was one notable exception: Donald Jamieson, who opposed Newfoundland's entry into Confederation, later became a federal Liberal cabinet minister and, later still, leader of the Newfoundland Liberal party.)[4]

THE ORGANIZATIONAL BEGINNINGS

The organizational beginnings of the Liberal party go back well into the nineteenth century, when riding organizations were created to elect Reformers to the pre-Confederation legislatures. Eventually modest provincial offices were established and, by the First World War, provincial policy conventions were held. Attended by hundreds of constituency delegates, they were held annually (or almost annually) in every province except Quebec and P.E.I. Thus, even though the party was soon dominated by its elected members, its origins nevertheless conform to Duverger's model of the mass-membership party—though membership was

[4.] In addition to the material mentioned in footnote 1, useful material on the early history of the Liberal party in the various provinces is contained in the following works: Martin Robin, ed., *Canadian Provincial Politics*; Hugh G. Thorburn, ed., *Party Politics in Canada*; H. Blair Neatby, *Laurier and a Liberal Quebec*; Norman Ward, ed., *A Party Politician: The Memoirs of Chubby Power*; Peter Neary, "Party Politics in Newfoundland, 1949-71: a survey and analysis", *Journal of Canadian Studies*, (November 1971); S.J.R. Noel, *Politics in Newfoundland*; L.G. Thomas, *The Liberal Party in Alberta: A History of Politics in the Province of Alberta, 1905-1921*; F.C. Engelmann & M.A. Schwartz, *Canadian Political Parties: Origin, Character, Impact*; W.L. Morton, *The Progressive Party in Canada*. See also my article, "Pressure Group Politics in Canada West before Confederation", *Canadian Historical Association Annual Meeting*, 1967. Wayne E. MacKinnon, *The Life of the Party: A History of the Liberal Party in Prince Edward Island*.

never large enough anywhere, with the possible exception of Saskatchewan, to really qualify for the adjective "mass".[5]

Before 1932, sporadic attempts were made to amalgamate these provincial associations into some kind of national organization: the policy convention of 1893, the creation in 1912 of a Central Information Office (with a young director by the name of Mackenzie King), and a National Liberal Advisory Committee three years later.[6] Typically, interest in party organization arose when the party was out of power and flagged when it got back into office.

The bitter party split over the conscription issue in the First World War gave the matter particularly pressing urgency. A convention was called in 1919, not only to elect a new leader, Mackenzie King, but also to deal with the party's organization. It approved the creation of the National Liberal Organization Committee with an executive (the leader and nine vice-presidents named by their respective provincial associations) and a national council (six from each province, including the provincial leader). A head office was set up in Ottawa with an organization branch and an information branch, incorporating the existing information office.[7]

As soon as the party regained power in 1921, everyone lost interest in the new organization. The provincial parties were slow to appoint representatives to the executive, as were the constituencies in meeting the $250 levy that was intended to finance the office.[8] Mackenzie King was wary lest it hobble him in his wheeling and dealing with both the Progressives and the factions within his own party. Gradually its functions were taken over by his ministers who, reverting to earlier practice, took it upon themselves to deal with the organizations in their respective provinces. The Central Office was kept active producing campaign literature in the 1921 and 1925 elections, but it was always short of funds.[9]

It was not until 1930 that, prompted by defeat and scandal, King was forced to reconsider seriously the establishment of a national organization. The scandal arose after it became known that the Beauharnois Power Corporation, which wanted a hydro-electric power

[5] Maurice Duverger, *Political Parties*, 2nd ed., Introduction and Book I. See also my article, "Ontario Political Parties: Fish or Fowl?" in Donald C. MacDonald, ed., *Government and Politics of Ontario*.

[6] Murphy Papers, vol. 34, folder 156, Party Organization, a memorandum printed for the 1919 convention; vol. 17, Laurier to Murphy, 17.11.15. Regenstreif, pp. 125-129.

[7] *The Story of the Convention and The Report of Its Proceedings*, pp. 203-204. Murphy Papers, vol. 17, folder 79, Murphy to Lemieux, 4.12.79; vol. 13, folder 59, Meeting of the Executive Council of the National Liberal Organization Committee, 24.2.20.

[8] Murphy Papers, vol. 17, folder 79, Murphy to Lemieux, 4.12.19; vol. 13, folder 59, Meeting of the Executive Council, 24.2.20; vol. 15, folder 72, Murphy to Kyte, 24.1.21.

[9] Neatby, pp. 327-328. Regenstreif, p. 134. Whitaker, p. 9.

concession on the St. Lawrence River, had given a large political donation to the party's chief organizer, Andrew Haydon. King got himself off a potentially dangerous hook by denying that he had any knowledge of the party's fund-raising activities. But the affair confirmed King's intention to institutionalize the distance between himself and those discredited individuals, the party's fund raisers.[10]

THE NATIONAL LIBERAL FEDERATION

In 1931, King revived the National Liberal Organization Committee which, a year later, gave birth to the National Liberal Federation. It was to be a true federation in which federal and provincial interests would have an equal voice and, in recognition of the federal principle, each provincial association would have an equal representation on the 69-member General Committee. (The name was later changed to Advisory Council and membership eventually increased to 236 in 1955). The smaller Executive Committee likewise recognized the principle of equal provincial representation.[11]

The Federation, unlike the earlier National Liberal Organization Committee, was to become a permanent fixture; however, there was an uncertainty as to what its functions should be—a situation that has a familiar ring today. Should it be the vehicle for gathering expert opinion on policy for the enlightenment of the parliamentary leadership or should it serve as a forum for the party rank-and-file to voice their policy concerns? Should it be responsible for keeping the party organization in good shape between elections? Would that in turn necessitate getting involved in patronage and fund raising? Should it run federal election campaigns or merely co-ordinate the campaigns of the provincial organizations? Should it confine itself simply to producing a newsletter or should it also get into the increasingly sophisticated business of advertising, marketing surveys, and public relations?

Vincent Massey—the patrician, first president of the Federation—gave his priority to policy and organized the first Liberal "thinkers" conference in Port Hope during the summer of 1933. Mackenzie King was, however, suspicious of Massey's attempts to shift the party to the Left and also saw the conference as interfering with the leader's prerogative to set party policy. Massey was allowed to hold the conference only if it had nothing directly to do with the Federation and King used the lure of an ap-

---

[10] Murphy Papers, vol. 11, folder 50, Murphy to Fraser, 18.8.26; vol. 28, folder 98, Murphy to Moore, 19.4.26. Regenstreif, p. 136. Neatby, *The Lonely Heights*, p. 385. K.Z. Paltiel, *Political Party Financing in Canada*, pp. 25-26.

[11] Regenstreif, p. 166-180. Interview with H.E. Kidd, 14.1.72.

pointment to the Canadian High Commission in London to make Massey promise that the Federation would restrict itself to organizational concerns in future.[12]

The Advisory Council of the NLF did provide a regular forum for policy debates and resolutions by party members, but it was not large enough to be considered a genuine gathering of the rank-and-file. With its deliberations held under the watchful eye of cabinet ministers, meetings generally praised the government; in fact, the absence of controversy prompted a later president, Senator Fogo, to tease delegates that they were not true Liberals in allowing so many resolutions to be presented and passed in such cursory fashion. Too much of the discussion went on in the smoking room outside the meeting hall and in the bedrooms of the hotel, he added. On the other hand, Brooke Claxton, a cabinet minister who described himself as "a kind of messenger boy" between the prime minister and the cabinet and the Council, warned the Advisory Council that, because the party was in power, they must be careful lest their resolutions put the government on the spot. On another occasion, recognizing that many of the delegates would like to have seen "resolutions put in sharper terms", he reminded them that the proper procedure was for the Council to pass general resolutions, which were put before the government confidentially—who then drafted the election platform. One wonders why he was so concerned, since the ministers kept careful control of the proceedings in any case.[13] Finally, meetings of the Advisory Council grew less frequent and, in the mid-fifties, took place at three-year intervals instead of annually as called for in the constitution. A suggestion made at the 1948 convention to hold a full-scale policy convention of rank-and-file delegates every four years was also ignored.

POLITICAL ORGANIZATION AND THE FEDERATION

While Massey's interest lay in the lofty concerns of policy, Norman Lambert, the first general secretary of the Federation (and later party president, when Massey got his high commissionership), was a master of political organization. But these concerns, like those of policy, encroached upon an area where the parliamentary party traditionally held sway.

From the days of Laurier, a system had evolved whereby key cabinet ministers from the various provinces took responsibility for party matters

---

[12.] Whitaker, pp. 37-43. H.B. Neatby, *The Prism of Unity*, pp. 38-39.

[13.] LPC, vol. 861, file: 1943 Advisory Council Proceeding of Meeting; vol. 862, file: 1948 Advisory Council. Meeting of; vol. 863, file: 1952 Advisory Council. Regenstreif, pp. 181-186.

in their own bailiwicks. The minister kept in touch with the MPs and defeated candidates in his province or region, looked for promising candidates, held nomination meetings, and was consulted by other ministers over the distribution of federal patronage in his area. Particularly in the later King ministries, these political lieutenants exercised formidable political power in their own right: such men as Fielding, Ralston and Ilsley from the Maritimes; Lapointe, Claxton and Power from Quebec; Murphy, Howe and Martin from Ontario; Dunning, Crerar and Gardiner from the Prairies. However, not every minister in King's cabinets had the appropriate talents. One who did, Chubby Power, commiserated with King: "Unfortunately, it is not always possible to make a good organizer out of a good Minister, and some of your best colleagues in the Cabinet were utterly incapable of understanding anything whatsoever about practical organization."[14]

A very different aspect of political organization under King was the completely informal network of personal contacts that he maintained throughout the country. The network was said to have consisted of several hundred names of people whom King had met in one way or another—a high school teacher, a farmer, a lawyer. Though not necessarily prominent people, they provided King with useful information about public opinion across the country on a level with which he, as a politician, had to deal. Although much of this was also done through his personal correspondence, every morning an official from the Federation presented King with a short list of those of his contacts who happened to be in Ottawa on that day. Depending on what was the current political problem, he might ask to have one of these people pay him a short visit. In a similar way, he kept in touch with his network whenever he travelled throughout the country. This had very little to do with the Federation; in fact, it was a function that a more active extra-parliamentary organization would have performed. In any case, it gave King a source of information that was very different from what came to him from the civil service, cabinet, or even the caucus.[15]

Because the party had been out of power when the Federation was established in 1932, Lambert had become very active in organizational matters. When the party returned to office in 1935, he hoped that the Federation would retain some responsibility in this area. He realized that it would have to have some influence over patronage, if it were going to exercise any real power. As long as Lambert was active, the party office did get involved in such matters, though more because of Lambert's un-

14. See my article, "President or Prime Minister" in Thomas A. Hockin, ed., *The Prime Minister and Political Leadership in Canada.* N. Ward, ed., *A Party Politician*, pp. 273-274.

15. Interviews with J.R. Scott, 2.9.72; Gordon Dryden, 18.9.79.

doubted talents than because of any formal recognition that this was an appropriate sphere for the Federation. Though it was described as "the gateway to department favours", the national office was not nearly as involved as Lambert would have liked. Ministers tended to know either too little or too much about what Lambert called the "business side" of party organization. Those who knew too little naïvely eschewed such partisanship; those who knew too much refused to share their patronage prerogative with anyone apart from cabinet colleagues.[16]

For his part, King regarded the whole patronage business as distasteful. Lambert was chafed by his leader's disdain, especially when it meant that King procrastinated over his appointment to the Senate. Years later, Lambert (by then a senator) was still bothered that the "business side" of political organization had "to be concealed from the public as something unclean and untouchable."[17]

Senator Fogo, who suceeded Lambert as general party factotum during the war and was formally elected president in 1945, was primarily a fund raiser and not active in party organization as Lambert had been. He believed that the party office should operate between elections only as a service branch with educational and promotional responsibilities and that it should not do very much even during elections. Allan McLean was styled National Director rather than General Secretary when he was appointed in 1945; but in spite of the grander title he seems to have been less of a force in the party than either Lambert or Fogo had been. In 1949, McLean was replaced by H.E. 'Bob' Kidd who, reverting to the earlier nomenclature, assumed the title of General Secretary. Kidd had formerly been an advertising executive with Cockfield Brown Inc., which handled the major share of the Liberal party's advertising business. His appointment has been interpreted as indicating a shift away from the traditional organizational practices of Lambert to the new emphasis on advertising, public opinion analysis and public relations. This, in fact, was where Kidd's responsibilities lay when he took up his position in the party office. Activity between elections was directed at maintaining a large mailing list (100,000 or more addresses) of people who "are potential points of strength throughout the country." But this concentration on so-called opinion leaders was diffficult to sustain. Publishing was very expensive, the provincial associations could not be counted on for distribution and it was difficult to get subscribers for the party's quarterly mag-

16. Whitaker, pp. 86-95.
17. LPC, vol. 86l, file: 1943 Advisory Council Proceeding of Meeting. Whitaker, pp. 91, 95-96, 103-104.

azine, *The Canadian Liberal,* even at the modest subscription price of $1.00.[18]

King may not have had much taste for party organization, but he saw the necessity for having people who did—and did not hesitate to blame them when things went wrong. With his successor, Louis St. Laurent, party organization got progressively less attention from everyone. Ministers became ever more preoccupied with the challenge of administering huge departments and could find neither time nor energy to undertake the inevitable travelling and speech-making required of those who became heavily involved in party affairs. In the immediate postwar period, Brooke Claxton, a cabinet minister from Montreal, had been the minister most active in such party matters as organization, advertising, publicity and general liaison with the Federation. When he retired in 1954, he left a gap which could not be filled by the remaining political ministers: an aging Jimmy Gardiner, a politically insensitive C.D. Howe and an ex-bureaucrat, Jack Pickersgill, for example.

The ministers may have become less politically-minded and less representative of their respective regions, but they refused to share their responsibilities. In 1945, the cabinet felt no compunction about summarily relieving the Federation of any campaign responsibilities without even consulting the party president, Senator Wishart Robertson. In the other postwar elections up to 1957, the Federation was usually represented on the campaign committee by its president, general secretary and associate general secretary; but campaign strategy, such as it was, remained firmly in the hands of the few politically-minded ministers. The result was that, according to John Meisel in his book on the 1957 election, there was really "no high command" in the campaign. The Federation had the more mundane task of acting as a "news exchange" and "clearing house". It produced a speaker's handbook, pamphlets, leaflets, free-time political broadcasts and helped with the leader's tour and national advertising. But even the important job of publicity was taken over by the party's advertising agency, Cockfield Brown, and the provincial party offices jealously guarded their own prerogatives in the campaign.[19]

---

[18] LPC, vol. 647, file: British Columbia Liberal Association, 1956-1957 1958-1959, Memo by Kidd, 24.9.57; file: Ontario Liberal Association 1950-52, Kidd to Hale, 30.3.51; file: British Columbia Liberal Assoc. 1953-55, Kidd to Deachman, 29.9.55. Interviews with Kidd, 14.1.72; Paul Lafond, 26.8.77. Whitaker, pp. 166, 185-194. Regenstreif, pp. 191-202.

[19] LPC, vol. 631, file: Office of the Prime Minister 1954-55, J.L. MacDougall to St. Laurent, 14.10.55; vol. 660, file: Ontario Liberal Association 1949, W.G. Hale to Kidd, 21.2.49; H.S. Hamilton to Kidd, 13.5.49; vol. 661, file: GE-1957 Ontario Liberal Association: Bulletins, "Organization Responsibility—Electoral Districts, 1952"; vol. 678, file:

By 1957 the Liberal party had become an extension of the cabinet and, when ministers went down like ninepins before the Conservative on-slaughts of 1957 and 1958, not much of the party was left.

CONSERVATIVE PARTY ORGANIZATION BEFORE 1957

It had always been part of the accepted political wisdom in Canada that federal success was dependent on having a strong provincial base, not least because of the value of provincial patronage in building a party organization. As one Conservative remarked, "Road Foremen are virtually Political Organizers."[20] Indeed, ever since 1896, a change of power federally had come in the wake of a series of victories by provincial wings of the same party. When the Liberals won the federal election of 1896, they held five out of seven provincial governments, having added two to the list within the preceding eight years. From 1900 to 1908, Conservatives replaced Liberals in the governments of four provinces and were on the point of winning a fifth, when they captured power federally in 1911. When the Liberals won the federal election of 1921, they held power in seven of the nine provincial capitals, having defeated four Conservative governments in the preceding six years. From 1923 to 1929, Conservatives wrested power from five Liberal administrations and won the federal election of the following year. The most spectacular affirmation of this pattern came in the next five years when Liberal governments replaced Conservative governments in six provinces and the Liberals, then holding power in eight provinces (if one counts the Liberal-Progressive government in Manitoba), went on to a landslide victory in the federal election of 1935.

Correspondence & Memoranda October to December 1961, Liberal Organization in the 1957 Campaign [written by Kidd]; vol. 647, file: B.C. Liberal Assoc., 1953-55, Memo by Kidd, "Record of Conversation with John L. Gibson, former Independent Liberal for Comox-Alberni, B.C.", 17.2.54; vol. 644, file: Working Group on Constitution (1), Report of the Committee Appointed to Study the Functions and Constitution of the National Liberal Federation [December 1959]; General Considerations, July 1959. Interviews with Pickersgill, 13.1.72; Kidd, 14.1.72; Lafond, 26.8.77. Whitaker, pp. 165-170, 179-194, 206-215. Meisel, pp. 63-72, 179.

20. PC, file P-4-G, Report of the Proceedings of the Organization Committee held at National Headquarters, 9-10.2.51. See also Murphy Papers, vol. 4, folder 17, Murphy to Bowman, 31.10.18. Claxton Papers, vol. 52, Claxton to MacDermot, 2.8.44; vol. 61, National Executive Committee Meeting, 24.2.54. LPC, vol. 715, file: Alberta Liberal Association 1963-65, Political Tape—Harper Prouse [sic], n.d.

The Conservative party accepted the traditional wisdom and, while the Liberals reigned in the 1940s and 1950s, the Conservatives hired a full-time national director, Richard Bell. They pioneered the establishment of an effective national office which operated between elections and which adopted the strategy of building up provincial Conservative parties, most notably in Nova Scotia, New Brunswick, Prince Edward Island, Manitoba and Saskatchewan. The Conservatives also sought to get on friendly terms with the Union Nationale in Quebec and the anti-Confederates in Newfoundland.[21]

Only Ontario was completely self-sufficient. Some associations, especially in the Atlantic provinces and Saskatchewan, depended heavily on financial assistance from outside to wage provincial election campaigns and to keep a provincial office open. There was even the occasional instance when the national headquarters took a direct interest in the "settlement of [a] Provincial leadership problem."[22]

The strategy of assisting provincial parties paid off. In the 1953 federal election, the two provinces (apart from P.E.I.) in which the party got its highest percentage of the popular vote were the two that the party held provincially. Although the 1957 election is remembered mainly for Diefenbaker's oratory, his victory owed much to the organizational base that had been built up in the provinces. The federal party got its highest percentage of the vote in the three provinces with Conservative governments and in another where it was soon to take power. The next highest per-

21. PC, file O-3-G, Memo from McRae, Chief Conservative Whip, 2.6.39; file O-5-G, Memo by Macdonnell, 23.12.46; file G-3-G, *passim.*; file P-4-G, Camp to Rowe, 6.11.56; vol. 11, Memo by R.A. Bell, 9.10.48; file H-9-G, A. Hamilton to G. Hees, 8.7.54; file M-5-G, Macdonnell to Bell, 26.6.48; Bell to Macdonnell, 8.7.48; files G-1-G and G-3-G, *passim.*; file: O-1-G, Bell to Drew, 14.4.49; W.H. Kidd to Drew, 9.11.51; file: P-4-G, Report of the Proceedings of the Organization Committee, 9-10.2.51. J. Granatstein, *The Politics of Survival*, pp. 157ff. J.R. Williams, *The Conservative Party of Canada: 1920-1949*, pp. 126-127. D. Camp, *Gentlemen, Players & Politicians*, pp. 50, 174, 180-184, 192, 216.

22. PC, file M-5-G, Macdonnell to Bell, 15.8.47; Bell to Macdonnell, 18.8.49; vol. 11, Memo by Bell, 9.10.48; file O-1-G, Bell to Drew, 23.8.49; file P-5-G, Kidd to Nowlan, 11.1.51; file F-4-G, Tory to Bell, 21.9.45, 3.1.46; Bell to L.W. Fraser, 11.10.45; Bell to Tory, 19.8.49. Camp, pp. 184, 192. The strategy could not be followed uniformly throughout the country. Coalition governments, in which provincial Conservatives were partners, complicated the situation in Manitoba until 1950 and, ostensibly, in British Columbia until 1951. There were doubts about the leadership of the Saskatchewan party. In Alberta no provincial Conservative party existed and federal Conservatives attempted to arrive at an "informal understanding" with the provincial Social Credit government and the federal Social Credit leader. The premier of Ontario, Leslie Frost, was cool to the federal PC leader, George Drew; although backroom relations between the two levels of the party were regarded as ideal and Frost supported Diefenbaker in the 1957 and 1958 elections. PC, file M-5-G, Macdonnell to Bell; file O-3-G, Report: Problems of Organization, file 1.11.44; file M-5-G, Macdonnell to H. Anscomb, 19.10.48; Bell to Macdonnell, 18.8.49; Macdonnell to Bell, 25.8.49; Kidd to Macdonnell, 16.11.50; files P-17-G, BC-B-1, BC-B-1a, *passim.* J. Manthorpe, *Power and the Tories,* pp. 45-46, 56.

centage but one was in Manitoba, where a revitalized Conservative party was to be victorious in the following year. The pattern of coming to power federally on the basis of provincial strength had been confirmed once again. The Liberals, one assumed, would attempt to follow suit.

CHAPTER 2. DEFEAT AND REVIVAL (1957-63)

When the voters surprised the Liberal party (and themselves) by not returning it to power in 1957, the situation did not look too serious—at first glance. In the popular vote, the Liberals had done marginally better than the Conservatives and held only seven fewer seats. But the Liberal party was not just a team who had lost the parliamentary Grey Cup by a mere seven points. The score was deceiving, since it did not reflect the fact that most of their star players had retired and their farm clubs had been losing for years! Key ministers such as C.D. Howe from Ontario, Stuart Garson from Manitoba, and Ralph Campney from B.C. were defeated and almost immediately withdrew from public life. The ministerialist underpinnings of the organization began to vanish like snow in spring rains.

Gordon Dryden, a young reform-minded lawyer from Toronto summed up the situation in a long memorandum which he wrote to Lester Pearson. He and his friend Boyd Upper had gone to Ottawa to discuss the party's problems with any senior Liberal who was willing to listen. Pearson was the only one who would. There were eleven political battlefields in Canada, said Dryden, and it was eighteen years since the Liberals had, as an opposition party, defeated an incumbent government. "Since 1943 we have been driven from control of 7 governments, in 4 by Tories under their own name and in 2 others by people more or less Tory under other names [presumably the Union Nationale in Quebec and Social Credit in B.C.]." In the United States, Dryden continued, the American parties appreciate the power and patronage that comes from controlling governments of key states. Our federal system provided similar opportunities in Canada, especially in Ontario where the time was ripe for the provincial Liberals to defeat "the strongest Tory government in Canada." A provincial victory there would help the federal party to win the additional Ontario seats which it needed to balance its preponderant strength in Quebec. It would also prevent the polarization between "Tories and Socialists" which had so weakened the British Liberal party. "When the party in the middle . . . gets down its leaders must be good politicians to keep the others on either side from joining battle on the issues over its prostrate body." In Ontario, the party had a good opportunity to demonstrate that it, rather than the CCF, was the alternative to the Conservatives. The object lesson would be no less relevant to the federal arena. A provincial Liberal revival in Ontario, then, was the key to ultimate success federally.

Dryden went on to outline the internal reforms which had to be made within the party before success could be won at the polls. The grass roots membership of the party had to have the opportunity of "being more than just cogs on a wheel in a machine thrown into gear every so often to elect someone else". At every level, executives could be made more effective if they were elected from below rather than appointed from above; general meetings at all levels had to be called more frequently; there had to be less secrecy in the party's finances—even if sources of funds could not be disclosed, reports could be given on how the money was spent.

While these reforms were urgently needed in every province and at the national level, Ontario was a good place to start. Dryden proposed amending the constitution of the Ontario Liberal Association so that more of the executive than just the president were elected by delegates to OLA annual meetings. The existing executive, he said, was weak and unable to direct the party's organization because the president was the only officer who had the authority which comes from having been directly elected. The Ontario office needed about five full-time organizers working in the constituencies to get good candidates nominated early. As well, research and publicity personnel were needed to counterbalance what the Conservatives got the civil service to do for them. Reforms of a similar nature had to be carried out at the national level of the party but, "while the federal field holds the glamour of the big league, it is in the Provinces that one finds the basis of political power in Canada." In fact, one of the basic assumptions of Dryden's plan was that there was one and only one Liberal party, federally and provincially; he did not question the Federation's original principle that "the provincial organizations together must make up the national organization". The federal leader had to become more involved in organizational matters than had been the case in recent years; but, if he tried to work either through members of Parliament or through members of the provincial legislatures, he ran the risk of reawakening old divisions. The answer lay in every province having a strong party executive which was "primarily responsible for organization" and was the common instrument for federal and provincial purposes.[1]

Initially, Dryden's memorandum had little effect. A leadership convention a few months later chose Pearson to succeed St. Laurent and

[1] LPC, vol. 724, file: Election Reports - 1965, "Memorandum concerning the Liberal Party in Canada after June 10, 1957." Letter from Dryden to the author, 26.5.75.

began to re-examine the party's structure and constitution. Within a few days, however, Parliament was dissolved for the second time in less than a year. The party was hardly prepared for its first election since 1935 as an opposition party. Senator John Connolly agreed to manage the federal campaign with the help of veteran Quebec politician, Chubby Power, and the Federation's general secretary, Bob Kidd. As Connolly recalled later, "We thought all we had to do was to push buttons and things would come alive; but there were no buttons. The former cabinet ministers had lost touch with the grass roots of the party; there were no lines to the provinces. There was simply no organization in the 1958 election".[2] The election results were an indication of how far the party's organization had slipped: the Liberals were reduced to just forty-nine seats and the Conservatives got the largest majority in Canada's history. It looked like they would be in power for a long time.

The Liberals were slow to recover. The parliamentary battle against the Conservative government had the first claim on Pearson's attention and he did not, at first, appear to show much interest in party matters. Much to their annoyance, Federation officials had to report not to him, but to his executive assistant, Mary Macdonald, who acted like a mother to Pearson and implied that she always knew what was best for him.[3] Bob Kidd, as General Secretary, continued his familiar preoccupation with expanding the national office's mailing list and saw better communications as the answer to the party's problems. Press coverage of the events that had preceded the party's defeat in 1957 had been marked by "a one-sidedness which was shocking", he said. The party could have "correct[ed] the impression" if only "we had had better communications within our party." (In the 1970s, this problem would be described as "a failure to explain our policies to the voters"!) The answer, according to Kidd, lay in "a list of names which runs to about 120 to 130 thousand, representing persons who are . . . .potential points of strength in the Liberal structure throughout the country. If we don't develop these points of strength, we won't have anybody who is prepared to stand up and answer an argument when it's presented to him in a neighbor-to-neighbor fashion."[4] Such an approach to political organization was soon to appear almost quaint in comparison to what followed.

---

2. Interview with Senator Connolly, 4.2.75.
3. Interview with H.E. Kidd, 14.1.72 and with J.R. Scott, 2.9.72.
4. LPC, vol. 647, file: British Columbia Liberal Association, 1956-57, 1958-59, Memo by Kidd, 24.9.57.

THE KINGSTON CONFERENCE AND THE NATIONAL RALLY, 1960-61

A first step in reviving the party came with the Kingston "Study Conference on National Problems" which was intended to produce policy ideas for the National Rally to be held in Ottawa four months later. The Kingston Conference was similar to the Port Hope conference of 1933 except that this time the suggestion for holding such a conference came from the leader himself. Like Port Hope, it was not to be an official party function; this was in order to attract "liberally minded people" who might not otherwise accept an invitation to attend a capital 'l' Liberal conference.[5] It was not the last time that the Liberals would thus attempt to lure new people into the party.

The Kingston conference did not give much evidence of democratization within the party because it was an elitist gathering of ex-ministers and prominent citizens who were unconnected with the party. In contrast to later conferences, it was of modest proportions—just ten papers were presented for discussion and there were only two hundred participants.

The National Rally was the first policy convention of rank-and-file constituency delegates since 1893. Pearson hoped that the Rally would produce resolutions that would become an electoral platform for the party. More shrewdly, those planning the Rally saw it as a means of recruiting "desirable supporters", of presenting to the public the image of a hard-working party, and of rekindling the enthusiasm of party members. To that end, the Rally was planned to give delegates plentiful opportunities to express their views and to break with the practice of King-St. Laurent conventions where delegates, often subjected to numerous ministerial speeches, had tended to feel "that they had come a long way at their own expense to act as rubber stamps."[6] The twenty-one policy committees engaged in what was, for the most part, free-wheeling debate. The proceedings were open to visitors, newsmen and delegates alike, but paternalistic supervision was still provided by Walter Gordon's Policy Committee, who felt obliged to kill a dangerously radical resolution which called for the admission of "Red China" to the United Nations! On this and other debates over medicare, withdrawal from NATO and NORAD, and free university education, the party's division into right and left wings was clearly perceptible, but mutually satisfactory compromises

---

[5] LPC, vol. 698, file: Meetings of the National Executive Committee 1959-60, Meetings of 5 & 8.12.59 and 19.2.60. *Mike*, III, 52. Walter Gordon, *A Political Memoir*, p. 86.

[6] LPC, vol. 687, file: Correspondence and Memos from October to December 1961, Dallas Taylor to Hellyer, 15.9.60 (Hellyer was co-chairman of the Rally Organization Committee); vol. 1134, file: Liberal Party of Canada Through the Eyes of Dick Stanbury, Feb., 1969

were eventually produced. Furthermore, the Rally did produce, as Pearson had hoped, a corpus of resolutions—like the promise to produce a national flag within two years of taking office—which gave the party an election platform as well as an agenda when they took power. While it was true that many of the ideas had their genesis in "thinker's" papers and that two years later Pearson spectacularly and unilaterally reversed the Rally's stand against Canadian acquisition of nuclear arms, the convention's resolutions at least gave the party leadership a framework of policy ideas from which it could and did work. They also provided the basis for a book by Walter Gordon, entitled *Troubled Canada* which was a polemical critique of Conservative government policies.[7]

REASSESSMENT OF THE NATIONAL LIBERAL FEDERATION

The redefinition of Liberal policies was accompanied by a re-examination of the party's constitution and organization. The old uncertainty about just what the Federation ought to do lingered on. The 1958 constitution declared that it was "the prime duty of the National Liberal Federation of Canada to foster study and research"; it also had "the power to co-ordinate the efforts of the provincial and district Liberal organizations throughout the Dominion". The provision of a standing publicity committee of the Federation implied a responsibility in this area; in addition, there were Advisory Council committees on credentials, constitution, resolutions, finance and organization, though these were to be set up only one month before an Advisory Council meeting.

The proper extent of the Federation's responsibilities was a bone of contention in the discussions that took place within the party over the next couple of years. The minimalist point of view was that the Federation was really responsible just for publicity and then only between elections, because an agency (in the past, Cockfield Brown) had taken over for election campaigns. The Federation had no responsibility, at any time, for collecting funds, which was done by a completely separate group of fund raisers. In the area of policy, a committee, appointed in 1958 "to study the functions and constitution of the National Liberal Federation", observed that "The Federation does not make party policy . . . Under the constitutional arrangements in this country responsibility for policy lies with the Leader and his elected associates"; it granted, however that "party members influence policy by resolutions and by dis-

7. D.C. Thomson, "Liberals Settle for the Middle Road", *Saturday Night*, 4.2.61. *CAR 1960, 1961*. Gordon, pp. 86-90, 97. Denis Smith, *Gentle Patriot*, pp. 77-81.

cussions at conventions and at meetings of the Advisory Council."[8] Lest that be too heady a whiff of power, Advisory Councils were admonished to give only "wise and prudent advice, and [to] be cautious of the responsibility and of the special problems which the Leader and his associates have when such advice is tendered. It is therefore important that the most representative and most responsible delegates possible should be sent to such meetings. A meeting of the Advisory Council can, and should, stimulate a loyalty to the Party and to the Leader."[9] The Committee dared to be more assertive on the subject of organization. It noted that, from 1945 to 1957, cabinet ministers in various regions of the country had gradually assumed responsibility for organization and "since the 1940 election there [had] been no official of the Liberal party holding the office or clothed with the authority of National Organizer as such." "The Party [had] had an object lesson in the campaign of 1958. Nine Ministers had been defeated and the gaps in organiation [sic] in that election were glaring." The consensus within the party was that there must be a national organizer to fill this gap.[10]

The maximalist, but minority, viewpoint, espoused by the Young Liberals, was that the Federation should be concerned with all five fields of publicity, policy, finance, research and organization:[11] Although this position appeared by 1968 to have won the day, in truth it cannot be said that the question is settled yet. One of the difficulties lay in how a major increase in the national office's responsibilities could be compatible with maintaining the federal structure of the party. The majority argued not only that the Liberal party had to remain a federation but that the drift away from the "fundamental concept of a federation based on a solid and well-grounded provincial foundation" had to be reversed. An Organization Committee Report to the 1958 Leadership Convention agreed that the increasing predominance of ministers in organizational matters up to 1957 had weakened the authority of the provincial executives and had been the cause of serious misunderstandings between them and the National Federation. The Report wanted a reaffirmation of the federal principle that gave primacy to the provincial parties, though it also saw

[8.] LPC, vol. 644, file: Working Group on Constitution (1) - National Liberal Federation, Report of the Committee Appointed to Study the Functions and Constitution of the National Liberal Federation, n.d. [probably December 1959]; vol. 864, file: 1958 Constitution.

[9.] Ibid., General Considerations, July 1959, no author.

[10.] Ibid., and footnote 8.

[11.] LPC, vol. 864, file: 1959 Advisory Council.

the need for a full-time national organizer who would act as a liaison between the leader and the various organizations and levels of the party.[12]

The maximalists who wanted to expand the Federation's responsibilities also pressed for changes in the structure which would have made it no longer a federation. Instead of Federation members consisting only of provincial associations and affiliated organizations they wanted *individuals* to be the members, thus making the party "a democratic body truly responsive to the wishes of the rank and file." In place of the provincial associations, it would be based on regional groupings of seven, eight or nine constituencies. This proposal was bandied about from one committee to another until it was finally rejected and the federal principle was reaffirmed once more. The only modest weakening of the federal principle was in the formula for provincial representation on the Advisory Council which was rechristened the National Council in 1961. Instead of equal representation by provinces, which had been the rule until then, the new formula took some account of differences in population. In general, however, the federal principle was reaffirmed and the centralized model rejected.

Finally, there was an attempt to ensure that conventions and Advisory Council meetings would occur regularly. During the mid-fifties, the Advisory Council had gone for three-and-a-half years without meeting, prompting an amendment in 1958 requiring that it meet annually. In 1959, for the first time, a clause appeared in the constitution specifying, with regard to national meetings or conventions, who was entitled to be a delegate and certain basic procedures to be followed in electing constituency delegates. A 1961 amendment required conventions to be called every five years.[13]

ORGANIZATIONAL REVIVAL

Apart from committee reports and constitutional amendments, there was not much interest taken in the party organization until the end of 1959. The first concerted attempt to address the shambles into which the party organization had fallen was taken by Walter Gordon at Pearson's request. Gordon recommended a personnel housecleaning at the national office

---

12. LPC, vol. 644, file: Working Group on Constitution (1), Draft - Confidential Preliminary Report of Organization Committee of National Liberal Convention - 1958.

13. LPC, *Ibid.*, Report of the Committee Appointed to Study the Functions and Constitution of the National Liberal Federation, 7.12.59; vol. 698, file: National Executive Committee Meeting December 1959. 1959-1960, Pearson to Matthews, 18.2.60; vol. 864, file: 1959 Advisory Council; file: Advisory Council Meeting - National Liberal Federation - 12.1.61.

and a campaign to raise funds from the usual corporate sources in order to eliminate debts and provide the national office with an operating budget. As a result of Gordon's continued prodding, James Scott, formerly executive director of the Ontario party, was appointed national director and Pearson approved the creation of a Leader's Advisory Committee, a strategy committee of his closest advisers which effectively bypassed such constitutional structures of the party as the national executive.[14]

Scott was a firm believer in the traditional techniques of riding organization: poll captains, house-to-house canvassing and even a thorough canvass by the candidate himself if he was nominated early enough to make that possible.[15] Such an approach to federal organizing suggested that the national director would have more direct contact with the constituencies than the federal model had permitted in the past. Scott and Connolly reassured provincial party spokesmen that Scott's work "would be co-ordinated with the activities of the existing provincial structures" and that the major responsibility would remain with the provinces until immediately before an election. A year later, Connolly reiterated that the appointment of a national organizer was not intended to centralize party organization through the national office but to facilitate co-operation "in the various provinces in order to achieve maximum results while maintaining the maximum of autonomy within the boundaries of each province."[16] The provincial presidents may have been reassured, but centralizing forces were at work nonetheless.

After just a year as national organizer, Scott had to resign for health reasons and Keith Davey, who had succeeded Scott as Ontario executive director, also followed him to Ottawa. The appointments of both national directors seem to have been made in a surprisingly casual manner. According to Davey, Pearson did not know that Scott was to be national director and Connolly first heard about Davey's appointment from Davey himself. (Connolly's recollection was that a committee including Pearson, Gordon, Martin and himself decided on Davey.)[17] In any case, when

[14] Denis Smith, pp. 57-59, 68, 83. LPC, vol. 698, file: Meetings of the National Executive Committee 1959-1960, Minutes of Meetings of the National Executive Committee, 5, 8.12.59.

[15] Before the 1955 provincial election, the candidate canvass was used as a model in four ridings held by the Conservatives: Bruce, Wellington South, Waterloo North and Kent East. In all four, the Liberal candidates—Ross Whicher, Harry Worton, John Wintermeyer and Jack Spence, respectively—won and continued to win in subsequent elections. Interview with Scott, 2.9.72.

[16] LPC, vol. 706, file: Executive Committee Minutes 1960-1961, Draft Minutes of National Executive Committee Meeting, 19.2.60; vol. 698, Meetings of National Executive Committee 1959-1960, Advisory Council 1959 Report of the Organization Committee; vol. 645, file: Hon. John J. Connolly, Connolly to Provincial Presidents, 14.2.61.

[17] Interview with Senator Davey, 15.1.72. Denis Smith, p. 371, n.42. Letter from Senator Connolly to the author, 20.5.75.

Davey arrived in Ottawa, he found that no one had a very clear idea of what he was to do. Officially, he had two bosses: Pearson, as party leader, and Connolly, as party president; in reality, but unofficially, he had one: Walter Gordon, who was the party's final authority on organizational matters.[18]

Keith Davey was a former broadcaster who had learned his first important lesson in practical politics at the age of twenty-three, as the campaign manager for a Liberal candidate in the solidly Tory riding of Toronto-Eglinton in 1949. There had not been much of an attempt at setting up a poll organization and, on the day of the election, Davey found himself with nothing to do. At five o'clock in the afternoon, he picked up a marked voters list and drove out to pick up eighteen Liberals who had not voted. The party lost the riding, but won that particular poll by one vote. After that, Davey was a firm believer in the value of a hard-working, carefully manned poll organization.

Davey had been a student at the University of Toronto where he met a number of other young Liberals who were all fascinated with politics. They started to become active in the party in the mid-fifties, but found that C.D. Howe and Walter Harris, who were the final arbiters for party matters in Toronto, had allowed the party to fall into the clutches of an ineffective, slightly corrupt group of hack Irish politicians with names like One-Eyed Sweeney and Chairman Mills. With the devastating Conservative sweep of all the Toronto and York ridings in 1958, there developed a Liberal power vacuum which this younger group moved quickly to fill. Calling themselves Cell 13, Davey, Dan Lang, Royce Frith, David Anderson, Gordon Dryden, Boyd Upper, Dick and Bob Stanbury, Jim Scott, Judy LaMarsh and Jim Service gathered together for dinner every Wednesday and plotted how to revitalize and take over the Liberal party in Toronto. It was surprisingly easy. Davey was elected president of Toronto and York Liberals in 1959. At his first meeting, he got the riding presidents to fill out questionnaires that asked for information on items such as riding constitutions, executive elections, frequency of meetings and size of membership. The Toronto riding organizations turned out to be largely a house of cards. Adopting the phrase—Work or Resign!—Cell 13 cleared out the dead wood in six months. In succeeding months, there were membership drives, campaign schools, policy committees and a dramatically transformed party in the heart of Tory Toronto.[19]

The national Liberal renaissance began in Ontario, where the whole organization was raised "like Phoenix from the ashes of 1957"—though it

---

18. Interview with Senator Davey, 15.1.72. Denis Smith, p. 83.

19. Interviews with Senator Davey, 15.1.72, 2.4.75. LPC, vol. 1134, file: Liberal Party of Canada Through the Eyes of Dick Stanbury, February 1969. *Globe and Mail*, 26.10.59. Denis Smith, pp. 81-82.

happened in a different way from that envisaged by Dryden in his 1957 memorandum. Under John Wintermeyer's leadership, there were signs of a provincial Liberal revival, but it petered out by the 1963 provincial election. Besides, provincial politics simply did not make the adrenalin of Cell 13 flow in the way that federal politics did.[20]

The members of Cell 13 were pragmatic, idealistic and naïve in more or less equal proportions and they all recall having had an enormous amount of fun with their politics. Their goal was to create a more open, democratic party, built on an active, involved grass-roots base, instead of relying on patronage to motivate the troops. But they also strove to establish a more efficient election organization which utilized the latest American techniques. Lastly, they wanted to seek out like-minded people throughout Ontario and the rest of the country who would assume leadership positions within the party and break up the tightly controlled riding associations which were all too common. For Stanbury, the movement was a "surge of democracy" which marked a dramatic break with the past. Other more prosaic commentators saw it as simply a stage in the familiar life-cycle, as one generation of party elders—having become more concerned with preserving their privileges than in demonstrating the energy and ability which got them there originally—is replaced by a new generation of young warriors.[21]

Davey described himself in his Toronto days as having been more activist and pragmatist than reformer; the same could be said of him as national director. A man with a big, expansive personality, a quick sense of humour and an agile mind that leaps from one subject to another as he talks, Davey's foremost concern in politics has always been to find out what will *work*, to come up with a *game plan*. His intuitions may not always have been right, but they were the product of a fertile, if unreflective, imagination. Davey had been the spark plug of Cell 13 and, as national director, he had more spark, flair and colour than any of his predecessors or successors, except possibly Lambert. He communicated frequently with Pearson and, at that time anyway, attempted to make the National Liberal Federation count for something. (In 1964, the name was changed to the Liberal Federation of Canada.) Davey's letters and memoranda to Pearson are fascinating, cogent documents; but party organization was not a subject that greatly interested Pearson and it is difficult to judge how much importance he attached to them. On the other hand, Pearson seems to have supported, at least in a general way,

---

[20] *Ibid.*, vol. 724, file: Election Reports - 1965 Post-Election, Memo, n.d., n. author [Dryden].

[21] Letter from Dryden to the author, 26.5.75. Interview with Senator Lang, 16.3.79. Godfrey Papers, A Commentary on Senator Stanbury's Paper "Liberal Party of Canada an Interpretation", 24.6.69.

what Davey and others were attempting to do or, at least, he did not oppose it. Of much greater significance were the ties between Davey and Gordon. Cell 13 had invited Gordon to join their group in the late 1950s and looked upon him as almost a revered father figure, a man who already had national prestige. Gordon, for his part, as a political neophyte, was anxious to make contact with people who could help him in his task of rebuilding the Liberal party. Until the miscue of recommending an election in 1965, he was Pearson's closest confidant on party matters; so, together with Davey, the party had direct access to the leader, though Gordon especially was often frustrated that Pearson's resolution so often lost the name of action.[22]

At his new post in Ottawa, Davey was anxious to use on the national level the methods which had worked so well in rebuilding the party in Toronto and Ontario. Later on, the new approach to stimulating greater involvement and more party democracy came to be called the "new politics"; initially, it simply meant getting new blood flowing faster through the old veins of the various provincial organizations. Dryden's prescription had been to rely on strong popularly elected provincial executives to revitalize their organizations, because interference from Ottawa would only exacerbate old divisions.[23] But, surveying the scene from Ottawa, it appeared to Davey that the existing provincial organizations could not be counted on to produce much rebirth according to the Ontario model. Newfoundland's provincial Liberal government could get Liberals elected in most of the province's federal ridings, but the premier, Joey Smallwood, along with the province's Ottawa representative in cabinet, Jack Pickersgill, ran the party in a completely autocratic manner. So much so that there were neither democratic nominations in the ridings nor a Newfoundland Liberal association to give even an illusion of democratic organization.[24] Similarly, New Brunswick produced its quota of "safe" Liberal seats in francophone ridings, but showed no signs of breaking with the traditional patronage politics that typified the area. Prince Edward Island was firmly in the grips of a Conservative government and so was Nova Scotia, where the Liberal party was controlled by older men with a losing record and a defeatist attitude.[25]

With the Quiet Revolution and an electoral victory in 1960, Quebec Liberals had achieved even more than their confrères in Ontario. For the

[22] Denis Smith, pp. 57-84. Interviews with Senator Davey 4.2.75; Senator Lang, 16.3.79; and Senator Frith, 24.8.78.

[23] LPC, vol. 724, file: Election Reports/65, Memorandum concerning the Liberal Party in Canada after June 10th, 1957.

[24] Interview with Pickersgill, 13.1.72. S.B. Wolinetz, "Party Organization in Newfoundland", Paper presented to the Annual Meeting of the CPSA, June 1975.

[25] LPC, vol. 794, file: Nova Scotia 1961-62, Memo from Davey to Pearson, 19.12.62.

moment, however, the provincial arena was the darling of reformers. A "New Guard" was beginning to take shape in the federal wing of the party and would eventually challenge the "Old Guard". But apart from the handful of English-speaking ridings in Montreal, Liberal affairs in Quebec, both federal and provincial, had traditionally been handled quite independently of the Federation and the Ottawa headquarters. John deB. Payne, an Anglophone Quebecker on the national executive warned Davey, "It is quite a jungle here and our French speaking friends will tolerate no interference, no matter how innocent, from an Anglo-Saxon."[26]

Before the 1962 election, Quebec Liberals decided on an innovation which marked a sharp break with autocratic traditions there. Instead of candidates being hand-picked by the Quebec federal leader, it was decided that there should be democratic nominating conventions in every riding according to ground rules agreed upon at the 1961 annual meeting of the Quebec Liberal Federation. The Conservative-held riding of St. Lawrence-St. George became a kind of "pilot operation" for the new procedures. As one of the so-called "English ridings" it was one which the national headquarters could monitor, but it put the party elite in a real dilemma. One of the candidates, William Pugsley, had the support of Claude Richardson, who had been the riding's MP from 1954 to 1958. In addition, Pugsley attempted to obtain the kind of official endorsement which used to be given, but Payne got Pearson to write to Pugsley saying that the convention would be "a free and open one." Pearson went on to assure him that "no one in Ottawa or in Montreal connected with the Party in any official capacity, and that includes myself, would try to impose any particular candidate on the delegates." The other candidate was a young lawyer by the name of John Turner. There was no question but that Payne and Davey preferred Turner and believed he was the only possible candidate who could win the riding. On the other hand, they wanted to "carry through with our plan to make the convention in St. Lawrence-St. George the most open and above-board convention on the Island." Pugsley and Richardson attempted to create all sorts of obstacles: they claimed that Turner had a letter declaring he was the chosen candidate and Richardson even talked of calling an independent convention. Payne assured Pearson that no one on the Montreal campaign committee had indicated any preference, although privately Davey promised Turner that Maurice Sauvé and Payne would work for him "to the extent that this is politically feasible." He added that "there would appear to be very little that I can contribute from here but I do want you to realize that you need only call if you wish me to intervene or assist in

[26.] LPC, vol. 742, file: John deB. Payne, Payne to Davey, 17.12.62 and *passim*.

any way." But that appeared to be unnecessary since, as Davey informed Pearson, "Turner should win in a completely democratic manner." If virtue could triumph virtuously, then let it do so!—the only suggestion of manipulation being a postponement of the nominating meeting from January until May 1962. There was general relief when Turner won, finally, and Davey could make the claim that "for the first time in the history of the Liberal Party of Canada in Quebec a nomination convention will be held in each one of the 75 ridings."[27] Democracy was well on the way in Quebec.

The situation in Manitoba was mixed. The new leader, Gildas Molgat, was loyal to the federal party and judged that a strong federal campaign would help him provincially. He was surrounded by youthful, Ontario-style supporters, but the provincial party had been in serious decline since the defeat of the Campbell government in 1958 and, federally, there was a dearth of "big name" candidates.[28]

The Saskatchewan provincial party was showing distinct signs of revival under its new leader, Ross Thatcher, who had rebuilt the party from its grass-roots base; but he intended to keep it tightly under his own personal control. In Ottawa, he was regarded as a right-wing, boorish, unprincipled demagogue—completely antipathetic to the new style. Ottawa Liberals were also convinced that Thatcher wanted to create some tension with them in order to show his voters that "Saskatchewan Liberals would be scrappy fighters for Saskatchewan's interests." They suspected him of making deals with federal Conservatives, of deliberately getting inferior candidates to stand in the 1962 election, and of putting federal campaign money into provincial party coffers. That may, of course, have been an act of retaliation against Pearson who had been reluctant to help Thatcher in the provincial election of 1960. Pearson had seemed less than sympathetic in explaining to Thatcher that he wanted to stay away from an election where the main target would be the CCF: "Such an intervention will be interpreted in the east and in other industrial centres in a very unfriendly way by certain circles which we are trying to win over to the Liberal Party." Keith Davey expressed the same sentiments less delicately during another provincial campaign four years later: "Reformers from coast to coast would be scandalized by the knowledge that we are in bed with Ross Thatcher. It seems to me that this would, once and for all, doom any possibility of expanding our Party to the left." Saskatchewan had only one prominent Liberal who was primarily interested in federal matters, Otto Lang, a law professor at the Univer-

[27] LPC, vol. 692, file: Election—Quebec Campaign 1961-1962, *passim.*; vol. 687, file: Corr. & Memos from Oct. to Dec./61, "Ottawa Report" by Keith Davey, n.d.

[28] LPC, vol. 766 & 767, files: Manitoba 1961-62, Manitoba Liberal Association in 1961, Memos from Davey to Pearson and Connolly, 25.9.61, 26.6.61.

sity of Saskatchewan; but Lang was completely rejected by the provincial organization and Thatcher's antipathy for him was not going to be easily overcome.[29]

The situation in Alberta could not have been worse. A provincial Liberal government had not been in power since 1921 and a revival in the early 1950s had petered out. Harper Prowse, who had led that revival, recalled that when he became a Liberal (he was elected first as "Servicemen's Representative"), he was "looked on as some kind of spy for the enemy down east." Thereafter the party was plagued with frequent leadership changes and it was even alleged that the federal wing was afraid to give them any help for fear of earning the enmity of the province's Social Credit government. The federal interests of the party had fallen into the hands of a group of politically ineffective patronage lawyers. Occasionally, there were young, aggressive, transplants from the East, such as Allan O'Brien, who were eminently acceptable in Ottawa's eyes; but their numbers were never more than a handful and it was clear that the party utterly lacked an indigenous base within the province.[30]

Relations with the British Columbia Liberal party were more satisfactory if only because the federal wing had been the dominant partner ever since the Liberal-Conservative coalition lost power in 1952. The provincial leader, Arthur Laing, and his successor after 1959, Ray Perrault, were, like Manitoba's Gil Molgat, anxious to help the federal party. But the provincial Liberals were disheartened by election defeats and torn by internal feuding. By the mid-fifties, Ottawa was coming to the conclusion that it could win federal seats even if the party was not strong provincially. Within a few years, however, reforms in the party's constitution and the change of provincial leadership coincided with the emergence of a new reform group who attempted to wrest control from the older party men in the ridings. This development would normally have been welcomed in Ottawa, but Davey and Gordon preferred an even newer group of Vancouver businessmen in the ever-factionalized world of B.C. politics. The latter, however, were looked upon by the reformers as "fairweather Liberals" who were uninterested in the provincial sphere and

[29.] LPC, vol. 747, file: Saskatchewan Provincial Election - 1964, "Saskatchewan Provincial General Election 1964" [probably written by International Surveys Limited]; file: Saskatchewan Liberal Association, 1963-65, Pearson to Thatcher, 24.2.60; Thatcher to Pearson, 26.2.60; Memo from Davey to Pearson, 3.3.64; vol. 745, file: Provincial Associations - General, Charles Templeton to Davey, 15.1.72. David Smith, *Prairie Liberalism: The Liberal Party in Saskatchewan 1905-71*, chap. 8.

[30.] LPC, vol. 715, file: Alberta Liberal Association 1963-65, Political Tape—Harper Prouse, [sic], n.d. Interview with Davey 15.1.72. LPC, vol. 757, A Report on Preliminary Research Conducted in the Prairies for The Liberal Party of Canada by International Surveys Limited October, 1963.

even had a "vested interest" in keeping Social Credit in power.[31]

A future British Columbia cabinet minister warned Pearson that reform control of the executive had produced bitter divisions which had bedevilled the party in a recent provincial election. These problems had to be avoided at all costs in the federal arena. "Someone must be appointed to have full authority over the campaign in this province with full power to decide any questions arising without necessarily referring to the local people. Unfortunately, our new officers are not the type who will be easily put on the sidelines during an election. Possibly the answer would be for you to appoint a personal representative in this province."[32]

PLANNING FOR THE 1962 ELECTION

This may have been the genesis of a device that was developed in order to deal with such an array of provincial problems and situations as was evident in the late fifties and early sixties. It was typical of Davey's approach to politics that the solution was a simple, straight-forward pragmatic one: set up a federal campaign committee in each province with a chairman appointed by Pearson as leader of the party. The official reason given for such centralization was that "A provincial executive's function is both federal and provincial, but the campaign committee is federal," or, more simply, that the leader appointed the committee chairman for the same reason that a campaign manager in a constituency was appointed by the candidate rather than elected by the riding association. The provincial executives were given assurances that only a federal campaign committee was being established in each province, *not* a separate federal organization;[33] but Davey admitted that the federal campaign committees gave "some kind of unilateral monolithic control—at least for purposes of the national campaign."[34] They were to provide, in each province, the same sort of urban, sophisticated, youthful, modern leadership which the resurgent Toronto-based Liberals were attempting to establish in Ottawa. The search for constituency candidates, who broadly fit the image which the party was attempting to project, was probably the

---

[31] LPC, vol. 647, 648, 649, 760, 761, 762, *passim.*, especially vol. 762, file: Vancouver Centre 1960-63, D.S. Moir to Davey, 22.1.62; vol. 761, file: B.C. Liberal Association 1961, Davey to Pearson, 21.9.61; Alistair Fraser to Pearson, 17.11.61. J.D. Ward, "Federal-Provincial Relations within the Liberal Party of British Columbia", M.A. Thesis, U.B.C., 1966, chap. V. Interviews with Senator John Nichol, 9.6.75 and with Professor Vaughan Lyon, 28.4.75.

[32] Confidential Source.

[33] LPC, vol. 737, file: National Campaign Committee, Minutes of Meeting—National Campaign Committee, 6.3.64, Denis Smith, p. 83.

[34] LPC, vol. 728, file: Federal Organization Confidential, Davey to Nichol, 31.1.66.

most vital function of the campaign committees. The "right candidate" might make the difference between winning and losing a constituency. They also had responsibilities in fund raising and in the renewed emphasis that was given to constituency and poll organization through campaign colleges for candidates and campaign managers, and campaign clinics for poll workers.[35]

Besides the federal campaign committee in each province, there was a national campaign committee with primary responsibility for two of the most important elements of the campaign: the leader and policy. It had grown out of the earlier Leader's Advisory Committee and, like the earlier body, was effectively under Walter Gordon's control. As the chief strategy planning committee for the next election, it virtually became the executive of the party and showed how easily the official party structures could be circumvented to suit the purposes of the party elite. It included the so-called "four horsemen" who led the parliamentary fight against the Conservatives: Pearson, Pickersgill, Martin and Chevrier; the president, past-president and national director of the party: Connolly, Matthews and Davey; and Pearson's closest advisers from the Opposition Leader's office: MacEachen, Lamontagne and O'Hagan.[36]

Not everyone was happy about these centralizing tendencies. One of the sternest critics of the innovation of the federal campaign committees was Norman Lambert. In correspondence with Pearson, he saw them violating the principle of "a democratically formed party organization" composed of two complementary parts: the parliamentary group and the Federation, the latter being "organized apart from the Parliamentary Party group in the form of local constituency and provincial associations to converge upon and to be served by the office of their national federation." Pearson replied that "it was largely due to the relative ineffectiveness of the Federation . . . that it became necessary to appoint Campaign Chairmen both at the Federal and Provincial levels", adding that "since 1957 we have passed through a revolutionary period in think-

[35] LPC, vol. 737, file: National Campaign Committee, Minutes for Preliminary Meeting for the Organization of the National Campaign, 9.12.61 (also in vol. 685); vol. 685, *Weekly Report*, 30.8.62, 22.2.62, 16.7.64, 12.11.64; vol. 693, file: Campaign Memoranda—Organization, Campaign Memorandum No. 1; vol. 696, file: Campaign Clinic.

[36] LPC, vol. 697, file: Leader's Advisory Committee 1961-1962; vol. 737, file: National Campaign Committee, Minutes for Preliminary Meeting for the Organization of the National Campaign, 9.12.61. Interview with Senator Davey, 15.1.72. Denis Smith, pp. 83, 371, n. 43. Smith quotes Tom Axworthy as saying that Connolly had been appointed president of the party instead of Gordon, partly to keep the traditionalists happy, and that the Leader's Advisory Committee was created in order to ensure that Gordon had effective control. Tom Axworthy, "Innovation and the Party System: An Examination of the Career of Walter L. Gordon and the Liberal Party", M.A. thesis, Queen's University, 1970.

ing of people in relation to political parties."

Lambert came back with the observation that the "revolutionary period" was really a "re-action to [the] excessive centralized direction and power" which had previously occurred during the Second World War and the following decade. During the thirties the provincial units of the party had been responsible for rebuilding Liberal strength, he said, but they had been rendered inoperative "by centralized domination of administration from Ottawa." C.D. Howe had become "the main-spring of the party organization" and "the disastrous result of 1958 was not so much a Conservative Party victory as a rebuke to 20 years of increasing centralized power". The provincial Liberal victory in Saskatchewan was an indication to Lambert that the pendulum was beginning to swing the other way. Under those circumstances, he concluded "that the greatest service which the National Liberal Federation Headquarters in Ottawa could perform would be that of a clearing house to integrate as far as possible and harmonize opinion throughout the Dominion, to be an accurate mirror and sounding board for the Prime Minister and the Parliamentary Party."

Commenting to Pearson on the letter, Davey agreed that the Federation should have a distinct and separate identity, "but I would fear for the parliamentary party's future if the organizational party was left to its own devices." What had prompted Lambert to write to Pearson was the appointment of the federal campaign chairman for Quebec. Yet Quebec was, said Davey, "a perfect case in point in proving the need of Federal Chairmen appointed by you. It will be a long time before the executive of the Quebec Liberal Federation gets around to worrying constructively about federal politics."[37]

Another important pre-election committee which revealed the extent of the party's new directions was the communications committee. It was first set up by Keith Davey after the 1958 election defeat as a Toronto-based public relations committee. Significantly, half of its members were politicians and half were professional advertising people, with many of the latter taking part in political activity for the first time.[38]

The national communications committee, which arose from its Toronto-based predecessor, included people such as George Sinclair, Hugh Horler, Richard O'Hagan, Alan Scott, George Elliott and Robert Smiley—all with MacLaren; Robert Gourd, president of a Quebec broadcasting company; John deB. Payne of Interprovincial Public Relations; Mike McCabe, a marketing executive with Lever Brothers; Joseph Clark, with a

[37]. LPC, vol. 744, file: PMO - L.B. Pearson 1964, Lambert to Pearson, 17.4.64; Pearson to Lambert, 27.4.64; Lambert to Pearson, 4.5.64; Davey to Pearson, 23.4.64.
[38]. LPC, vol. 686, Davey to Gordon, 26.9.61.

Toronto public relations firm; and two others with extensive broadcasting experience, Royce Frith (also president of the Ontario Liberal Association) and Don Jamieson. The chief political members were Walter Gordon; L.G. 'Bob' Giguère, a Quebec party organizer; Paul Lafond from the Ottawa party office; Tom Kent, Pearson's policy adviser in the leader's office; and Jack Pickersgill, MP. The committee was, however, chiefly composed of men who were professionals in the communications field, so its main thrust was clear. The committee oversaw the work of George Elliott at MacLaren and made recommendations on such questions as what public opinion surveys should be done, how Pearson should be prepared for television, and why advertising decisions should be centralized in Ottawa.[39]

ELECTION STRATEGY 1962

For good and ill, the new approaches espoused by these committees were very evident in the party's election strategy. So was the influence of the American pollster, Louis Harris, who provided the disturbing news that the public retained its admiration for Diefenbaker, if not his government, and saw Pearson as too indecisive. Gordon concluded that Liberal strategy should avoid attacks on Diefenbaker and concentrate on just a few "positive aspects of the Liberal program in simple concrete terms." "Pre-Campaign Strategy", written by Tom Kent in the summer of 1961, took for granted that Diefenbaker would again try to take an opposition stance, forcing the Liberals to defend the years of Liberal government before 1957. A Liberal offensive against the Conservatives, however, would ensure that the campaign was fought on issues which favoured them, he argued.[40]

The Liberals were not really sure how to present their leader. Many of them, such as Keith Davey, were greatly impressed with J.F. Kennedy and the Kennedy campaign of 1960. Indeed, they acknowledged using T.H. White's *The Making of the President, 1960* as a bible. They were aware, however, that Lester B. Pearson was a different sort of leader from John F. Kennedy. Having just turned sixty-five at the beginning of the 1962 campaign, Pearson was a generation older than Kennedy. He had a boyish charm which, although particularly ingratiating at the level of a small, informal gathering, was nevertheless quite different from Kennedy's athletic, masculine presence. Pearson's career, before becoming

[39] LPC, vol. 698, file: Public Relations and Communications, *passim.* Gordon, pp. 101-102.
[40] Denis Smith, pp. 87-88. LPC, vol. 692, file: Pre-campaign strategy 1961-62, "Pre-Campaign Strategy."

leader, had been devoted almost entirely to international diplomacy, whereas Kennedy had been brought up in the partisan atmosphere of Massachusetts Democratic politics. Even their wives were different— Jackie Kennedy, glamorous, thirtyish, from an aristocratic (if somewhat decadent) American family; Maryon Pearson, a grandmother better known for her quiet, acerbic wit.

Pearson's reputation as a statesman, which his Nobel Peace Prize served only to emphasize, was considered something of an embarrassment by party strategists. Because international affairs were thought to be of little concern to Canadians, Pearson was told to stick to domestic issues so that he could come across as a man of the people. His "reputation as 'foreign affairs expert - domestic affairs novice' . . . continues to be his very serious handicap.[41] "The leader is 'Mike'. He does best to sign his letters L.B. Pearson, but we should all talk about him as Mike." ('Lester', considered not to be a "strong name", was to be avoided completely.[42]) At its worst, this degenerated to an eternal fussing over Pearson's "image". On television, Pearson should wear a straight tie instead of his accustomed bow tie; when speaking before an audience, he should not use gestures and should keep his glasses off; he should not appear alone on television; he should revise his style completely, "abandoning all the trappings of oratory"; he should not appear to be haranguing his audience. If anything, such advice no doubt served only to increase Pearson's uneasiness.[43]

If Pearson could not be remade into a John F. Kennedy, at least the contrast with Diefenbaker should be emphasized in the campaign, said the party strategy: Diefenbaker's personality as opposition leader may have suited the mood of the country in 1957; but, after five years of Conservative government, the country was now looking for the "vigorous and calm" leadership that Pearson offered. Alternatively, because the party's surveys showed that the public had no very clear conception of Pearson, there were plans to portray Pearson as a leader who could "attract and lead a team that gets things done competently and sincerely in the national interest."[44]

One interesting device for promoting Pearson's leadership—though it never really got off the ground—was "Citizens for Pearson." This was an

---

41. LPC, vol. 712, file: Publicity Program 1961, "Suggestions for a Liberal Promotional Campaign."

42. LPC, vol. 692, file: Pre-campaign strategy 1961-62, "Pre-Campaign Strategy"; vol. 767, file: Manitoba Liberal Association 1961, Davey to O'Sullivan, 11.10.61.

43. LPC, vol. 694, file: Election 1963 Correspondence & Reports, Davey to Gordon, 19.3.63; Gordon to Pearson, 20.3.63; Belliveau to Pearson, 11.3.63; vol. 698, file: Public Relations & Communications, passim.

44. LPC, vol. 692, file: Pre-campaign strategy 1961-62, "Pre-Campaign Strategy", "Campaign Strategy; No. 1". Gordon, pp. 99.

idea that was obviously borrowed from the United States, where such committees are established in communities across the country to raise money and win support from individuals who might not wish to be associated with a political party. To Liberal organizers, it had the additional advantage of getting around "the encumbrances of the federation principle of Liberal Party control in each of the provinces."[45] But for whatever reason, this plan did not get very far.

On Diefenbaker himself, Liberal strategists were hesitant. They agreed that Diefenbaker was running a one-man government, but they did not think the voters cared about that. Furthermore, their surveys showed that Diefenbaker was more popular than his party, so the Liberals were extremely reluctant to attack Diefenbaker himself. Ten days before the election, Walter Gordon wrote to all candidates: "Rule One is don't attack Diefenbaker . . . Never—repeat never—refer to him. Always attack the Tories, without names." The official reasoning was that Diefenbaker would relish the role of martyr, but one senses that the Liberals were still more than a little wary of the man who, in 1958, had turned Pearson's first parliamentary sally against him into a rout of the new Liberal Opposition Leader.[46]

The chief organizational innovations of the Liberal campaign in 1962 were three: public opinion surveys and statistical analysis; standardized, nation-wide advertising; and campaign managers' workshops, called campaign colleges. The Liberals' employment of Kennedy's pollster, Lou Harris, is well known—though it was not publicly acknowledged at the time for fear that the Conservatives would cite this as another instance of American, or even worse, American *governmental* influence—within the Liberal party. At one time or another both Jim Scott and Keith Davey dismissed surveys as just confirming what was known already; but, after the election, Davey agreed that it was "not possible to overestimate the significance of the contribution Lou Harris made to our campaign" and he went on to acknowledge that surveys could be used even more widely throughout the country in the next campaign.[47]

Just as important as surveys were the statistical analyses of ridings developed by Daniel Lang, the Ontario federal campaign committee chairman. On the basis of such information, resources, both financial and organizational, were concentrated in those ridings which the party sup-

45. LPC, vol. 686, Peter A. Cadeau to James J. Moore, 9.8.61.

46. LPC, vol. 689, file: National Office, General Correspondence, Elections 1962-63, "Campaign College. How to Present and Stick to National Issues"; file: Election Campaign 1962 General Corr., Gordon to all Candidates, 7.6.62. Gordon, pp. 98.

47. LPC, vol. 769, file: Ontario Correspondence 1962, Davey to Winters, 9.7.62; vol. 698, file: Public Relations and Communications, Minutes of Meeting of Communications Committee, 18.7.61. Inteview with Scott, 2.9.72. Gordon, pp. 97-99.

posedly had the best chance of winning.[48] It also led to the overall decision to make a regional concentration of effort on Ontario and Quebec. The Liberals assumed that they could easily win at least sixty seats in Quebec. The Conservatives' extraordinary feat of winning two-thirds of Quebec's seventy-five seats in 1958 could not be repeated what with a Liberal government having won power in Quebec and Diefenbaker having been reluctant to give prominence to his Quebec ministers. A riding-by-riding analysis indicated that there were forty "winnable" seats in Ontario, twenty of them among the twenty-seven seats in the Clear Grit heartland of southwestern Ontario. It was calculated that, historically, no party had won 100 seats in Ontario and Quebec without forming a majority government; so from the spring of 1961, all pre-election effort was concentrated in Ontario.[49]

Before the 1962 election, the value of a good riding organization was rediscovered. Apathy, it was argued, had been a factor in the Liberals' crushing 1958 defeat in Ontario. The lower the turnout, the better the Conservatives did. Both Liberal experience and the information gathered from surveys suggested that the less committed voters tended to vote Liberal if they voted at all. It followed that an efficiently manned election day organization was vital in order to ensure the high turnout necessary to improve Liberal chances. Door-to-door canvassing has been a feature of election campaigning in Canada since the nineteenth century. Periodically, however, a party grows lax: new poll workers are not recruited and trained, and the poll organization—the infantry of a political party—becomes decrepit. By the early 1960s, the Liberals' poll organization in Ontario was in such a bad state that they started again to build it up "from point zero." David Greenspan developed the campaign college to train a whole new generation of campaign organizers. It was an intensive two-day course for candidates and campaign managers to teach them how to organize a riding campaign, how to deal with issues in accordance with party strategy, and how to project the candidate's personality. There were at least four such campaign colleges in Ontario before the 1962 election, as well as in British Columbia and New Brunswick.

In a properly organized riding, poll captains had to contact all their voters personally, but were told to give their attention to only two groups of voters: the uncommitted and the committed Liberals. In dealing with the "undecided", the main thing was simply to get the voter to associate the local candidate with the *Liberal party* because people voted for the

---

[48.] Interview with Senator Lang, 16.3.79. Gordon, p. 94. LPC, vol. 685, Davey's Weekly Report, 18.10.62.

[49.] LPC, vol. 707, file: MacLaren Advertising Co. Ltd. Correspondence 1960-1961, Minutes of fourth meeting of National Liberal Federation Plans Board, 13.4.61. Interview with Senator Davey, 15.1.72.

party rather than the man. (At that time, no party designation appeared on the ballot, so the connection between the candidate and the party was vital in riding campaigns.) Basically, though, it was more important to locate the known Liberals than to influence the others. The campaign through the media was "designed to sell and convince the voters en masse." It was the job of poll captains to locate the *individual* voters who had responded favourably to the media campaign and make sure that they cast their ballots on election day. Canvassers were not supposed to get involved in policy discussions—the fear being that New Democratic Party supporters would tie up Liberal canvassers with endless arguments.[50]

Several months before the campaign began, Alan Scott of MacLaren had argued that riding organization would be less important in the election than an intensive national advertising campaign. But, when the election was over, Arthur Ford, the veteran editorial writer of the *London Free Press*, gave credit to Ontario Liberals for having built an organization "which functioned more shrewdly and smoother than any political machine I have ever watched since the days when General A.D. MacRae was the campaign manager for Rt. Hon. R.B. Bennett in 1935."[51]

Looking at the election results, one could hypothesize that, if Alan Scott had been right, then the swing to the Liberals would be fairly uniform across the country. On the other hand, if an increase in voter turnout were accompanied by a larger Liberal vote, this would be evidence of riding organization effectiveness, especially if Liberal losses in 1957 and 1958 had been due, as some surmised, to Liberal absenteeism at the polls. Because campaign colleges had been used most extensively in Ontario, one could expect to see there a high correlation between turnout and increased Liberal vote, assuming that all riding organizations would not have been equally effective. A scatter diagram (Chart I) of the results provides more evidence for the impact of riding organization as opposed to that of national advertising, although it is far from conclusive. Both among the various provinces and within Ontario, swings were actually less uniform than they had been in 1949 and 1953. The overall turnout in

[50.] LPC, vol. 686, Jack Milne to Davey, 5.9.61; vol. 688, Davey—Correspondence & Memos 1962 (3), Dryden to Davey, 29.5.62; vol. 760, file: B.C. Liberal Association 1962, Press Release by D. Dunwoody, 12.4.62; vol. 685, file: Davey's Weekly Reports, 22.2.62; 30.8.62; vol. 769, file: Ontario Correspondence 1962 (1), Davey to John Paul, 9.7.62; vol. 693, file: Campaign Memoranda—Organization 1963, "Campaign Memorandum No. 1", 1963; vol. 696, file: Campaign Clinic. Interview with Senator Davey, 15.1.72. Public Archives of Ontario, "To the Liberal-Conservative Party of Ontario", pamphlet. PC, file: O-5-G, Hon. A.W. Roebuck, "Campaign Management and How to Win Elections", pamphlet.

[51.] LPC, vol. 686, file: Davey—General Correspondence & Memos, A.J. Scott to Davey, 2.8.61; vol. 769, file: Ontario Correspondence 1962 (1), clipping of *London Free Press*, 23.6.62.

Chart I **RELATIONSHIP BETWEEN TURNOUT AND THE LIBERAL SWING IN ONTARIO (1958-62)**

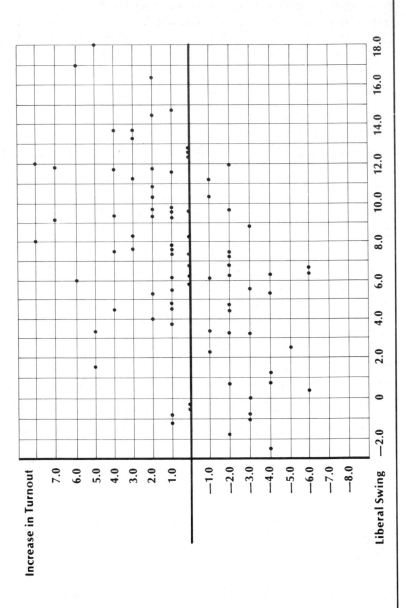

Ontario hardly changed between 1958 and 1962 and, although there is a rough correlation between turnout and the Liberal vote from riding to riding, many of the variations appear to be due also to regional and historical factors.[52]

Although the Liberal party had made a dramatic comeback since 1958, the election on 18 June 1962 did not return a Liberal government. The results were Conservatives 116, Liberals 100, Social Credit 30, NDP 19. The Conservatives lost almost a hundred seats, but the Liberals picked up only half of these. The concentration on Ontario had paid off with the most dramatic gain in seats anywhere in the country. From fifteen, the Liberals went to forty-four, overshooting their goal by four. They picked up six extra seats in the Atlantic provinces, half of those coming from the traditionally Liberal strongholds in New Brunswick. In the West, despite some substantial increases in the popular vote, especially in Manitoba and British Columbia, they won only six seats—although this was an improvement from zero in 1958. But the most disturbing failure in Liberal calculations came in Quebec, where the party won just over half of the sixty seats anticipated. The Conservatives had lost heavily, as predicted, but Social Credit—a movement of rural protest which had appeared almost overnight—took twenty-six seats which the Liberals had expected to fall into their hands.[53]

John Payne attributed the disappointing Quebec results to "the failure of the federal Liberals to recruit new, energetic and young candidates, relying instead upon 'old hands'". The Liberals had lacked an effective Quebec spokesman, said Payne, and Caouette, the Social Credit leader in Quebec, had gone unchallenged. "His dialogue, though irresponsible, was in a language of the people. He aroused their emotions and their curiousity [sic]. He spoke as though he alone understood them and had a plan to solve their problems. The people were fed up, cynical and ready to gamble on almost everything." For the future, Payne advocated "an intelligent and skilfully executed propaganda campaign" with a distinctly regional character, conducted through the local media and relating Liberal policies to regional issues.[54]

---

52. For 1958-62, the standard deviation for Liberal swings in Ontario constituencies was 5.43; in 1949-53 and 1945-49, it was 4.55 and 5.03 respectively. (Constituencies affected in a major way by redistribution were excluded.) See also, J. Wearing, "How to Predict Canadian Elections", *Commentator* (February 1963), 2-4.

53. For a discussion of various aspects of the 1962 election see John Meisel, ed., *Papers on the 1962 Election*; for analyses of the rise of Social Credit in Quebec, see Maurice Pinard, *The Rise of a Third Party: A Study in Crisis Politics* and Michael B. Stein, *The Dynamics of Right-Wing Protest: Social Credit in Quebec.*

54. LPC, vol. 694, file: Election 1963 Correspondence & Reports, "Caouette, Social Credit and Quebec".

Across the country, candidates, organizers and provincial campaign committees agreed that, though the campaign had gone well in many respects and had got off to a strong start, it had faltered in the last two weeks. This view was confirmed by the Gallup poll which indicated that the party had lost the support of 7% of the electorate during the course of the campaign. There was also general agreement that the idea of the Pearson *team* had never really come across during the campaign. The party's pre-campaign training was well received, especially Ontario's campaign colleges. The attempt to standardize local advertising was generally supported in spite of having been only moderately successful. Liberals from the eastern and western provinces, however, complained that the national advertising campaign had been insensitive to the particular concerns of their regions and they asked for better representation on the National Campaign Committee. As we shall see, this resistance to the centralized campaign developed into a crescendo of criticism over the next few years.[55]

1963 CAMPAIGN

It was obvious that the Twenty-Fifth Parliament would not last very long. The minority Conservative government was seriously divided over the question of whether Canada should accept American nuclear warheads for the Bomarc missiles, which were placed in Canada as part of the NORAD defence system. Some Liberals, notably Walter Gordon, were convinced that the electorate would not maintain this faltering government in power and were eager for another election. It came following the defeat of the government on a non-confidence motion in February. Liberal hopes were buoyed up by a Gallup poll which gave them an eleven-point lead over the Conservatives.

It is often said that opposition parties do not defeat governments, that they defeat themselves. But one might have expected the Liberals in 1963 to have waged an aggressive campaign in order to do all they could to hasten the government's self-destruction. However Tom Kent, who wrote the Liberals' "Strategy for Victory, 1963" struck an oddly defensive note when he warned, "A lot of . . . people would still like to find reasons for not voting for us. We must avoid giving them reasons." As in 1962, Diefenbaker was an opponent whom the Liberals were not quite sure how to handle. The government was in such disarray that the Conservatives would probably not have much of a national strategy, said Kent. Die-

55. LPC, vol. 688, file: Davey—Correspondence and Memos 1962 (3), "Campaign Appraisal"; vol. 689, file: National Office: General Corr. Elections 1962-63, Davey to Elliott, 21.1.63; Stephen E. Patterson to Davey, 6.2.63. Denis Smith, p. 103.

fenbaker would no doubt want to run a campaign based on attacking the Liberals, but how much control would he have over his party's campaign? Furthermore, if the election became one in which politicians indulged in their favourite political sport of attacking the other parties, the Liberals would be outdone by Diefenbaker, Kent later recalled thinking. On the other hand, there was so much going against the government that Diefenbaker might actually be able to arouse voters' sympathies. These considerations led Kent to recommend an unusual strategy for an opposition party: "So far as criticism of the government is concerned, this must be the quiet campaign. The arguments against the government have to be stated—clearly and strongly. But all that means is stating the facts briefly; the facts make our case for us." The country wanted a decisive, purposeful government who "can face up to the problems instead of evading them . . . . If we don't get their votes, it will be because we don't look as if we truly have decisiveness and purpose."

A few weeks earlier, Pearson had upset many Liberals (including Walter Gordon) when he unilaterally changed the party's non-nuclear policy to one of accepting nuclear warheads so as to honour the Conservative government's NATO commitments. According to Kent's interpretation of the first unveiling of his strategy statement to the party's National Council and National Campaign Committee (which included Pearson), he had, in effect, gently reprimanded the party leader and warned against further such aberrations when he went on to say, "We have a programme which we put forward only last year. That programme was built on the statements of Liberal policy which were adopted five years ago, at the leadership convention of January 1958. It's a consistent programme. Either adding to it or subtracting from it at this stage would only be interpreted as political expediency." On economic policy, there was a Kennedyesque flavour to the notion that a Liberal Government would get the economy expanding again and thereby obtain the revenue needed to start contributory pensions and medicare. "Those measures are the second, not the first, priority. If we don't say that, they are unconvincing promises . . . . The basic need is to make our economy more prosperous, more productive." Lastly, though issues were crucially important, leadership was considered equally so. In 1962 the emphasis was supposed to have been on the Pearson *team*, even though that had never really been developed. In 1963, Kent judged that the mood of the country had changed in one short year. "The Diefenbaker style of leadership has failed. Another style of leadership is what is needed. We have it and we should make the most of it. Our campaign should emphasise Mr. Pearson personally. The team is still important, but it's secondary."[56]

56. LPC, vol. 689, file: National Office: General Corr. Elections 1962-1963, 12.2.63. Gordon, chap. 7. Kent to author, 21.8.80

As the campaign progressed, the Liberals' momentum seemed to peter out, as it had in 1962, and this was confirmed by the polls. Diefenbaker's counter-attack was much more successful than anyone could have anticipated when his divided government had been defeated in February and the Gallup poll showed that, by a narrow margin, Canadians still preferred Diefenbaker to Pearson. One of Pearson's aides floated the suggestion of "a slam-bang counter-attack on Diefenbaker . . . fight[ing] fire with fire, half-truth with half-truth"; but Davey continued to oppose an all-out attack on Diefenbaker. He suggested instead "a dramatic personalized ending" in which Pearson would give a list of specific pledges of what his government would do in "99 days to get the country rolling." The more immediate concern, however, was to get the Liberal campaign "rolling again"! Pearson accepted the idea though, as a historian, he was sensitive to any comparison with Napoleon's Hundred Days and changed it to "Sixty Days of Decision".[57]

The 1963 campaign organization was, in many ways, a continuation of what had been set up for 1962. But there were some significant changes. In Quebec, Bob Giguère, an experienced "backroom" organizer, replaced the more courtly but less effective Lionel Chevrier as chairman of that province's federal campaign committee and a search for new candidates produced men of high calibre such as Guy Favreau and Jean-Luc Pépin, although Pearson's about-face on nuclear arms kept Pierre Trudeau and Jean Marchand from becoming Liberal candidates until 1965. Ignoring Payne's call for distinctively regional advertising, the Quebec campaign of 1963 was more integrated into the national campaign than had been the case in 1962. The same advertising material that was supplied to the rest of the country was to be translated into French for Quebec. Davey told Pearson that "if the Quebec campaign was autonomous last June [1962] this time it is semi-autonomous". The surveys done for Giguère by International Surveys were remarkably accurate in revealing that, while Social Credit was gaining strength in ridings which the party did not hold, its strength was declining in ridings which it had won. This, together with an increased Liberal vote, would mean fifty seats for the Liberals, Giguère predicted. The actual results gave the Liberals forty-seven—a gain of twelve over 1962.[58]

In the western provinces, several initiatives were taken to improve the party's poor standing. Davey attempted to bring the Saskatchewan fed-

[57] Confidential Source. LPC, vol. 694, file: Election 1963 Correspondence & Reports, Davey to Gordon, 19.3.63. Gordon, chap. 7. J.M. Beck, *Pendulum of Power*, "Twenty-Sixth General Election."

[58] LPC, vol. 698, file: Reports to Hon. L.B. Pearson from Keith Davey—Election 1963, Davey to Pearson, 1.3.63; vol. 698, file: Public Relations & Communications, Minutes of Meeting of Communications Committee, 18.7.61, Memo from Moore to Davey; vol. 694, file: Election 1963, K. Davey, Giguère to Pearson *et al.*, 15.3.63.

eral campaign committee into line with the new Liberal style, as it was conceived in the East, by replacing Thatcher as campaign chairman. He met with Thatcher and Thatcher's chief fund raiser, McConnell, who looked to Davey like a 450-pound Goldfinger. They discussed the possibility of a new chairman. "It's got to be some bastard we like", said McConnell. Thatcher interjected, "There's no bastard in Saskatchewan I can't get along with." "Otto Lang?" suggested Davey. "That's the one bastard I couldn't get along with", replied Thatcher. But Lang was appointed, Thatcher's aspersions notwithstanding.[59]

In Alberta, a survey by International Surveys indicated that disillusionment with the Liberals and Conservatives was producing a swing to Social Credit, though half the electorate were thought to be uncommitted to any party and would decide on the basis of issues or candidates. Popular concern about unemployment and the need for a stable government was working to the Liberals' advantage. But Pearson was not a popular figure, particularly among female voters, and Liberals in general were viewed by some Albertans as *"mud slingers* and *whiners,* who had *no definite policies."* [60] The projected swing to Social Credit did not in fact materialize, but neither was there much of an increase in the Liberals' percentage of the vote. In Saskatchewan, the former CCFer, Hazen Argue, was unable to hold the Liberals' only seat; Otto Lang lost by a large margin in Rosthern and even the popular mayor of Saskatoon, Sidney Buckwold, made only modest inroads into the Conservatives' large majority. In Alberta, the victory of another well-known mayor, Harry Hays in Calgary South, suggested that the search for well-known local candidates paid off, at least in the short run, even though Hays had had no previous affiliation with the party.

Finally, British Columbia Liberals, although still beset with their own internal divisions, were nevertheless confident enough of how to appeal to B.C. voters that they decided to use their own advertising material instead of what was provided nationally.[61] Whether this had an appreciable effect on the campaign in that province is difficult to say; in any case, the Liberals' gain in the popular vote was better than average and parliamentary representation increased by three seats.

Overall, the campaign had been something of a disappointment. Again, as in 1963, the Gallup Poll indicated that the Liberals had *lost* support during the campaign, falling from 44% in February to 42% in the election. Although the Liberals won enough seats to form a government,

---

59. Interview with Davey 15.1.72.
60. LPC, vol. 694, file: Election 1963, K. Davey, George McKimm to Davey, 19.3.63, "Strategy for Victory". Emphasis in original.
61. LPC, vol. 698, file: Reports to Hon. L.B. Pearson from: Keith Davey—Election 1963, Davey to Pearson, 1.3.63.

they were four short of an overall majority. In the national office, there had been concern over the growing disenchantment of the electorate as the campaign had progressed. Newspaper reports and editorials had revealed a "weird atmosphere", a tendency to dismiss both parties with "a plague on both your houses." The campaign was seen as having failed to convince thoughtful voters that Pearson was the "truthful, down-to-earth, no-frills leader" that they apparently wanted. [62]

The Sixty Days of Decision had attempted to address this problem; but, significantly, party records reveal surprisingly few misgivings about certain other aspects of the campaign. Although the party had a program which it had developed in 1960 and 1961, it was overshadowed by campaign gimmicks like the Truth Squad—the Liberal keepers of Diefenbaker's conscience who kept track of his statistical and factual "errors" at Tory election meetings—and the colouring books, which lampooned Diefenbaker. Pearson himself blurred the party's program as he backed away from the commitment to medicare and overturned the party's stand on nuclear arms (although, by contrast, his clear and forthright support of bilingualism in December 1962 was certainly one of the chief reasons why the Liberals gained more seats in Quebec than in any other province). Campaign colleges and national advertising were not enough for a convincing electoral victory; but, even though the party had developed a program, the leader exercised enormous discretion to use it as he saw fit. Davey often declared that, as national director, he should express no views on policy, even privately; presidents of the party were, for the most part, equally reticent. Ironically, the national campaign committee had complete authority over the leader's travels about the country and were constantly giving him advice on *how* he spoke; but they provided no check on *what* he said even when, as in the case of the nuclear arms reversal, this caused serious problems within the party. It had been a carefully controlled, centralized campaign—except in one vitally important aspect.

CONCLUSION

Although the Liberals were just short of a majority in 1963, the party had, since 1957-58, made an impressive comeback. After April 1963, the extra-parliamentary wing faced another test. Would it retain its vitality and integrity as a separate body or would it again come under the domination of the parliamentary wing—especially the cabinet—as had happened after 1935? The manner in which Pearson had changed his

---

62. LPC, vol. 694, file: General Corr. Election 1963, K. Davey, Pat (PJP) to Davey, 20.3. [63].

position on nuclear arms was disturbing. The federal campaign committees were supposed to stimulate democratic revival in the provincial associations and had had some success. But they could just as easily become the means for imposing centralized control from the top. The next few years would be critical ones for the party.

CHAPTER 3. THE "NEW POLITICS" IN POWER (1963-68)

The Liberal party's return to power in April 1963 was both a vindication of the party reform movements which had begun in Ontario, Quebec and British Columbia, and a challenge to the effectiveness of the new party structures. For six years, the rebuilding of the party had been a central concern of many of the leading figures in the party who, since they were not MPs, used the extra-parliamentary party as a vehicle for their activities. Suddenly the position changed. The two elections brought a dramatic increase in the number of MPs; the acquisition of power created Liberal ministers, executive assistants, and a Liberal Prime Minister's Office. Inevitably, the significance of the extra-parliamentary party—the Federation, the national office—paled in comparison. Ministers had departments to run, cabinet meetings to attend, and the particular concerns of the party organization fell into the background. This is nowhere better illustrated than in the career of Walter Gordon. From having had the primary responsibility for putting together a national electoral organization, Gordon now had primary responsibility for reviving the Canadian economy.

The Federation's principal liaison with cabinet and caucus was through the regular meetings which Keith Davey, as national director, had with Pearson. Before April 1963 the arrangement had worked well, according to Davey; but afterwards it became much more difficult. Pearson was frequently presented with detailed memoranda on current party problems and with Davey's advice for action on those matters which the Federation could not settle alone. But Pearson was not one for taking immediate decisions at any time—except in the midst of a crisis—and too often party matters were allowed to drift in spite of Davey's prodding and Gordon's concern that essential decisions on party organization were not being made.[1]

---

[1] LPC, vol. 728, file: Federal Organization Confidential, Davey to Nichol, 31.1.66. Walter Gordon, *A Political Memoir*, pp. 188, 220. Interview with Senator Nichol, 9.6.75.

As national director, Keith Davey was anxious to maintain high visibility for the party—not least because the new minority Parliament was not expected to last long. People at the Federation were well aware of the historical problems of maintaining a good organization between elections, particularly when the parliamentary wing of the party was thoroughly engrossed in the business of government and parliament. Remembering that the St. Laurent cabinet had been blamed for allowing the party organization to atrophy after the 1953 election, there was concern about not dissipating the effort which had gone into building up the Federation between 1958 and 1963. It was absolutely essential, Davey told Gordon, that the parliamentary wing of the party not be allowed to gain control of the party organization. This was the opinion, he said, of the "new and younger wing of the Party", including most of the key campaign people, who were "genuinely concerned that the Party organization maintain its vigorous approach."[2]

More specifically, Davey saw four challenges facing the party: the need to broaden its electoral support on the left of the political spectrum; the need to alleviate strained relations with the new Quebec Liberal Federation; the need to broaden the party's base of financial support; the need to have grass-roots consultation over patronage. The way to meet these challenges, Davey told Pearson, was by continuing the process of party reform which had begun in Toronto with Cell 13, by applying at the national level the methods which had worked so well in Ontario. The key was to get new people involved in party activities; from this involvement would come a sense of commitment to the party, further recruitment by new members and a consequent ripple effect throughout the community. The new people who came into the party would bring with them new ideas, enthusiasm and idealism; the old, undemocratic, self-serving cliques would be pushed aside. Davey christened it the "new politics." "In the organizational sense, the new politics means new approaches to both political morality and practical political organization. I would suggest that the key words are 'involvement' and 'communications'. I think these two factors were an integral part of our campaign success . . . . The people who were primarily responsible for our 1962 and 1963 campaigns were primarily motivated by a mixture of altruism and affection for the Leader. These motives remain, but their interest can be sustained only if we succeed in finding new ways and means of involving these people between elections". To go back to the original challenges: democratizing the party's structures would attract small "l" liberal support which had gone to the NDP and to prairie Conservatives in the last election; the strained relationship with the Quebec Liberal Federation was

2. LPC, vol. 728, file: Federation Organization Confidential, Confidential Memorandum by A.B.M., 7.5.63; Davey to Pearson, 9.5.63.; Davey to Gordon, 30.5.63.

primarily due to the undemocratic way in which two by-election candidates were chosen—"a valid grievance", which could not be met by democratizing the organization there; the party leader should insist on contributions from individual party supporters in order to end the party's primary reliance on large corporate donations; the party should be consulted on patronage matters as a means of ensuring that popular, meritorious appointments were made. Davey concluded that "an integral solution to *all* of these problems is equally a first step towards 'the new politics': specifically, democratizing the Party structure."[3]

Davey urged Pearson to speak to these questions at the 1964 meeting of the National Council (the new name for the old Advisory Council) not as prime minister, but as leader of the Liberal party. With just a hint of hyperbole, he declared that it would be "the most significant speech on political organization which has ever been made by a Liberal Prime Minister." He made five suggestions:

1. To broaden the party's fund-raising base, announce the initiation of a National Liberal Union—a purely honorary club with a fee of $100

2. Call for a revision of the party's program by another thinkers' conference to take place in Kingston in September 1964; and by

3. A National Rally in January 1965 with the same format as the 1961 rally

4. Urge all Canadians to engage in political activity at the constituency level by joining the party of their choice

5. Announce that political patronage is being abolished.

As we shall see later, Davey was never quite able to make up his mind as to what should be done about patronage, and he granted that the last suggestion "would antagonize some of the 'old guard' and some of the Party faithful, particularly in the boondocks."[4]

At a party meeting in Toronto, Pearson took up the theme of the "new politics", defining it as "the dropping of narrow and nasty, short-sighted and selfish partisanship . . . politics that makes the appeal to the people that John Kennedy made in his inaugural address . . . . the fullest democratization of our party, in the sense that authority and policies must flow upwards from what we call the rank and file to those who have been chosen to fill positions of responsibility and authority in the party. That requires work on the part of the members of the party . . . so that the in-

---

3. LPC, *Ibid.*, 9.5.63; 4.2.64.
4. LPC, vol. 737, file: National Council Meeting, 1964, Davey to Pearson, 19.11.63.

volvement of the individual can be mobilized for the determination and pursuit of national purpose through national parties."[5]

At the National Council meeting, a number of changes were made in the party's constitution to give some concrete recognition to these goals. Party conventions were to be held every two years instead of every five. (The interim constitution committee had recommended that they be held every three years, but Pearson took the more populist position of having them every two years and, not surprisingly, the delegates supported him.) By providing that the convention—rather than the National Council—would elect the party officers and amend the party constitution, the convention effectively became the highest authority in the party. The other major change was to clarify the position of party committees. Before 1961, they had been only committees of the Advisory Council and had ceased to exist once it adjourned. The 1961 constitution had provided for standing committees of the Federation, while maintaining some of the Advisory Council committees; but the frequency of elections had prevented any of the committees from being activated. In 1964, they were all made committees of the Federation and were expected to become an important aspect of the "new politics". One major constitutional change which was rejected was a proposal by the president of the Young Liberal Federation, Michel Robert, to require a vote of confidence in the leader at a convention after every general election. Time, however, was on the side of Robert.[6]

COMMITTEES

Davey described the decision to reactivate the standing committees as "perhaps the most important step towards broadening grass roots participation in the formulation of Liberal policy." The policy committee, it was hoped, would become as active as the Quebec party's well-known Political Commission. The Committee decided, however, not to draft policy but to concentrate on setting up research facilities and directing programs such as the Liberal forums. These grass-roots assemblies were to be provided with written material by policy development groups, each composed of a few dozen people with expertise in various areas, while discussion leaders kept everything on track. Finally, in the "Party to People" stage, those who had attended the policy forums were to form poll subdivision committees, each of whom were to visit five homes a month to discuss topical questions and report back the the party's MPs.

[5] Quoted in LPC, vol. 685, file: Davey's Weekly Report, 26.3.64.

[6] LPC, vol. 1155, file: Minutes of National Council Meeting, June 1-2, 1964. *Globe and Mail*, 2.6.64.

Even on paper, the scheme was ambitious, but twenty-seven such forums were held throughout Toronto on the third Monday of each month. The policy committee and its chairman, Dick Stanbury, wanted to extend this format to the rest of the country as a means of involving "as many people as possible across Canada in the discussion and development of party policy and to provide machinery whereby a two-way flow of information and opinion could be created between the Parliamentary section of the Party and the Organizational section." Stanbury warned Pearson, however, that everyone involved in the forums had asked whether the government and the MPs were really going to pay attention to their deliberations. The committee itself wondered how seriously it would be taken by the cabinet when it was only rarely that even the caucus was consulted before government policy was announced in the House. Betraying its wishful thinking, the committee hoped that "pressure from the executives of the constituencies would be required to invoke a sense of thousands requiring cabinet to take notice."[7]

If the policy committee had difficulty carving out a sphere of influence for itself vis-à-vis the cabinet, some of the other committees had a similar problem with respect to the campaign structures. The organization committee, for example, had no responsibility for electoral organization except between elections when the federal campaign committee lapsed; but as long as there was minority government, that was unlikely to happen. Similarly, the finance committee was to look after financing only non-campaign activities and the Federation itself. The committee on communications and publicity was distinct, as well, from the committee that looked after campaign advertising; the former committee was concerned with such matters as a party newspaper. The committee on constitution and structures at least had an unencumbered mandate—it was asked to look at party procedures such as nominations and conventions with a view to encouraging large numbers of individuals to become involved in party affairs.[8]

The five standing committees apparently got off to a good start as far as their provincial level of operations was concerned. Nationally, they ran into problems. With the political situation so uncertain throughout 1964 and the first half of 1965, the standing committees tended to be overshadowed by the provincial campaign committees that were still active. Also, in a country as large as Canada, where communications entail enormous telephone bills and travel expenses, each committee had a budget of just $500 a year. It was not long before the policy committee in

---

7. LPC, vol. 685, file: Davey's Weekly Report, 15.10.64; vol. 738, file: NLF-Standing Committees, Stanbury to Pearson, 25.11.64; Minutes of Meeting of Policy Standing Committee, 20-21.11.64.

8. LPC, vol. 1155, file: Minutes of National Council Meeting, June 1-2, 1964.

particular concluded that it must lower its sights. Without any research staff at the national office, they could not attempt to have Liberal forums operating in every riding. The Federation did not hire its first researcher, Linda Walters, until 1966, by which time the committee had decided to concentrate its attention on promoting regional policy conferences. Although a research director, Dr. Dan Coates, was hired a year later, the policy committee realized that the Federation might not be able to finance a proper staff and wondered if a separate policy research foundation might not be more feasible.[9] As we shall see in chapter 5, this idea was pursued further. For the time being, however, it was premature to judge whether any of the standing committees would fill the important role for which they had been cast in the "new politics."

PATRONAGE AND THE "NEW POLITICS"

It seems that Davey was never completely sure whether he wanted to reform the way patronage was distributed or to abolish it completely. He was sure, however, when the Liberals first took office, that ministers had to be prevented from using their patronage prerogative to gain control over the party organizations in their respective regions of the country as had occurred in the past. Under the "new politics" as *Realpolitik,* the party organization was to be given some prestige and clout by having something to say in how patronage was distributed.[10]

Davey was apparently unaware that his predecessor, Norman Lambert, had had the same concern when the party had regained power in 1935. The Federation was then only a few years old and Lambert was of the opinion that only by having some control over patronage could it be assured of permanence. In addition, Lambert had been chief fund raiser as well as chief organizer and, as has been mentioned, he wanted a close link between patronage and fund raising. Whitaker found that Lambert was often influential in getting loyal Liberals small contracts, purchase orders, and legal business, though the Federation was "certainly not an automatic 'pass key' to the public treasury." Indeed, Lambert frequently experienced frustration over not getting co-operation on patronage

---

9. LPC, vol. 685, file: Davey's Weekly Report, 3.6.65; vol. 744, file: PMO - L.B. Pearson 1964, Davey to Pearson, 3.12.64; file: PMO - L.B. Pearson 1965-66, Davey to Pearson, 11.2.65; vol. 737, file: National Executive Committee, Nichol to Members of National Executive, 13.12.65; vol. 1028, file: Confidential. Policy and Research, Dan Coates to Stanbury, 8.4.68, "Report of Standing Committee on Policy, Liberal Federation of Canada, 1968"; vol. 1155, file: Minutes of National Council Meeting, June 1-2, 1964. Interview with Allan O'Brien, 24.8.77.

10. LPC, vol. 728, file: Federal Organization, Confidential (2), Davey to Gordon, 30.5.63, Davey to Pearson, 9.5.63.

questions from ministers who either disdained such partisanship or practised it selfishly.[11]

In any case, the experiment was repeated in 1963, with the difference that this time the federal campaign committees were to be the key to the whole operation. Normally after an election, the campaign committee in a riding dissolves and responsibility for party affairs reverts to the riding executive. One might have expected the same thing to happen to the federal campaign committees at the provincial level, but the committees were retained—ostensibly to tackle by-elections and to keep the party prepared for an election which, under minority government, was always a possibility. But the committees had additional responsibilities which, beyond merely fighting elections, also provided evidence of the new centralizing tendencies which, potentially at least, were in conflict with the "new politics." Firstly, they were to provide a mechanism for rejuvenating provincial Liberal executives by bringing new people into the federal campaign committees. These people would, in turn, challenge tired and lacklustre provincial executives. Nova Scotia, for example, was considered to be the "number one organizational problem" in June 1964, on account of an apathetic provincial executive which purveyed unrelieved gloom. The first step in revitalizing the party was to appoint a new federal campaign committee chairman who would look for a new provincial party president. In fact, there were two chairman in fairly rapid succession and, within a year, a young Halifax lawyer, MacLeod Rogers, successfully challenged the incumbent president.[12]

Secondly, in order to advance the cause of the "new politics" of "involvement" and "communication", the federal campaign committees were to serve as political sounding boards and "to facilitate grass-roots consultation when the cabinet is considering appointments." Significantly, it was the federal campaign committees rather than the elected provincial executive that were to be the means by which the extra-parliamentary organization had a hand in patronage. Only new bottles were fit to receive old wine.

The word "patronage" has an aura of the unsavoury about it and, when it involves influence-peddling, uneconomic use of public funds, or wholesale firings of competent civil servants, the opprobrium is justified. Much of the flagrant appointments and contracts patronage that existed years ago has been eliminated by various reforms in Canadian public administration. On the other hand, there remain important areas where governments feel they must have discretion in filling positions with spe-

[11] Whitaker, *The Government Party*, pp. 90-111.

[12] LPC, vol. 744, file: PMO - L.B. Pearson 1963, Davey to Pearson, 10.6.64; vol. 685, file: Davey's Weekly Report, 19.11.64, 29.4.65, 26.8.65; vol. 728, file: Federal Organization, Confidential, Davey to Nichol, 31.1.66.

cially qualified people from outside the civil service or with people who are in sympathy with governmental aims in a particular area.[13] This sort of patronage, so the argument goes, makes it feasible for a government to be responsible to the voters for what its officials are doing. Another argument for the appointment of active politicians is that the weaknesses or faults of anyone who has been in the spotlight of an election become known—better than if the appointee has, for example, led a sheltered academic life—at least that is the contention! There is another sort of petty business patronage which, for example, takes the form of routine legal or engineering work which can be done adequately by any law or engineering firm. The public interest is not being violated if the party in power takes its business to its friends. Volunteer work for a party is often time-consuming, tedious and thankless; and, for someone like a lawyer or an accountant, it may entail actual foregone income. The possibility of patronage is the carrot which keeps the party workhorses going. Admittedly, the actual distribution of patronage may bring more disappointment than gratitude; but if a party in power pretends to ignore patronage opportunities, it runs the risk of appearing ineffectual or hardhearted. Harper Prowse, a senator from Alberta, put it this way: "Look, how far do you think you are going to get . . . in the confidence of people if they say - these are Liberals. This man has given 20 years of his life to this party, for peanuts . . . Now, if we are just going to toss that guy aside and say - well, we have no responsibility - how does that create, in the people who are asking us to run their affairs, confidence that we will have a [sic] compassion or concern, for them." As a former leader of the Alberta Liberal party, Prowse had, one might say, first-hand knowledge on the subject of thankless labour on the party's behalf![14]

"Political opportunity" in the new Pearson administration was divided into five categories:

1. Major appointments to such prestigious posts as the Senate, the Bench, commissions and boards

2. Minor appointments like that of crop insurance adjustors and surveyors for the Dominion Bureau of Statistics

3. Legal lists of the lawyers to whom the government takes its legal business; these were broken down into four categories: Justice, Central

---

13. An interesting instance of the latter argument is contained in M. Brownstone's article "The Douglas-Lloyd Governments: Innovation and Bureaucratic Adaptation" in *Essays on the Left: Essays in Honour of T.C. Douglas.*

14. LPC, vol. 715, file: Alberta Liberal Association 1963-65, "Political Tape - Harper Prouse" [sic]. Interviews with Nick Taylor, 6.6.75 and with Dan Murphy, 2.8.77. See also, "William Johnson in Quebec: Within reason patronage is proper", *Globe and Mail,* 31.8.79.

Mortgage and Housing Corporation, Sales Tax - Weights & Measures, Veterans Loan Act

4. Major suppliers (over which political influence was relatively limited, except perhaps in recommending one firm among three suggested by a department)

5. Minor suppliers, such as the gas stations, contractors, paper cup and sanitary suppliers, etc., with whom the government might have to do business in the various constituencies throughout the country.[15]

Davey was "staggered by the scope of government appointments" and surprised by "the people who have their hands out"—or, as a cabinet minister observed, "The lines form on the right even before rigor mortis sets in."

The aim of the new system of dealing with patronage was that, instead of a minister relying on the advice of a few friends, there would be wide consultation in order to produce the best recommendations. A minister was supposed to inform the federal campaign committee in his province of upcoming appointments; the committee would then consult throughout the province and make up a short list of suitable nominees for the minister to consider. The minister might consult with others and his authority to have the final say was unquestioned, but the committee was to be a privileged adviser—more so, even, than other ministers. Contribution to the party cause was not to be the sole criterion for making recommendations. The "principle consideration" was to get "good people"; "the best possible appointment is the best possible politics." The Liberals vowed they would be more responsible than their predecessors—one of the Conservative appointments to the Board of Broadcast Governors was a man whose only qualification, Liberals alleged, was that he was Diefenbaker's dentist![16]

A simpler procedure was to be used for legal lists and minor suppliers. Each minister was to get an "approved" list of contacts in each constituency in the event that his department had business there. MPs would do the same thing for their own constituencies and, in ridings not held by the Liberals, the provincial campaign committee would designate someone

[15] LPC, vol. 737, file: National Campaign Committee, Minutes, 31.7.63; vol. 728, file: Federal Organization, Confidential, Memo from Davey to Gordon, 30.5.63; vol. 744, file: PMO - L.B. Pearson 1963, Memo from Davey to Pearson, 22.5.63; vol. 750, file: London.

[16] LPC, vol. 737, file: National Campaign Committee, Minutes, 31.7.63, 6.3.64; vol. 728, file: Federal Organization, Confidential, Davey to Pearson, 9.5.63, 4.2.64; Memo from Davey to Gordon, 30.5.63. Another dentist, who ran *against* Diefenbaker, was rewarded by the Liberals with an appointment to the Freshwater Fish Marketing Corporation. *Globe and Mail,* 13.6.77.

in the constituency to draw up the lists. Traditionally, this job would have been given to the defeated candidate, but a memo to all federal campaign committee chairmen pointed out that "such a system obviously encourages some people who we do not want to run again. You and your committee will have to make this decision and while defeated candidates should be given every consideration, their appointment should not be automatic."[17]

The new system apparently got off to a good start with the help of Senator John Connolly who, as party president and a member of the cabinet, had a good vantage point on patronage questions. However, it soon ran into problems. A minister traditionally had considerable influence over appointments made in his own province by another department and some ministers did not want to share this privilege with their federal campaign committees. (In the case of New Brunswick, however, it was apparently the provincial Liberal government which had control over federal patronage there.) Furthermore, consultation proved to be cumbersome. Ministers were either too busy to provide advance information about openings or committee chairmen did not reply to requests for names. Davey reported that there was, in fact, "precious little consultation."[18]

The attempt to reform patronage ran into other sorts of difficulties with some of the party's grass roots. It came as a shock to some that the "new politics" apparently entailed passing over Liberals whose only virtue was to have laboured for the party "through the heat of the day", or that it meant keeping Conservative appointees in their jobs if they were working satisfactorily. The argument for a more partisan distribution of patronage had a certain cogency. In the farm areas, for example, the government's agricultural administration was crucial to its image. Many of the appointments, like Prairie Farm Assistance adjustors, had originated as Liberal patronage under Jimmy Gardiner and were still politically sensitive because the appointees dealt directly with the people. The Conservative appointees were allegedly still loyal to the former Conservative Minister of Agriculture, continually reminding farmers of the benefits they had received under the former government, but the Liberal Minister of Agriculture decided not to recommend any changes except in cases of incompetence.[19] There followed cries of alarm and disbelief. Patronage

---

17. LPC, vol. 728, file: Federal Organization, Confidential, Davey to all Federal Campaign Chairmen, 15.7.63.
18. LPC, vol. 744, file: PMO - L.B. Pearson 1964, Davey to Pearson, 10.6.64; vol. 737, file: National Campaign Committee, Minutes, 5.1.65; vol. 728, file: Federal Organization, Confidential, Davey to Nichol, 31.1.66; vol. 724, file: "D" General, David M. Dickson to Davey, 11.11.64.
19. LPC, vol. 734, file: Mc and Mac General, A.G. McLean to Davey, 10.6.63; file: M, W.G. Morrow to Davey, 1.12.65.

was held to be "an essential lever in motivating lethargic individuals - and in giving an organization a sense of power and effectiveness. We have sat and watched Conservatives continue to hold agricultural patronage posts while our constituency presidents were being slowly politically castrated. The end result is a total loss of respect for the job and for the Party."[20] The "new politics" was interpreted as evidence of a general indifference to the Prairies and of a failure to understand its problems.

As well as doing without the grease of patronage, the new politics of "involvement" and "commitment" were supposed to operate without the paid poll worker in the constituency during elections. Here again, the democratization of the party met resistance from the Demos itself. Davey was convinced that "paid workers just can't measure up against inspired volunteers", but an organizer in rural southwestern Ontario complained that "everywhere I have been there is the same gripe. The conservatives pay their workers much better than the Liberals." "Just wait until the poll clerks etc. have to be appointed in this riding. Did you ever stand over a robin's nest when she was feeding her young? The whole nest is obscured with wide open mouths. Well you will not be able to view the anatomy of these individuals. They will be using both hands to open wide their pockets to hear the jingle of the money they will be smacking their lips in anticipation of receiving. We will be pikers of the first water unless we pay them $18.00 per day and expenses." A good lady from Preston, Ontario voiced the opinion that to expect party supporters to work for the party without being paid "sounds like Communist, I am surprised that in a Country like Canada, it is allowed."[21]

Finally, Davey had to concede that the attempt to provide for a more rational, democratic and less partisan distribution of patronage had failed. Not only did the ministers fail to consult the party office, but when the federal campaign committees *did* get involved in patronage, they invariably created misunderstandings. In October 1964, the Federation formally withdrew from all "economic" patronage, though it intended to remain active in "appointment" patronage. Three months later, Davey, acknowledging "the political facts of life", relieved the Federation and the federal campaign committees of all responsibility in "political opportunity."

The whole matter of patronage raised a basic dilemma which the party had not been able to solve. Davey and all the other reformers were convinced that a viable party could not be built on patronage. The Liberal re-

[20] LPC, vol. 734, file: M. General, J. Cameron Millikin to Davey, 10.10.65.

[21] LPC, vol. 685, *Weekly Report*, 12.11.64; vol. 716, file: Beaton, Gordon - Reports and Correspondence "Gordon Beaton's report on Wellington Dufferin (Prov.)", 23.4.65, 13.4.65; Beaton to Davey, 27.6.65; vol. 716, file: C General, Crosbie to Pearson, 27.12.65.

vival in Toronto had been started by middle- and upper-middle-class people who really did not understand patronage politics but whose energy and enthusiasm had won more Toronto seats than the old petty patronage gang had ever been able to win. In Toronto, as Davey commented to Nichol, "it really couldn't matter less where the RCMP buys its gas." In Digby, Nova Scotia, however, what was a laughing matter in Toronto was serious politics! Patronage was a bread-and-butter issue in the Maritimes; in the Prairie provinces, while its importance lay in its being a symbol of power. In the long run the reformers were surely correct in judging that a viable, winning party could not be built by catering to a handful of "patronage lawyers", but Davey conceded to Nichol "that there was an amazing parallel between our electoral failures and the relative importance of patronage in the area concerned." He concluded wistfully, "it seems to me in this area we have reaped the worst of both worlds. Either we played the patronage game very badly or we failed to make a sufficient virtue of the new politics."[22]

Although the national office was not able to solve the question of how it should be involved with the old parish-pump politics in the era of the "new politics", it did remain active in what might be called upper-middle-class or "metropolitan" patronage. At least two provincial supreme court justices believed that Davey had had much to do with their appointments. Furthermore, the advent of advertising and media men into the party's highest councils, such as the Communications Committee, produced lucrative departmental accounts for their firms when the party returned to power.

The employment of advertising agencies by government goes back to the First World War. Within the following decade, political parties had begun to use them as well. Before 1957, Cockfield Brown Inc. was the principal agency for the party's election campaigns and even had H.E. 'Bob' Kidd on its payroll while he was general secretary of the Federation. In return, Cockfield Brown received a large proportion of the advertising business done by government departments and, for at least a number of years, Norman Lambert collected donations to the party based on a 5% kickback on contracts which Cockfield Brown received. The Conservatives were just as wedded to this modern form of patronage and duly shifted departmental accounts from Liberal to Conservative agencies after they took power in 1957.[23]

[22.] LPC, vol. 728, file: Federal Organization, Confidential, Davey to Pearson, 4.2.64; Davey to Nichol, 31.1.66; vol. 737, file: National Campaign Committee, Minutes, 6.3.64, 5.1.65; vol. 744, file: PMO - L.B. Pearson 1965-66, Davey to Pearson, 12.1.65; vol. 738, file: National Liberal Federation Employees, Davey to Nichol, 27.10.64; vol. 1094, file: Nova Scotia Liberal Association 1966-68, President of Digby Liberal Association to Allan MacEachen, 21.10.66. Interviews with Senator Davey, 15.1.72, 4.2.75.

[23.] Whitaker, pp. 216-263.

Cockfield Brown must have doubted the wisdom of having become so closely allied with the Liberals, especially when the Conservatives won such a huge majority in the 1958 election. Neither they nor Walsh Advertising, who had also done work for the party, even bothered to send representatives to a meeting of the Toronto and District publicity committee, called by Keith Davey to examine the party's relationship with its advertising agencies. On one occasion, Kidd had consoled the B.C. provincial leader, Ray Perrault, by observing that an agency would be willing to make a good deal with an opposition party by gambling on the "reward of advertising accounts when you become Premier of British Columbia". Perrault never became premier but, in the dark days of 1959, MacLaren Advertising gambled that Lester Pearson would become prime minister. MacLaren came to the party's assistance by granting it credit and by subsidizing the salaries of Richard O'Hagan, Pearson's press officer, and Paul Goulet, who worked in the Federation office as public relations director. Five years later, MacLaren was rewarded with $1.3 million worth of annual government advertising (30.5% of all departmental advertising) and other Liberal firms in Toronto and Montreal got virtually all the rest. (The Crown corporations spent almost as much on advertising as the departments, but they were not as amenable to political direction and preferred to remain with their existing agencies, which were mostly Conservative.) The allocation of departmental business among the various Liberal agencies always involved a good deal of negotiating—ministers had their favourites; considerations of "merit" sometimes conflicted with "political" considerations; John Aird, the chief fund raiser, was opposed to transferring any of MacLaren's business to Quebec agencies as long as Quebec contributed nothing to the costs of the national campaign or the national office. Even in the face of conflicting pressures, the obligation to MacLaren was not forgotten. The short-term solution, Davey told Pearson, was to increase the government's advertising business by insisting that all government departments do their advertising through agencies. Parenthetically, a more radical solution, he said, would be a Government of Canada Advertising Agency, though he admitted that "certainly the advertising agencies would be up in arms."[24]

FINANCING THE PARTY

The "new politics" and the traditional fund-raising operation were uneasy bedfellows, not because the traditional fund-raising methods were

[24] LPC, vol. 744, file: PMO - L.B. Pearson 1964, Davey to Pearson, 7.10.64. vol. 647, file: B.C. Liberal Association 1956-59, Kidd to Perrault, 22.7.59.

actually so bad, but because they *looked* so questionable. Everything was cloaked in secrecy. There was no public accounting of how much was raised from whom or how much was spent where—except that it was generally suspected to have come in large amounts from rich individuals and large corporations who conceivably expected something in return, and to have ended up often as bottles of whisky and ten-dollar bills that put the voters in good humour as they went to the polls. The Conservative party's Pacific scandal and the Liberal party's Beauharnois scandal confirmed everyone's worst suspicions, though, in retrospect, the Beauharnois scandal seems to have been more a case of the donor having been "played for an out-and-out sucker by the collection agents" than of the Liberal party having been corrupted.[25]

Even an "insider" like Richard Stanbury, who was party president from 1968 to 1973, apparently misunderstood the fund-raising operation, according to one of the fund raisers. In his paper, "The Liberal Party of Canada Through the Eyes of Dick Stanbury", he says that, before 1958, the regional lieutenants in the cabinet used their powers over patronage to assist them in their fund-raising responsibilities within their respective regions. He described C.D. Howe as "the inheritor of several generations of the practice of concentrating financial power in the same leaders who held organizational and policy power." Senator John Godfrey, himself one of the fund raisers during the 1960s and 1970s, chided Stanbury for having perpetuated a "popular myth." The chief fund raiser in Ontario throughout the 1940s was Senator Peter Campbell, who had no ministerial responsibilities; while, with the exception of C.D. Howe and Jimmy Gardiner, the ministers "took very little interest in fund raising and had to be continually prodded for assistance", according to Godfrey. Even Howe, he said, did little of the actual fund raising. His role was to be the cabinet minister whom businessmen knew best and in whom they had confidence—the reassuring business pipeline to the cabinet and to the prime minister. A request from one of "C.D.'s boys" for a party donation was not ignored. Mention has already been made of the little influence which Norman Lambert claims to have had with ministers and the prime minister—myths to the contrary—in spite of being the chief fund raiser during the thirties, as well as sometime general secretary and sometime president of the Federation. The fund raisers, or the "Treasury Committee" as it is called, operated in a kind of political no man's land. The leader appointed them, but after that he preferred to have as little to do with them as possible. Many of the ministers never met the fund raisers. After Lambert, their involvement with the party's operations became less

---

[25]. Quoted in Whitaker, pp. 19-21.

and less. According to the division of labour within the Liberal party, the fund raisers got the money which other people spent.[26]

Lambert's influence with the cabinet may have been exaggerated, but he was nevertheless effective as a fund raiser, getting donations of $5,000, $10,000 and occasionally more from many of the well-known Canadian companies. He was assiduous in keeping lists of companies who got government business; but, though he seems not to have indulged in "toll-gating" (requiring a donation to the party before a firm can get a government contract), he did raise money by means of the strictly legal, though ethically questionable practice of "kickbacks" (asking for 1½ to 2½ percent of a contract *after* the company has received it). Whether any contributors were able to get special treatment in return is difficult to say. One fund raiser claimed that the only ones who ever wanted to make deals were the $100- or $200-donors, who could be easily turned down. Whitaker points out that one of the party's most generous individual contributors was interned as an enemy alien by the government during the war![27]

Still, there was no doubt that the *manner* in which fund raising operated was completely out of keeping with the "new politics." "Involvement" and "commitment" by armies of volunteers were unidimensional, if only time but no money was given. Furthermore, it made no sense for a supposedly democratic, responsible organization to have no authority over its fund raisers or its funding procedures. The executive of the Federation did not even see the Federation's own financial statements, let alone those of the federal campaign committee.[28]

The first major review of the party's finances under Pearson was done by Walter Gordon in 1959. He recommended a fund-raising campaign of the traditional type to meet a national office operating budget of $600,000 from January 1960 to June 1962, when the next general election was expected to come. That worked out to an annual budget of $240,000 compared to the $30,000 budgets of the late 1930s, though they had gone as high as $224,000 in the election year of 1957, which was also the party's last year in power. The campaign was generally successful, although the national office was not, in the end, funded to the extent that either Gordon or Davey wanted. A year later, the party president, John Connolly,

---

26. LPC, vol. 1134, file: Liberal Party of Canada &c., Feb., 1969. Godfrey Papers, A Commentary on Senator Stanbury's Paper &c., 24.6.69. Whitaker, p. 96.

27. Whitaker, *passim*. Interview with Colin Campbell, 14.6.74. See also J.L. Granatstein, "Financing the Liberal Party, 1935-1945" in M.S. Cross & R.D. Bothwell, eds., *Policy by Other Means*, pp. 181-199. K.Z. Paltiel & J.B. Van Loon, "Financing the Liberal Party, 1867-1965" in Committee on Election Expenses, *Studies in Canadian Party Finance*, pp. 147-256.

28. Godfrey Papers, Godfrey to Stanbury, 27.3.75.

expressed his concern to General Matthews, the chief fund raiser, that the party had an alarming overdraft of $140,000.[29]

It was always more difficult to raise money in the traditional way for the less glamorous purpose of maintaining a party office between elections than it was to get campaign funds. So the party considered new ways of developing a broader base of contributions which would be used solely for meeting the Federation's annual expenses. The party's finance committee (not the fund raisers, but one of the five committees that had been set up in 1964) recommended that the provincial associations gradually assume responsibility for financing the Federation, beginning with 20 percent of the budget in 1965; but later the idea was abandoned as being unrealistic,[30] conceivably because the other provinces traditionally relied on Ontario and, to a lesser extent, Quebec to carry the burden. Furthermore, they all had enough trouble funding their own offices.

There were also various proposals from people such as Paul Hellyer for the institution of a national membership plan—this in spite of the constitutional problems that it would create in a federated party, and without apparently being aware of the 1933 campaign for popular subscriptions which had raised only $1,942.83. A more feasible suggestion was that province-wide memberships be co-ordinated by the Federation, providing uniform Liberal membership cards and subscriptions to the Federation's periodicals. Quebec and the western provinces eventually instituted province-wide memberships, but as long as the largest province, Ontario, retained its traditional and haphazard practice of allowing individual constituencies to create their own rules for memberships, a national scheme was doomed.[31]

By far the most effective new means of raising money lay not in emulating the low-fee, mass-membership European working-class parties, but in seeking out larger donations in the manner of middle-class American parties. Fund raisers in all fields know that it takes less time and effort to raise a given amount of money by going to a few large donors than to get it in small amounts from a large number of contributors. The historical concentration of Liberal fund-raising efforts on a relatively few large cor-

---

[29] Smith, *Gentle Patriot*, pp. 57-59. Whitaker, pp. 112, 203. LPC, vol. 698, file: Finance (James Scott) Expense Accounts - 1960, Lafond to Matthews, 15.9.60; vol. 645, file: Hon. John J. Connolly, Connolly to Mathews, 29.3.61.

[30] LPC, vol. 728, file: Finances - Confidential, Davey to Nichol, 16.6.65, Davey to Aird, 23.8.65; Confidential Memorandum by A.B.M., 7.5.63.

[31] LPC, vol. 686, file: Davey - General Correspondence & Memos, J.E. Belliveau to Davey, 14.3.62; Hellyer to Davey, 21.8.61; vol. 698, file: National Executive Committee Meeting December 1959, Advisory Council 1959, Report of the Finance Committee; vol. 737, file: National Executive Committee, National Executive Committee Minutes, 26.5.65; vol. 744, file: PMO - L.B. Pearson 1965-66, Report of Interim Finance Committee.

porations was a recognition of this principle. The next step towards a somewhat more democratic, but still efficacious means of fund raising was to get medium-sized contributions from a rather large number of individuals. So, in 1959, Ontario Liberals established the Liberal Union, which aimed to get 1,000 donations of $100 each. These funds were used exclusively for maintaining the provincial and federal offices and none went into election campaign coffers. Alberta and British Columbia instituted similar schemes and Manitoba held dinners at $100 a couple. Such fund-raising methods were the wave of the future; but, for the present, the national office still had to be partly funded out of what could be saved from election campaign money. Fortunately, John Aird, the chief fund raiser during the sixties, was tough enough with the campaign committees to keep them (in their enthusiasm or panic) from using all the money that had been raised for the election. There was usually enough left over to keep the national office running for several months.[32]

In 1962, the Liberal platform contained a promise to legislate a limit on election campaign expenditures and a system of election subsidies out of public funds. After the party took office, Davey urged Pearson to act on this pledge as a way of implementing the "new politics." A Committee on Election Expenses (the Barbeau Committee) was duly established by the government and, when it reported, it recommended far-reaching changes in Canadian election laws to provide for the registration of parties, public subsidization, spending limits, disclosure of income and expenditures, and tax credits for individuals who contributed to political parties. A special party committee was asked to give its reactions to the executive of the Liberal Federation and, by and large, it endorsed the Barbeau Report. It was particularly enthusiastic about giving tax relief to those who made political contributions. The party wanted to establish a national Century Club of $100-donors and it felt that this would be successful only if tax relief were provided. The party committee, however, preferred to see contributions as a deduction from taxable income, instead of the tax credit which Barbeau recommended, so that political contributions would be seen in the same respectable light as charitable donations (and possibly to improve the tax break of contributors). The party committee also differed with Barbeau in preferring that disclosure apply only to donations over $1,000; nor did they like the proposed prohibition of paying party workers on election day. Finally, they were not enthusiastic about putting any limits on advertising expenditures until the rest of the recommendations had been successfully implemented. John Aird, however, went further than his colleagues: he was of the opinion that campaign fund raising should be stopped and that all election ex-

---

[32] LPC, vol. 739, file: National Liberal Union, *passim.*; vol. 744, file: PMO - L.B. Pearson 1965-66, Report of Interim Finance Committee.

penses should be met from public funds.[33] In spite of prodding from the party, the government was slow to bring in legislation embodying the Barbeau Committee's recommendations. Consequently, the party's plans to institute some kind of nation-wide fund raising along the lines of a national Century Club were left in limbo.

One of the most effective practitioners of traditional fund-raising methods was John Aird, who was chief fund raiser in the mid-sixties. As a Bay Street corporation lawyer who attended Upper Canada College, Osgoode Hall and was now a member of the Toronto Club, as well as many corporate boards, Aird had all the personal connections which are essential for raising big sums of money. (As Mackenzie King said, you need millionaires to get money from millionaires.) He was more effective than his predecessor, General Bruce Matthews (whose father had been a Liberal fund raiser in the 1930s) and managed to give the party real financial security. Davey told Aird that "for the first time since I have been here I honestly feel confident about the state of Party finances." Davey's only concern was that Aird might have difficulty giving enough time to his fund-raising duties and urged Pearson to appoint Aird to the Senate so that "he does not lose interest."[34] The appointment duly followed. (When Aird ended his fund-raising activities, he resigned his Senate seat and turned to other interests.)

Aird claims that it never occurred to him to use a kickback system as Lambert had done and he informed the national campaign committee that toll-gate practices would not be tolerated. In fact, he found that companies expected to give money to political parties, so fund raising was not particularly difficult. By his own estimate, he had raised $6,000,000 for the Liberal party by 1968, when he retired as chief fund raiser. One of his most effective arguments was to point to the automatic checkoff system that unions used to collect money for the New Democratic Party. The corporations must give *their* support to the two-party system, he said — in other words, donate to the two "free-enterprise" parties. A variation on this line of attack was developed by John Godfrey, who suggested to corporation executives that they should give equal amounts to the Liberals and Conservatives instead of the traditional sixty/forty division be-

<hr>

[33] LPC, vol. 728, file: Federal Organization, Confidential, Davey to Pearson, 4.2.64. Godfrey Papers, Report of the Special Committee on Finance, re: the Report of the Election Expenses Committee. R. Haggart, *Toronto Telegram*, 14.5.68. D.O. Carrigan, *Canadian Party Platforms 1867-1968*, p. 269.

[34] R. Haggart, "The bagman who wants to lose his job", *Toronto Telegram*, 14.5.68. LPC, vol. 728, file: Federal Organization Confidential, Davey to Pearson, 4.2.64; file: Finances - Confidential, Davey to Aird, 20.11.64; vol. 744, file: PMO - L.B. Pearson 1964, Davey to Pearson, 10.6.64; vol. 737, file: National Campaign Committee, Minutes, 5.1.65. Interviews with Godfrey, 30.9.77; with Aird, 6.9.78; with Lang, 16.3.79. Whitaker, p. 58.

tween government and opposition parties. Most of them liked the Conservative party better, he said, and the fifty/fifty idea put them into a better humour for giving a Liberal donation.[35]

Within the party, Aird operated in a detached manner. He stuck to his fund-raising job and took little interest in party business or party committees. (He is the sort of person who would have little patience for endless political discussion.) By his own admission, he did not have much influence in party affairs and did not want to. Neither Pearson nor Trudeau had much to do with his fund-raising activities and he claimed not to have had ten minutes discussion with either on the subject.[36]

THE 1965 ELECTION

When Pearson decided, finally and reluctantly, to ask for a dissolution of Parliament in September 1965, it was done primarily for the sake of short-term political tactics. The experience of governing with a minority had been a demoralizing experience for the Liberals, especially because a succession of scandals had given the opposition ample ammunition. Furthermore, voting surveys done by Lou Harris's company, Oliver Quayle, showed that the Conservatives were out of touch with public opinion on such issues as the Liberal proposal for a distinctive Canadian flag and they indicated that the Liberals would get an overall majority. In addition, party strategists, such as Davey and Gordon, were confident that, as long as Diefenbaker remained leader of the Conservative party, the Liberals could get a majority. The Conservatives, however, were making moves to oust Diefenbaker and the Liberals could not count on him for long. On the other hand, it was generally agreed that the public were not anxious to have an election called for the third time in just over three years. In the end, Gordon convinced Pearson that the redistribution of parliamentary seats in the following year and the Canadian centennial celebrations in 1967 would effectively eliminate the possibility of an election during 1966 and the first half of 1967, thus leaving the government at the mercy of the opposition parties.[37]

The election revealed two liabilities which the party had incurred over the last two-and-a-half years: the failure to renew the party's program and the failure to involve ministers sufficiently in the party organization.

The 1965 election was the third fought by the Liberals on the program which had been developed in 1960-61. That program had given the gov-

---

[35] *Ibid.*

[36] Interview with Aird, 6.9.78.

[37] Gordon, pp. 217-233. LPC, vol. 737, file: National Campaign Committee, Minutes, 31.7.63, 5.1.65.

ernment a clear agenda on taking office in 1963. Two years later, its record of accomplishment included such measures as the Canada Pension Plan, the adoption of a new Canadian flag, and a minimum wage; but future plans were hazy apart from medicare and a federal welfare program.[38]

In May 1965, a memo from Nichol, Gordon and Davey to "Key Liberals Across Canada" urged them to talk about what the government had accomplished: the Canada Pension Plan, the fall in the unemployment rate to less than 4%, the 1965 tax cut, and the flag. It concluded with the now-familiar refrain, "As always, we should avoid personalities: above all, the Leaders of the opposition parties." Davey, in the midst of the campaign, even went so far as to reprimand Pearson for scoring a debating point on Diefenbaker in a press conference. The public, he said, were sick of this kind of "gut politicing" [sic]; the image they wanted to avoid was that of the champion and his chief challenger slugging it out for the last round of their careers. This seemed like wise advice, but it effectively left the field open to Diefenbaker who was by no means reticent in attacking Liberals, especially the French Canadian ministers who had been tagged with scandals, both large and small. Later, in his memoirs, Gordon admitted that, when Pearson rejected the campaign strategy and replied to a Diefenbaker attack, he gave his best television performance of the campaign.[39]

At the final meetings of the national campaign committee after the election, it was agreed that the lack of any real program for the future had created a serious problem. John Payne pointed out that there had been no party manifesto as in 1962 and 1963. Larry Jolivet, the B.C. campaign co-chairman, added that, without specific policies, the party had not been able to explain to the voters why it wanted a majority. Gordon agreed that the absence of a precise program had been "one of our weak points" and that, because the Liberals had been unable to keep the campaign on issues of their own, the Conservatives had put theirs in the forefront. There was a consensus in the campaign committee for getting a specific, detailed manifesto ready for the next campaign.[40] When it occurred, however, a manifesto could not be prepared in time and hardly seemed necessary in any case. Before long, what was almost an inadvertent omission in 1965 had become a habit.

The campaign showed an even more pronounced tendency to focus attention on the leader than had been the case in 1963. According to Gor-

[38]. Gordon, *loc. cit.*

[39]. LPC, vol. 724, file: Campaign Strategy, Memo, 11.5.65; vol. 1028, file: PM's Office, General Correspondence, Davey to Pearson, 19.9.65. Gordon, p. 230.

[40]. Gordon, p. 231. LPC, vol. 737, file: National Campaign Committee, Minutes, 14.1.66.

don, Pearson was determined to fight the election on his own. The national campaign committee in effect went along with this by deciding to use Pearson in all free-time television broadcasts because he was the "only . . . man in this Party who is of major interest to all the people everywhere in the country who are reached by a national network."[41]

The various ministers did not shoulder the campaigning duties as their predecessors had done. This was due partly to disinterest and partly to neglect. The one fed on the other. Judy LaMarsh complained in her memoirs that the cabinet never discussed the organizational state of the party and had very little contact with the national office. This was less serious when Connolly was president, because he was also a member of the cabinet; but his successor, John Nichol, was not. In November 1963, a political advisory committee was created to take the place of the leader's advisory committee which had operated before the party took office. The new committee was supposed to keep Pearson (who acted as chairman) informed of "the political thinking of some of our key members who are not in the House of Commons", but after a "rather abortive and unsuccessful beginning" it was disbanded. LaMarsh recalls that the ministers were never allocated responsibility for various regions of the country, even though this had been a basic feature of the political organization of earlier Canadian cabinets. It was finally done in February 1967, though with certain anomalies: Ontario was divided among eleven ministers instead of one being designated as the "senior" or "political" minister; also, J.J. Greene was given responsibility for the two Renfrew constituencies in Ontario (one of which he represented) and, as minister of agriculture, Alberta and Saskatchewan, because there was no Liberal member from either province.[42]

In some instances the inadequate liaison between ministers and the party was due to their own lack of interest in the party's needs. According to Davey, "one of the most unpleasant jobs which the federation does, is to supply speakers for various functions across the country." Ministers were supposed to inform headquarters when making trips out of Ottawa, so that speaking engagements could be arranged with local Liberal groups; but, in spite of continual reminders, ministers seldom kept the national office informed. They were indifferent about undertaking speaking commitments and, when they did, sometimes cancelled them at short notice, even during the election campaign. No doubt there were often

---

[41.] Gordon, p. 230. LPC, vol. 737, file: National Campaign Committee, Minutes, 21.9.65.

[42.] Judy LaMarsh, *Memoirs of a Bird in a Gilded Cage*, pp. 144-147. LPC, vol. 742, file: Political Advisory Committee, *passim.*; vol. 1026, file: Cabinet Organization Responsibility, Nichol to Pearson, 27.2.67; vol. 1028, file: Liberal Federation of Canada - General Corr., *passim.*; vol. 1026, file: Communications, Communications Committee Report, 8.12.64.

good reasons or circumstances over which the ministers had no control, such as a prime-ministerial summons. Early in 1965, Davey challenged Pearson about a rumour to the effect that he had instructed all ministers to accept no speaking engagements. "Not *all* engagements", Pearson replied "but priority must be given to Parl[iament] for the next few weeks." (And 1965 turned out to be an election year!) Even when ministers did get away from Ottawa, the Federation's speakers bureau found that they tended to concentrate their visits in parts of the country where the party was already strong—metropolitan Toronto, urban Quebec, British Columbia, Newfoundland—while the rural areas of the country, where the party had virtually no representation, were neglected.[43]

A number of Liberals were also unhappy about the lack of attention given to the recruitment of new, outstanding candidates. Before 1963, Pearson himself had been very active in persuading new people to become active in the party. The party's back-bench strength after 1963 bore ample testimony to his efforts, but these apparently weakened in the face of the preoccupations of government. A report from British Columbia three weeks before the election was remarkably accurate on a seat-by-seat prediction, but in four cases the party had evidently "muffed it" by nominating poor candidates. In October 1963, International Surveys declared that the "overwhelming problem" for the party on the Prairies was "that there is no Western leader of the Liberal party" to interpret government policy to the people of that region; the Liberals had no individual or idea that could make the party "mean something" in the West. A couple of years later, Pat McGeer, a British Columbia MLA, outlined a plan of action for the Liberals in the West: in addition to making a number of specific policy recommendations, it urged that the prime minister and the cabinet participate in recruiting outstanding candidates in the West, because the party organization by itself could not. When the election was over, McGeer had nothing but praise for the organizational work that Davey had directed, but he again expressed disappointment over the failure of the prime minister and the cabinet "to undertake those measures which would win support in this part of the country." By contrast, the recruitment of major candidates in Quebec was successful. Lamontagne, Giguère and Sauvé finally got Marchand to run as part of a team with Gérard Pelletier and Pierre Trudeau. It could not be coincidental that Quebec was the only province where the Liberals made major gains. Elsewhere, Robert Winters, a former St. Laurent cabinet minister and

[43.] LPC, vol. 717, file: Ministerial Engagements Cab. Mins. Itinerary, Davey to Pearson, 19.5.64; vol. 724, file: Election Night Coverage - '65 Campaign, Gordon Blair to Davey, 20.10.65; vol. 728, file: Federal Organization Confidential, Davey to Nichol, 31.1.66; vol. 744, file: PMO - L.B. Pearson 1965-66, Davey to Pearson, 11.2.65; vol. 1030, file: Speakers' Bureau, Bobbie O'Neill to Provincial Organizers, 23.11.67; vol. 1031, file: Speakers Liaison Service, O'Neill to Nichol, 6.11.67.

executive with Rio Tinto, was the only other well known public figure to join Liberal ranks. Mackenzie King's "system" had depended on the recruitment in virtually every province of lieutenants who all carried considerable political weight of their own; but it was being replaced, either unconsciously or by default, by a new system, marked not by the contribution of regional lieutenants, but, more and more, by election campaigns which focused on the leader. That new "system" did not begin with Trudeau.[44]

THE END OF THE DAVEY-GORDON ERA

The disappointment of still being short of a majority after the 1965 election led to important changes in the Liberal party. The two men who had been most closely associated with guiding Liberal campaigns over the last four years, Gordon and Davey, had also been the strongest advocates of an election which, they had predicted, would return a Liberal majority. Consequently, Gordon felt obliged to offer Pearson his resignation from the cabinet and Davey resigned as national director shortly afterwards.[45]

Inevitably the centralized campaign structure, which Davey in particular had been instrumental in constructing, came in for reassessment. He was credited by one organizer with having been "mainly instrumental in building the Party organization from a disenchanted, bickering disco-ordinated group, to a well oiled machine." Davey himself maintained that the campaign committees had been useful in providing "some kind of unilateral monolithic control" over national campaigns.[46] However, even in strictly electoral terms, success had been uneven. By 1965, the party held forty-one of the fifty-six seats in the six largest cities or metropolitan areas. In the one hundred and seventeen non-metropolitan seats of Ontario and Quebec, they did almost as well, winning seventy seats. But of the ninety-two remaining non-metropolitan ridings outside central Canada, the Liberals took only twenty and all of these had been traditionally Liberal seats before 1957. In fact, almost all of the seats that the Liberals won in 1965 had had long Liberal histories except for the Toronto and

44. LPC, vol. 737, file: National Campaign Committee, Minutes, 14.1.66, 21.9.65, 5.1.65; vol. 724, file: Election Night Coverage - '65 Campaign, Don McColl to Davey, 15.10.65; vol. 757, file: A Report on Preliminary Research Conducted in the Prairies for the Liberal Party of Canada by International Surveys Limited, October 1963; vol. 734, file: Mc & Mac, McGeer to Pearson et al., 29.6.65, McGeer to Davey, [November 1965]. J. Wearing, "President or Prime Minister" in T.A. Hockin, ed., Apex of Power: The Prime Minister and Political Leadership in Canada, p. 250.

45. Gordon, pp. 232-233.

46. LPC, vol. 734, file: M General, Millikin to Davey, 10.11.65; vol. 728, file: Federal Organization Confidential, Davey to Nichol, 31.1.66.

York ridings and a dozen other ridings in southern Ontario, and even the Toronto ridings had gone Liberal occasionally. Outside southern Ontario the party, at best, returned to the *status quo ante* and, on average, it did worse. Before 1957, the Liberals could usually count on winning about half of the hundred-odd seats in Atlantic Canada and Western Canada; but in 1965, they won only twenty-three. A dozen seats in suburban Ontario did not make up that deficiency.

There were various explanations tendered within the party as to why this had happened. The author of an unattributed memorandum entitled "A Party in Crisis" blamed Gordon and Davey for an excessive reliance on "slick advertising", "public relations gimmicks" and public opinion polls. Though credit was given to Pearson for bringing many young, dynamic, talented people into politics, many of them—like John Turner, John Munro, Pauline Jewett, Jack Davis—were still on the backbenches, while "in the cabinet could be found many who showed not the slightest tinge of political purpose." Even worse, the re-entry into federal politics of Robert Winters, "a C.D. Howe Liberal" who represented all that Canada rejected in 1957 "hover[ed] over the Liberal Party like the Ghost of Christmas Past, threatening to undo all the progress that has been made since the 1958 debacle."[47]

Others argued that a centralized campaign which was right for Toronto did not necessarily work in places like the Annapolis Valley, the Bruce Peninsula or the South Saskatchewan River. In 1962 and 1963, for example, unemployment was said to be the wrong issue in Alberta, where the unemployment rate was well below the national average. Similarly, the 1965 advertising campaign, which was directed to the urban areas, was inappropriate in the West, where "the only urban city . . . is Vancouver. The rest are cities populated by peoples with distinct rural mentalities either coming directly from farm areas or only one generation removed. It is therefore imperative that we, in the West, be allowed to tailor our own programmes." Another Liberal from the Maritimes declared that the party's campaigns in that region had been "inept" because they had failed both to come to terms with the regional outlook of Maritime voters and to counter the predominant influence of the Conservative media in the region.[48]

The appeal to an urban or even a metropolitan electorate was, at least partly, a conscious decision. As Keith Davey said, there were more seats in Toronto and York county than in any Prairie province and anyway the

---

[47.] LPC, vol. 724, file: Election Reports/65.

[48.] LPC, vol. 734, file: M General, Millikin to Davey, 10.11.65; vol. 715, file: Alberta Liberal Association 1963-65, Political Tape - Harper Prouse [sic]; vol. 689, file: National Office: General Corr. Elections 1962-1963, Stephen E. Patterson to National Headquarters of the Liberal Party, 6.2.63.

Liberals had, on average, won only two-and-a-half seats in Alberta since it became a province.[49] But there was a basic flaw in Davey's arithmetic. The appeal to a metropolitan electorate gave the party a base which was both too narrow and too volatile. The gains in southern Ontario did not compensate for the failure to regain the respectable totals that the Liberals had usually had in the West and the Atlantic provinces. The Liberals were never able to win a clear majority in the early 1960s and, without the disdained machine politics of Eastern Canada and the historical advantages which it had with French Canada and Catholic voters, the Conservatives would have won every election. Furthermore, experience in the 1970s would show that Toronto could abandon the Liberal party as readily as it had earlier created a Liberal bandwagon.

An important aspect of the centralist strategy was the responsibility that the federal campaign committees had for reviving the Liberal party at the provincial level. By 1966, Davey was pleased to note that they had achieved their goal of electing "as provincial presidents in each province the kind of able, progressive people who we originally recruited to be campaign chairmen."[50] In chapter 1, we noted how the federal wing of the Conservative party had, in the 1950s, adopted this strategy of building on provincial successes, though with the difference that federal Conservatives tended to accept provincial Conservatives as they found them. Over the years, this has been the traditional Canadian strategy, especially for the opposition in Ottawa. But in the 1960s, the Liberal party went about it differently, inasmuch as the Ottawa leadership had a pretty clear idea of the sort of people who should lead the provincial revivals, and these people were appointed to the federal campaign committees. However, the federal campaign committees in Manitoba, Alberta and British Columbia, while matching Ottawa's prescription almost perfectly, had not been able to get their provincial parties to make much headway against well-entrenched governments, although the Liberals were the official opposition in Manitoba and Alberta. In Ontario, the federal Liberals got their man, Andrew Thompson, into the leadership of the provincial party in 1964. But he ran into bad luck and the leadership, almost by default, went to Robert Nixon. Partly because the federal wing monopolized the talents and energy of its key people in Ontario, the provincial party languished in the doldrums throughout the sixties.

Provincial Liberal parties were in power in Saskatchewan, Quebec, New Brunswick and Newfoundland, but not as the result of any Ottawa-directed revival. The provincial wing in Quebec was actually more reformist and democratic than its federal counterpart, which was split be-

[49] Interview, 4.2.75.

[50] LPC, vol. 728, file: Federal Organization Confidential, Davey to Nichol, 31.1.66.

tween old and new guards in the early 1960s and, in 1964, the two Quebec wings formally severed their connections—though admittedly, this was more in appearance than in reality at the riding level. In spite of differences between the two, it seemed to be an advantage to have a Liberal party in power provincially. The same was true, only more so, in New Brunswick and Newfoundland, where ruling provincial Liberals could be relied upon to elect federal members and did. On the other hand, Davey was obviously uncomfortable about having to rely on provincial parties which were far from being practitioners of the "new politics" as he defined it. Sooner or later, he told Nichol, there will be, in both provinces, "a reaction to some pretty powerful machine politics."[51]

Nova Scotia was seen as the province where an Ottawa-directed revival was most likely to bear fruit. A new provincial executive was followed by a new leader, Gerald Regan, and Davey was full of praise for what his Nova Scotia friends were doing. Davey's successor was much more pessimistic about Liberal prospects. Ironically, when to everyone's surprise Gerald Regan led his party to victory in 1970, the electoral benefit to federal Liberals over the next several years was barely perceptible.[52]

Saskatchewan, even more than Nova Scotia, illustrated the hazards of the centralized strategy for building up provincial Liberal strength. A Saskatchewan Liberal government took office a year after the federal Liberals came to power, but Ottawa disapproved profoundly of Thatcher's right-wing Liberalism and viewed his party as more of a hindrance than a help in federal elections. For his part, Davey remained convinced by surveys of Western attitudes that the Liberal party should be small 'l' liberal and left-of-centre throughout the West.[53] But, even if their brand of liberalism was not admired in Ottawa, the fact was that the Thatcher Liberals were in power in Saskatchewan.

Admittedly, it was difficult for Ottawa Liberals to decide, in other cases, whether a provincial Liberal group truly reflected a genuinely idiosyncratic provincial outlook or whether they were simply an ineffective clique who should be eased out. Indeed, Davey wondered whether, in view of the growing divergence between federal and provincial interests within the party, a unitary structure might not be better for the party than the existing federal one. In any case, the Davey strategy marked a profound break with Mackenzie King's approach which had, as an essential feature, the *acceptance* of regional differences within the Liberal party, along with strong cabinet ministers who were spokesmen for those re-

---

51. *Ibid.*
52. See chapter 4 for a discussion of the Liberal party in each province.
53. Interview with Davey, 4.2.75.

gional differences. As his biographer said, "King accepted the regional and cultural particularisms instead of defying them."[54]

The powerful position of leader of the Quebec caucus was still as important as ever and, in spite of more centralized campaigns, Quebec particularism got ample recognition. That was not so true elsewhere. A number of key Prairie Liberals regretted that no strong regional lieutenant had emerged to challenge Diefenbaker and Alvin Hamilton (the former Conservative Minister of Agriculture). Their voters were largely insulated from national concerns, they argued, and needed spokesmen who identified with local causes—popular leaders like Jimmy Gardiner, the Saskatchewan politician who had been Minister of Agriculture for twenty-two years in King's and St. Laurent's cabinets. King may not have liked Jimmy Gardiner's style of politics, but he respected his political power. Eventually Ottawa did acknowledge Thatcher as the *de facto* political boss of Saskatchewan and conceded control over federal matters, including patronage and elections, in his province. Also, in deference to the Saskatchewan Liberal executive, Hazen Argue replaced Otto Lang as Saskatchwan federal campaign chairman. But that did not mark the end of the attempt to make Otto Lang the leading federal Liberal in Saskatchewan.[55]

According to one westerner, Keith Davey's view of Canada was what he could see from the top of the Toronto-Dominion Centre on a clear day. Like most caricatures, it had its element of truth; but, to be fair, Davey recognized the problem when he said in 1965, "Today in Canada, we really have two majorities. One in Eastern Canada which is predominantly Liberal and one on the Prairies which is predominantly Conservative. I think I understand why this has happened but I really must confess I don't know what we can do about it. Particularly since attempting to build a base in the West could easily jeopardize our base in the East."[56] Perhaps he saw the problem too starkly in terms of opposing forces instead of regional variations; indeed, by the end of his time as national director, he also saw the need for allowing the federal campaign committees to be more representative of provincial points of view.

The centralized strategy had been an interesting experiment, especially as it had attempted to achieve something which Canadian reformers have

54. H. Blair Neatby, "Mackenzie King and the Historians" in J. English and J.O. Stubbs, eds., *Mackenzie King: WideningshDebate*, p. 4.

55. LPC, vol. 737, file: National Campaign Committee, Minutes, 14.1.66; vol. 715, file: Alberta Liberal Association 1963-65, Political Tape - Harper Prouse [*sic*]; vol. 744, file: PMO - L.B. Pearson 1964, Davey to Pearson, 10.6.64; vol. 685, file: Davey's Weekly Report, 22.10.64, 3.12.64; vol. 724, file: Campaign '65 - Memos, etc. to Candidates, Provincial Campaign Chairmen/65. David Smith, *Prairie Liberalism*, pp. 303-304.

56. Interview with Nick Taylor, 6.6.75. LPC, vol. 716, file: "C" General, Davey to Walter Cook, 6.12.65.

so often longed for—a strategy which attempted to find a commonality *across* regions and provinces, a *consistent* appeal which meant the same thing everywhere.

THE 1966 NATIONAL MEETING

By the end of 1965, it was clear that the cabinet no longer consisted of regional lieutenants who ran the party in their own provinces: the old Mackenzie King system was dead. It was also clear that turning the system on its head, through having centrally nominated federal campaign committees who infused the "new politics" into provincial units, was not working either—or was producing only minority governments. What was working, however, was the attempt to involve greater numbers of people in a Liberal party that was more open and more democratic than it had ever been before. This movement really took root at the 1966 National Meeting and flowered at the 1968 Leadership Convention.

The 1966 National Meeting was the policy committee's most notable achievement. The format of the conference was an innovation insofar as a Liberal party in power gave free rein to delegates in their deliberations on policy. There were no resolutions prepared in advance and no resolutions committee to guide those deliberations. The policy committee restricted itself to setting out alternative policies in the form of questions which were put before the delegates in the workshop sessions. The conference was planned on the perhaps naïve and idealistic assumption that fifteen hundred delegates could come to a conference, having thought about the issues raised by fifteen background papers totalling over two hundred pages; that they could ponder in the workshops the questions posed by the policy committee and consider the summaries of resolutions which had been sent in from across the country; that they could draft their own resolutions which would be forwarded to the plenary sessions; and, finally, that they could do all this in seventeen hours spread over three days![57]

The debates were intense, especially on two issues which threatened to turn a talkfest into a gladatorial contest. They were the government's decision to postpone the implementation of its new medicare program and the question of whether the government should take steps to reverse the high level of foreign ownership of Canadian industry. The two issues became personified in the former finance minister, Walter Gordon, and

[57] LPC, vol. 1028, file: Confidential. Policy and Research, Coates to Stanbury, 8.4.68; "Report of Standing Committee on Policy, Liberal Federation of Canada, 1968." J. Wearing, "Party Leadership and the 1966 Conventions", *Journal of Canadian Studies* (February 1967), 23-27.

his successor, Mitchell Sharp. Gordon, a strong proponent of extending the country's social welfare programs and of curbing foreign economic domination, had earlier in the year published *A Choice For Canada,* which challenged the party to take a clear stand on such issues. Sharp was more concerned about the country's finances not being over-extended by costly new welfare programs and more sympathetic to those who wanted to maintain an open door on foreign capital. Opposing blocs formed before the convention: Ross Thatcher, the new Liberal premier of Saskatchewan, called a meeting of western Liberals to oppose Gordon's views; while Andrew Thompson, the Ontario Liberal leader, began to organize support for Gordon in Ontario until illness hampered his efforts. The debate itself was anti-climactic. Although the press re-ported a dramatic clash between right and left wings of the party, in real-ity Liberal abhorrence of having to make a clear choice carried the day. On both questions, agreement was reached on compromise resolutions. A caucus of delegates from both sides of the foreign investment issue pro-duced a resolution which favoured positive rather than punitive measures to expand Canadian investment. Unanimous approval was given to a res-olution which "deeply regret[ted] the postponement of Medicare and strongly affirm[ed] its determination to have Medicare implemented as soon as conditions allow, and certainly not later than July 1st, 1968." Still, it was clear that Gordon had failed to rally the convention behind him.[58]

Some of the other resolutions indicated directions in which the govern-ment later moved: recognition of Red China, agricultural national mar-keting boards, a federal portfolio of urban affairs, liberalized abortion laws. In addition, several important changes were made to the party's constitution in order to enhance further the authority of such con-ventions. Firstly, the policy convention was given the power to establish the "basic policies of the Party"; secondly, a member of the cabinet (or of caucus, if the party is out of power) was to report to each convention on the consideration given to the resolutions passed by the previous con-vention; the convention might then refuse to ratify the leadership's deci-sion; thirdly, at the policy convention following a federal election, an automatic resolution calling for a leadership convention was to be voted on by secret ballot.[59]

Mackenzie King would certainly not have approved. He told the 1948 national convention that a prime minister was responsible only to Parlia-ment and not to any party organization. "The substitution, by force or otherwise, of the dictates of a single political party for the authority of a freely elected Parliament is something which, in far too many countries,

---

[58]. Gordon, pp. 242-251. Smith, pp. 286-292.
[59]. Constitution of the Liberal Federation of Canada [1966], Clause No. 9, H and I.

has already taken place. It is along that path that many nations have lost their freedom. That is what happened in fascist countries. A single party dictatorship is, likewise, the very essence of Communist strategy."[60]

King notwithstanding, the second amendment, the so-called "accountability clause", was thought at the time to be a significant breakthrough in giving the extra-parliamentary party real authority. Within days, however, Pearson had repudiated two of the more impractical resolutions: one calling for a North American-Caribbean free trade area and the other asking that all federal civil servants in bilingual areas be bilingual. In spite of what the party's constitution now said, he declared that the convention's resolutions did not "establish policy" but would be taken "very seriously as a guide to policy." Indeed, the medicare resolution was apparently an important factor in the government's later decision not to consider a second postponement.[61]

The 1966 meeting may not have been the dramatic "surge toward democracy" that some of the accountability delegates had believed it to be, but it was significant in breaking with the older type of convention which had been so dominated by the parliamentary elite.[62] The 1961 meeting had produced a more comprehensive refashioning of the party's program, but it was essentially an occasion for getting the party rank and file to approve the policies which had been drafted by a small group who worked closely with Pearson. The 1966 meeting saw the beginning, though imperfectly realized, of a very different sort of policy convention —one where the rank and file worked very hard to indicate where they thought the party should be moving. The latter sort of convention will almost certainly not produce the carefully phrased policy statements which can be more readily achieved at the former type of convention. It is, instead, a reflection of what the party rank and file from across the country (or, more accurately, the local party elites from across the country) consider to be the best direction for the party for the next few months or years. Expert opinion is not what is wanted, so much as man-on-the-street opinion—rather like what Mackenzie King's personal network used to produce. At this stage, no one was really sure what the format or the goals of such a conference should be. At times the conference verged on being a meandering seminar on current problems—a kind of Couchiching-on-the-Rideau—while at other times, such as in the debate on the medicare postponement, the delegates were attempting to second-

60. Quoted in Whitaker, p. 175.

61. *Globe and Mail*, 15.10.66. "National Meeting 1966 and Liberal Party Conference: Proceedings of Plenary Sessions." Interview with Michel Vennat, 11.6.70.

62. See, for example, Dalton Camp's recollections of the utter frustration which he felt as an erstwhile Young Liberal at the 1948 convention. *Gentlemen, Players and Politicians*, pp. 1-12.

guess the government. But a contemporary newsman's assessment was that for 1,700 people to talk policy for three days instead of meekly accepting what was decreed by the leader, "may not sound remarkable, but, in fact, it is revolutionary."[63] In subsequent conferences, the party continued to experiment on just how this new sort of party conference should work.

THE 1968 LEADERSHIP CONVENTION

The leadership convention caught the imagination of the Canadian public perhaps more than anything that the party had done for years—though no more than the Conservative leadership convention the year before. The excitement of the race need not concern us here.[64] As far as the history of the party organization is concerned, several features of the convention stand out. It was more genuinely open and democratic than any previous Liberal leadership convention had been; it was won by a man who had been a member of the party for less than three years; no policy resolutions were passed and very little policy discussion occurred throughout the whole leadership campaign, in spite of the central role supposedly given to policy in the "new politics."

According to both Chubby Power and Richard Stanbury, the constituency delegates at earlier conventions were often named by their MP and voted as he directed them. In 1968, not only were there many more rank-and-file delegates, both absolutely and relative to the number of ex-officio delegates, but in many constituencies lively contests took place for the six delegate positions. Since 1959, the party's constitution had set down procedural guidelines that constituencies were to follow in electing delegates; furthermore, there was so much talk about "open conventions" and "independent delegates", that the old kind of parlia-

[63] A. Westell, "The New Liberals: Ideas are more important than votes", *Globe and Mail*, 15.10.66. For another assessment, see "The Opinions of Gérard Pelletier, *Montreal Star*, 18.10.66.

[64] For accounts and analyses of the convention, see Peter C. Newman, *The Distemper of Our Times*, pp. 435-469. Martin Sullivan, *Mandate '68*, pp. 273-353. George Radwanski, *Trudeau*, pp. 85-117. John C. Courtney, *The Selection of National Party Leaders in Canada, passim.* L. Leduc, "Party Decision-making: Some Empirical Observations on the Leadership Selection Process", *CJPS* (1971), 97-118. D.V. Smiley, "The National Party Leadership Convention in Canada: A Preliminary Analysis", *CJPS* (1968), 373-397. C.R. Santos, "Some Collective Characteristics of the Delegates to the 1968 Liberal Party Leadership Convention," *CJPS* (1970), 299-308. R.R. March, "The 1968 Federal Liberal Leadership Convention", Paper presented to the CPSA, May 1976. J. Wearing, "The Liberal Choice", *Journal of Canadian Studies* (May 1968), 3-20.

mentary control of the extra-parliamentary party seemed no longer acceptable.[65]

There was, nevertheless, much talk about "deals" between candidates (in spite of John Turner's somewhat sanctimonious disapprobation) and two of the leading candidates, Mitchell Sharp and Paul Hellyer, did make public pledges of support for other candidates when they withdrew from the race—for Trudeau and Winters, respectively. It would seem though that, when most of their supporters followed suit, they did so on account of their own preferences (especially in the case of Hellyer's supporters), rather than because they had been so directed.[66] The secret ballot, the milling about of delegates as they went to cast their ballots, and the comparatively short length of time between ballots—all these factors militated against delegates being herded into negotiable blocs.

The contest tended to divide candidates and delegates along attitudinal lines, although the divisions cut across one another and produced some strange bedfellows (Gordon and Sharp, for example, both of whom ended up supporting Trudeau). Some candidates were thought to be on the Right, others on the Left; regional loyalties came into play, as did personal likes and dislikes among the candidates. One of the most important features of the convention was the effect it had on determining who, among the party elite, moved into the inner circle and who moved out. The Toronto reform group, which had been so influential during Pearson's leadership, did not really have a candidate. (At one time it might have been Walter Gordon, though he had decided by the summer of 1966 not to contest the leadership; any remaining hopes that he might reconsider were effectively quashed when he failed to carry the 1966 National Meeting with him.) Keith Davey and Judy LaMarsh were with their former Cell 13-mate, Paul Hellyer. Jerry Grafstein, one of the younger generation of Toronto Liberals, was a key organizer for Turner. Walter Gordon and former MP, Pauline Jewett, wanted Jean Marchand to run. Others were ready to support either Marchand or Trudeau, if either one or the other entered the race. By that time, however, the key Trudeau nucleus had already formed in Montreal and Ottawa. It eventually included a few Quebec party veterans like Bob Giguère, the Quebec federal campaign chairman in the 1963 and 1965 elections; there were also new Quebec Liberals like Jean Marchand, the Quebec federal leader; Jean-

---

[65] Norman Ward, ed., *A Party Politician: The Memoirs of Chubby Power*, p. 371. LPC, vol. 1134, file: Liberal Party of Canada Through the Eyes of Dick Stanbury. There were certainly instances of supporters of one candidate or another attempting to "pack" the meetings in which delegates were chosen; but Lele, Perlin and Thorburn are too categorical in thus concluding that "constituency elections afford the elite an opportunity to effectively control the party rank and file." See their article, "The National Party Convention" in Hugh G. Thorburn, ed., *Party Politics in Canada*, 4th ed., pp. 77-88.

[66] Leduc, pp. 103-108.

Pierre Goyer, MP; Claude Frenette, president of the Quebec Liberal Federation and the executive director, Pierre Levasseur. What was particularly distressing to the Toronto stalwarts, though, was that the Trudeau inner core also included a number of people whom they had never heard of before. These "amateurs" (as Trudeau described them, in both senses of the word) gave to his campaign organization an improvisatory freshness which contrasted, quite intentionally, with the Hellyer and Martin machines that evoked memories of the "old politics." When Sharp dropped out of the race the day before the convention began, he brought several members of the Pearson Liberal "establishment" with him into the Trudeau camp, although there were problems in meshing the two organizations.

Three months before the convention, most commentators had given Trudeau little chance of winning; but his last-minute candidacy excited great interest with the media and the Canadian public. As it became increasingly apparent that Trudeau was actually in the lead, there was a flurry of activity among key members of the Hellyer, Winters, Martin and even Turner camps who sensed that new people were about to take over the party. Neither Martin nor Turner were interested in a "stop Trudeau" movement, but Hellyer threw his support to Winters before the last ballot. Because it took Trudeau four ballots to beat Winters, and then only by a slim margin, it looked as if the party might be seriously divided. A survey of delegates after the convention, however, showed that a very high proportion thought the convention had made a satisfactory choice.[67] With the euphoria of a victory in the general election, Trudeau had a basically united party behind him.

Before the convention, Senator Nichol, the party president and co-chairman of the convention organization committee, had said that "the Convention should be oriented to policy as a function of leadership." But the convention organizers decided that the delegates would be so caught up in the leadership race that they would not be interested in discussing policy. There were other problems. All but one of the candidates (former Quebec minister, Eric Kierans) were members of the federal cabinet and saw difficulty in reconciling the principle of cabinet solidarity with debate among themselves on policy questions. To some extent, this was subterfuge, since the Pearson cabinet had been notorious for leaks and public differences of opinion. More to the point, the question of a second postponement of medicare had resurfaced at a candidates meeting early in the campaign. A potentially acrimonious split gave the candidates such a scare that they invoked cabinet solidarity as an excuse for avoiding confrontations over policy during the remainder of the campaign. They even agreed to say nothing publicly about two important policy

[67] Leduc, pp. 109-110.

areas which had been the subject of independent reports to the government: tax reform and foreign ownership. The reports were so recent that collective responsibility for cabinet decisions was really not an issue. Nevertheless, the candidates treated both subjects almost as if they were *sub judice.*

Some policy positions were spelled out. Pierre Trudeau's views on the constitution were clearly enunciated in his collection of articles, *Federalism and the French Canadians;* Eric Kierans took concrete policy positions on a range of issues, both in his book, *Challenge of Confidence,* and in his campaign speeches. But Trudeau was non-committal on questions other than those concerning the constitution and all the candidates refused to get into a debate with Kierans.

At the convention itself, workshops on "Our Country", "Our Economy - Our World", and "Our Life" were held simultaneously on the first day. Each candidate answered questions for half an hour in the workshops, while delegates milled about aimlessly and showed only passing interest, except when Trudeau spoke. Not surprisingly, the convention became a media-oriented personality contest. (A major consideration was how the convention would look on television—even the platform from which the candidates spoke was constructed like a stage-set by a design firm which was hired for that purpose.)

Admittedly, there is a chicken-and-egg problem about a party choosing its leader and its policies. It is temptingly easy to say that the leader should be bound by the party's policies, whenever they are passed; but that is naïve even in the case of parties with stronger traditions of policy formulation by their extra-parliamentary wings. Having a policy convention coincide with a leadership convention would at least have induced the candidates to engage in more policy debate. The other alternative—having a policy convention a year after a leadership convention—has the advantage of making the new leader's views an important factor in the policy debates. In 1968, however, the Liberal party had neither, because Trudeau took advantage of the rising crest of Trudeaumania to ask for a dissolution. The temptation to have an election was overwhelming and, in the event, it produced the first Liberal majority government since the 1953 election. As for the longer term, it might well be asked whether the absence of an agenda, similar to that which the Pearson government had from the 1961 policy rally, was not at least partly responsible for the Trudeau government's sense of drift between 1968 and 1972 and the electorate's disillusionment which brought the party to the brink of defeat in 1972.

Although completely overshadowed by the leadership contest, a new party president was also elected. When it looked, before the convention, as if Richard Stanbury was going to be the only candidate, John Nichol, the retiring president, made sure that he was acceptable to all the leadership candidates. He was, although Trudeau hardly knew him. It was the first time that the president had not been hand-picked by the leader. But it was wrong to conclude that, with a Cell 13 alumnus as president, the party was still in the hands of the Toronto reform group. Important changes had taken place and they were to become evident over the next few years.

CHAPTER 4. THE LIBERAL PARTY IN THE PROVINCES

It is an important part of Liberal mythology that the party, like the country itself, is a federation. Life may be less complicated in the Conservative party with its more simplified structure as an association which does not attempt to incorporate the provincial parties as distinct units. But the official Liberal position, ever since Mackenzie King, has been that the Liberal Federation rests on the pillars of strong provincial units which speak for rank-and-file Liberals in each province. In practical terms, the differences between the two parties have been exaggerated. As we saw in chapter 1, both parties traditionally adopted the strategy of building upon success in provincial elections in order to achieve power federally. On the other hand, the Liberals in the 1960s created a more centralized campaign structure which sometimes bypassed the provincial associations or even attempted to remodel them to suit the purposes of the federal elite. In recent years, Liberals in Quebec, Ontario and Alberta have come to recognize that the divergent interests of federal and provincial wings, even within the same province, cannot be well served by a single, provincial organization and, as a result, they have created two separate ones. In each of these provinces, however, the federal wing has continued as a distinct unit within the national party; to that extent, the party remains a federation. The question of whether the pattern set by those three provinces should be followed throughout the country is a contentious subject in Liberal circles. Some would even go so far as to suggest that the federal structure be abandoned altogether. Before going any further, we must examine in more detail the position of the party in each province, paying particular attention to how the federal and provincial wings relate to each other. That relationship is, as we shall see, enormously complex and variable. (Liberal results in seats and votes for both federal and provincial elections are set out by province in Chart II.)

Chart II LIBERAL RESULTS IN SEATS AND VOTES FOR FEDERAL AND PROVINCIAL ELECTIONS BY PROVINCE (1956-80)

NEWFOUNDLAND

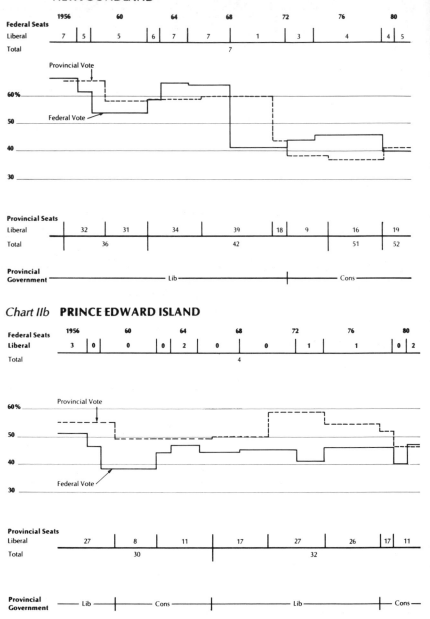

Sources: Paul W. Fox, ed., *Politics: Canada*, 4th. ed.
Hugh G. Thorburn, ed., *Party Politics in Canada*, 4th. ed.
Canadian News Facts

Chart IIc NOVA SCOTIA

Federal Seats	1956		60		64		68		72		76		80	
Liberal	10	2	0	2	5	2		1	1		2		2	5
Total			12						11					

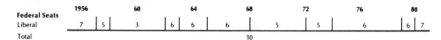

Provincial Seats							
Liberal	18	15	4	6	23	31	17
Total		43			46		52

Provincial Government

——————————— Cons ——————————— | —————— Lib —————— | — Cons —

Chart IId NEW BRUNSWICK

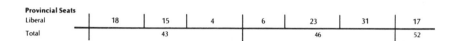

Federal Seats	1956		60		64		68		72		76		80	
Liberal	7	5	3	6	6	6		5		5		6		6	7
Total							10							

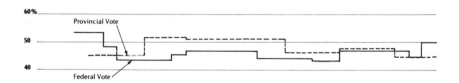

Provincial Seats						
Liberal	15	31	32	32	26	25	28
Total		52			58		54

Provincial Government

—— Cons —— | —— Lib —————— | —— Cons ——————

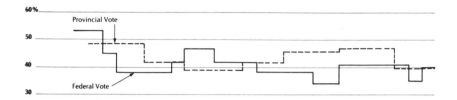

Chart IIe QUEBEC

Federal Seats	1956		60		64		68		72		76		80	
Liberal	66	62	25	35	47	56		56		56		60	67	74
Total			75						74				75	

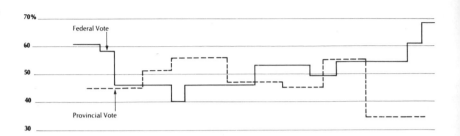

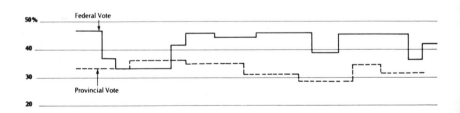

Provincial Seats												
Liberal	20		52		63		50		72		102		26
Total		93			95			108				110	

Provincial Government		UN		Lib		UN		Lib		PQ

Chart IIf ONTARIO

Federal Seats	1956		60		64		68		72		76		80	
Liberal	51	21	15	44	52	51		64		36		55	32	52
Total			85						88				95	

Provincial Seats												
Liberal	10		21		23		27		20		36		34
Total		98			108			117				125	

Provincial Government		Cons	

Chart IIg MANITOBA

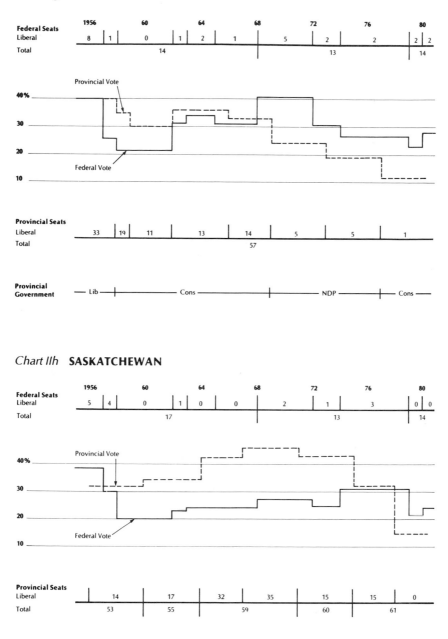

Federal Seats	1956		60		64		68		72		76		80	
Liberal	8	1	0	1	2	1		5	2		2		2	2
Total			14						13				14	

Provincial Vote

40%

30

20

Federal Vote

10

Provincial Seats									
Liberal	33	19	11		13		14	5		5		1
Total						57				

| Provincial Government | — Lib —|— | Cons — |— | NDP — |— Cons — |

Chart IIh SASKATCHEWAN

Federal Seats	1956		60		64		68		72		76		80	
Liberal	5	4	0	1	0	0		2	1		3		0	0
Total			17						13				14	

Provincial Vote

40%

30

20

Federal Vote

10

Provincial Seats								
Liberal		14		17		32		35		15		15		0
Total		53		55		59		60		61

| Provincial Government | ———— CCF ———— |— | Lib —|— | NDP ———— |

Chart IIi ALBERTA

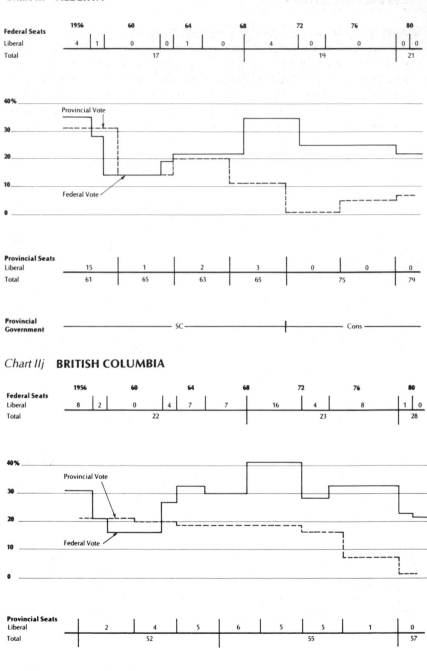

Federal Seats

	1956		60		64		68		72		76		80	
Liberal	4	1	0		0	1	0		4		0		0	0	0
Total			17						19				21		

Provincial Seats

Liberal	15		1		2		3		0		0		0
Total	61		65		63		65			75			79

Provincial Government

———————————— SC ———————————— | ———————— Cons ————————

Chart IIj BRITISH COLUMBIA

Federal Seats

	1956		60		64		68		72		76		80	
Liberal	8	2	0	4	7	7		16		4		8		1	0
Total			22						23				28		

Provincial Seats

Liberal		2		4		5		6		5		5		1		0
Total		52						55					57

Provincial Government

———————————— SC ———————————— | NDP | ——— SC ———

NEWFOUNDLAND

During the first twenty years of Newfoundland's history as a Canadian province, the Liberal party was simply Joey Smallwood, the leader and premier. He had built a personal base of support among those in the fishing outports who had listened to him make the case for Confederation in the broadcasts of the 1946 convention which had been called to determine the fate of the former bankrupt Dominion. For the next twenty years, every federal and provincial election in Newfoundland was really a referendum on Joey Smallwood and Confederation; he won them resoundingly. Even though there existed something called the Liberal Association of Newfoundland, it consisted of little more than a president and a secretary-treasurer (who was also Smallwood's fund raiser). What counted was his own one-man organization, based on lots of personal contact, provincial contracts and federal welfare payments. In a province with a population of less than half a million, his organization could operate without middlemen. Federal elections were such utterly Smallwood ventures that he picked the candidates and managed the campaigns himself. His executive assistant, Ed Roberts, informed Keith Davey that the publisher, editor, chief staff writer and copy editor of the 1962 Liberal campaign newspaper were all Joey Smallwood. Available resources were mobilized to the extent that every cabinet minister was a poll captain and every taxi in the city was booked to take Liberals to the polls on election day. "You have the all-out support of a superb organization, by far and away the best provincial 'machine' in Canada," said Roberts.[1]

In time, the very prosperity that Confederation had brought to Newfoundland diminished Smallwood's base in the depopulated outports; his government, tainted by scandal and wracked with the desertions of those who chafed at his one-man rule, became increasingly unpopular. Provincial politics were so pre-eminent that, when the Liberals lost all but one of the island's seven seats in the 1968 federal election, it was no reflection on Trudeau and the federal Liberal government, but a clear indication that Smallwood's hold on the province was waning. The setback prompted Smallwood to announce that he would establish a genuine grass-roots party and then resign as premier. The grass-roots organization was reputedly intended to prevent the leadership from falling into the hands of the St. John's commercial elite, whom Smallwood, the populist and former socialist, despised. But when John Crosbie, who came from a

---

[1] LPC, file: Liberal Association of Newfoundland, 1960, Roberts to Davey, 4.6.62. Richard Gwyn, *Smallwood the unlikely revolutionary*, p. 125. Steven B. Wolinetz, "Party Organization in Newfoundland", CPSA Papers, 1975. S.J.R. Noel, *Politics in Newfoundland*.

wealthy St. John's family (and was later minister of finance in Joe Clark's federal Conservative government), appeared to be the only candidate, Smallwood entered the race himself. The contest for delegates led to the recruitment of 30,000 members into the new provincial association, but after Smallwood reaffirmed his hold on the leadership, the new grassroots membership organization began to wither. There was, in any case, no tradition of political organization in a province where small communities were until recently very isolated from each other.

In 1971, Smallwood's government was defeated and he resigned the leadership shortly afterwards. He was succeeded by his protégé, Edward Roberts, who was described as a new breed of Newfoundland politician—an urbane St. John's lawyer and an admirer of J.F. Kennedy. Since then, however, the party has been bedevilled with leadership problems and party feuding. Smallwood was not the sort who could adapt easily to the role of retired politician. After failing to regain the leadership from Roberts, he led a breakaway group of Liberals for a year.

Four leadership conventions in eight years stimulated considerable activity in the new riding associations and, in 1977, Newfoundland Liberals held their first policy conference. One could not say with any assurance, however, that internal party democracy has finally taken root now that the twenty years of Smallwood's one-man rule have ended. The latest change in the leadership occurred just after a provincial election had been called and without the benefit of a leadership convention. William Rowe, the previous leader, had called a convention to settle questions about his leadership after he was accused of leaking confidential police reports to the media. The Conservative premier, unable to resist the temptation of exploiting the Liberals' internal problems, called an election. Not to be caught out on a limb, the party executive convinced Rowe that he should resign so that they could invoke a clause in the party's constitution to replace him immediately. Their choice was Donald Jamieson, who had just lost his job as federal cabinet minister with the defeat of the Trudeau government a few days before. A columnist in the *Evening Telegram,* the afternoon daily newspaper in St. John's commented on the incident:

Don Jamieson was not elected by anybody to be the leader of the Liberal Party of Newfoundland. He was picked by a small group of backroom Liberals who had finally decided to sink the knife into party leader Bill Rowe. This brand of politics is extremely dangerous. If it becomes accepted it means that any small group of men at the core of the party can ignore all the customs and traditions of politics and impose their will on the party.[2]

2. Wick Collins in the St. John's *Evening Telegram,* 29.5.79.

Even with the quick change (or, as some commentators said, because of it), the Liberal party lost the election. In spite of everything, though, the Liberal vote in both federal and provincial elections has held up better than one might have expected of a one-man machine after the departure of that man, Joey Smallwood.

It was rumoured that the installation of Jamieson was one of the last political exploits of the former PMO. If and when he is confirmed as provincial leader, one could expect that the provincial wing of the party will once again become the predominant partner. It must be of small comfort to federal Liberals knowing that their strength in Newfoundland is dependent on a situation where the rules are few and the game is played in such earnest.[3]

MARITIME PROVINCES

The three Maritime provinces are the only part of the country where Gilbert's lines in *Iolanthe* are as valid today as they were when they were written a hundred years ago:

> That every boy and every gal
> That's born into the world alive
> Is either a little Liberal
> Or else a little Conservative!

The highest percentage of the vote that a third party has ever received there was 20 percent for the United Farmers in New Brunswick in 1920. In the Nova Scotia provincial election of 1978, the NDP got 15 percent of the vote and thus equalled the record high which the CCF achieved in 1945. Neither ideology nor major policy questions have much to do with party lines—the last big issue to divide Liberals and Conservatives was that of entering Confederation over a hundred years ago. But political loyalties are nevertheless as fundamental to a Maritimer's self-perception as are religious beliefs—and just as well known.

In New Brunswick especially, linguistic and religious rivalries have often required delicate political management. A case in point was the federal constituency of Westmorland. This was "traditional country where they haven't caught up on Ecumenism", a federal organizer told

---

[3] St. John's *Evening Telegram*, 19,21.3.77; 14,18.4.79; 5.5.79; 23.6.79; 14.7.79. *Montreal Star*, 30.10.69. *London Free Press*, 21.2.76. Wolinetz, "Party Organization in Newfoundland." Ralph Matthews, "Perspectives on recent Newfoundland politics", *Journal of Canadian Studies* (May 1974), 20-35. Peter Neary, "Party politics in Newfoundland: 1949-71", *Journal of Canadian Studies* (November 1971), 3-21. Susan McCorquodale, "Newfoundland, The Only Living Father's Realm", in Martin Robin, ed., *Canadian Provincial Politics*, pp. 134-167.

Keith Davey in 1964. Just under half of the county were francophone Acadians and the ratio of Roman Catholics to Protestants was almost equal. Homogeneous communities of French Catholics and English Protestants were concentrated in opposite ends of the riding, except for the principal urban centre of Moncton in which the various groups were well represented. Historically, the riding had usually been held by an English Protestant but, more recently, Acadians had been demanding that an Acadian get the Liberal nomination. In the face of those competing claims, an Irish Catholic was regarded as a good Westmorland compromise. Another possibility, which would have been ideal for the 1964 by-election, was to nominate L.G. DesBrisay, an English Protestant with a French name! Unfortunately, he also happened to be a member of Robichaud's provincial government and Robichaud would not let him switch to the federal arena. The second choice was the former member's widow, Margaret Rideout, an English Protestant who was on good terms with French and Irish Catholics. She was nominated and won the seat.[4]

In recent years, religious and linguistic antagonisms have subsided. In 1954, the possibility of a Roman Catholic winning the leadership of the Nova Scotia Liberal party had led to bitter divisions at the convention. Eleven years later, the leadership was won by a Catholic, Gerald Regan, without producing another Battle of the Boyne. In 1958, it was considered a remarkable feat for Louis Robichaud to win the leadership of the New Brunswick Liberal party, since it had been led almost exclusively by English-speaking Protestants. Twenty years later, there were two Acadians in a five-man contest and support for the various candidates cut across linguistic lines as if they no longer existed. When one of the Acadian candidates withdrew, he gave his support to a non-Acadian. The eventual winner was Joseph Daigle and for another Acadian to have become the New Brunswick Liberal leader was by now thought to be quite unexceptional.[5]

Politics is also an important facet of the economic life of this region, where economic development has lagged behind the rest of the country and where government is a comparatively bigger employer and spender than it is elsewhere. Patronage and pork-barrel are considered legitimate and necessary functions of government, though voters tend to overlook subtle distinctions as to which level of government is constitutionally responsible for what. A P.E.I. correspondent informed Connolly, when he was president of the Liberal Federation, that local issues were important

---

4. LPC, vol. 794, file: New Brunswick 1960-1962, file: Westmorland 1964-65, Belliveau to Davey, 16.6.64; 9.7.64. Hugh G. Thorburn, Politics in New Brunswick, pp. 78-82.
5. Thorburn, p. 110. Halifax Chronicle-Herald, 16.6.65; Ottawa Journal, 13.5.78; Saint John Telegraph-Journal, 18.5.78; Financial Post, 6.5.78; Calgary Herald, 6.10.76.

even in a federal by-election because so little distinction was made between the two governments. The by-election in question (Kings, May 1961) boiled down to a competition between Conservative and Liberal largesse. "The fact that we we have spent more is very likely going to have considerable influence on a large number of the voters. These people live under rather desperate circumstances and their limited understanding of the role of government is, I think, understandable." Even the heavy snowfall that winter had aroused anti-government feeling and it was suggested that, when Pearson visited the riding, he should make a joking reference to this. Furthermore it did not apparently hurt either candidate to be publicly regarded as a suppliant for government welfare — quite the contrary, in fact. The Conservative candidate was seen to be deserving of an MP's salary because she was the widow of the former member; on the other hand, the Liberal candidate had been the member before 1957 and by re-electing him the voters could ensure that he had enough years as an MP to qualify for a pension. Whether they sympathized more with the widow or whether, in fact, Conservative campaign generosity to the voters ultimately turned out to be more impressive than the Liberals' is not recorded. In any case, she won.[6]

Although patronage has been an accepted fact of political life, it became an issue in New Brunswick in 1973 when the Justice Department was accused of having interfered with an investigation by the RCMP into allegations that the Conservative party was collecting kickbacks from firms which had been given government business. Reports in the *Financial Post* suggested that the practice was very widespread.

It's the very poverty of regions such as New Brunswick that creates a climate ripe for kickbacks. Few individuals are wealthy enough to give political donations. The party in power is tempted to use the kickback system as a source of income. And because the government and its agencies are the biggest buyers of goods and services in the province, few firms can resist the governing party's demands.[7]

At first, the Liberal leader, Robert Higgins, was reluctant to take up the issue — apparently because a similar scheme had been in operation when the Liberals were in power. A couple of years after the initial revelations had been made, Higgins did call for a Royal Commission into every aspect of party finance. The government replied by setting up a judicial inquiry to investigate only the charges about interference with the RCMP and ignored the larger question of whether there was an illegal kickback system. The inquiry exonerated the Justice Department and Higgins felt

---

6. LPC, vol. 794, file: New Brunswick Liberal Association 1960-1962, Ned Belliveau to Davey, 18.8.61; vol. 796, file: Prince Edward Island, 1960-61, W.J. Morris to Connolly, 9.5.61.

7. Philip Mathias, *Financial Post*, 28.5.77. See also, 9.11.74.

obliged to resign as Liberal leader. It was yet another instance of what a Liberal organizer had said years before: "Down here they play politics for keeps."[8]

The traditional, fiercely competitive two-party systems of the Maritime provinces simplify relations between the federal and provincial wings of both parties. The enemy is the same in both federal and provincial arenas and one organization runs the party campaign at both levels. In New Brunswick, especially, provincial Liberals have not been hesitant to do whatever they could to assist their federal counterparts. (This is less true in Nova Scotia.) Ottawa was informed, for example, that the federal campaign of 1962 would be handled by the premier himself even to the extent of his searching for suitable candidates.[9]

The primacy of provincial politics has usually meant, however, that the Ottawa leadership has not had much room for independent initiative. After a trip to New Brunswick in 1961, for example, Davey reported to Pearson that the revival of federal Liberal fortunes there was due largely to the provincial Liberal victory in 1960 and was therefore quite different from the increased support that the federal party was getting on its own merits in Ontario and Western Canada. By the same token, Maritime Liberals were generally left to their own devices, especially when a provincial Liberal government was in power. There was no question, for example, about attempting to impose an Ottawa nominee as federal campaign chairman for New Brunswick. On the other hand, when a provincial party was hard pressed, federal assistance has occasionally been provided. In the 1960s, the national office paid J.E. (Ned) Belliveau, a native New Brunswicker and Toronto advertising man, to lend aid to provincial Liberal campaigns in the Maritimes as well as in Ontario. He was a kind of Liberal equivalent to Dalton Camp, helping out with publicity, platform writing, and candidate recruitment for Liberal parties who were out of power. Nelson Rattenbury, Robichaud's chief bagman, gave him much of the credit for the Liberals' victory in the 1960 provincial election in New Brunswick and thanked General Matthews, the Liberal Federation president, for having made his services available.[10]

8. LPC, vol. 794, file: New Brunswick Liberal Association 1960-, Belliveau to J. Scott, 13.4.60. CAR (1974), 214. Ottawa Journal, 13.5.78.

9. LPC, vol. 794, file: New Brunswick Liberal Association 1960-1962, W.J. Morris to Davey, 23.6.61; vol. 795, file: Nova Scotia Liberal Association, 1960-, Orval Troy to J. Scott, 11.8.60. Interviews with Frank Matheson, 28.6.78; Alan Abraham, 28.6.78; J.G. Simpson, 29.6.78. Provincial and federal treasury committees are separate at least in Nova Scotia.

10. LPC, vol. 794, file: New Brunswick Liberal Association 1960-, Belliveau to J. Scott, 11,13.4.60; Belliveau to Matthews, 15.6.60; Rattenbury to Matthews, 18.7.60; file: New Brunswick Liberal Association 1960-1962, Davey to Pearson, 28.6.61, 22.11.61; Belliveau to Davey, 18.8.61.

The principal exception to the rule of non-interference from Ottawa occurred in the mid-1960s when, as we saw in chapter 3, the Nova Scotia Liberal party seemed to be a perfect instance where a federally directed revival would pay eventual dividends in the federal sphere. After losing power in 1956 and suffering worse defeats in 1960 and 1963, the Nova Scotia Liberal party was in the hands of a gloomy old guard. With federal and provincial politics being so intertwined, there was "no question that the provincial leadership situation is having a telling and negative effect on federal Party fortunes", Davey reported to Pearson. "It is a fact of life that Earl Urquhart [the provincial leader] will have to be replaced—and the sooner the better. He expects some kind of a federal appointment (and in my opinion he should get it). Then, we have to come up with an aggressive new leader."[11]

The revitalization was to start with a new, Ottawa-appointed federal chairman who could then look for someone to challenge the incumbent president of the provincial association at the next annual meeting, even though the president had always been hand-picked by the leader. Soon afterwards, Jack Cruickshank, a thirty-two-year-old broadcaster was appointed federal campaign chairman for Nova Scotia. Then Davey got a popular thirty-seven-year-old lawyer, MacLeod Rogers, to run for the presidency. In spite of having the support of the nominating committee, the incumbent, Eric Balcom, was beaten by Rogers and so began a new era which Davey described glowingly in his "Weekly Report" to key Liberals across the country.[12]

The third step in reconstruction came when Gerald Regan, an MP and former sportscaster, ran for the leadership—reportedly as the result of some federal arm-twisting—and won. The Nova Scotia organization was flooded with bright, young, energetic people and Davey rejoiced at "dealing with up-tempo types in Nova Scotia."[13]

After that, things did not work out quite as planned. Rogers and the other young reformers got frustrated with Regan, who in turn did little to encourage them. A year after he won the leadership, the Ottawa assessment was that Regan was a "loser" and had failed to build an effective organization. The party was divided into factions and no one was providing any leadership—not the provincial leader, nor the provincial president, nor the federal minister from Nova Scotia. There were com-

11. LPC, vol. 744, file: PMO - L.B. Pearson 1964, Davey to Pearson, 10.6.64; vol. 794, file: Nova Scotia 1961-62, Davey to Pearson, 19.12.62.

12. LPC, vol. 685, Weekly Report, 19.11.64, 29.4.65, 26.8.65; vol. 739, file: Nova Scotia Liberal Association 1962-1965, Davey to Rogers, 21.9.64, Davey to Barrow, 1.12.64. Interview with J.G. Simpson, 29.6.78.

13. LPC, vol. 1094, file: Nova Scotia Liberal Association 1966-1968, Davey to Pearson, 10.3.65; vol. 1037, file: Nova Scotia, Report by John Cruickshank, 22.6.65. Halifax Chronicle-Herald, 6.7.65.

plaints that the minister, Allan MacEachen, had failed to support the young reformers and that he was not giving Regan the opportunity to participate in federal patronage decisions and announcements of federal works projects in Nova Scotia. Rumours of a "palace revolution . . . to divest Allan [MacEachen] of all rights" as the political minister for Nova Scotia were dispelled, however, with the promise of wider consultation over patronage.[14]

In October 1970, Gerald Regan led the Liberal party in what the *Canadian Annual Review* described as a "stunning and totally unexpected defeat" of the provincial Conservative government. After the fact, everyone had a theory to explain it:

- Efforts to involve party members in policy development
- The creation of a new positive image for Regan by not allowing him to attack the Conservative government
- Saturation television advertising in the Halifax area
- A cash contribution from Ontario to the Liberal campaign fund
- A Conservative self-inflicted defeat
- A leadership-oriented campaign by the Conservatives based on the slogan: "When you think about it, is there anyone you would rather have as premier of Nova Scotia than Premier Ike Smith?"
- The re-establishment of the "normal" Liberal majority which had been broken only because of the popularity of Smith's predecessor, Robert Stanfield.[15]

What was clear was that Regan was beholden to no one in Ottawa for his victory. Even before he became premier, Regan had been burned by getting too closely associated with the federal party. In the first federal election soon after becoming leader, he campaigned vigorously for Liberal candidates. But Stanfield, the Conservative premier, took advantage of Regan's activity to turn it into a campaign on provincial issues and the Conservatives swept the province.[16] After that, Regan was

---

14. LPC, vol. 1094, file: Nova Scotia Liberal Association 1966-1968, O'Brien to Pearson, 11.8.66, Rogers to O'Brien, 14.12.66, Stanbury to O'Brien, 28.8.68, O'Brien to Trudeau, 24.10.68; vol. 1096, file: Stanbury - Correspondence & Memos, 1968, Harry Flemming to Stanbury, 8.7.68; vol. 1139, file: Information - Nova Scotia 1968-72, Stanbury to Fairclough, 1.8.68; Fairclough to Stanbury, 7.8.68; Report on Nova Scotia Convention October 25th, 26th, 1968 by J.M. St.-Laurent; Stanbury to Wylie, 30.7.69. Interview with Allan O'Brien, 24.8.77.

15. LPC, vol. 1138, file: National Executive Meeting, 18-19.9.71. Ottawa *Citizen*, 16.10.70. Interviews with Torrance Wylie, 8.9.71; William Simpson, 29.6.78. P. Aucoin, "The 1970 Nova Scotia provincial election", *Journal of Canadian Studies* (August 1972), pp. 25-35. Godfrey Papers, Godfrey to Stanbury, 27.3.75.

16. Halifax *Chronicle-Herald*, 13.11.65.

more circumspect; as premier, and like other Liberal premiers before him, he found that it was wise to take a strongly provincial stance in dealings with the federal government. Regan never became a fairy godmother to the federal party in the way that Smallwood and Robichaud did; while Allan MacEachen, for his part, never built up a powerful Nova Scotia base as Nova Scotian lieutenants before him had done, in spite of being a Nova Scotian MP for over twenty years. The Liberals did not win more than two of the eleven or twelve federal seats in Nova Scotia in any election between 1958 and 1979, except for 1963, when they won five. Ironically, that high point came just as the Ottawa-led revitalization had begun. (In 1980, they again won five seats.)

Traditionally, political parties in the Maritimes have been dominated by the leader and the legislative caucus. It was only in 1961 that Prince Edward Island Liberals held their first leadership convention instead of having the caucus choose the leader. Allan O'Brien reported in 1969 that the New Brunswick party was "run as it has been for some time by a very small group of people who have not seen fit to build a broadly spread, democratically structured political organization in the province . . . the limit of our jurisdiction in that province under the circumstances, does not provide us with too many opportunities to influence the present situation more than encouraging the organization and the leadership in a discreet way." Nevertheless, the huge attendance (relative to provincial populations) at party functions is one indication of a high level of political participation: there were 1,481 registered delegates at the 1978 Liberal annual meeting in Nova Scotia and 2,252 registered delegates at the 1978 New Brunswick leadership convention.[17]

In Nova Scotia, the federal party's participatory experiments in the early 1970s were parallelled by similar efforts to restructure the party, to increase membership, to raise money more widely through a Century Club, to draft detailed party programs and to make the leadership accountable. After eight years in office, however, a Halifax columnist, Peter Meerburg, reported that the party had grown "fat, arrogant and careless." The 1978 annual meetings was primarily a media event and the party's own television crew were there to film footage for an imminent election campaign. "The so-called accountability session at the weekend conclave was a joke. Each of the 14 questions asked by the audience contained an element of congratulation of [sic] adulation for the govern-

17. LPC, vol. 1094, file: Organization - Special Memorandum, O'Brien to Stanbury, 20.1.69. Frank MacKinnon, "Prince Edward Island: Big Engine, Little Body", in Martin Robin, ed., Canadian Provincial Politics, pp. 248-252. Robert S. Best, "The Organization of Provincial Parties", in Donald C. Rowat, ed., Provincial Government and Politics: Comparative Essays, 2nd ed., pp. 407-435. Halifax Chronicle-Herald, 11.4.78. Ottawa Journal, 13.5.78.

ment. It would be folly for any serious Liberal to pose a nasty or embarrassing question under those circumstances."[18]

The provincial party lost the election but, with almost 40 percent of the popular vote, it remains a potent, resilient force in that province.

QUEBEC

Thirty years ago, the Quebec Liberal party was as undemocratic and loosely structured as any party in the Atlantic provinces. Today it is certainly more highly organized and perhaps even more democratic than any other Liberal party across the country. The party is the most wilful, independent, exasperating, but also the most brilliant and faithful daughter of that secular church—the Liberal Party of Canada. Formerly, there was hardly a trace of democracy in its structures. There was no constitution, there were no constituency associations, no formal members, but only rival cadres of ministers, organizers and fund raisers, based in Quebec City, francophone and anglophone Montreal, and Ottawa. Sometimes the federal wing predominated; at other times it was the provincial wing. The whole operation was made to run with a liberal application of patronage and paid election workers.

Old guards and new guards

It was the provincial wing of the party which took the first steps to set up formal party structures based on constituency associations, members, membership fees, conventions, commissions and executives. As always with Liberals, it was electoral defeat that spurred them to action. After the end of World War II, the provincial wing experienced a series of disastrous defeats, the worst of which was in 1948, when they won only 8 out of 92 seats in the legislature. The federal Liberals, by contrast, had held power since 1935. For the provincial MLAs, who saw themselves as the poor relations of their federal cousins, the Fédération libérale provinciale or FLP, established in 1955, was a way out of the morass of defeat. (The name was changed later to the Fédération libérale du Québec or FLQ— not to be confused with the Front de Libération du Québec—and later still to the Parti Libéral du Québec or PLQ.) From the beginning, the FLP was unsure about what sort of relationship it should have with the federal party, some arguing that the principles of Liberalism were the same in both federal and provincial affairs and that "un rouge à Québec" was

[18.] Halifax *Chronicle-Herald*, 11.4.78; 10,12.3.79; 16.3.74; 20.9.71. LPC, vol. 1138, file: National Executive Meeting, 18-19.9.71.

"un rouge à Ottawa." Others argued that the logic of federalism's division of powers between two levels of government necessitated two separate Liberal parties. Theory apart, account also had to be taken of the informal non-aggression pacts which many federal MPs had with Union Nationale MLAs whose provincial ridings overlapped with theirs. It is not surprising that they saw little benefit to themselves in this new provincial Liberal structure.

Even within the federal Liberal party, Quebec Liberals tended to be a law unto themselves. Before 1957, there was no Quebec Liberal party with membership in the National Liberal Federation of Canada, inconceivable as it may seem. (Before 1957, the Quebec representatives on the Advisory Council were named by the Quebec ministers.) The Quebec Liberal caucus and federal election campaigns in Quebec were managed separately under the authority of the leader of Quebec MPs in Ottawa. The Quebec "lieutenant", so called, was, in effect, more like a viceroy within his own political domain. His wide control over patronage, including nominations and even cabinet posts, gave him an authority which was diminished only on those rare occasions when the party lost power federally or in the more frequent periods when provincial Liberals held the reins in Quebec City. Just a few months before the 1949 election the director of the national headquarters, commenting on the organizational preparedness in English Canada, added that of course he had no direct knowledge of what was going on in Quebec[19] and this would not have been atypical.

The attitude of federal Quebec Liberals changed with the Conservative victory in the federal election of 1957 and even more with their unwonted rout in Quebec a year later. The Conservatives and the Union Nationale were now a common enemy and shared adversity produced a community of interest. In 1957 the FLP requested affiliation with the NLF and was accepted. For a time, at least, the principle of "rouge à Ottawa; rouge à Québec" was granted.[20]

The "double allegiance" rule created few problems as long as both federal and provincial Liberals were out of power, but the provincial Liberal victory of 1960 and its even greater victory of 1962 provided a new perspective, this time for the provincial Liberals. As supporters of a gov-

[19] LPC, vol. 614, Kidd to Bruce Brown, 25.2.49.

[20] Whitaker, The Government Party, pp. 269-302; Norman Ward, ed., A Party Politician: The Memoirs of Chubby Power. LPC, vol. 672, file: Fédération libérale du Québec, 1957-1958, Gérard Brady to Lafond, 29.1.57. Gérard Bergeron, "Les partis libéraux du Canada et du Québec (1955-1965) (aspects bilingues et biculturels)", Etude préparée pour le Service des Recherches de la Commission Royale d'Enquête sur le Bilinguisme et le Biculturalisme (1966), p. 21. David M. Rayside, "Federalism and the Party System: Provincial and Federal Liberals in the Province of Quebec," CJPS (1978), 499-528.

ernment that was confident and increasingly nationalistic, a number of them argued that, in their confrontations with federal authority, they should be free of encumbering ties with a federal party. Also, as a reformist, left-of-centre party, the provincial Liberal party was the only home for like-minded provincial voters, whereas in federal elections there was also the NDP and, for rural populists, the créditistes. The "double loyalty" rule was perceived as an encumbrance to the provincial Liberals—at that time, no one envisaged it working the other way round! The advent to power of a hesitant minority Liberal government in 1963 served only to exacerbate the situation. When the separation of the two levels of the party was first proposed in 1963 by René Lévesque, François Aquin and other left-wing members of the Policy Commission, the idea was vigorously opposed by the party establishment. Within a year, however, Lesage had changed his position, arguing that affiliation was a nuisance both to a federal Liberal government and a Quebec Liberal government. According to Judy LaMarsh, who was a federal cabinet minister at the time, Guy Favreau, the Quebec federal leader, had also come to the conclusion that the federal wing would do better on its own. Federal Liberals resented the influence that Lesage was able to exert in federal affairs through his domination of the combined party, and they were also concerned about the growing strength of separatist-leaning groups within the provincial wing. It would be easier, they believed, to recruit outstanding federalists from Quebec if the federal wing were free of such entanglements.[21]

In 1964, the provincial FLQ dissociated itself from the federal party and two years later, the founding convention of the new federal Quebec Liberal party was held. The structures of the Liberal Federation of Canada (Quebec) or LFC(Q) were closely modelled on those of the FLQ. (Coincident with the change in the name of the federal party in 1970, the Quebec party was renamed the Liberal Party of Canada (Quebec) or LPC(Q).) The principal body was to be the board of directors, consisting of the executive, three representatives of the federal caucus, and seventeen regional directors, each elected at the annual congress by the delegates from that region. The larger, more inclusive general council, in addition to the board members, also included the presidents and secretaries of all the riding associations, all Liberal Quebec MPs, the secretaries of the six permanent commissions and six delegates from each affiliated federation, such as women and youth. The board of directors had to report to it every six months and the only body with superior authority was the annual congress, composed primarily of delegates from the riding associations. The three most important committees were con-

---

[21.] Bergeron, pp. 96-99, 105. Judy LaMarsh, *Memoirs of a Bird in a Gilded Cage*, pp. 143-144. Interview with Torrance Wylie, 5.8.70.

cerned with organization (the Electoral Commission), finance, and policy (the Political Commission. Its upper limit of eighty-five members would be superfluous in other provinces, where the thankless task of drafting policy statements is regarded as much less exciting than organizing election campaigns. Quebec's Political Commission, however, had become a mammoth and controversial body, attracting many non-Liberal radicals and leftists.) Finally, the constitution laid down many guidelines to which its member constituency associations had to adhere. Federal associations had to be distinct from provincial ones, but a considerable overlap of membership was expected and it was later reported that there was a 90 percent duplication of membership in the federal and provincial county associations.[22]

For some provincial Liberals, separation was seen as casting adrift the weak sisters of the federal Liberal caucus. While provincial Liberals were revelling in the heady atmosphere of the Quiet Revolution, the federal Quebec party presented a gloomy, uninspiring image. Lip service was paid to the necessity of attracting young, reform-minded Quebeckers to Ottawa, but Pearson's first cabinet was hardly reassuring, including as it did such old-guard Liberals as Azellus Denis and Jean-Paul Deschatelets and only one genuine member of the new guard, Maurice Lamontagne. A Quebec member of the party's national executive, John deB. Payne, described the old guard as wanting "neither new men nor new ideas. All they want is protection of their imagined cabinet posts, judgeships and senatorships . . . . [They] represent the old ways—patronage, spoils and no intellectual participation in the affairs of government or in party politics. They are not really interested in governing. The new group—the Lamontagnes and the Sauvés—want to participate in government policy for the whole of the country not just Quebec. None of them are interested in the spoils or patronage in the old classical sense." Pearson's Quebec lieutenant, Lionel Chevrier, a franco-Ontarian without any real power base in Quebec, was inclined not to challenge the old guard and further appointments made towards the end of the Pearson government's first year of office included Yvon Dupuis, as a member of the cabinet, and Guy Rouleau as parliamentary secretary to the Prime Minister. Payne described them as "young old men" and both were later seriously implicated in the scandals which engulfed so many of Pearson's Quebec ministers, both old and new guard.[23]

The change in generations and the shift to a new style of politics resembled what was happening in Ontario, except that the Ontario old guard collapsed without a struggle to the challenge from Cell 13. In the begin-

---

[22.] Bergeron, pp. 160-180. *Globe*, 9.4.66.

[23.] LPC, vol. 742, file: John deB. Payne - Correspondence, Payne to Davey, 17.12.62, Payne to Davey, 5.5.64. P.C. Newman, *The Distemper of Our Times*, chap. 20.

ning there was really no comparable group in Quebec. The initial fight against the old guard was carried on almost single-handedly by Maurice Sauvé, a brilliant loner who did not disguise his contempt for the parochial, patronage-minded Liberals of the older generation. He wanted Quebeckers to be represented in the federal Cabinet by authentic spokesmen, who understood the new, changing Quebec, and by ministers of such high calibre that they could not be ignored by their English-speaking colleagues. So long as Quebec had mediocre representation in Ottawa, said Sauvé, its interests would be neglected. He also demanded that the new party structure, the LFC(Q), exercise its democratic control over party funds and organization in place of the shadowy cliques who had traditionally held those responsibilities. At first, Sauvé's imprecations produced no results, in spite of some well-orchestrated support from prominent journalists. Pearson persisted in keeping the old guard in his cabinet; Lamontagne refused to join Sauvé's crusade; and Favreau depended on the old guard as the indispensable masters of the mysteries of election organization, about which he professed to know little.[24]

Ironically, the separation of the provincial party from the federal party had much to do with the eventual salvation of the latter. After the separation, Lesage, in one of his more conservative moods, became increasingly unhappy with the growing strength of the nationalist, leftist wing, led by Lévesque and Aquin from their power base in the Policy Commission of the FLQ. Over the next several months, he carried out a purge of the Policy Commission. Two years later, at the party convention of November 1966, the more conservative wing of the party blocked a reform slate that sought to end the leader's exclusive discretionary control of the party's finances and to give financial control to the FLQ itself. John deB. Payne predicted that this "garrotting party" of provincial Liberal reformers would drive some into creating a separatist party of the Left and would drive others, the young federalist reformers, into the arms of the newly created federal Liberal party, where they could find "an acceptable political home and the intellectual climate they seek." He was right. Jean-Luc Pépin and Jean Chrétien had already joined its ranks in 1963 and two years later, the famous "Three Wise Men"—Jean Marchand, Gérard Pelletier and Pierre Trudeau—were finally persuaded to become federal Liberal candidates. Finally, when Marchand took over as Quebec lieutenant in 1967, the new guard were at last firmly in power in Ottawa;

[24.] Interviews with J. deB. Payne, 13.1.72 and Claude Frenette, 3.10.79. Bergeron, pp. 209-231.

Quebec federal Liberals could now hold their own with their Quebec City counterparts.[25]

Not all the new guard came through unscathed. As Sauvé carried on his struggle to reform the federal party in Quebec, some commentators noted an inherent contradiction in his position: he called for more democratic selection of riding candidates and, at the same time, for a higher calibre of candidates. What if the people did not want to be represented by new guard Liberals? What indeed! A cruel fate allowed Sauvé to experience that dilemma at first hand. The nominations in Quebec ridings in the 1968 election were probably more democratic than any in the province's history, but Sauvé himself failed to win the Liberal nomination in the safe new riding of Gamelin and, though he was eventually nominated in St. Hyacinthe, he was defeated by the incumbent Conservative, Théogène Ricard. The man who had led the initial fight against the old guard was not to savour the fruits of that victory.[26]

The world keeps turning and it was not long before the ever-flowing tides of change produced a new generation of reformers. The original new guard had consolidated its position when Pierre Levasseur was appointed executive director of the Montreal office of the LFC(Q) in 1967 and Claude Frenette was elected president in early 1968. Both about thirty years old, they were representative of a new generation of high-powered French Canadian business executives. They were also both convinced federalists and admirers of Pierre Trudeau and their presence secured the loyalty of the LFC(Q) for the impending leadership contest.[27]

The office of the new LFC(Q) was a shambles, but the two men proceeded to demonstrate that a party could be effectively organized according to established business and military principles and that the old guard had no monopoly on the part of political organization. Frenette also became an enthusiastic advocate of both democratization within the party and participation by the party in ministerial decision making. The latter, as we shall see in chapter 5, took the form of provincial advisory groups or troikas. Through these, the provincial party president and the chairman of the provincial caucus of MPs could discuss prospective appointments and political matters generally with the minister who had political responsibility for party matters in that province. Under this scheme, Quebec would cease to be a province "pas comme les autres"

[25] Interview with B. Deschenes, 31.10.78. LPC, vol. 1028, file: Payne, John deB., "The Quebec Liberal Conference, An Appraisal", 22.11.66 with addenda. Don & Vera Murray, de Bourassa à Lévesque, pp. 29-35 Montreal Gazette, 1.4.66. Montreal Star, 15.4.67. Martin Sullivan, Mandate '68, pp. 93-118.

[26] Bergeron, pp. 221-229.

[27] Martin Sullivan, pp. 240, 264-267.

with its lieutenant (or "roi nègre" as Trudeau himself had called the position years before).

Jean-Paul Lefebvre, a former MLA who was appointed executive director in 1970, was also a strong advocate of collegial decision making and (that typically francophone concept), "l'animation sociale." He attempted to expand the party bureaucracy and to make the party a genuine mass movement. However, he soon found himself isolated from both Frenette and Marchand, who suspected he wanted to become a kind of federal equivalent of Paul Desrochers, the powerful general secretary of Bourassa's provincial Liberal party organization. It also became clear that the new-guard Marchand was a traditionalist when it came to collegial sharing of the Quebec lieutenant's old patronage prerogatives. Although the troika worked well for a few months, it finally stopped meeting after Marchand made some decisions without having consulted the troika. Marchand was also opposed to such measures of internal party reform as publishing the LFC(Q)'s financial statements or giving the LFC(Q) a large enough budget to promote participatory activities by party members. Lefebvre was disappointed that Trudeau, after his initial support of the participatory concept, had stayed out of party affairs and declined to enter the fray against Marchand. After a year and a half as executive director, he resigned with the parting comment that it had not been easy to create a democratic party.[28]

Jean Fortier, who was elected president in 1971, was as committed to democratization as Frenette and Lefebvre. But in the case of riding nominations, conflicting considerations were no less a problem than they had been in the sixties. The party constitution had been amended to prevent two of the most common abuses—a riding clique keeping tight control over the issuance of new memberships; or a candidate packing a nominating meeting through the sale of last-minute memberships to his friends and relations. The new constitutional provisions declared, firstly, that anyone could become a member of his or her constituency association by applying directly to the provincial secretariat with the right of appeal to the board of directors of LPC(Q); secondly, that recruitment of new members was automatically suspended when a general election was called; thirdly, that riding conventions were to be chaired by representatives of LPC(Q).[29]

As evidence that these changes had been efficacious, Fortier pointed to the nominating conventions which had been held in all seventy-four

28. *La Presse*, 30.9.71; 16.10.71; 19, 21, 26.1.74. *Le Devoir*, 1.10.71. Interview with Claude Frenette, 3.10.79.

29. Liberal Party of Canada (Quebec), Constitution for Constituency Associations, 1971, 2.B. Constitutional Documents of the L.P.C.(Q), Document D: Rules of the Convention, A.4., B.7.

Quebec constituencies in the 1972 election and claimed that the LPC(Q) had successfully defied Michel's Iron Law of Oligarchy in transforming itself from a traditional party of cadres or cliques into a democratic organization. Total party membership in the province was 53,403 and 60 percent of them had attended the various nominating conventions throughout the province, for an average of 440 per convention.

There were still, however, some checks on the power of the rank-and-file members. The party constitution also provided that "Due to special circumstances and in the general interest of the Party, the Leader of Quebec can dispense with a Convention in a county and designate the official candidate after consulting with the Electoral Commission and the Executive Committee of the County Association." In 1972, this power was used when democratization conflicted with another equally commendable goal—that of getting outstanding women into Parliament. Quebec riding associations had been particularly reluctant to nominate women, especially in ridings where they had a good chance of winning. Monique Bégin, formerly the executive secretary of the Royal Commission on the Status of Women, was one whom the members of the party establishment were particularly anxious to have as a Liberal candidate. She attempted first to get the nomination in Duvernay but could not overcome the strong support which had been garnered by a local accountant, Yves Demers. Even the presence of a minister, the Hon. Jean-Pierre Goyer, and of eleven MPs could not prevent Bégin from losing 630 votes to 748. But a few weeks later, at the St. Michel riding convention, the former MP, Victor Forget, suddenly withdrew at the last moment and the convention was informed that, because no one else had filed nomination papers, Marchand (with the Electoral Commission's concurrence) had designated Bégin as the candidate. "The departure of Forget was a study in political brutality" commented the *Gazette*. "Until the eve of the nominating meeting, Forget did not know what was about to hit him. When it did, he was reduced to tears . . . A few days after the nomination meeting, Forget became a citizenship court judge, which pays between $26,000 and $20,000."[30] As for Bégin, her subsequent career as a prominent member of the Quebec caucus and eventually as a cabinet minister tended to vindicate Marchand, but the incident clearly illustrates the limits of party democracy in the LPC(Q).

The next round between "participationistes" and "electoralistes" came with the election of a new president at the 4th party congress in January 1974. Minority government from 1972 to 1974 had made it both nec-

---

[30] Constitutional Documents of the LPC(Q), Document D: Rules of the Convention, D.25. Montreal *Gazette*, 19.12.77. Interviews with Micheline Côté, 3.11.78; Jean Fortier, 29.10.79. *La Presse*, 21.8.72. *Globe and Mail*, 9.9.72; 25.7.70; *Le Devoir*, 23.10.72; 13.6.70.

essary and inevitable that electoral considerations outweigh any attempts to increase popular participation with activities like regional policy conferences. As retiring president, Fortier called for a renewed emphasis on participation, but many MPs and ministers dismissed such talk as "dreamy idealism." The contest for the presidency produced a confrontation between the Montreal "participationistes" and the Ottawa "electoralistes", with Maurice Labelle as the càndidate of the former camp and Senator Jean-Pierre Côté representing the latter. With the defeat of Labelle, Gagne in *La Presse* commented that the democratization effort of Fortier and Lefebvre had come to an end.[31]

When Marchand resigned as Quebec leader in February 1975, Trudeau appointed Marc Lalonde to succeed him. Marchand was a lovable, unpredictable man who might make a decision on a whim; but he could be inveigled into changing his mind. Lalonde was the opposite: fair, rational, respected rather than loved, and too cool, too disciplined ever to reverse his own final decision. Lalonde's appointment further confirmed how tightly the reins of power were held in the Quebec party. Authority came, as it has done for decades, directly from the federal party leader through a man who has always been close to the leader, even "an extension of the arm of the Prime Minister."[32] Even if he had not the moral authority of Jean Marchand, the powers which he exercised were considerable:

Tout ce qui concerne le Québec, que ce soit au niveau des relations avec les dirigeants provinciaux, ou encore des organisations de comtés, du choix des candidats, du choix des secrétaires parlementaires, tout passe par lui. En outre, et ce n'est pas peu dire, il a la mainmise sur la machine libérale, celle qui bon an mal an retourne sa cinquantaine et plus de députés.[33]

No president since Fortier and no executive director since Lefebvre has ever attempted to challenge the power of the Quebec leader. Senator Côté, Fortier's successor, is described as having been, very clearly, the boss of the 1974 federal campaign in Quebec, but only because his authority came directly from the prime minister.[34] His successor, Dalia Wood (later appointed a senator) consented to become a last-minute candidate for the party presidency when Jacques Bouchard was forced to withdraw following allegations that his advertising agency held $5 million in government contracts. She also became acting executive director when Jean-Pierre Mongeau resigned to become chairman of the federalist forces in the referendum. Wood had been the president of Trudeau's Mount Royal constituency association and she was not one to chal-

[31]. *La Presse*, 21.1.74; 26.1.74; 19.1.74; *Le Devoir*, 19.1.74.
[32]. *Montreal Star*, 27.2.75.
[33]. *Le Soleil*, 1.3.75.
[34]. Interview with Roger Hébert, 2.11.78.

lenge the authority of his right-hand man in Quebec. Jean Marchand succeeded her, but resigned as president a short time later, complaining that the Quebec party no longer allowed party members to express their opinions. Plus ça change . . . .[35]

A model machine

If party militants remain dissatisfied with the extent to which democracy has been realized within the LPC(Q), there is no doubt that it is nevertheless an impressive, well-organized party which keeps in close contact with its grass roots, unlike the Liberal party in other provinces which often gives the impression of being little more than a loose liaison of similarly loosely structured riding associations. The office of the LPC(Q) on St. Catherines Street West in Montreal exudes an atmosphere of cool efficiency personified in Mrs. Dalia Wood, the brisk, fiftyish, immaculately groomed acting director, who is an impressive example of the perfectly bilingual Quebec anglophone. Her second in command is a charming, good-looking man by the name of Roger Hébert, who obviously thrives on the details of political organization. With a staff of twenty-five and an annual budget of $600,000, the Montreal office is more like the Ottawa headquarters than any provincial party office—except that it is just a bit more chic than Ottawa. As an illustration of the LPC(Q)'s tight structure, the party office maintains a central list of its 120,000 members and, as already mentioned, application for membership can be made directly to the central office or to a riding association; in order to ensure that due notice of meetings is given to all members of each riding association, all the mailings are done from the Montreal office.

One of the most important means by which the LPC(Q) can exercise its clout is through the Electoral Commission, the powers of which are fully set out in the party's constitution; similar committees in other provinces have no constitutional recognition and function solely at the discretion of the federal campaign committee. The Electoral Commission includes a minister who represents the party leader, the party president, the executive director and the chairman of the Quebec caucus. The Commission is responsible for finding suitable candidates and, to this end, it has considerable powers. All prospective candidates must apply to the Commission and be approved by it, though appeals can be made to the executive committee of the LPC(Q). This is no mere formality—in 1974, five applicants were refused permission to enter nomination contests. The Com-

---

[35.] *Montreal Star*, 12.3.76. *Globe and Mail*, 24.8.79.

mission is also empowered to recognize riding associations; it can designate persons to act for it when no association is recognized; and it has to approve the date and location of each riding's nominating convention.[36] Periodically, there are pre-election reports that the Electoral Commission is going to conduct a "housecleaning" of the Quebec caucus in order to clear out the dead wood and, if the actual results of these purgations are usually less extensive than the initial claims, it should be remembered that such exercises would not even be contemplated in other provinces.[37]

The highly articulated nature of the LPC(Q) is also apparent in the party's policy committees, election-day organization and fund raising. Ever since the days when the FLP's Political Commission laid the groundwork for the Quiet Revolution in the 1950s, Political Commissions of both the federal and provincial parties have had a prestige unrivalled by Liberal policy committees in other provinces. Recent chairmen of the LPC(Q)'s Political Commission like Céline Payette and Micheline Côté have looked upon the position as being almost a full-time job. Under Côté, the Commission had a membership of forty people and met fortnightly. In her own assessment, the position gave her more influence than the average backbench MP and the Commission's confidential suggestions to the prime minister appeared not infrequently as government policy, although she became disillusioned when the government apparently paid no heed to the Political Commission's views on the Gens de l'air issue in the summer of 1976. The policy conferences organized by the Political Commission are impressive exercises in grass-roots democracy. Each of the twenty regions into which the province is divided has its own day-long policy conference attended by two- to three-hundred people on average. These activities culminate in the policy deliberations of the LPC(Q)'s biennial conventions. Voting is by secret ballot and the results are published a few weeks later. In 1976, for example, one hundred resolutions were approved, some of which were critical of the government's alleged leniency with criminals and its refusal to help in dealing with the Olympic deficit. One cannot help but be struck by the faith that Quebec policy people have in their policy process. As Payette said, "You cannot use just experts to develop policy, you have to use 'real' people. They may not know the answers but they know how to articulate the problems."[38]

[36.] Constitutional Documents of the LPC(Q), Documents B and D. Interviews with D. Wood, 1.11.78 and R. Hébert, 2.11.78.

[37.] Montreal Star, 5.2.72; Windsor Star, 18.2.72; Le Devoir, 25.7.78; Interview with R. Hébert, 2.11.78.

[38.] Interviews with Céline Payette, 2.11.78 and Micheline Côté, 3.11.78. Le Jour, 18.3.76; Le Devoir, 8.4.76.

It is perhaps a small point, but even the election-day organization adds a layer which does not appear in the typical Ontario constituency and which helps to tighten the whole structure. That is the group of sector heads each of whom oversees the activities of seven to ten poll captains. In an Ontario riding, a ward chairman is likely to have forty or fifty poll captains under him; he has to leave them more or less on their own on election day and there is really no way for him to be sure that his poll captains are really energetic in getting known Liberal supporters to the vote in the last crucial three or four hours before the polls close — often, in fact, they do not even fully understand what their function is! In Quebec, this extra layer of sector heads between the ward chairmen (or *chef de région*) and the poll captain (or *chef de section de vote*) keeps the organization better articulated, a characteristic feature of the Quebec party.[39]

The Quebec party's fund-raising activities have set an example for the other provinces. Before the 1974 election-expenses legislation, Quebec was always accused of being a drain on funds collected nationally. In 1975, the General Council of LPC(Q) decided to make the constituencies responsible for collecting their own campaign funds through annual fund-raising drives and to end their dependence on corporate donations and $100/plate *dîners bénéfices* which had been organized by the Montreal office. Since then, the constituencies have had four annual, province-wide, fund-raising drives which have each collected more than $1 million, mostly in amounts of $150 or less. The funds are divided as follows: 25 percent remains with the constituency to finance year-round activities; 40 percent is held in trust for the constituency's next federal campaign; 25 percent goes to the LPC(Q) for annual office maintenance and 10 percent is held in trust for the province-wide federal campaign. By the time of the 1979 election, every Quebec constituency had raised enough money that it could spend the full amount allowed under the Election Expenses Act. In no other province was the riding-level fund raising so impressive. LPC(Q) also runs a "sectoral" or provincial-level campaign directed at medium-sized contributors; the provincial headquarters gets 75 percent of this for annual office expenses and the remaining 25 percent is held in trust for Quebec's federal campaign. (The Quebec party is not involved in the national fund-raising campaign which is directed at the large head offices; but it negotiates for a share of the thirty cents per elector, which the national office receives as a subsidy from public funds.)[40]

39. Interview with R. Hébert, 2.11.78. "Resumé du cours Leadership en Organization", mimeographed study prepared by the LPC(Q), 1978.

40. Interviews with B. Deschenes, 31.10.78 and D. Wood, 1.11.78. *La Presse*, 9.6.75. *Globe and Mail*, 9.6.75; 14.9.77. *Le Devoir*, 18.2.76; 19.2.79. Montreal *Gazette*, 18.2.76. "*Dialogue*" (April 1976), 10.

Finally Quebec's separation of the federal and provincial wings into distinct parties has become a test case for the other provinces. While separation was originally advanced out of the self-interest of the provincial wing and even, by some, as a means of advancing the nationalist cause, it later proved its tactical usefulness for the federal group as well. The federal party may have been the weaker, less popular party in the mid-1960s, but by the mid-1970s, the position was reversed and the members of the federal party were glad to keep their distance from the luckless provincial Liberals—preferring instead to maintain their own, impressive party structures which were exclusively devoted to federal politics. The fluctuation in the relative strengths of the two parties is certainly going to continue over the years ahead, so self-reliance is appropriate and no doubt beneficial. Similar considerations induced the Ontario provincial wing to strike out on its own in 1976. One might ask, then, is complete separation the ideal for every province? Two qualifications should be made. Firstly, where either wing is very weak, indifference to its fate by the stronger wing ultimately damages both, as we shall see in the case of the western Liberal parties. Secondly, separation in any case is not complete, even in the case of Quebec. Although the two hierarchies are now composed of quite different personnel, there is a considerable overlap at the riding level. Moreover, the federal party could not be indifferent to the declining popularity of both Lesage and Bourassa; in fact, both men's resignations followed stinging attacks on them by federal Quebec Liberals. Even—indeed, especially—on such a vital issue as leadership, there is no such thing as watertight compartments.[41]

ONTARIO

The largely personal feud that Mitch Hepburn waged against Mackenzie King in the late 1930s and early 1940s probably marked the lowest point every reached in the relations between federal and provincial wings of the same party. Certainly no other Liberal premier has ever condemned the policies of a federal Liberal government as Hepburn did in the notorious Ontario War Resolution of 1940.[42] But those days have long since passed and, throughout most of the period presently under review, the federal Liberals regarded their relationship with the provincial wing in Ontario as ideal; provincial Liberals were less certain.

Following Hepburn's sudden retirement from politics, the provincial Liberals suffered a devastating defeat in the 1943 election and an even worse one in 1945, when Hepburn briefly attempted a comeback. The

[41]. *Globe and Mail*, 9.4.66; 2.9.69. Montreal *Gazette*, 8.3.76.
[42]. Neil McKenty, *Mitch Hepburn*, pp. 208-209.

federal party did not fare quite so badly in the federal election which followed the second provincial one, but it lost every seat but one in Toronto. The party's bad performance in the federal election produced a split in the Toronto organization and David Croll, the only Toronto Liberal MP, became the moving spirit behind a new rebel Toronto and Yorks Liberal Association (formerly the Toronto Central Liberal Association). For over a year two rival associations fought for control of the various riding organizations amidst charges that Tammany Hall tactics were being used. Ottawa then moved determinedly to ensure that the party came into loyal hands. C.D. Howe, as the senior Ontario political minister, dissolved the renegades' association and got his man, J.D. McNish, elected as chairman of a reunited Toronto Liberal Association, though the insurgents won seven of the eight executive seats. A few years later, the association was renamed Toronto and Yorks—apparently conceding that the rebel group had had the best name—McNish was re-elected president and was, effectively, the Liberal boss in Toronto.[43]

From 1945 to 1958, the Ontario party was completely oriented to the federal arena and the federal wing did not expect much assistance from a generally moribund provincial group. This was partly due to very severe leadership problems experienced by the provincial party, beginning with Hepburn's abortive return in 1945, Walter Thomson's disastrous showing in the 1951 election and four stints under Farquhar Oliver, either as leader or as acting leader, when no one else wanted the job.[44]

As we saw earlier, the plan for rebuilding the party after 1958 was supposed to start at the provincial level in Ontario and, at the provincial leadership convention of 1958, the federal wing of the party pushed for Walter Harris, who had been finance minister in St. Laurent's government until its defeat. However, the party showed some encouraging signs of life and threatened to split over what was regarded as an attempt "by a group of men in Toronto who couldn't win an election for poundkeeper" to foist Harris on the provincial Liberal caucus. John Wintermeyer, an MPP, won a third-ballot victory over Harris in one of the most closely contested leadership races that the provincial Liberals had ever held. Liberal standings in the legislature doubled at the next year's election, and for a while, it looked as if a provincial Liberal revival was indeed occurring, though not under federal auspices nor with much federal help. The revival petered out, however, and Wintermeyer lost his seat in the 1963 election. Following this period of relative independence from the federal wing, the two levels were once more securely knit together when the

---

[43] Interview with Gordon Dryden, 3.4.74. *Globe and Mail*, 24.1.45; 20, 24.11.45; 12.2.47; 21.3.47; 31.3.48; 28.3.50.

[44] Interview with Boyd Upper, 19.6.74. LPC, vol. 660, file: Ontario Liberal Association 1949, R.M. Campbell to Kidd, 12.5.49.

leadership was won by Andrew Thompson, a protégé of Keith Davey and Walter Gordon. Because Thompson was a member of the party's reform wing, his leadership of the provincial party served to advance a strategy which Davey was promoting then—a broadening of the party's support to include the NDP or its voters—in the province where it was most likely to pay the greatest dividends. Since the Conservative party constituted the principal opposition to the Liberals in both federal and provincial arenas, the strategy did not work against the interests of the provincial party in the way that it did for provincial Liberal parties in the West; but Thompson's more conservative caucus at Queen's Park was noticeably less enthusiastic than their leader to work for the federal cause or to fit into a left-of-centre mould.[45]

Both Gordon and Thompson resigned their respective positions within a year of each other in 1965-66 after some bad luck—Gordon's was political, Thompson's personal—and Gordon's departure left a serious gap in the leadership of Ontario Liberals that has never been filled. Robert Nixon, who succeeded Thomson as leader, continued the practice of close co-operation with the federal wing of the party and that was reciprocated. He was invited to join the Ontario advisory group or troika and that was an indication of the harmonious relations between the two wings of the party in Ontario, since, in the original conception of the troika, the provincial president was seen as the sole representative of the provincial wing. While Nixon was leader, the provincial wing of the party seems to have been consulted more often over federal appointments than had been true earlier. Nixon confessed that he was not greatly interested in the individual cases, but he appreciated the symbolic importance of being known as someone who *was* consulted by federal Liberals. For their part, federal Liberals regarded their relations with the provincial wing as ideal. Indeed, it *was* ideal. The provincial Liberals were strong enough in provincial elections to reinforce many voters' Lib-

---

[45] J. Wearing, "Ontario Political Parties: Fish or Fowl?" in D.C. MacDonald, ed., *Government and Politics of Ontario*, pp. 328-329. *Globe and Mail*, 12,17-22.4.58. The quoted remarks are by one of the other leadership candidates, Ross Whicher, MPP. *Montreal Star*, 10.5.66. *Canada Month*, February 1964. LPC, vol. 741, file: Ontario Provincial Liberal Party, Gordon Awde to Davey, 21.4.64, 8.9.64; vol. 744, file: PMO - L.B. Pearson 1965-66, Davey to Pearson, 28.9.65; vol. 1027, file: Government Advertising, R.M. Campbell to Nichol, 28.10.66; vol. 1037, file: Ontario Campaign Committee, Dan Lang to Davey, 7.2.64; Davey to Lang, 14.12.64. Interviews with Colin Campbell, 14.6.74; Robert Nixon, 5.9.78; Boyd Upper, 19.6.74. Davey, when he was national director, told Wintermeyer bluntly that he had surrounded himself with a remarkably weak group of advisors. Wintermeyer responded by offering to make Davey Toronto campaign director; like a true federal Liberal, Davey pleaded the pressure of his Ottawa job, though he did consent to join the campaign committee. LPC, vol. 741, file: Ontario Provincial Election-1963, Davey to Wintermeyer, 27.5.63; Davey to Campbell Calder, 28.5.63. Even when Wintermeyer was leader, the provincial party received financial and organizational help from the federal wing. J.E. Belliveau to the author, 11.12.79.

eral identities, but after being in second place for so long the provincial wing was not exciting or glamorous enough to be a serious drain on the energies of key Liberals. In fact, federal Liberals were so anxious to maintain this sort of uneven balance that, when it looked as if the provincial wing might catch fire under a new leader in 1973, one federal strategist admitted that he voted to renew Nixon's mandate at the provincial leadership convention. With a minority Liberal government in Ottawa facing the possibility of an election at any time, the "feds" did not want Ontario Liberals to start getting too interested in provincial politics.[46]

The 1975 provincial election was a moment of truth for Ontario Liberals. Throughout the period of minority government from 1972 to 1974, provincial party concerns were relegated to their customary position of second place. The 1974 annual meeting in Sudbury, for example, had been planned to focus primarily on provincial policy questions, drawing on the momentum generated by two striking provincial by-election victories in the last couple of years. When the annual meeting convened in late April, however, it was apparent that the minority Liberal government in Ottawa was about to be defeated and that an election was imminent. Ontario's federal ministers appeared in force along with Trudeau himself and the meeting became, in effect, a launching for the federal election campaign.

Even more, the 1975 provincial election itself raised questions about the wisdom of provincial Liberals having too close a relationship with the federal wing. When the federal Liberals regained their majority in 1974, they promised to use all their prestige, money and organization to help the Ontario wing, reputedly for the first time. The provincial Liberals looked as if they were going to have their best chance in forty years of defeating a Conservative government. But instead of winning, they came third, albeit with a substantial increase in popular vote and legislative seats. Various factors were cited to explain why victory had eluded their grasp, apparently in the last week or two of the campaign. One was the final televised leaders' debate that degenerated into a shouting match between Davis and Nixon. Another factor was supposedly John Turner's sudden retirement as federal finance minister just one week before the election. The latter served to underline the growing public concern about the economy and made provincial Liberals sensitive to Davis's taunt that they were the "kissing cousins" of the increasingly unpopular Trudeau government.[47]

Whatever the reasons for the outcome, the important point to consider in our analysis is that new Liberal MPPs especially became convinced that the federal link was hurting them in the eyes of the electorate and

---

[46] Interview with Nixon, 5.9.78. Confidential Source.

[47] Globe and Mail, 10.2.75; 20.3.76. CAR 1975, pp. 136-143.

that the "feds" had no sensitivity for the provincial wing of the party. It was also argued that the separation of the two wings would allow for the development of two distinct teams—one working exclusively for the provincial party, the other for the federal party. Previously, there had been a good deal of overlap between both campaign committees, for example, and there was, of course, only one executive, one provincial office, and one annual meeting to serve both federal and provincial interests. Did the executive director of LPO, for instance, spend 80 percent of his time on provincial party matters and 20 percent on federal? Or was it the other way around? Not surprisingly, both sides tended to believe that the sharing arrangement worked to their respective disadvantages.[48]

Nixon's nine years at the helm of the Ontario Liberal party ended the many unsettling leadership changes that the party had endured since the Hepburn era. But with the third and most disappointing election defeat, Nixon resigned. Nixon has said that he would have asked for a separation of the two wings if the party had won the 1975 election. In any case, this was also the commitment of his successor, Stuart Smith. A few months after the convention, the last annual meeting of the Liberal Party in Ontario duly carried out the separation that gave birth to the Liberal Party of Canada (Ontario) and the Ontario Liberal Party (LPC(O) and OLP respectively). There were emotional appeals from the floor to maintain the unity of the Liberal cause, but both the federal and provincial elites supported the move as a means of increasing the efficiency of the two wings. In any case, some kind of financial independence became mandatory under the Ontario election-expenses legislation which prohibits more than token transfers from a federal party to a provincial party.[49]

Since 1976, the most notable effect of separation has been the development of two distinct campaign teams for the federal and provincial parties, as well as two separate offices for organization and fund raising. It is questionable whether the supposed strategic advantage of the parties appealing separately to their electorates has made any difference. One study of Ontario voting behaviour suggests that Ontario Liberals exercised a certain degree of discrimination even before the 1976 separation:

48. Interviews with Sean Conway, 5.9.78; Paul Klie, 18.8.78; David Collenette, 18.8.78. A study of three Hamilton ridings found that more Liberal riding officials were active in federal elections than in provincial ones and that 39 percent of them participated only federally. These differences in activity levels were substantially greater than for the other two parties. Henry Jacek et al., "The Congruence of Federal-Provincial Campaign Activity in Party Organizations: The Influence of Recruitment Patterns in Three Hamilton Ridings", CJPS (1972), 190-205.

49. LPO, Ad Hoc Constitution Committee, "Why Reorganization?" [1976]. Globe and Mail, 20.3.76; 24,26.4.76. Interviews with Robert Nixon, 5.9.78; Kathy Robinson, 6.9.78; Sean Conway, 5.9.78.

the smaller Liberal vote in provincial elections was explained in part by the abstention of many federal Liberals in provincial elections. Ironically, since 1975, the Liberal vote in provincial elections has been closer to federal strength than it was before, although this is because the popularity of the provincial party has gone up, while that of the federal party has declined—and both for separate reasons.[50]

Funding the party in Ontario

In comparison with its counterpart in Quebec, the Liberal provincial office has been a modest operation. Partly this is because the Quebec office is not simply a provincial office "like the others", but more or less a French language equivalent of the national office. Furthermore, the structure of the Ontario party is more decentralized. For example, even though standard membership cards were introduced in 1969, a centralized membership system has only recently got started in earnest and so far only fifteen ridings participate.

The funds for running the party office are raised separately from those used for elections. Ever since John Aird started fund raising in 1956, election campaigns have been properly financed, but fund raising for the between-elections organization has not been nearly as successful. The Liberal Union, which was initiated in 1969 to get donations of $100, was the main source of funds for the Liberal Party in Ontario (LPO). But it was not very dependable: in 1969, for example, the Liberal Union raised only half its goal. In 1972, proceeds from the Liberal Union and its federal equivalent, the Red Carnation, contributed $38,000 to LPO, but that fell to $22,000 in the following year. A more lucrative money maker was the Prime Minister's Dinner, an annual affair sponsored by the Toronto and District Liberal Association (T&D). It netted $42,000 in 1969, rising to $204,000 in 1978. (T&D kept 5/12 of the proceeds to finance its own staff in the LPO office and the other 7/12 went to LPO.) Because of the vagaries of fund raising and the undulating cycles of election activity, the party office has expanded and contracted like a wheezing accordion. In the early 1960s, the annual budget was between $50,000 and $70,000, but in 1966, the party president complained that they could employ only an executive director and one organizer to service 115 provincial and 85 federal ridings and that the NDP's manpower was much more impressive. Again in 1971, LPO reported serious financial problems and the staff was

[50] John Wilson & David Hoffman, "The Liberal Party in Contemporary Ontario Politics", *CJPS* (1970), 177-204.

reduced to one executive director, an executive secretary and two clerk-typists.[51]

The near defeat of 1972 forced everyone to take LPO more seriously. A new executive director was appointed—David Collenette, who had already proved his abilities with T&D. For the first time, the federal treasury committee made a substantial contribution of $30,000 to the annual expenses of LPO and, the following year, this was increased to $60,000. This allowed LPO to hire three field organizers for the first time in several years as well as an assistant executive director. Expenses, which had been running between $60,000 and $80,000 in the early 1970s—in other words, not much more than they had been ten years earlier—jumped to almost $200,000 in 1974 (excluding the extraordinary expenses for a provincial leadership convention).[52]

Once the election was over, however, the federal contribution was cut off abruptly and Trudeau insisted that the 1975 Prime Minister's Dinner would be his last one. As one Ontario Liberal commented, that was "like getting cut out of your rich uncle's will"; but Trudeau had disliked the image of a plutocrats' dinner, which the $100-a-plate occasion conveyed. Besides, he always seemed to give a bad speech in Toronto. There was no dinner in 1976 but, in 1977, it was revived as a Confederation Dinner with Trudeau's undeclared rival, former finance minister John Turner, as the principal attraction. Then Trudeau was told bluntly that the party was in a perilous financial state and that, if he did not want to do another dinner, then he should find himself a new party. The argument won him over. He addressed the 1978 and 1979 dinners.[53]

Comparing the Ontario offices of the three parties, it is very apparent that each has its own approach to party organization in a federation. The NDP operation is based on its provincial level. A single office at Main and Gerrard in the east end of Toronto services the provincial organization and takes on a federal orientation only in the lead-up to a federal election. Liberal party matters are dealt with in three offices. Since 1976, LPC(O) on King Street has been solely concerned with federal party business. Two other offices serve the provincial party: OLP on St. Mary Street and a separate corporate fund-raising office on University Avenue which is responsi-

[51] LPC, vol. 740, file: Ontario Liberal Association 1963-65, David Anderson to Walter Gordon, 18.12.63; vol. 1029, file: Ontario Liberal Association, Gordon Blair to Nichol, 25.4.66; vol. 1137, file: Executive Committee Meeting, 13-14.9.69; file: National Executive Meeting, 26-27.6.71; vol. 1139, file: Ontario General, 1968-69, Notes on the Liberal Party in Ontario, n. author, n.d. LPO, Treasurer's Report, [1973], [1974]. *Liberal Action*, December 1969. Interviews with David Collenette, 23.3.74; Gordon Edick, 13.6.74; Robert Nixon, 5.9.78. *Globe and Mail*, 5.5.76.

[52] LPO, President's Report [1973]; Standing Committee on Finance, Report to the Annual Meeting [1975]. Interview with Collenette, 23.3.74.

[53] Interviews with Robert Nixon, 5.9.78; Paul Klie, 6.11.79.

ble, not to the party executive, but to the provincial leader. In 1979, LPC(O)'s $400,000 budget equalled the combined budgets of the two provincial offices; altogether they slightly exceeded the one NDP office. The Conservatives have four offices: two for fund raising, federal and provincial; and two for party organization, federal and provincial. At $1.4 million, their two provincial offices have much higher expenses than the other two parties. The federal party's operations, however, are much more centralized in Ottawa than is the case with the Liberals and the NDP. Its Toronto offices are just regional branches for the national headquarters with budgets totalling about $200,000.[54]

Party democracy—policy conventions and riding nominations

The policy role of LPC(O) and its predecessor has been at best, hit and miss. The office itself has no policy staff and gives most of its time to organizing conventions, party communications, fund raising, and ensuring that riding associations perform their minimal prescribed functions such as holding annual meetings and electing presidents. Policy development rests with the volunteer side of the party, chiefly through policy standing committees such as agriculture, policy and women, and labour-management. (There are also committees for party affairs such as communications, finance, and organization.) They tend to be more active than the national committees chiefly because a Toronto core can usually be counted on to attend, but even the provincial committees go through long periods of inactivity and doubtful effectiveness.[55]

In 1971, the provincial Liberals went through an ambitious process of policy development including a "thinkers' conference", and a full policy

---

54. J. Wearing, "Ontario Political Parties: Fish or Fowl?" in Donald C. MacDonald, ed., *Government and Politics of Ontario*, 2nd ed. Interviews with Andrew Duncanson, 12.11.79; Sandra Burke, 28.6.79; Michael Perik, 28.6.79; Penny Dickens, 5.7.79; Bernard Nayman, 9.7.79; Jack Heath, 17.7.79. LPC(O), Statement of Revenue and Expenditure and Surplus, 1978. *Fifth Annual Report of the Commission on Election Contributions and Expenses*, 1979. *Ontario Liberal*, Minutes of the Executive Board Meeting of the Ontario Liberal Party, 17.2.79.

55. Interviews with Harvey Bliss, 14.9.78; Paul Klie, 18.8.78. LPO used to participate in a joint federal-provincial tabloid called *Liberal* in the late 1960s. In the early 1970s, until separation, it published, on its own, a four-page monthly magazine called *Communique*. The 1979 defeat predictably stimulated a renewed interest in intra-party communications. Currently, *Liberal Outlook* has the same format as *Communique*; it is supplemented by a more frequent mimeographed publication, aptly titled, *The One Pager*. Party publications never seem to exist for very long. Depending on whether or not electoral needs are foremost, they serve a variety of purposes: reporting on party activities, stimulating intra-party discussion, or (so it is said) providing key Liberals with ammunition to use at cocktail parties!

rally in Ottawa, very much along the lines of what the federal party did in 1969-70. The provincial party, however, went further and produced a detailed, thirty-two page booklet which incorporated a large number of the policy rally's resolutions. During the election, the Conservatives gleefully attacked "Blueprint for Government" as wildly extravagant and since then much less prominence has been given to formal convention resolutions. In the next few years after that unsettling experience, there was almost always an election, either federal or provincial, and the policy committee lowered its sights. Instead of seeing itself as the body that sought to keep the party both honest and active, it modestly limited itself to assisting campaign committees and the leader's research staff.[56] Participation was soundly put to sleep both in Ontario and in Ottawa.

Although no policy committee in Ontario has been as active as the Quebec Political Commission, the Ontario party has frequently led the way in other areas of party reform. In 1966, the Toronto and District Association got leadership review and accountability clauses into the provincial party's constitution and these became the model for similar amendments made to the federal party's constitution later that year, as we saw in the previous chapter.

Major changes were also initiated in 1964, when the Ontario party's constitution brought in certain requirements for riding associations. Because the latter had pre-dated any province-wide organization, they had developed their own rules and practices for membership, nomination meetings and election of executives. On occasion, these loose arrangements led to questionable irregularities. One such difficulty occurred before the 1963 federal election in Ottawa East. Yves Parisien, who had lost the riding nomination for the 1962 election by just seventeen votes, was understandably unhappy when the local executive decided that another nomination meeting for the new election would be unnecessary, since last year's nominee, Jean Richard, had won the seat. Parisien formed a rival Ottawa East Liberal association along with two others who had resigned in protest from the original executive and he was duly nominated at the convention called by the new association. Under pressure from the provincial party office, the original executive decided it must hold a nomination meeting after all, but it did nothing to help the new challenger, Bill Boss. He was told at the last minute that his nomination papers had to be signed by ten members from the riding, but he could not see the membership list until three hours before the deadline for filing nominations and then was allowed to copy only fifteen names. Boss had time to collect only seven signatures and, at the meeting, his nomination was ruled unacceptable. In the election, the two rival Liberal

[56] LPO, Standing Committee on Policy & Research, Report to the Annual Meeting, 1975.

candidates, Richard and Parisien, placed first and second respectively, but the whole fiasco prompted the provincial party to insert into its own constitution basic democratic procedures to which all riding associations had to adhere: they must have written constitutions; they must give proper notice of nominating conventions and annual meetings; they must allow a representative of the provincial president to chair such meetings. As with the leadership review and accountability provisions, these changes became the model for similar amendments which were made to the federal party's constitution in 1970.[57]

In 1978, more nomination scandals prompted further re-examination of the party's constitution. The problem arose from the fact that making the party more open and democratic did not necessarily mean, as we saw in the case of Quebec, that a riding would nominate the candidate whom the party elite believed was the best qualified, nor did it mean that the nomination contests would be models of decorum. In order to ensure that nominations were not decided by a closed group in the constituency, the provincial constitution provided that anyone whose membership application was refused by a riding association could appeal to the district board of LPC(O) and it gave a vote at nomination meetings to new members who had joined up to just three days before the meeting. Candidates seeking riding nominations naturally took advantage of such easy entry by enrolling new members who were likely to support them. Indeed, nomination contests have been regarded as a good way to recruit new members, to shake up a moribund clique, and to test a candidate's drawing power.[58]

In 1977-78, however, things got out of hand. Since the current polls indicated that the Liberal party's popularity was high, a Liberal nomination was highly sought after, particularly in Toronto. In one constituency (Scarborough Centre), a man who was not known to be a prospective candidate presented the riding executive with a list of 569 new members just before the seventy-two-hour deadline and announced his candidacy, taking the other declared candidate completely by surprise. In another constituency (Parkdale-High Park), the candidates had agreed to submit no more than one hundred new names a day; but again, just before the deadline, two new "candidates" appeared, each with one hundred new members. It turned out later that they were "front men" for one of the original candidates and had entered the race solely for the purpose of getting two hundred more of his supporters into the nomination meeting. In

---

57. LPC, vol. 724, file: Constitution - National Liberal Federat., Memo by Gordon Dryden, 8.1.64; 5.2.64; vol. 694, file: Election 1963, K. Davey, Gordon Blair to Nixon, 11.3.63; 27.3.63; Blair to Dan Lang, 27.3.63.

58. Constitution, Liberal Party of Canada (Ontario), 1976, Article XII, f, k. Interviews with Kathy Robinson, 6.9.78; Paul Klie, 18.8.78.

yet another case (Don Valley East), the first candidate to enter the race packed the riding's annual meeting and got the date of the nomination meeting moved forward a month so that his recently declared opponent had almost no time to recruit new members.[59]

Scarborough Centre, in particular, was a real shock to the Ontario campaign committee. Because the party office had had no field organizers since 1976, they had been forced to rely on ministers' inexperienced executive assistants for their political intelligence on what was going on in the ridings. Scarborough Centre convinced them that they had to hire two experienced political organizers who then proceeded to work in a score of nomination contests from February 1978 until the election. Did the campaign committee interfere with the ridings' democratic right to choose their own candidates? One party official justified the move by saying that there are two principles involved. One is the ridings' obligation to get as many people as possible involved in the political process; the other is the campaign committee's obligation to recruit the best candidates it can. If the campaign committee had no preference in a particular contest, it stayed out. If it did have a preference, the political organizer did nothing on behalf of the preferred candidate that could not have been done by anyone else—except that the professional organizer had much more experience to draw on. After that, the campaign committee usually got the candidate it wanted—and even induced the Scarborough Centre winner to withdraw, eventually.[60]

At the party's next annual meeting in November 1978, one of the main items of business was to consider more formal ways of closing loopholes in riding nomination procedures by making certain amendments to the constitution. The following were accepted:

1. Membership applications must be duly signed (that is intended to prevent a candidate from buying memberships on behalf of people who have only a minimal interest in joining)
2. A candidate must announce his or her intention to stand at least ten days before the nomination meeting
3. The riding executive (not the annual meeting) has the power to set the date of the nominating convention for which fourteen days notice must be given
4. New members must have joined at least seven days prior to the nominating convention in order to be able to vote
5. An existing provision, whereby 25 percent of the members may live outside the riding, was retained; but they are now required to have been members at least six months prior to any convention or meeting
6. The president of LPC(O) can designate an impartial person to receive membership applications in a riding

[59] *Globe and Mail*, 9.2.79. Confidential Sources.
[60] Confidential Source.

7. In an "electoral emergency" determined by the provincial president, the minimum time periods may be reduced.[61]

The Ontario party is still substantially more decentralized than its Quebec counterpart. A minimum age requirement, for example, was defeated. Furthermore, although the party hierarchy can use all manner of persuasion to induce an undesirable candidate to give up a nomination—and have done so—no one has proposed a central veto power such as that held by the Quebec Electoral Commission.[62]

Ironically, even later in the spring of 1978, the steep decline in the government's popularity had changed the situation dramatically and the problem became one of finding good candidates to run and keeping good candidates from resigning in the face of the several election postponements.

The changes in the LPC(O) constitution do not fundamentally change the party's nomination procedures: signing up new members is still the way to win in Ontario as well as in the other provinces, but this undignified scramble tends to devalue a party membership. On the other hand, the alternatives seem worse. In Britain, candidates are chosen at the constituency level by a relatively small committee (a Conservative executive council or a Labour general management committee). Particularly in the case of the Labour party, these committees are sometimes controlled by extremists who are quite unrepresentative of Labour voters or even Labour members in the constituency. One writer has commented with respect to both parties that "it would be difficult to devise a method by which fewer people are involved or less knowledge of aspirants is assured than the present system for selecting a parliamentary candidate." At the other extreme, American primaries have essentially taken away the function of candidate selection from the political parties.[63] The Liberal party and, with minor variations, the other two major Canadian parties, have attempted to steer a middle course between these two extremes.

THE WESTERN PROVINCES

In the four western provinces, the internal organization of the Liberal party is of less immediate interest than the question of mere survival. That will be the focus of this section.

---

61. Constitution, Liberal Party of Canada (Ontario), Article XII.

62. A Manitoba riding executive dropped a candidate who had publicly criticized Trudeau. *Globe and Mail*, 7.3.79.

63. Richard Rose, *The Problem of Party Government*, pp. 256-264. Ruth K. Scott & Ronald J. Hrebenar, *Parties In Crisis: Party Politics in America*, pp. 122-130.

The really serious decline occurred in the decade beginning with 1968 and is like a Greek tragedy in its apparent inevitability. Put into perspective, we can see that the provincial wings of the party often acted in a counterproductive manner by continually changing leaders and ideological positions. But many of their problems arose from their relations with the federal party—its unpopularity, its failure to provide leadership and its reluctance to help when conditions were difficult.

Before 1957, the electoral position of the Liberal party in western Canada was reasonably strong. A Liberal government was in power in Manitoba. In Saskatchewan, it constituted the only viable opposition party and, historically, it had been a powerful political force throughout the province's history. Alberta, traditionally the graveyard of Liberal hopes, had seen a Liberal post-war revival under the provincial leader, Harper Prowse; but it was soon to face competition from the Conservative party which, having disappeared completely after 1940, was being painstakingly rebuilt by a young and determined leader, Peter Lougheed. Only in British Columbia was the party reduced to a third-place position, following the sudden appearance of Social Credit in 1952. But even in B.C., the provincial Liberals could count on a steady 20 percent of the popular vote. Throughout the four provinces, the federal popular vote approximated provincial strength: a respectable 35 to 40 percent in Manitoba and Saskatchewan; a bit lower in Alberta and 20 percent in B.C. The vagaries of the electoral system sometimes worked to the disadvantage of the federal party; provincially, it was protected to a limited extent by preferential and single transferable vote systems, which were used from 1926 to 1959 in Alberta. Manitoba used similar systems until 1953.[64]

Before 1957, the Mackenzie King system, under which a senior federal minister was recognized as having political responsibility for his province, was still in full flower. Stuart Garson, a former premier of Manitoba, was in charge of that province; Jimmy Gardiner, another former premier, managed federal Liberal affairs in Saskatchewan; responsibility for Alberta was handled less effectively by George Prudham; and in B.C., the home of political factions, Ralph Campney and Jimmy Sinclair (later Pierre Trudeau's father-in-law) competed for supremacy. Within each province, the provincial wings of the party were circumspect in their relations with the federal party. They expected some benefit from federal patronage and fund raising; but, especially in Manitoba and Saskatchewan, strict adherence to party lines did not preclude keeping the federal wing at a judicious arm's length, even to the extent of publicly

[64]. Alan C. Cairns, "The Electoral System and The Party System in Canada, 1921-1965", *CJPS* (1968), 55-80. T.H. Qualter, *The Election Process in Canada*, pp. 131-136. LPC, vol. 650, file: Alberta Liberal Association, 1957-59, T.L. Perras to Kidd, 6.7.59.

chastizing the federal Liberal government when it was not sufficiently attuned to western problems.[65]

The Davey strategy for revival

The Diefenbaker sweep of 1957-58 changed everything. The federal victories reinforced Conservative provincial revivals which were already well under way in Manitoba and Alberta; over the longer term, Conservative federal strength throughout the West allowed the party to become a relevant provincial force, even in Saskatchewan and British Columbia where it had all but disappeared. After the Conservative victory in the Manitoba provincial election of 1957, the Liberals were out of office everywhere in western Canada and, as we have seen, Liberal strategists in Ottawa decided to break with past practice (to the extent that they knew what past practice was!) by rebuilding the four federal wings along preconceived lines and with as few concessions as possible to provincial idiosyncracies. The Ottawa plan was to encourage a Toronto-style renaissance throughout the West by getting young, upwardly mobile, energetic, urban, reform-minded Liberals to take the key positions in the principal metropolitan centres. Such a strategy was bound to produce friction. In Manitoba, the party was dominated by conservative Ontario-born farmers from the southwestern wheat belt and the old families of the Winnipeg Grain Exchange establishment; in Saskatchewan, an equally farm-dominated party was led by a former CCFer, Ross Thatcher, who had all the anti-socialist zeal of a convert; in Alberta, the provincial revival had died with Prowse's retirement and the party had become querulous and resentful of intruders; finally, in B.C. the party was ridden with factionalism and big-city machines.[66]

In spite of these obstacles, federal campaign committees, which filled Ottawa's prescriptions almost perfectly, were put together in Manitoba, Alberta and B.C. The B.C. campaign committee effectively sidelined a reform group which had taken over the party executive just the year

[65] David E. Smith, *Prairie Liberalism: The Liberal Party in Saskatchewan*, p. 184. Denis Smith, "Liberals and Conservatives on the Prairies, 1917-1968" in David P. Gagan, ed., *Prairie Perspectives*, p. 36.

[66] T. Peterson, "Manitoba: Ethnic and Class Politics in Manitoba" in Martin Robin, ed., *Canadian Provincial Politics*, pp. 69-115. Christine McKennirey, "Voting Patterns in the Prairie Provinces", unpublished essay. Lloyd Stinson, "The Campbell Years", *Winnipeg Free Press*, 20.2.71. D.E. Smith, *Prairie Liberalism*, pp. 272-316. Gordon A. Anton, "The Liberal Party in Alberta: An Organizational Case Study", M.A. Thesis, U. of Alberta, 1972. Judith B. Ward, "Federal-Provincial Relations within the Liberal Party of British Columbia," M.A. Thesis, U. of British Columbia, 1966. Interview with L.C. Jolivet, 11.6.75. LPC, vol. 757, file: A Report on Preliminary Research Conducted in the Prairies for the Liberal Party of Canada by International Surveys Limited, October, 1963.

before. They were suspected of being more interested in federal than provincial party matters, but that could also be said of the provincial leaders themselves. All of them, with the exception of Dr. Patrick McGeer, either moved from the House of Commons to the provincial leadership (David Anderson), or moved from the provincial leadership to the House of Commons (Arthur Laing and Raymond Perrault), or tried unsuccessfully to get elected as MPs after resigning the provincial leadership (Anderson again, and Gordon Gibson). In any case, the new federal team, led by L.C. Jolivet and George Van Roggen, were reported to have produced "the kind of harmony which would have seemed impossible in B.C. several years ago."[67]

The federal campaign committee in Alberta was the centre of considerable controversy. Davey saw it as the only way to overcome the Liberals' reputation in Alberta as "the Party of political immorality"; but many local Liberals saw it as a group of outsiders who held "clandestine meetings" and were part of a plot to create a separate federal organization answerable only to Davey and Gordon. They also accused the campaign committee of interfering with the very democratization that the device was supposed to be promoting elsewhere. At the root of the problem was the almost obsessive interest that Alberta Liberals took in patronage. But they themselves were in utter disagreement as to how that delicate matter should be handled. For some, federal patronage took on a symbolic significance because it allowed Alberta Liberals to experience some of the fruits of victory which in that province could otherwise only be had vicariously. They feared that the federal campaign committee would be oblivious to the debts owing to party "regulars" who had worked long and hard.[68] Another group, led by party presidents Nick Taylor and David McDonald, justified their concern about patronage because, as Taylor said, "it makes a party responsible for what the civil servants are doing." Accordingly, the party's democratically elected executive must be recognized as the authoritative voice of the party and consulted seriously over such matters as finances and appointments, including the appointment of the campaign committee itself. (This was also a point of controversy with one of the provincial leaders, Adrian Berry, who resigned over the issue

67. LPC, vol. 760, file: British Columbia 1962, Gilmour to Davey, 16.12.61; vol. 761, file: B.C. Liberal Association 1961, Davey to Pearson, 21.9.61; vol. 762, file: Vancouver Centre 1960-63, Donald S. Moir to Davey, 22.1.62; vol. 1037, file: British Columbia Campaign Committee, Davey to Pearson, 17.5.65. Interview with John Nichol, 9.6.75. Judith Ward, chap. 5.

68. LPC, vol. 1037, file: Alberta Campaign Committee, Davey to Pearson, 2.12.63; J.F. O'Sullivan to Taylor, 9.9.63; vol. 734, file: M. Cameron Millikin to Davey, 10.11.65; Davey to Millikin, 4.8.64; W.G. Morrow to Davey, 1.12.65; vol. 715, file Alberta Liberal Association 1963-1965, Political Tape - Harper Prouse [sic], n.d.

in 1966.)[69] Finally, there were even some Alberta Liberals who held that patronage had had a "perverse and pervasive effect" on the party. It had attracted lawyers who participated only in federal politics and who had a vested interest in keeping the party a closed group that lost elections. Two defeats as a Liberal candidate in Alberta earned you a judgeship—or so it was alleged![70]

In Saskatchewan, Thatcher exercised such complete control that only one suitable Liberal could be found who was interested primarily in federal matters, and that was Otto Lang. As the dean of the law faculty in Saskatoon, Lang was worlds apart from the traditional Saskatchewan Liberal typified by Jimmy Gardiner, and Thatcher would have nothing to do with him. When Thatcher became premier, Ottawa had to concede his control over the federal wing by allowing him to name Hazen Argue as federal campaign committee chairman, but Thatcher was barely on speaking terms with Ottawa Liberals.[71]

The situation in Manitoba was probably the happiest. Gildas Molgat, who won the leadership in 1961, represented a bridge between the party's rural, conservative past and its progressive, urban present. He was fully committed to the federal wing and even managed to lead a modest provincial rival.[72]

In spite of some unhappiness with the federal campaign committee structure, the Liberals' popular vote in federal elections increased throughout the West during the 1960s and surpassed the party's provincial vote everywhere except in Saskatchewan. (See Chart II on pages 82 to 85.) The Trudeau sweep may not have been as extensive in western Canada as it was in Ontario and Quebec, but the Liberals actually won more seats in Alberta, for example, than they had won there since 1953. Throughout the West, 1968 was the high point. After that, the decline was unrelenting and rapid.

[69]. LPC, vol. 715, file: Alberta Liberal Association 1963-1965, Nick Taylor to Connolly, 26.8.63; vol. 1029, file: Alberta Liberal Association, David McDonald to Nichol, 17.2.67; Liberal Association of Alberta, Annual Report of President, 28.1.67; McDonald, "The Uses of Power and the Democratization of the Liberal Party", 4.12.65; Taylor to Aird, 22.11.66. Interview with Taylor, 6.6.75.

[70]. LPC, vol. 1143, file: Staff Meetings, Minutes; vol. 1082, file: Liberal Party in Alberta 1968-69, C.M. Robinson, "Patronage has no place in a Just Society", 1.11.68; Nick Taylor to Stanbury, 17.1.69; Robert Russell, Edmonton Journal, 14.1.70. Interview with Taylor, 6.6.75.

[71]. LPC, vol. 744, file: PMO - L.B. Pearson, 1964, Davey to Pearson, 10.6.64. David Smith, pp. 303-304.

[72]. LPC, vol. 757, A Report on Preliminary Research Conducted in the Prairies for the Liberal Party of Canada by International Surveys Limited, October, 1963.

Allan O'Brien
Former National Director

Gordon Gibson
National Director, 1979

Senator Keith Davey
Former
National Director

Gordon Ashworth
National Director,
November 1979

Senator John J. Connolly
President, The Liberal Party
of Canada
1961-64

John L. Nichol
President, The Liberal Party
of Canada
1964-1968

Senator Richard J. Stanbury
President, The Liberal Party
of Canada
1968-1973

Senator Gil Molgat
President, The Liberal Party
of Canada
1973-1975

Senator Al Graham
President, The Liberal Party
of Canada
1975-

Decline in the provinces: indigenous factors

Two problems were particularly evident at the provincial level: frequent changes of leadership and the ravaging effects of polarization. Frequently a provincial election came just after the change of leadership— too soon for the leader to rebuild the party or to establish himself with the voters. As in the case of Ontario a decade earlier, it was easier to get rid of a leader than to keep one in the face of adversity. Molgat led the Manitoba Liberals from 1961 to 1969, but four by-election losses on the eve of a provincial general election discouraged him, perhaps unduly, and he resigned. Over the next nine years there were three leaders: Robert (Bobby) Bend, I.H. (Izzy) Asper, and Charles Huband. Unhappily, one suspects that xenophobia is often a factor in Manitoba politics. Molgat himself thought the provincial party was better off not to be led by a French Canadian (himself), when the federal leader was also a French Canadian. Later, under Asper, there were rumblings within party ranks about being led by a big-city Jewish lawyer.[73]

Saskatchewan has changed leaders only twice since Thatcher's death in 1970: D.G. Steuart and E.C. (Ted) Malone. Alberta holds the record with six leaders in the fifteen years after Prowse: Grant MacEwan, David Hunter, Adrian Berry, Mike Maccagno, Jack Lowery, Robert Russell. Since 1974, the party has finally settled down with Nick Taylor, a millionaire oilman who can afford to lead the party without having a seat in the legislature. B.C. Liberals were led by Ray Perrault from 1959 to 1968, but since then the party has had four leaders: Dr. Patrick McGeer, David Anderson, Gordon Gibson, and Jev Tothill. B.C. leadership conventions, unlike those in the other provinces, have not been so much contests as rituals to confirm what internal party machinations have produced as the "obvious choice." That is except for the last one held in 1979. A virtual unknown won the leadership of the party, when it held not a single seat in the legislature.[74]

The B.C. case also illustrates how, more so in the West than elsewhere, the perils of polarization have contributed to Liberal travails. B.C.'s political history has been marked by a dichotomy between Big Business and Big Labour. During World War II, a Liberal-Conservative coalition got the support of the former, and faced a CCF opposition which represented the latter. With the collapse of the coalition in 1952, Social Credit appeared from nowhere to fill the void and, while the party was essentially *petit bourgeois*, the premier, W.A.C. Bennett, consolidated all the business in-

---

73. *Winnipeg Free Press*, 12.7.68; 16.8.74. *Globe and Mail*, 27.2.69; 10.8.74; *Toronto Star*, 24.2.69. Confidential Source.

74. *Globe and Mail*, 30.1.71. Gordon Anton, chap. 1. Vancouver *Sun*, 26.9.75; *Edmonton Journal*, 27.7.72; *Globe and Mail*, 19.2.79.

terests behind him by making Social Credit the party of "anti-socialist unity." Polarization acted as a centrifugal force on the provincial Liberal party. In the 1969 election, the party was doing well under Dr. Patrick McGeer, but Bennett, in a last minute appeal, warned electors not to split the free enterprise vote and held Liberal gains to a minimum.[75]

Three years later the situation became even more difficult. In spite of Bennett again warning that the "socialist hordes" were at the gates, it was clear that a majority of British Columbians were ready to end twenty years of Social Credit rule. Some Liberals thought that the party would be in a better position to capitalize on that discontent under a new leader, so McGeer was eased out and replaced by David Anderson. Unfortunately for the Liberals, the election was called just two months later. The parties that benefited from the fall in the Social Credit vote were the NDP and, to an even greater extent, the Conservatives, who had virtually disappeared in the two previous elections.

The impact of an NDP government on the Liberals was more devastating than Social Credit had ever been. Although Bennett had been unable to revive polarization in 1972, it came back with a vengeance soon afterwards. Those British Columbians who were determined to hold the NDP to one parliamentary term sought out every likely avenue to consolidate the anti-socialist vote. There was considerable popular interest in the idea of bringing Conservatives, Liberals and Social Crediters into one free enterprise Majority Movement. This acted as a catalyst on Liberal and Conservative MLAs who were impatient with having been perpetually in the opposition and who were, on the other hand, disturbed by the sheer incompetence that they saw in both the NDP and Social Credit caucuses.

All three party leaders, however, rejected the idea of a unity party. In Anderson's case, this was partly because he felt the pull of federal loyalties, as did the party president, Doreen Braverman, who vowed that B.C. Liberals would not "sell the federal party down the river." On the other hand, one of the attractions of the unity party for the Liberal MLAs who supported the idea was the prospect of being free of ties with a federal party. A party convention backed Anderson and, when premature revelations about the unity talks killed the idea itself, three of the five Liberal MLAs opted to sit as independents. It was only a matter of time before they took the only option that remained—that of joining Social Credit, which became, in effect, the new unity party. It won the election of 1975 and Bennett *fils* included six ex-Liberals in his cabinet and two former

---

[75] Martin Robin, "British Columbia: The Politics of Class Conflict" in his *Canadian Provincial Politics*. G.L. Kristianson, "The Non-partisan Approach to B.C. Politics: The Search for a Unity Party - 1972-1975", *B.C. Studies* (Spring 1977), 13-29. LPC, vol. 1127, file: B.C. provincial election 1969, *passim*. Vancouver *Sun*, 16.8.69. *Edmonton Journal*, 27.7.72.

Conservatives out of a total of fourteen positions.[76] A subsequent Social Credit victory in 1979 reduced the Conservative party to 5 percent and annihilated the Liberals.

In Alberta, a futile attempt to form an alliance with Social Credit was initiated by the Liberal leader, Jack Lowery, in 1969. In recent years, two former Social Crediters, H.A. (Bud) Olson and Harry Hays, had run successfully as Liberals in federal elections and, with the declining popularity of the provincial Social Credit government, it looked as if some sort of accommodation might be possible at the provincial level. Some Liberal MPs, like Olson and Pat Mahoney, apparently favoured the move as a step towards creating a separate federal organization in Alberta and also (or so it was alleged) because they needed Social Credit help to keep their seats. Before talks got beyond the preliminary stage, however, rumours got into the press and Lowery's strategy blew up in his face. His provincial executive were firmly opposed; they demanded and got his resignation. "There *is* a difference between Social Credit and Liberalism" said Mel Hurtig, a Liberal candidate in 1968, who told Trudeau that Olson should be "severely reprimanded for his part in the incredible fiasco." Another harsh critic was Bob Russell, even though, as executive director of the party a few years earlier, he had strongly supported a merger with the NDP. The man with foresight was the party's only MLA, William Dickie, who joined the Conservatives.[77] His prescience was rewarded when he became a minister in Lougheed's government.

Under the present leadership of Nick Taylor, the Alberta Liberal party has sought to emphasize its distinctiveness by raising environmental concerns, although Taylor himself admits that, to warn Albertans of the dangers of overdevelopment, is like "talking to a bunch of buffalo hunters who want to shoot all those goddamn buffalo, get the hides, grab the money and go back to Montreal as fast as they can."[78] Unlike B.C., however, the problem in Alberta is less one of polarization than what might be called "diluvialization", where topsided government majorities swamp the opposition. (The first party to sweep the province in 1905 with 61 percent of the votes and twenty-two out of twenty-five seats was, incredibly, the Liberal party, which has never recovered from the Farmers' sweep in 1921.)

[76] Interviews with David Anderson, 12.6.75; Charles Campbell, 10.6.75; Allan Williams, 12.6.75. G.L. Kristianson, *op. cit. Edmonton Journal*, 27.7.72. Vancouver *Sun*, 22.6.74; 19.10.74; 3,7,21,22,24,26,28.5.75. *Globe and Mail*, 31.5.75.

[77] LPC, vol. 1082, file: Liberal Party in Alberta 1970-1974, Hurtig to Trudeau, 7.1.70; Lowery to Wylie, 21.1.70; vol. 715, file: Alberta Liberal Association 1963-65, Russell to Davey, 23.12.65; 18.2.64; Davey to Russell, 7.1.64. Anton, pp. 54-56. Toronto *Telegram*, 16.1.70. *Globe and Mail*, 31.12.69. *Edmonton Journal*, 14.1.70.

[78] Calgary *Herald*, 23.2.79.

In Saskatchewan and Manitoba, provincial Liberals have attempted to deal with polarization by adopting a flexible approach. In the 1964 Saskatchewan election, Thatcher moderated his anti-socialist posture on the advice of a Montreal public relations firm and even dropped his attacks on the CFF's controversial medicare program because opinion surveys showed that it was widely accepted by the time the election came. His party won that election; but, when his government was defeated seven years later, Saskatchewan Liberals agreed that he had moved the party too far to the Right. Thatcher's chief lieutenant, D.G. Steuart, won the leadership and pledged to move the party back to its former position at the centre of the political spectrum. He also called for more rank-and-file participation in policy making. In 1972, a policy convention—described as the first real policy convention for years—passed resolutions which were then studied for two years before being given final approval at the 1974 convention to become the party's platform for the 1975 election.

When the election came, however, Steuart gave less attention to the party's methodically drafted program and more to reviving the old socialist bogey by attacking the government's takeover of the potash industry simply on the grounds that the potash companies represented free enterprise. This did not prevent the party from falling further in the popular vote (though it kept the same number of seats), nor did it prevent the emergence of the Conservative party as a force at the provincial level for the first time since the 1930s. Since then, polarization has taken its toll on the Liberal caucus, as it has in B.C. Ted Malone, who won the leadership in 1976, rejected an anti-socialist alliance with the Conservatives; but Thatcher's son, Colin, described his own political position as being "not Liberal, but anti-NDP. In Alberta, I would be a Conservative and in B.C., I would be a Socred." Two years later, he and another Liberal MLA left the Liberal caucus to join the Conservatives.[79]

In the 1978 provincial election, the Liberals, astonishingly, failed to win a seat and the Conservatives emerged as the principal opposition in the province. However, even one of the province's leading newspapers disagreed with itself about whether the Liberal demise was related to their problems with the political spectrum. An editorial in the Regina *Leader-Post* commented that:

The old political spectrum analysis, with the Liberals roughly in the centre and the Tories more or less on the right, no longer holds water. And the election results

---

79. LPC, vol. 747, file: Saskatchewan Provincial Election - 1964, "Saskatchewan Provincial General Election 1964"; vol. 744, file: PMO - L.B. Pearson 1964, Davey to Pearson, 10.6.64. *Globe and Mail*, 4.12.72; Regina *Leader-Post*, 30.11.72; 4.12.72; 10, 17.11.73; Saskatoon *Star-Phoenix*, 16.11.73; Editorial, 6.12.75; 30.7.75; 7.11.77. *Ottawa Journal*, 9.12.74.

should leave no doubt that for the Liberals, generalized antagonism to socialist statism is far from enough.

The opposite opinion was voiced by an editorial writer in the same paper:

It may have been his [Malone's] failure to mount a hard-hitting ideological campaign that was a major cause of the Liberal's electoral disaster. The NDP and the Conservatives, both of which did well in the election, stressed ideology heavily. There was never any doubt they were making it a left wing/right wing fight. Where were Malone and the Liberals? No one seemed to know. They had policies, but all of us like labels because they make it easier to sort out things. The Liberals simply didn't have a label for their politics.[80]

But it is in Manitoba that the attempt to play ideological politics has been most inept. It began when Molgat was succeeded in 1969 by Robert (Bobby) Bend, who described himself as "slightly right of centre but . . . progressive-minded." The *Montreal Star* thought him "the dullest Liberal leader since Douglas Campbell" and saw his victory as marking a return to the Bracken-Garson-Douglas tradition of cautious, conservative Liberal-Progressive leaders and an attempt to win back the farm support that had once been the backbone of the party.[81] While the Liberals moved to the Right, the NDP saw the opportunity to break out of the working-class ghetto to which it had been confined by Winnipeg's class-conscious politics, and chose a reassuringly moderate MP, Edward Schreyer, as provincial leader a month later. At the election that followed in a few weeks, the Liberals suffered the sharpest drop in their popular vote since the 1930s and were reduced to just five seats in the legislature, while the NDP took office for the first time in the province's history.

The party's executive council concluded that, under Bend's leadership, it had been simply a second conservative party and must return to a middle-of-the-road position. Two months after the election, Bend resigned as leader and, at a highly emotional executive council meeting, an urban reform group, led by Lloyd Axworthy, called for a restatement of the party's philosophy and purpose by means of rank-and-file participation much along the lines of what the federal party was attempting at the same time with its three-stage policy development (see chapter 5). The following year, in a reversal of the usual process, the party first held a policy convention—which passed a generally reformist program, including a guaranteed annual income proposal—and then called a leadership convention, which was won by a Winnipeg tax lawyer, I.H. (Izzy) Asper. The party seemed determined to shake off its "right-wing conservative tag", although Asper himself was described as "a contradictory

-

80. 25.11.78.
81. *Globe and Mail*, 12,15.5.69. *Montreal Star*, 15.5.69.

figure. Like all Liberals, he is a social progressive and economic conservative."[82]

The experience of an NDP government subjected the party to various cross-pressures. One Liberal MLA, Laurent (Larry) Desjardins, who was attracted to Schreyer's moderately left-of-centre politics, crossed the floor and eventually became an NDP minister. Others, including the *Winnipeg Free Press*, urged the Liberals to form an alliance with the Conservatives in the "best interests" of the province. Possible co-operation was discussed "unofficially" and even the federal minister for Manitoba, the Hon. James Richardson, talked vaguely about the need for a new party, even though the idea was rejected by the Conservatives, who no doubt judged correctly that they were the most viable alternative to the NDP and did not need Liberal help in gathering up the anti-socialist vote.

When a provincial election came in 1973, the Liberals further blurred their newly acquired reformist label by attempting to capitalize on a welfare backlash with advertisements that started off: "Welfare shouldn't mean you pay for people who won't work." Although the Liberals were credited with having the best slate of candidates and an aggressive door-to-door campaign, their popular vote slipped again.[83]

Afterwards there was more talk about making a decisive break with their right-wing image and, this time, the break was made in earnest. The party's new leader, Charles Huband, shifted the party's policies to the Left and even promised that, if a choice became necessary after the 1977 election the parties would support the NDP rather than the Conservatives. But, just as in 1969, the party found itself in the wrong place at the wrong time: in 1977 the electorate moved to the Right and elected a Conservative government headed by Sterling Lyon, one of the most avowedly right-wing leaders in the party's history. Not to be daunted, Huband proposed a union with the NDP the day the Conservatives were sworn into office, but the idea was subsequently rejected by both parties.[84]

According to a study of the Liberal party which was done at the time of the 1973 election, Manitoba voters found the Liberal party's image colourless and unclear. With all the changes of direction over the past decade, that is hardly surprising.[85]

[82.] LPC, vol. 1135, file: General - Manitoba 1969, Gerry Robinson to Wylie, 5.9.69; Robinson to Stanbury and Wylie, 6.10.69. *Winnipeg Free Press*, 22.9.69; 15, 17.11.69; 22.6.70; 30, 31.10.70; 2.11.70; 26.3.73.

[83.] *Winnipeg Free Press*, 8.7.69; 14,17.11.69; 30.10.70; 9.6.71; 20.11.72; 9,15.6.73; 12.9.73; 16.8.74. Ottawa *Citizen*, 19.6.73. *Globe and Mail*, 27.6.73. LPC, vol. 1135, file: Manitoba General - January 1970 to Dec. 1971, Robinson to Manitoba General File, 17.6.71; News Release by Asper, 12.10.71.

[84.] *Winnipeg Free Press*, 5.2.75; 6.12.76; 4,10.11.77; 5.12.77.

[85.] John Wilson, "The Decline of the Liberal Party in Manitoba Politics: A Preliminary Analysis", CPSA Papers, 1974.

Some political scientists argue that, as a society becomes more advanced economically, class divisions lead to the emergence of a two-party system in which a party of the Right faces a party of the Left.[86] This would appear to explain what has happened to the Liberal party in the western provinces and, if that is true, then polarization was bound to eliminate the party no matter what it did. There are some problems with the analysis, however. There is first of all the anomaly of Alberta, where a Social Credit government was itself transformed from a protest movement to a party of the rural Right during its thirty-six years in office and was finally defeated by a party of the urban Right. The second problem with the polarization thesis is that it fails to explain the case of the most economically advanced province, Ontario, which has had a remarkably persistent three-party system since 1943, thus confounding political analysts who periodically describe it as being in a "transitional phase" in which the future of the Ontario Liberal party is "bleak."[87] Thirdly, the British party system, which is the usual model for demonstrating the impact of economic development, appears to be getting less polarized. Recent elections show a decline in the two-party vote and, as social mobility has increased, class voting has become blurred.[88]

In any case, the experience of the Liberal party in the four western provinces suggests that a party which tacks back and forth across the political spectrum, hoping to catch the shifting tides in the current of public opinion, is pursuing a dangerous and ultimately self-defeating course. On the other hand, a party that simply defines itself as being in the centre between two opposites runs the risk of ultimately standing for nothing in the electorate's eyes. As Allan Williams, one of the B.C. ex-Liberals put it: "The problem with being the centre party is that it becomes just a garbage can for people who are dissatisfied with the right or the left." Gordon Gibson, speaking to an Alberta Liberal convention was surely right to warn of the "middle-of-the-road trap." "To stay alive through the long, dark nights ahead", he said, "It is necessary for the party to develop a Liberal philosophy based on principles rather than expedience . . . That philosophy must focus on the individual, promising equality of oppor-

[86] John Wilson argues persuasively that the Canadian party system can be more readily understood if one accepts that each province has a distinctive political culture and that the federal party system is in many respects an aggregate of ten provincial systems, which can themselves be grouped into different stages of economic and, thus, political development. His analysis becomes less convincing, however, when he argues that Alberta and Saskatchewan are the most advanced provinces. "The Canadian Political Cultures: Towards a Redefinition of the Nature of the Canadian Political System", *CJPS* (1974), 438-483.

[87] John Wilson & David Hoffman, "Ontario: A Three-Party System in Transition" in Martin Robin, ed., *op. cit.* and "The Liberal Party in Contemporary Ontario Politics", *CJPS* (1970), 177-204.

[88] *The Economist* (10-16.11.79), 34.

tunity and personal responsibility."[89] Some of the most successful parties in western Canada have been those that have ignored spectrum politics and defied an easy placement on the Right, Left, or Centre: the Roblin Conservative and Schreyer NDP governments in Manitoba; the early Thatcher Liberal and Blakeney NDP governments in Saskatchewan; the Lougheed Conservative government in Alberta; the W.A.C. Bennett Social Credit government in B.C. (when it was being the government rather than waging an election campaign!). Indeed, each of those parties defined for itself the political perspective in its respective province and forced other parties to come to terms with it. Of the western Liberal parties, the tiny Alberta Liberal party has best grasped this notion.

Provincial decline: exogenous factors

While the provincial Liberal parties undoubtedly aggravated their problems by changing their leaders too often and by getting preoccupied with the political spectrum, many of their difficulties arose from their relations with the federal wing of the party. Unlike the Maritimes, where provincial politics tends to be foremost, grievances against the federal Liberal government often became issues in provincial elections. Provincial Liberals found themselves having to answer for federal government policies on bilingualism, transportation, the White Paper on tax reform, the alleged federal threat to provincial control over natural resources, and Trudeau's famous rhetorical question: "Why should I sell your wheat?" An editorial in the *Winnipeg Free Press* in 1969 put the blame on the federal Liberal government for the difficulties in which Molgat and the Manitoba Liberals found themselves:

Many of Mr. Molgat's difficulties arose from the fact that during much of his term of leadership a Liberal government was in office at Ottawa which had almost no Prairie representation. The federal government paid scant attention to Western Canada. 'We don't need them' seemed to be the attitude of the Liberals toward the Prairies, and Western Canada was largely ignored in the formulation of party policy. This is an attitude that some people feel still exists. Some Prairie farmers see in Ottawa a lack of interest in the problems of the grain farmer, for example. Manitoba Liberal organizers believe that the recent byelections were fought on federal, not provincial, issues; and this was a factor in the defeat of local Liberal candidates.[90]

[89]. Interview with Williams, 12.6.75. Calgary *Herald*, 28.8.78.

[90]. *Winnipeg Free Press*, 27.2.69. See also, for example, *Toronto Star*, 24.2.69; 7.5.69; *Globe and Mail*, 10.8.74; Regina *Leader-Post*, 14.11.73; 6.11.76; Saskatoon *Star-Phoenix*, 16.11.73; 24.7.75.

The premiers of Saskatchewan and Alberta went further and very explicitly used provincial elections in order to strengthen their own positions in dealing with the federal government. In that context, a vote for the provincial Liberal party was almost tantamount to a betrayal of one's own province.[91]

In spite of these problems, provincial Liberals were, for the most part, unwilling to follow the Quebec example of separating from the federal wing of the party. Indeed, it was almost an article of faith (in spite of breaches to the contrary) that all Liberals worked for the same cause within a single organization. Just as the Ontario party had changed its name in 1964 from the "Ontario Liberal Association" to the "Liberal Party in Ontario" to signify that one organization encompassed both wings, so the Liberal associations in B.C., Manitoba and Alberta adopted a similar format in the late 1960s. In Saskatchewan, the approach taken by Thatcher to the idea of Liberal unity was different, as we have seen. He simply wanted the provincial organization to run everything, as had Saskatchewan leaders before him all the way back to Walter Scott, the first Liberal premier of the province. After Thatcher's death, Saskatchewan Liberals reaffirmed the principle of one organization serving both wings, though on the basis of the two wings being equal. The single-organization concept met with reservations in Ottawa. Torrance Wylie, while he was national director, told a Manitoba Liberal, Graeme Garson, "I personally have felt for a long time now that it is practically impossible for one organization to effectively serve both the provincial and the federal political responsibility. My reading of Canadian history is that there are two competing perceptions of politics in Canada, one of which is provincial and one of which is federal, and that any organization that trys [sic] to combine the two inevitably finds itself in the position of serving both badly, or one dominating at the expense of the other."[92] Party history over the next ten years showed that Wylie's comments had been very perceptive.

It was perhaps logical that the weakened provincial parties maintain close ties with the governing federal party in order to take advantage of federal patronage, federal fund raising and a federal minister (or senator) to keep the party happy; but such was not always forthcoming. Previous party history would suggest that the federal wing might take advantage of provincial weakness to dominate the provincial wings and, during the 1960s, we saw that Ottawa Liberals did attempt to exert control through

[91] Tex Enemark, "A Time to Discuss some Fundamentals", "Dialogue" (Winter 1976), 14, 18. *CAR* (1975), 207.

[92] LPC, vol. 1135, file: General - Manitoba 1969, Wylie to Garson, 12.11.69. vol. 1092, file: Liberal Party in Manitoba June 1966 - October 1968; *Globe and Mail*, 13.12.71. David E. Smith, *passim*.

the federal campaign committees. Allan O'Brien, who succeeded Keith Davey as national director in 1966, was more inclined to believe that provincial success would eventually accrue to the benefit of the federal party; but, after he left in 1969, most Ottawa Liberals were dubious about the value of the provincial wings and often feared that too much time and money were going into provincial activities.[93] Although the provincial organizations were supposed to serve both levels of the party, they could expect little help from Ottawa when they got into trouble, even though the federal wing inevitably suffered as a consequence. On several occasions, a provincial party found that its local financial supporters had cut off its funds as a way of forcing it into some kind of political alliance with another party. But, even when Ottawa took the position that the provincial wing should stay out of any entanglements and maintain a Liberal presence provincially, federal money was not provided to make up the shortfall. An example of this problem can be seen in the case of Manitoba in 1971 when potential contributors were hoping to force the provincial party into a coalition with the Conservatives to defeat the NDP. As a result, the Liberal party in Manitoba did not have the money to hire organizers and to run the office which was intended to serve both levels of the party, but federal fund raisers refused to help.[94]

In Saskatchewan, the provincial leader, E.C. (Ted) Malone, became embroiled in an argument with the federal minister, the Hon. Otto Lang, over the division of party funds. Because there is a federal tax credit on contributions to political parties, Saskatchewan Liberals had decided to raise all money jointly and deposit it in the federal fund so that contributors could receive the tax credit. The money was to be divided equally between the two wings, but, according to Malone, Lang was slow in giving the provincial wing its share. This sort of pecuniary jousting is commonplace within a political party, but ironically, it occurred soon after Malone had won the leadership, defeating E.F.A. (Tony) Merchant, who had advocated separation of the party on the Quebec-Ontario model. The situation became serious when the provincial Liberals lost every seat in the 1978 provincial election and failed to qualify for any public subsidization. The party fired all its staff and seriously considered selling its office building to pay off a debt of between $150,000 and $200,000.[95]

[93] Judith Ward, p. 193. LPC, vol. 1094, file: Organization - Special Memorandum, O'Brien to Stanbury, 20.1.69, O'Brien to Stanbury, 5.7.68; Interviews with Wylie, 5.8.70; 21.7.78; Senator Lafond, 26.8.77; Gerry Robinson, 4.2.77.

[94] LPC, vol. 1138, file: National Executive Meeting, 27-28.11.71. See also, *Winnipeg Free Press*, 11.1.78.

[95] Regina *Leader-Post*, 31.7.76; 6.8.77; 10.3.79. Saskatoon *Star-Phoenix*, 5.7.76.

In Alberta, Bob Russell, who was provincial leader in the early 1970s, had no seat in the legislature, had no party staff, and got no help from the province's four Liberal MPs in the provincial election. Two years later, the party still did not have either a provincial organizer or an executive director—surely a minimum staff—and Russell, who had to run a full-time business while being party leader, decided, not surprisingly, that it was more than he could manage. He resigned.[96]

The B.C. Liberal party seems to have fared only slightly better. Early in 1975, there were reports that B.C. industrialists and lawyers who did business with the federal government had been advised to "think twice before embracing Young Bennett or the Majority Movement" and that federal fund raising would go to help the provincial party directly. Even by the end of that year, however, the provincial Liberal leader, Gordon Gibson, reported that the party would be spending less than $30,000 in the provincial election compared with $240,000 in the previous one. "We just cannot collect a cent out of the business community", he said.[97]

Besides starving the provincial parties, the federal wing has occasionally even gone so far as to discourage provincial activity in the hopes of currying favour with provincial Social Credit governments. Harper Prowse alleged that Alberta's federal minister, George Prudham, cut provincial Liberals out of federal funds when Prowse was leader in the 1950s and discouraged Alberta oil companies from contributing to the provincial party in the hope that the province's Social Credit government would refrain from wholeheartedly supporting federal Social Credit candidates. In a similar vein, one Alberta MP in 1971 called on the provincial party to disband because it had nothing to contribute. In 1979, Bill Bennett, the B.C. premier, cleverly called a provincial election in the midst of the federal campaign. With only two token candidates in the federal election, Social Credit could concentrate its resources at the provincial level and hope that the Liberals and Conservatives would put their main effort into the federal contest. Taking up the bait, the Liberal campaign committee in B.C. strongly discouraged provincial candidates and only five ran. Federal interests came first, but that did not stop the party from being decimated federally as well as provincially.[98]

[96] LPC, vol. 1082, file: Liberal Party in Alberta 1970-74, Gibson to Wylie, 22.9.71. *Edmonton Journal,* 26.9.73.

[97] Vancouver *Sun,* 21.2.75; 2.12.75.

[98] LPC, vol. 715, file: Alberta Liberal Association 1963-65, Political Tape - Harper Prouse [*sic.*] *Globe and Mail,* 31.5.75. *Edmonton Journal,* 6.1.71. David E. Smith, "Grits and Tories on the Prairies" in Hugh G. Thorburn, ed., *Party Politics in Canada,* 4th ed., p. 280. Interview with Bob Russell, 5.6.74. Confidential Sources. According to Gordon Ashworth, LPC National Director, only five candidates *wanted* to run provincially. Interview, 6.3.80.

The failure of federal leadership

Although the Liberal party's problems in western Canada have got worse in the last decade, they can be traced back at least to the St. Laurent government and an insensitivity to western economic and cultural distinctiveness. In the Trudeau era, the government's wheat acreage reduction program, LIFT (Lower Inventories for Tomorrow), was seen as a threat to traditional values like the family farm and bumper crops, and the Liberals came to represent eastern "centralized control and management." The failure to understand fed upon itself. Meagre representation of the West in Liberal caucuses meant that Liberal governments had to rely, as Manitoba MP Lloyd Axworthy said, "upon civil service solutions for Western Canada." Western Canada had regional needs, but Liberal governments in Ottawa for the most part lacked effective spokesmen for these regional points of view. Even after 1968, when ministers were formally given political responsibilities, western ministers failed to provide much political leadership in their respective provinces. On the other hand, there was little indication that the prime minister acceded to them as provincial lieutenants as Mackenzie King did with Gardiner, for example, or as most Liberal prime ministers have done with their Quebec lieutenants.[99]

The succession of ministers in Manitoba—Hon. Roger-Joseph Teillet, Hon. James Richardson, and Hon. Joseph Guay—was little short of disastrous. Teillet formally abdicated political responsibility to Douglas Everett, the federal campaign chairman in Manitoba (and later Senator). Incredible as it may seem, he even lost his own bid for renomination in St. Boniface before the 1968 election. Richardson, who was political minister for Manitoba after 1968, had considerable personal stature, but seemed incapable of giving any leadership to Manitoba Liberals in the stormy aftermath of Bobby Bend's election defeat. There were also complaints from the Manitoba troika (called the "federal affairs committee") that Richardson was not sufficiently sensitive to the "political significance" of the appointments that came under his responsibility and, in the fall of 1969, the other members of the committee resigned, claiming that they had received no co-operation from the minister. Richardson himself resigned from the cabinet in 1976 and Guay became Manitoba's minister

[99.] David E. Smith, pp. 273-289. LPC, vol. 763, file: Alberta - 1963 Campaign, Nick Taylor to Davey, 18.10.62. Tex Enemark, "A Time to Discuss some Fundamentals", "Dialogue" (Winter 1976), 14, 18. Lloyd Axworthy, "How to Win the West!", "Dialogue" (Autumn 1975), 9-11. The PMO was very involved in patronage even after the regional desks were disbanded.

apparently for the sole reason that he was, by then, the province's only Liberal MP.[100]

In Saskatchewan, even after Ottawa Liberals conceded to Thatcher as *de facto* leader for federal party matters and allowed him to name the federal campaign chairman for the 1965 election, the Liberals won no seats in that province for the second time running. Three years later, they won two seats and Thatcher's *bête noire*, Otto Lang; was made the minister responsible for Saskatchewan. Lang created an unofficial federal organization, the key members of which were christened the "Silver Seven"; within a few months, Allan O'Brien, the National Director, gave Lang much of the credit for "a remarkable improvement in our relationship with the federal ridings and the provincial executive." But Thatcher's attitude had not changed. He got the 1969 annual meeting to reject the idea of any kind of separate organizations for federal and provincial party affairs—a vote that was considered a setback for Lang's incipient organization.[101]

Lang certainly worked hard at his political responsibilities, but his political fortunes were constantly fluctuating. He was alternately booed and cheered at annual party meetings in Saskatchewan (1969 and 1971). In 1974, he got three Liberals elected on the highest popular vote the Liberals had received since 1953 and he organized support at the 1978 federal policy convention for a resolution calling for $600 million to be spent on prairie rail rehabilitation—a proposal that was subsequently approved by cabinet. But in 1979, all the Liberal candidates in Saskatchewan were beaten on a popular vote which was almost as low as the nadir of 1958. The consensus was that Lang was never able to unbend enough to acquire the common touch that is so essential in Saskatchewan; but John Embury, the Saskatchewan provincial president and a man who had often clashed with Lang, claimed that he had done more for western Canada than any other minister in the last fifty years.[102]

[100]. LPC, vol. 721, file: Veterans Affairs, Teillet to the other ministers, 22.10.63; vol. 1135, file: General - Manitoba 1969, Graeme Garson to Richardson, 6.11.69; Gerry Robinson to Wylie, 5.9.69; Wylie to file, 8.9.69; Robinson to Stanbury and Wylie, 6.10.69; 17.10.69; vol. 1143, file: Selkirk - General Info, Selkirk By-election, 20.4.70 [written by Robinson]. *Winnipeg Free Press*, 22.9.69.

[101]. David E. Smith, *Prairie Liberalism: The Liberal Party in Saskatchewan 1905-71*, pp. 77, 303-304. LPC, vol. 1094, file: Organization - Special Memorandum, O'Brien to Stanbury, 20.1.69; vol. 1126, file: Activities Report, 1969-72, Robinson to Wylie 4.12.69. Regina *Leader-Post*, 6.8.77.

[102]. LPC, vol. 1143, file: Saskatchewan General 1969-70, Nancy Morrison to Michel, 30.11.69 (copy to Gerry Robinson); vol. 1126, file: Activities Report, 1969-72, Robinson to Wylie, 4.12.69. Resolutions Report, Liberal Party of Canada Convention 1978, #218. *Globe and Mail*, 13.12.71; 20.7.74. Regina *Leader-Post*, 13.12.71; 27.2.78. The Winnipeg Conference, 13.10.79.

In Alberta, where the party organization was very weak and given to "regional jealousies, vindictive in-fighting and back-biting", the short-term solution lay in recruiting "star" candidates who had no previous connection with the provincial party. Three became ministers: two former Social Crediters—Harry Hays in 1963 and H.A. (Bud) Olson in 1968—and, most spectacularly, Jack Horner, who was plucked from the Tory frontbench in 1977. It would be an understatement to say that they did not fit in with the left-of-centre image that Ottawa strategists were attempting to project across the country, especially in the 1960s. The argument that only conservative Liberal converts could get elected in Alberta would have been more convincing if any of them had been re-elected; but none were.[103]

British Columbia was the only western province that did not suffer from a dearth of potential ministers. If anything, it suffered from the opposite problem, particularly when the 1968 election returned sixteen B.C. Liberals who achieved a reputation for never being able to agree on anything! In Pearson's cabinet, there was rivalry between the two B.C. ministers: the Hon. Arthur Laing, who had a loyal political following dating back to the 1950s when he had been provincial leader; and the Hon. John Nicholson, who had been chairman of the B.C. federal campaign committee until he resigned to become a candidate. Not surprisingly, Nicholson and the federal campaign committee counted for more with Pearson than Laing and the B.C. Liberal association. When Nicholson retired in 1968, Laing was formally recognized as the minister responsible for B.C., while two new ministers, the Hon. Ronald Basford and the Hon. Jack Davis, jockeyed for position. Laing, as we shall see in chapter 5, was a staunch defender of the old-style approach whereby the minister was the political "boss" of the province. But he was not infrequently overruled and his *de facto* power was held in check by the campaign committee (who now also held positions on the provincial executives), which included men like L.C. (Joly) Jolivet, George Van Roggen (appointed to the Senate in 1971), John Nichol (also appointed to the Senate, when he became party president in 1964), Paul Plant, and Alex Walton. Laing resigned from the cabinet in 1972 and the election cut B.C.'s fractious caucus from sixteen to four. For a while, Davis and Basford were rivals again. When Raymond Perrault was appointed to the Senate after losing his Commons seat, he became the political minister. By 1976, Trudeau finally decided that Basford was worthy of the post; he was made

103. LPC, vol. 1037, file: Alberta Campaign Committee, Davey to Pearson, 2.12.63; vol. 1082, file: Liberal Party in Alberta 1970-1974; vol. 1094, file: Organization - Special Memorandum, O'Brien to Stanbury, 20.1.69. *Lethbridge Herald*, 8.2.66. Interview with John Patrick Day, 2.6.74.

the political minister and became one of the most effective of the Trudeau era until he retired in 1978.[104]

The future

The federal Liberal party cannot divorce itself from the fate of its provincial wings. There are many different theories about the relationship between provincial and federal voting patterns in Canada.[105] Provincial strength does not always translate into federal strength, but provincial weakness *is* carried over. (See Chart II on pages 82-86.) One fact does stand out—rarely has a party maintained its federal strength while it has been weak provincially. The Conservatives were able to win fifty out of seventy-five seats in Quebec in 1958, but lost almost all of them at the next election; the Liberals won sixteen out of twenty-three seats in B.C. in 1968 and lost all but four at the next election. There was simply no dependable base. (Conservative strength in B.C. since 1974 appears to be an exception.)

On the other hand, experience has shown that provincial parties are wise to keep some distance between themselves and their federal counterpart, especially if the federal party is in power. When Nick Taylor became Alberta's provincial leader, he urged Alberta Liberals to set up a separate organization on the Quebec-Ontario model in order to be "rid of the albatross of having to explain every asinine move Ottawa makes." The plan was approved at the party's annual meeting in 1977. It is remarkable that the other provincial parties have all opted for single organizations in spite of what D.V. Smiley sees as "a group of pervasive influences at work in the direction of autonomous federal and provincial party systems in Canada."[106] The traditional model of a single organization with the provincial wing predominant may well be appropriate for Liberals in the Atlantic provinces. However, the only recent instance in the western provinces—that of Saskatchewan in the 1960s—was not propitious. On the other hand, the model that was prevalent throughout the West in the 1960s and 1970s—that of co-equal wings (more or less) within a single organization—seems to have been the worst sort of compromise. Western Canadian history suggests that provincial

---

[104] Confidential Sources.

[105] See, for example, F.H. Underhill, "The Canadian Party System in Transition", in his *In Search of Canadian Liberalism*, pp. 192-202. S. Muller, "Federalism and the Party System in Canada" in J.P. Meekison, ed., *Canadian Federalism: Myth or Reality*, 1st ed., pp. 119-132.

[106] *Globe and Mail*, 2.3.74. Calgary *Albertan*, 5.1.77. *Edmonton Journal*, 7.2.77. Interview with Taylor, 6.6.75. Smiley, *Canada in Question: Federalism in the Seventies*, 2nd ed., p. 102.

Liberal parties have to be able to reflect their respective provincial outlooks and to be strong spokesmen for provincial rights. Some provincial Liberals would go further and abandon the "Liberal" label, replacing it with names like the "Alberta party" or the "Western Canada party." However, as long as there are Conservative and NDP parties at the provincial level, the federal Liberal party would be at a serious disadvantage without provincial Liberal parties of some sort, if only because of the automatic identification that some voters carry from one level to the other, even if they constitute a minority.

The federal party, for its part, might well reconsider the idea of a Prairie Liberal party that was proposed by Wylie and several Prairie Liberals around 1970, but was not enthusiastically received by Political Cabinet. Occasionally western Liberals have banded together, as they did very successfully in Regina before the 1966 policy convention or as they did in Vancouver before the 1973 convention. But, without some kind of permanent structure, such initiatives had little follow-up.[107] The federal Liberal party desperately needs an effective voice for the West within the extra-parliamentary organization in order to counterbalance, at least to some extent, the western weakness in the Liberal parliamentary caucus.

The unrepresentative parliamentary caucus is, as Alan C. Cairns pointed out, a serious problem for all parties. Useful proposals for combining some form of proportional representation with our existing single-member constituency system were contained in the former Liberal government's constitutional bill and in the report of the Pépin-Robarts Task Force on National Unity.[108] These merit consideration by all parties. For the Liberal party, which in the last election got 24 percent of the vote in western Canada and 3 percent of the seats, proportional representation would be a major step in dealing with the party's problem in the West.

Ironically, the loss of power federally in 1979 provided the Liberal party with its best opportunity in years to make a comeback in western Canada because western Liberals had been temporarily freed of the albatross of an eastern-based Liberal government in Ottawa. As opposition leader, Trudeau acknowledged that organizational rebuilding in the West

[107] LPC, vol. 1135, file: General - Manitoba 1969, Robinson to Wright, 4.12.69; vol. 1096, file: Stanbury R.J. - Correspondence 1968-1970, Wylie to Stanbury, 9.3.70; vol. 1082, file: Liberal Party in Alberta 1970-1974, Speech by Pat Mahoney to Calgary South Federal Liberal Association, 26.2.70. *Globe and Mail*, 16.7.73. Wylie to the author, 21.12.79. In 1976, the LPC national executive established a Western Commission to study the party's problems in the West, but the commission's report had not been made public at this writing and was not made available to the author.

[108] Canada, *The Constitutional Amendment Bill*, 1978, Section 64. Canada, The Task Force on Canadian Unity, *A Future Together: Observations and Recommendations*, pp. 104-106.

would necessitate massive funding,[109] and the decision to hold the 1980 policy convention in Winnipeg was an indication of intent. But the 1980 election came too soon. With the loss of its only seat in B.C., the party's western base shrank to a narrow South Winnipeg-St. Boniface enclave. Back in power with a caucus dominated by its Ontario and Quebec members, the party hierarchy will be tempted to view the problems of the four western Liberal parties as casually as they did in the 1970s. If that happens, the party can write itself completely out of the western half of Canada.

109. *Globe and Mail*, 17.11.79.

CHAPTER 5. CHARISMA AND PARTICIPATION (1968-71)

In the winter and spring of 1967/68, the tradition-bound world of Canadian politics was transformed—or so it seemed at the time—by Pierre Elliott Trudeau. Popular fascination with Trudeau's novel and colourful style swept the party and the country. The phenomenon which the media christened Trudeaumania looked initially like an instance of what the German sociologist, Max Weber, called charismatic leadership. For Weber, such leadership was a stimulant to popular participation and a challenge to existing bureaucracies, though eventually charisma produced its own institutions and routines. The interest in Trudeau did indeed bring thousands of new faces into party ranks at the leadership convention and in election committee rooms across the country and, especially during the leadership convention, there was an assumption—albeit not very clearly articulated—that Trudeau's victory would blow winds of change through the encrustations of the civil service establishment. During the election campaign, "participatory democracy"—already a popular phrase in North America during the sixties—became almost a campaign slogan which raised great expectations. True to the Weberian model, when the excitement of the election had subsided, Trudeau called on the party's national executive for practical implementation of the participatory ideal. For the next three years, the Liberal party was consumed with the experiment.[1]

There were at least three different possibilities. Participation might simply mean the sense of involvement felt by those who were mobilized to support a popular leader, as with the populist, mobilizing parties that have been prominent in Third World countries since 1945. Secondly, participation might mean that the traditional party structures were made more responsive to local party elites throughout the country. That was really what Davey and Pearson had meant by the "new politics." Thirdly,

[1] H.H. Gerth & C. Wright Mills, eds., *From Max Weber: Essays in Sociology*, pp. 52-54. "Report of the President, Liberal Federation of Canada to the Liberal Policy Convention, 1970."

the general public might have greater access to government through a variety of channels not restricted to the party, as when the party set up task forces or when the government published white papers and gave research grants to interest groups to gather opinions from the public on various policy questions. All these conceptions were present in the discussions that ensued, but not everyone in the party agreed on what was meant by that evocative catch phrase, participatory democracy, and this was part of the reason for the ensuing disillusionment.

In a somewhat bizarre attempt to get an expert opinion on the meaning of political communication within the context of participatory democracy, a seminar was arranged with Marshall McLuhan in the fall of 1968. The session was attended by two MPs; two cabinet ministers, Donald Macdonald and Paul Martin; Pierre Levasseur, Marc Lalonde and Jim Davey from the Prime Minister's Office; George Elliott of MacLaren Advertising; four members of the national office, including the national director, the research director, and the director of communications; and Gordon Dryden, the party treasurer. In the first of what was supposed to have been a series of monthly seminars, McLuhan must have reaffirmed the faith of the assembled Liberals when he announced that Trudeau was one of the few people in the world who could identify with the young generation who had become members of the global community. In contrast with how some others perceived Trudeau, McLuhan saw him as having "a delicate, sensitive, responsive personality which is not in any sense overbearing." He told them not to allow Trudeau, as prime minister, "to waste his time being plugged into the bureaucracy. He has excellent Ministers who can look after the bureaucracy. His job is to work in close relationship with the people, probing and working towards solutions to specific problems, keeping himself in a position to recognize patterns of behaviour and respond to them."

The reactions afterwards by those who had been exposed to McLuhan's insights were mixed. One of the PMO staff was doubtful about the claim that Trudeau had a unique rapport with young people after having witnessed quite the opposite in a discussion with students at 24 Sussex Drive. Several were perplexed as to how a political party could adapt to the society which McLuhan had described. The voters in McLuhan's world were "almost totally alienated" and reacted against any establishments, including political parties, which set out fixed positions. George Elliott was disturbed that inconsistencies apparently did not matter in McLuhan's world, where realities were "basically the pictures on the television that come in one on top of the other so that there are no longer degrees of remoteness from or proximity to the real thing." Allan O'Brien confessed that the discussion left in a quandary those like him who were committed and comfortable "working within highly structured goal-oriented political organizations . . . How do we as political people communicate with and establish empathy with a society which to some degree at least tends to reject the very institution that we operate through."

McLuhan, as it turned out, had some traditional prejudices of his own. He declined to continue the seminars without being paid what was to Stanbury "a very substantial fee . . . well beyond the resources of the Party." He also thought the seminar had been attended by too many staff people whom he regarded as "paid party hacks", but he let it be known that he would be pleased to continue the discussions with Trudeau himself. George Elliott agreed with McLuhan inasmuch as he thought the experiment should come to an end. "I feel very strongly that we have gotten all the stimulation out of McLuhan there is." At the very least, the McLuhan seminar demonstrated that new approaches were disorienting.[2]

The task of attempting to apply the ambitious ideals of participation in some kind of concrete terms was undertaken by the new party president, Richard Stanbury. (An amiable, round-faced lawyer, his garrulity sometimes tried Trudeau's patience, especially when it took the form of long, discursive memoranda.) For Stanbury, the party was central to the participatory process—continuing the reforms begun in 1960—but he also looked for a much broader participation by the general public than ever before. He saw four areas where changes had to be made in order to implement participation:

1. The national office of the Federation had to be professionally staffed and properly financed
2. Channels of communications had to be established between the Federation and the cabinet so that the latter's decisions took account of party views
3. Programs had to be developed at the riding level to open up the party to the public
4. Channels of communications had also to be developed to explain the actions and intentions of the government to the party and the public.[3]

The Toronto *Globe and Mail* commented that "cynics will not hesitate to brush aside the just-announced reform of Liberal Party machinery as a flashy trick for institutionalizing the Trudeau cult", but it saw in Stanbury's "obvious earnestness and realism" evidence that the reforms were "more than window-dressing." Opinions from the parliamentary caucus

---

[2.] LPC, vol. 1096, file: Stanbury, R.J. - Correspondence 1968-1970, Memorandum by Stanbury on Seminar with McLuhan, 16.10.68; Elliott to Stanbury, 23.10.68, 7.11.68; Jim Davey to Stanbury, 22.10.68; O'Brien to Stanbury, 5.11.68; Levasseur to Stanbury, 23.10.68; Stanbury to Trudeau, 12.11.68.

[3.] LPC, vol. 1134, file: Liberal Party of Canada Through the Eyes of Dick Stanbury, Feb., 1969. "Report of the President, Liberal Federation of Canada to the Liberal Policy Convention, 1970."

were more circumspect. Public participation had to be meaningful, said one MP; people had to feel that their ideas had really been considered. Another warned that "we will have to be very careful not to deceive the public as to exactly what we are endeavouring to achieve" and he expressed some apprehensions lest the exercise lead to eventual embarrassment.[4]

Before we proceed to look at how these reforms were accomplished, something has to be said about the changes of personnel that took place after Trudeau won the leadership. Three of the key positions in the Liberal Federation were held by people who were strong proponents of the participatory ideal: the new party president, Richard Stanbury; the English-speaking co-chairman of the policy committee, Allen Linden; and Torrance Wylie, who became national director at the beginning of 1969. But many of the people, who had been associated with the reform movements of the Pearson period and had taken leadership positions within the party structures at the time, found themselves on the sidelines after 1968. At the leadership convention, antipathies had developed between the various candidates' teams, especially those of Trudeau and Turner. After the election, many of the key Liberals who had supported leadership candidates other than Trudeau found that their telephones did not ring. They were no longer on hand to provide support when things got tough for the three who carried the main burden of implementing the post-1968 reforms. On the other hand, most of the people who made up Trudeau's immediate entourage at the leadership convention were relatively new to Liberal party politics. After April 1968 they went directly into executive and administrative positions in the government and few of them became very active in the party organization or showed much interest in making the party a vehicle for participation.[5]

THE NATIONAL OFFICE

While in one sense the apex of the party, the national office of the Liberal Federation—the link between the provincial organizations and the elected members of parliament—is an apex without real levers of power, and performs mainly service and co-ordinating functions. It can never be sure that party members accept the proposition that "without a strong Party Headquarters, there can be no hope of a strong National Liberal Party." In the past, said Stanbury, "one of the reasons the Federation has been ig-

---

4. "The politics of easy access", 17.9.68. LPC, vol. 1096, file: Stanbury - Correspondence and Memos 1968, Jean Roy to Stanbury, 7.8.68; D.A. Hogarth to Stanbury, 16.8.68.

5. Confidential Sources.

nored is that it has deserved to be ignored. It has not been able to provide to the Parliamentary Wing of the Party any service which the Parliamentary Wing of the Party regarded as being significant."[6]

With the new age of participatory politics, however, there issued forth a veritable avalanche of ideas as to how the party headquarters might justify its existence. There were to be questionnaires, voting surveys, constituency intelligence files, film and voice-tape banks, dial-a-news-item services in major cities and television seminars for MPs and an extraordinarily ambitious Party-to-people program that would entail monthly visits by Liberal poll captains to one-twelfth of the homes in every poll across the country in order to gather responses to various policy questions.[7]

Even if only some of these ideas were implemented, it was obvious that the party office would have to be expanded significantly. For a long time, it had been located in an old house on Cooper Street, a declining residential area about a mile from the main governmental and business section of Ottawa. Though cheap to operate, the building was thought to be inadequate and an outmoded holdover from an older era. The party brought in a management consultant to advise on the organization of the new office. He recommended a larger staff with more specialized experience than the generalists of the past and advised dividing the office into departments on functional lines: Administration; Organization and Liaison; Communications; Policy Research and Information; Finance; and Programs.[8]

Under *Administration* came the routine operation of the party office with a director, an accountant, two secretaries, a receptionist and five people working on addressograph and duplicating equipment. *Organization,* with two directors and a secretary, was responsible for maintaining liaison with the provincial and constituency organizations, and with the development of election training programmes and organizational strategy for the next election. It was also to provide the secretariat for the new advisory groups which will be discussed later. *Communications,* consisting of a director, a French-speaking associate director, a co-ordinator of the speakers bureau, and a secretary, handled public relations and media relations for the Federation; in addition, the

---

[6] Stanbury Papers, vol. 14, Bill McAfee, Appraisal of Role of Communications Department, Liberal Federation of Canada, November 1968. LPC, vol. 1094, file: Organization - Special Memorandum, Memorandum to the New Leader of the Liberal Party of Canada, n.d., Stanbury. The fact that Stanbury felt it was necessary for the national office of the extra-parliamentary party to justify itself to the parliamentary wing is indicative of the deference felt even by as staunch a party supporter as Stanbury.

[7] LPC, vol. 1094, file: Organization - Special Memorandum, What should be the elements of the new party.

[8] Stanbury Papers, vol. 14, D.M. Ferguson to Stanbury, 22.8.68.

Diagram I **LIBERAL PARTY OF CANADA EXECUTIVE OFFICE (1968)**

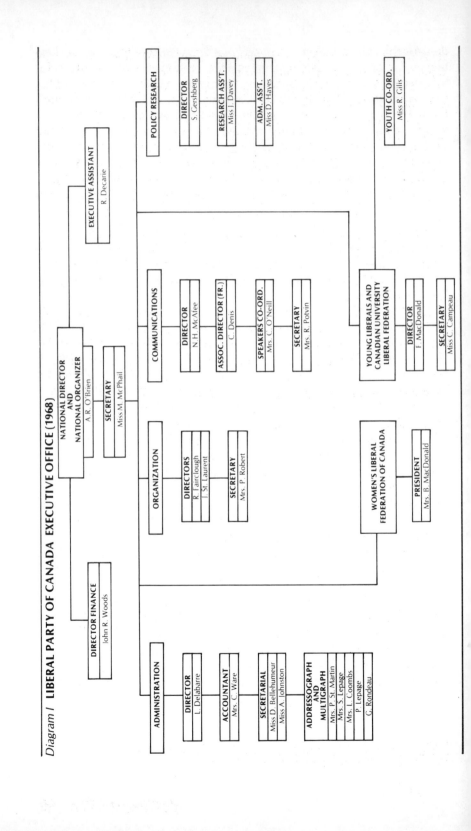

NATIONAL DIRECTOR AND NATIONAL ORGANIZER
A. R. O'Brien

SECRETARY
Miss M. McPhail

EXECUTIVE ASSISTANT
R. Decarie

DIRECTOR FINANCE
John R. Woods

POLICY RESEARCH

DIRECTOR
S. Gershberg

RESEARCH ASS'T.
Miss J. Davey

ADM. ASS'T.
Miss D. Hayes

COMMUNICATIONS

DIRECTOR
N. H. McAfee

ASSOC. DIRECTOR (FR.)
C. Denis

SPEAKERS CO-ORD.
Mrs. C. O'Neill

SECRETARY
Mrs. R. Potvin

ORGANIZATION

DIRECTORS
R. Fairclough
J. St. Laurent

SECRETARY
Mrs. P. Robert

ADMINISTRATION

DIRECTOR
L. Delabarre

ACCOUNTANT
Mrs. C. Ware

SECRETARIAL
Miss D. Bellehumeur
Miss A. Johnston

ADDRESSOGRAPH AND MULTIGRAPH
Mrs. P. St. Martin
Mrs. S. Lepage
Mrs. L. Coombs
P. Lepage
G. Rondeau

WOMEN'S LIBERAL FEDERATION OF CANADA

PRESIDENT
Mrs. B. MacDonald

YOUNG LIBERALS AND CANADIAN UNIVERSITY LIBERAL FEDERATION

DIRECTOR
F. MacDonald

SECRETARY
Miss C. Campeau

YOUTH CO-ORD.
Miss R. Gilis

department was responsible for mailings for party members, a speakers bureau for constituencies requesting MPs, and technical assistance for MPs in their dealings with the media. One of the biggest headaches of the Communications Department was the production of a party news-letter. For many years, a Liberal news-letter had been published, though on a very irregular basis. The provincial parties had their own newspapers, but increases in postal rates and printing costs had severely strained provincial budgets. In 1969, the national executive adopted a proposal for a combined federal-provincial bi-monthly Liberal newspaper. The *Canadian Liberal* was to be an eight-page newsprint tabloid with three pages of provincial content determined by each province, one page of provincial-federal promotion and four pages of federal news. Bulk printing and mailing would result in considerable savings, so it was argued. The paper was lively and eye-catching, but there was always trouble adhering to regular publishing dates and it was never possible to get all the provinces to participate.[9]

The *Policy Research Department,* with a director and two assistants, was responsible for stimulating and developing policy discussions at all levels of the party; it was directly responsible for running federal policy conferences and acted as a secretariat for the Standing Committee on Policy. It was also supposed to deal with all policy emanating from the membership—promoting it aggressively with the cabinet and reminding ministers that they must account to national conventions on how policy developed by the party membership had been dealt with. The Director of the *Finance* department was the most recent addition to the staff. His appointment indicated that the Federation intended to get control of its own finances, as will be discussed in the section on "Finances." The Finance Director managed the budget of the Federation and was responsible for developing new methods of raising funds from a broader base. He was also expected to make recommendations to cabinet on the new party finance legislation that was before cabinet.

Programs (with a staff of three in addition to the Women's president), in the first instance, gave executive direction to the Women's and Youth affiliated organizations and, with their hoped-for demise as separate organizations, Programs was in due course intended to develop ways of promoting greater participation in party activities by members and the general public. Programs for the involvement of youth and women's activities would then become just one aspect of this department's work. The Women's Federation and the Young Liberals were eventually phased out — only to resurface in a different guise as commissions—and a Program

9. LPC, vol. 1137, files: Executive Committee Meetings, 23.11.69; 14-15.3.70; 20-21.6.70; 12-13.9.70; 13-14.2.71; 27-28.11.71; 18-19.9.71.

Director with broadened responsibilities was never appointed, apparently because the budget did not permit it.

By 1968, the party office had a staff of twenty-six to twenty-eight with the cost of operations up dramatically from $146,375.98 in 1963 to $376,772.38 in 1969/70.[10]

In spite of these increases, however, the national office did not have staff or funds commensurate with what it was expected to accomplish. The chairman of the communications committee pointed out that, at less than $10,000 a year, the budget of the communications department was just over 1 percent of the advertising budget for the Ontario Milk Marketing Board. A more direct comparison could be made with the Prime Minister's Office, which had doubled its staff and tripled its budget in approximately the same period. The PMO had a staff of eighty-five with a budget of $900,000 in 1970 and half of that office—in the Correspondence Section and the Regional Desks—carried out tasks which in some respects overlapped with the communications and organizational responsibilities of the party office.[11] Not surprisingly, the problem of the national office's credibility and status remained. Stanbury was dismayed that the party office was regarded as no more than "some sort of foreign agency" by many of the ministers' offices. Allan O'Brien agreed that no matter how well the national office performed its duties, the question of status was "no less important in Ottawa than it is in any other community of impressionable people . . . it's important to us and to the Party's presence in Ottawa, but it is a delicate strategy that must not be over played."[12]

LIAISON - ADVISORY GROUPS, POLITICAL CABINET, PRIME MINISTER'S OFFICE

One of Stanbury's chief concerns was how to achieve effective co-ordination among the various segments of the party: the Federation, the caucus and the cabinet; and how to give the extra-parliamentary party a larger role than it had had previously. Except during election campaigns, the three segments of the party all went their separate ways. Before 1958,

[10] LPC, vol. 728, file: Finances - Confidential, Memo from Lafond to Connolly, Davey, Matthews, Aird, 27.1.64; vol. 1137, file: Executive Committee Meeting, 12-13.9.70.

[11] LPC, vol. 1138, file: National Executive Meeting, 18-19.9.71. Anthony Westell, *Paradox, Trudeau as Prime Minister,* pp. 114-115.

[12] LPC, vol. 1094, file: Organization - Special Memorandum, O'Brien to Stanbury, 5.7.68; vol. 1134, file: Liberal Party of Canada Through the Eyes of Dick Stanbury, Feb., 1969. See also vol. 1140, file: Organization, *passim.*

co-ordination had not been a serious problem. Caucus and the party membership had been generally docile. When aroused from their somnolence for election campaigns, their activities had been co-ordinated by the cabinet ministers. Between 1958 and 1968 the Federation and the continuing campaign chairmen had shared responsibility for party organization, but no organizational responsibilities had been formally assigned to cabinet ministers or the parliamentary party after the return to power in 1963. "The result was frustration on the part of the Party organization because, while there was permissiveness and sympathetic assistance from the Leader for its development, there was no real support of its role and no attempt to make effective use of its resources in co-ordination with the work of the Cabinet and Caucus." The Federation, Stanbury, continued, had to have a continuing involvement in party affairs, but past attempts at having regular meetings of cabinet, caucus, and the Federation had not been successful and the Federation had been ignored.

Stanbury's device for linking together 155 MPs, 29 ministers, the prime minister and a party membership estimated at 500,000 was the advisory group or troika. As envisaged, it was intended to give the party membership, represented by the Federation, a far larger role in government than it had ever had before—indeed, far larger perhaps than that enjoyed by any party in a Western democracy, because of the *continuing* input which the party would have at the highest levels.

Each province was to have an advisory group, consisting of a representative of the cabinet, a representative of caucus and a representative of the provincial party membership. The first would be named by the prime minister, the second by caucus and the third by the party's provincial president. The advisory group was seen as co-ordinating the activities of the varous segments of the party in the province and providing a channel of communications through which political problems could be referred from the province to Ottawa. Each member of the advisory group was expected to consult with his "constituency" and together they would take responsibility for the "health and welfare" of the party in matters of policy, finance, organization, and appointments within their respective provinces. It was still recognized, however, that the minister retained the right to make the final decision. At the apex, a national advisory group would deal with national questions that were beyond the scope of the provincial groups and it would act as a continuing campaign committee for strategic planning. The advisory groups were to occupy a key, pivotal position inasmuch as other co-ordinating channels—such as the Political Cabinet, Regional Desks and meetings of ministers' executive assistants—were expected to follow up the recommendations of the advisory groups. The organizational department of the party office was to act as the secretariat to the advisory groups by preparing background papers, drawing up agenda, calling regular meetings and following up recommendations.[13]

Stanbury was attempting what Norman Lambert and Keith Davey had tried before him: to give the party clout by having it participate in patronage decisions. The only difference was that Stanbury's aims were broader and his structures on paper were more sophisticated. No mention is made in party documents about examining these earlier attempts, nor does it appear that models were sought among the political parties of other Western democracies. Indeed, none could have been found. The British Labour party's National Executive Committee is probably the most powerful extra-parliamentary party body in Western democracies. The NEC includes members of the cabinet (or shadow cabinet) and the party headquarters acts as a secretariat for it, though not for other co-ordinating committees with Labour cabinets. The NEC, however, has been more interested in policy than appointments. It shares responsibility with the parliamentary front bench for approving Labour's election manifesto, but is not consulted over government appointments when the Labour party holds office. In fact, for a party secretariat to have power over appointments, one has to look to Communist countries; and that was certainly not the model that Stanbury had in mind for his advisory groups. Ministers were to retain the final decision-making power, so the amount of leverage that the Liberal party could exercise through the advisory groups would be strictly limited. On the other hand, it is clear that Stanbury wanted to give the party, the Federation, a more important role than it had had and that the successful implementation of the advisory group idea would have entailed a decisive shift of influence to the Federation. For that to happen, there had to be acquiescence from the ministers, encouragement from the Prime Minister, a determined pressure from the party membership and an alliance between the Federation and the caucus. The first was especially crucial.[14]

The advisory groups were set up in late 1968, but they were by no means enthusiastically received. Many of the caucus were suspicious of the new arrangements. Rather than seeing the advisory groups as a

[13.] LPC, vol. 1094, file: Organization - Special Memorandum, Memorandum to the New Leader of the Liberal Party of Canada, n.d., Stanbury; What should be the Elements of the New Party, n.d., [Stanbury]; vol. 1134, file: Liberal Party of Canada Through the Eyes of Dick Stanbury, Feb., 1969; vol. 1140, file: Organization, Notes for Address to National Caucus, 30.10.68, Stanbury. In 1963, Nick Taylor, the president of the Alberta Liberals, had suggested a similar four-member "opportunity committee" for each province. Vol. 1037, file: Alberta Campaign Committee, Taylor to Connolly, 28.6.63.

[14.] R. Rose, *The Problem of Party Government*, pp. 340-344. R. T. McKenzie, *British Political Parties*, pp. 330-333, 451-453, 524-527. G. Braunthal, "The Policy Function of the German Social Democratic Party", *Comparative Politics* (1976-77), 127-145. I. Deutscher, *Stalin: A Political Biography*, chap. VII. LPC, vol. 1134, file: Liberal Party of Canada Through the Eyes of Dick Stanbury, Feb., 1969.

means of improving communications within the party, some MPs saw them as a threat to the traditional personal relationships which they had been able to build up over the years with individual cabinet ministers. Stanbury did not see how it was possible, in these more complex times, for 155 MPs to have personal relationships with 29 ministers and the prime minister. Writing to Barney Danson, then a backbench MP, he was at a loss to understand what the MPs did not like about the advisory groups. "It has been my impression listening to the agonized frustration of the MPs that they would dearly love to have some vehicle that had more muscle than they have individually themselves." Did they want more caucus representation on the groups? Did they resent the presence of party representatives? "Some MPs, particularly those from British Columbia, feel that the [party] organization has no part in the between-elections functions of the political party. I think these would rather be able to organize caucus in such a way that they have all the muscle themselves. But if, in so doing, they alienate the interested members of the Party organization, they will find themselves subject to the same charges as they are now levelling at the Cabinet. What I am trying to do is to give each part of the Party a part in the decision-making process and, by so doing, strengthen the arm of both the caucus and the organization."

Danson replied that most members simply did not understand the function of the advisory groups and saw them as "a quiet operation locked up by those directly involved. It's just one of those old hang-ups about backroom boys that seem to concern the members who don't seem to get consulted adequately on many matters that are decided by the Provincial Advisory Groups." More consultation with caucus would correct the situation, he thought. In Stanbury's opinion, some ministers were handling caucus well, but most were not. "The Members are too bright and too aggressive to accept blindly the cipher role which the parliamentary system imposes upon them, unless they have an opportunity within their own party to understand the question and to make the representations which they feel are necessary. *Meaningful involvement of the caucus in the process leading to government decision* will do all that can be done to remove the frustrations on policy matters. Explanation of the Advisory Groups, some examples of their effective use by the Members as channels to government should persuade Members that this is a more effective way of getting things done than by the old way." But Stanbury and Danson could not help concluding, half jokingly, half in earnest, that their great insights into the parliamentary process were not widely shared.[15]

---

[15] LPC, vol. 1126, file: Advisory Groups - General, Stanbury to Danson, 20.8.69; Danson to Stanbury, 4.9.69. Emphasis in the original.

The biggest obstacle to the effective operation of the advisory groups, however, was the cabinet. In Stanbury's estimation, its members had not learned to work together either as a team or in partnership with the rest of the party. New policy departures were being planned without any reference to other wings of the party and in that respect the cabinet, if anything, had slipped backward. "There is a resistance to cooperating with the Party Office in matters of opportunities, policy information, uses of the Cabinet Ministers' time—in fact in almost every aspect of Party life." The caucus and the party would respond quickly if they believed the cabinet really wanted input from them. But "there has not been a single request from a single Cabinet Minister to test any policy question on the Party membership and the public through them. The structure exists but it will atrophy through disuse, unless the Cabinet shows it means business." The cabinet, he thought, was still relying too much on the civil service, special interest groups and the media—all elite groups—for their policy ideas.[16]

By September 1969, a province-by-province survey revealed that some of the advisory groups were working with reasonable effectiveness, but others were not meeting at all. Those in the central provinces and the prairie provinces met fairly regularly; though consultations with their respective constituencies were not as extensive as they were supposed to be. Just as with the earlier attempt under Davey to have greater consultation over appointments, the system proved to be cumbersome and time consuming. Insufficient advance warning and inadequate information precluded consultation on many questions and the groups spent so much time on patronage recommendations that there was little time left for looking at the "health and welfare" of the party in the province—except insofar as "health and welfare" meant patronage! In Saskatchewan the provincial organization stayed clear of any active involvement and the groups representing British Columbia and the Atlantic provinces had not met at all. The senior minister from British Columbia, Arthur Laing, was totally opposed to the whole scheme. His argument, as he set it out to Stanbury, was not an unreasonable one. MPs, he said, were aware that their political influence had steadily grown smaller. "Within their capacity to make decisions on appointments, wise Ministers will consult with the elected members from their regions as well as fellow Ministers. It might well be deemed 'the last straw' if the Federation were to become still another layer between the Minister and the back bench." The way for the Federation to acquire influence and respect was not through "Jobs", he said, but through the Federation being sufficiently independent that it could guide and goad the party through thinkers' conferences

---

[16.] LPC, vol. 1134, file: Liberal Party of Canada Through the Eyes of Dick Stanbury, Feb., 1969.

not dominated by ministers and MPs. In other words, too much co-ordination and co-operation between the Federation and cabinet was a bad thing.[17]

In spite of opposition, Stanbury kept plugging away at the advisory groups concept and wider consultation gradually became the rule rather than the exception. Forms and names changed from one province to another. Even Arthur Laing started to consult with the president of the Liberal party in British Columbia. The Ontario troika, as it was called, broke down over disagreements between the Ontario minister and the caucus chairman, but under Judd Buchanan, who became the Ontario political minister in 1977, it is reported that wide consultation took place. Initially, as we saw, the party office was supposed to have functioned as a secretariat, but the job proved to be more than the party office could handle and it ceased to have any formal involvement with patronage. In later years, notice of appointments was handled in a very systematic way by the PCO and the PMO. Once a month, a thick memorandum listing every upcoming federal appointment was circulated to ministers and key party people in the provinces and, once a week, the ministers from each province met to discuss the recommendations that were forwarded to them.

Whether the government exercised its patronage powers in a more or less partisan way than previous governments is difficult to say, partly because the number of positions to be filled by Order-in-Council (i.e., at the government's discretion) is over 600 a year. A few non-Liberals were appointed to the Senate although, in the months leading up to the 1979 election, these appointments were the most blatantly political of all because they went to opposition MPs in ridings which the Liberals had hopes of winning. Legal appointments became genuinely less political when Trudeau, as Justice Minister in 1967, began the practice of asking the judicial committee of the Canadian Bar Association to comment on prospective senior court judges. There were indications that considerations of quality rather than party affiliation were uppermost in appointments to highly visible bodies like the Canada Council; to be too readily identified as a Liberal was occasionally a disqualification. On the other hand, at least one minister, the Hon. John Munro, frankly admitted that patronage was a fact of political life. "Is it wrong to favor a past political supporter over someone else if the two have equal ability? Of course it isn't." One study found that, between 1968 and 1977, at least 200 former Liberal candidates (or their spouses) had received appointments, to which the Hon. Allan MacEachen replied, "When I looked at the list

---

17. LPC, vol. 1125, file: Advisory Groups - General, Robinson to Stanbury and Wylie, 30.9.69: Fairclough to Stanbury, 7.3.69; Meetings of the Saskatchewan Advisory Group, 12.2.69, 4.3.69; vol. 1096, file: Stanbury, R.J. - Correspondence and Memos 1968, Laing to Stanbury, 3.9.68.

this morning, I was quite impressed with the quality of persons who were available for this kind of service in Canada."[18] (The report did not indicate the position of his tongue when the remark was made!) The whole question comes down to the propostion that, whenever there is discretion, there is the potential for patronage. Should such decisions be made by civil servants or by politicians? The latter are at least publicly accountable.

POLITICAL CABINET

Political Cabinet was another co-ordinating body that was created in 1968 partly to complement the work of the advisory groups. Described as cabinet without its administrative or executive responsibilities, it consisted of the entire cabinet plus the party president, the national director, the chairman of caucus and the prime minister's principal secretary, but no civil servants. Besides dealing with unresolved problems referred to it by the advisory groups, it examined the broad political impact of the government's actions. More bluntly, it was conceived by the Federation as a means of politicizing a cabinet which was considered to be dangerously apolitical, especially when compared with pre-1957 cabinets. It got off to a good start, meeting for two or three complete days, up to six times a year, and about every six weeks during minority government. The Federation drew up the agenda and chose to have discussed subjects such as election finances; western alienation; the Liberal party's policy formulation process; the advisory groups; various by-elections; student unrest. At first, party people professed to be amazed at how much impact they were having on cabinet, but soon the familiar complaints about lack of communication were heard. By the end of 1972, one party official concluded that, as a device for bringing the party and the government closer together, Political Cabinet was actually counter-productive. It "seemed to be nothing more than two hours of confrontation during which the party accused the Cabinet ministers of being non-political, lazy, poor communicators, excessively bureaucratic and so on. For their part the ministers seemed to believe that party representatives were naïve or at best simplistic, chronic bitchers, disorganized, non-supportive of their efforts." Gradually the emphasis was shifted so that Political Cabinet became more an opportunity simply to explain party programmes, activities and problems, than to sit in judgment on the political performance of

[18.] Interviews with Senator Stanbury, 4.8.78; Paul Klie, 18.8.78; John deB. Payne, 13.1.72; Colin Kenny, 29.9.78. *Globe and Mail*, 2.7.74; 28.4.76; 13,14.6.77; 17.4.79. Geoffrey Stevens, "Appointment System Improved" in Paul Fox, ed., *Politics: Canada*, 4th ed., pp. 548-550.

ministers. A few years later, the general assessment was that the inclusion of the whole cabinet along with party officials made it just too cumbersome and it stopped meeting. That gap was filled by the smaller, more effective Political Planning Committee which used to meet weekly for up to an hour-and-a-half and whose membership consisted of the party president, the national director, the PM's principal secretary, the chairman of caucus, the co-chairman of the national campaign committee and just the senior political ministers.[19]

PRIME MINISTER'S OFFICE

Ever since the days of Sir John A. Macdonald, the prime minister has had his own personal political staff, but when Trudeau doubled the PMO soon after becoming prime minister, alarmed observers feared that he intended to make it into a Canadian equivalent of the White House Office. According to Marc Lalonde, Trudeau's first principal secretary, the expansion took place in order "to establish more effective collective control over the administration and better communication with the people at large." The PMO staff answered his mail, made his travel arrangements, handled his relations with the media, and helped him with strategic political planning. The party office feared that an enlarged PMO would invade its area of jurisdiction and that fear was shared from differing perspectives by the cabinet, the caucus and the Privy Council Office.[20]

From the Liberal Federation's point of view, the greatest potential for overlap came from the new post of program secretary, who advised the prime minister on long-term policy goals and political strategy, and from the regional desks, who gathered political intelligence in the various regions of the country.

The regional desks were, in part, a pragmatic solution to a practical problem: Liberal parliamentary representation was weak on the prairies —eleven out of forty-five seats were held by Liberals—and additional channels of communication were needed in order to keep abreast of issues and problems as they arose in those three provinces. The Federation, on the other hand, did not have the funds necessary to employ enough

---

[19] Blair Williams to the author, 3.8.76. Interviews' with Senator Stanbury, 6.4.70; Torrance Wylie, 5.8.70, 8.9.71; Gerry Robinson, 4.2.77. LPC, vol. 1137, file: Executive Committee Meeting, 14-15.3.70; 12-13.9.70; 13-14.2.71.

[20] D. Smith, "President and Parliament" in T.A. Hockin, ed., Apex of Power, 2nd ed., p. 232. W. Stewart, Shrug: Trudeau in Power, pp. 2-3. A. Westell, Paradox: Trudeau as Prime Minister, pp. 107-122. Marc Lalonde, "The changing role of the Prime Minister's Office", Canadian Public Administration (1971), 510-529. Thomas D'Aquino, "The Prime Minister's Office: Catalyst or Cabal?" in Paul Fox, ed., Politics: Canada, 4th ed., pp. 394-408.

staff to fill the vacuum, so a Western Desk was set up in the PMO as a pilot project. One might well ask why public funds should be used to alter what prairie voters had determined to be appropriate Liberal representation in Ottawa. The reply was that the regional desks were supposedly concerned more with issues and only secondarily with helping the party. In any case, there was bound to be friction, especially in a province like Alberta where local Liberals lacked self-confidence and were sensitive to slights at the best of times. In order to quiet apprehensions that the new system might be a threat to established power bases, initial contacts were confined to party officials who were asked to outline what the regional desk could do for them. At first, similar arrangements for Ontario and Quebec were considered unnecessary because those provinces had so many Liberal MPs. P.E.I., with no Liberal representation, was thought to require a different approach from that conceived for the Prairies since concerns there were almost exclusively to do with patronage, and it was thought best to leave that with the Federation. In New Brunswick, too, where half the seats were held by Liberals, patronage concerns predominated. "We are also politely reminded—and we agree—that the established authority must not be by-passed" observed a progress report on the regional desks.[21] Even in these two provinces, however, the obsession with patronage created a different sort of void which regional desks might have to fill, according to the report, and that was the capability of foreseeing upcoming local issues. If the party did not work through advisory groups to "pick up the slack", then regional desks would have to become "a substitute for the Party structure."

Eventually, regional desks were created to service all four regions of the country. Following further discussions between party representatives and Pierre Levasseur, who was in charge of the regional desks, it was agreed that they should also "act as a non-party political intelligence source for the Prime Minister", communicating with citizens "who would not normally make their representations through the Members of Parliament or through the Party organization. These would include provincial and local government officials, special-interest groups, youth groups", and so forth.

Relations between the PMO and the Federation steadily deteriorated into what was described by one national office staff member as a "two-armed-camps atmoshpere." The PMO tended to be disdainful of party activities and saw the party as "something to be gotten around or managed." Stanbury noted a widespread concern that the prime minister's staff was "over-protective, that it lacks political experience and judgment, and that it is arrogant in purporting to act for the Prime Minister."

21. LPC, vol. 1141, file: PMO General 1968-1973, "Regional Desks: Progress Report", 20.9.68 (no author) Document #3.

In rationalizing their fields of endeavour, he insisted that the PMO should keep out of Liberal party affairs. "The Prime Minister's Office has no role in the Leader's exercise of the leadership of the Party organization. The relationship there must be a direct one between the Leader and the Party President." Not mincing words, Stanbury declared, "there is nothing worse . . . than to have the decisions of the National Executive questioned or investigated by members of the Leader's staff." As far as the regional desks were concerned, they should have no dealings with party people; if the Leader was unhappy with the intelligence he was getting through the party organization, he should take up the problem with the party president.[22]

PARTICIPATION AND THE 1970 POLICY CONVENTION

The 1970 policy convention in many ways marked the culmination of the movement to refashion the Liberal party as a membership-based, internally democratic, participatory party. It also provided the decisive test as to how much support there was for these goals within the party.

The party's constitution was again the subject of re-examination in the light of these goals. Under that constitution, as we have seen, membership in the Liberal Federation of Canada consisted of only the twelve provincial and territorial associations. (Diagram II) An individual could only be a member of his or her provincial association or, in some cases, only of a riding association. A federated structure, however, conflicted with the mobilization model of a participatory party, because the intermediate bodies, in a sense, broke the direct link between individual Liberals and their charismatic leader. As a champion of the participatory party, Stanbury was logically consistent in favouring a change in the constitution so that individuals could join through a national membership system. For Gordon Dryden, the party's unoffical constitutional lawyer, a different model was relevant—that of a political party in the common sense. Dryden drew a nice legal distinction between a party under common law and one created by statute. The latter defined its membership, whereas anyone could declare himself to be a member of a party of the first type. Dryden's distinction was useful in pointing out the Berkeleian nature of party membership in both of the two older Canadian parties; that, for many, party membership exists in the mind of the beholder: self-declared and self-defined. Accordingly, Dryden was in favour of amending the constitution in order to recognize both kinds of membership.

The discussion of membership also led to consideration of a change in

22. Bill McAfee to the author, 2.2.79. G. Radwanski, *Trudeau*, p. 253; also p. 148. LPC, vol. 1134, file: Liberal Party of Canada Through the Eyes of Dick Stanbury, Feb., 1969.

Diagram II · **LIBERAL PARTY OF CANADA (1970-79)**

LPC Constitutional Structures

Quasi-Unofficial   Parliament   Government

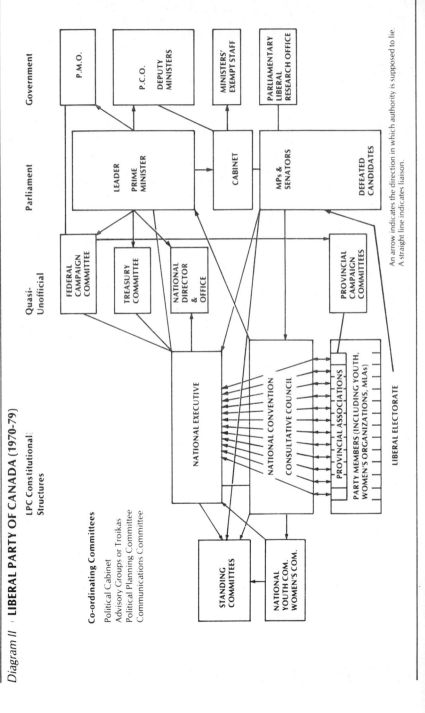

Co-ordinating Committees

Political Cabinet
Advisory Groups or Troikas
Political Planning Committee
Communications Committee

An arrow indicates the direction in which authority is supposed to lie.
A straight line indicates liaison.

the party's name. By calling it a federation, the implication was that it consisted only of the member associations. Changing the name to the Liberal Party of Canada avoided that suggestion. John Varley, the president of the Student Liberals, favoured changing the name also in order to get away from the notion that the Liberal Federation was simply the party office on Bank Street and that the parliamentary party was therefore separate from and superior to the Federation. All Liberals, he argued, should be considered members of the same body.[23]

The somewhat illogical outcome of the whole debate was that the name *was* changed; but, because of continuing resistance to the concept of individual membership, the twelve associations remained the only members. The goal of internal democracy received recognition in a new clause, 2-C, which was added to the membership section. It set out in some detail certain minimum standards for the democratic and constitutional procedures which the provincial and territorial member associations had to follow. Every member association had to have a written constitution that specified procedures for obtaining membership, as well as appeal procedures if an application was rejected; the member's constitution also had to provide for holding regular general meetings, election of officers, and procedures for amending its constitution; finally, they were bound to "strive to assure that the constituent Liberal organizations affiliated therewith in their respective provinces and territories adopt a written constitution similar in spirit to their own and, as much as possible, to the fundamental principles enumerated herein." The clause was admirable as far as it went in attempting to ensure that there was a common denominator of written procedures governing the practices followed by the widely varying provincial Liberal parties across the country. Considering that even a written constitution was a comparatively new experience for three of the associations, the common denominator had to be very low and there was no attempt to specify what those various procedures should be—only that they should exist in writing. The federal party was simply following the lead of some provincial associations who had already adopted more stringent minimum standards for their constituency associations.

In keeping with the increased emphasis on rank-and-file participation in the policy process, a new clause 5 provided for a kind of continuing policy convention called the Consultative Council. Delegates to a convention were to be consulted by the National Executive by mail at least twice a year on "important political issues" and those representing fed-

---

23. LPC, vol. 1129, file: C.O.C. Constitution, Dryden to Robinson, 8.7.70; Memo by Varley, Report on Proposed Changes to Clause 1 and 2A, n.d.

eral constituencies would have to be elected annually by their ridings.[24]

A "tidying" amendment, which has not yet been seen in operation, was clause 8-H-2. It requires leadership candidates to file nomination papers signed by at least seventy-five party members at least two weeks before the convention. As an attempt to eliminate nuisance candidates, the amendment is limited in scope, since it is so easy to obtain memberships. Virtually anyone with seventy-five friends could become a properly accredited leadership candidate. A more effective requirement would have been the signatures of seventy-five *delegates* or, going further, the commitment of their first-ballot *votes*. The provision of a closing date for nominations was no doubt inspired by the spectacle of Diefenbaker's last-minute entry into the 1967 Conservative leadership convention—not the first time that the Liberals have attempted to learn a lesson from the problems of their rivals.

In a new preamble to the constitution, the party attempted to show that it was serious about defining its basic political principles. It was felt that the existing statement of purposes in clause 1-B put too much emphasis on the party as a purely electoral organization and the new preamble attempted to say something about the basic values that united as amorphous a body as the Liberal Party of Canada. As one might expect of a "liberal" party, the preamble subscribes to "the fundamental rights and freedoms of man under the rule of law" (though without attempting to spell these out); more unexpectedly, in searching for the party's most basic principle, the preamble returns to the humanist Renaissance concept of "dignity"—"the dignity of each individual man and woman is the cardinal principle of democratic society and the primary purpose of all political organization and activity in such a society." It is perhaps significant that this statement won out over two alternative versions which have a more contemporary ring to them. The first stated that the Liberal party was an "association of the politically active and reform-minded community, and a force for the stimulation and education of those who are alienated." The second (in part written by the Hon. John Roberts, later Secretary of State) declared that the "authority for government rests in the consent and command of the citizens"; that political parties are the instrument for direct citizen participation and for holding the government responsible to the citizenry; and that a political party, as well as supporting candidates for public office and forming a responsible government, must act as a stimulator within society.

While the approved version stated categorically that "all citizens have

[24.] The Consultative Council replaced the National Council, which had in turn replaced the old Advisory Council. Numbering over 225, the National Council was supposed to have met in years when conventions were not held, but in fact it never met. LPC, vol. 1129, Lafond to O'Brien, 30.1.69; Report to the Standing Committee on the Constitution, 12.9.70.

access to full information" (and thus put the party in apparent conflict with the government on the Freedom of Information issue), it declined to give pride of place to the political party as the principal participatory vehicle in the Canadian political system. Instead the Liberal party sought "to provide a flexible and democratic stucture" giving citizens conceivably one opportunity among many (including pressure groups as well as political parties) "to participate in open and public assessment" of public policies and leadership and "the right to advocate, by all lawful means, such modifications of policies and leadership as they deem desirable to promote the political, economic, social, cultural and general well-being of Canadians." While the preamble was undoubtedly accurate in describing, implicitly, the Liberal party as simply a vehicle—and not an especially privileged one—for the membership to advocate certain policies, the preamble was oddly self-depreciatory in implying that party members had the opportunity only to *advocate* changes in the leadership of the state, especially in the light of the "accountability" amendments which had been added in 1966.[25]

The foregoing amendments, proposed to the convention by the executive, were all accepted; but two of the executive's amendments were voted down. The first would have increased the guarantees for women and youth representation in the delegations elected at the constituency level by requiring that, of the six delegates, two would have to be women, two under the age of twenty-five and—as if to avoid the charge of discriminatory anti-discrimination—two would have to be men. The convention, however, preferred the more modest existing guarantees of clause 9-D-8 (it became 8-D-8 in the new constitution), which stipulated that every riding should be represented by at least one Liberal Woman and one Young Liberal. The other defeated amendment was one that would have extended ex-officio representation at national conventions to regional and district elected officers. While a limit was placed on the number of such ex-officio representatives (their number was not to exceed one quarter of the number of federal electoral districts in the province), such a change would have, for example, increased the potential ex-officio representation at the 1968 leadership convention by 10 percent.[26] There was little support for watering down the strength of the so-called "grass roots" component at a national convention.

Although the 1970 policy convention was the fourth to be held by the party without the added excitement of a leadership race, it was innovative in a number of ways and marked a new stage in the party's history. Previous policy conventions had occurred as isolated events—indeed,

---

[25.] LPC, vol. 1129, file: C.O.C. Constitution, "Report to the Standing Committee on the Constitution", 12.9.70.

[26.] J.C. Courtney, *The Selection of National Party Leaders in Canada*, p. 118. Liberal Federation of Canada, "Constitutional Amendments" [1970].

very isolated events, since the first two were separated by a gap of sixty-five years. Coming at the required interval of two years after the 1968 leadership convention, the 1970 policy convention thus confirmed the party's declared intention to hold regular national meetings.

The 1970 convention was the first major attempt to put into practice the goal of enabling the party "to act as the major link and vehicle between the people and the government." There was to be an ambitious three-phase program, culminating in a giant policy convention, which, according to Stanbury, would "convince the public that the Party really wants its participation." These new structures would service a two-way flow of communicating government intentions to the party and the public and of providing "to the public and the expanded party a credible and responsible means of effecting the course of government."[27] "The Politics of Participation" described the ambitious three-phase program leading up to the 1970 policy convention as the "most important development" since 1968 "to stimulate and ensure meaningful participation."

The three phases were to begin with a "thinkers' conference" at Harrison Hot Springs, British Columbia, in November 1969. This would be followed by a series of grass-roots meetings in which ordinary citizens as well as party members would react to the experts' ideas and formulate their own proposals in constituency meetings. The third phase was to be a normal policy convention (with constitency delegates) at which, according to the party's constitution, "the basic policies of the party shall be established."[28] Throughout the three stages, the emphasis was to be on getting the maximum participation.

It was perhaps an indication of the residual effect of Marshall McLuhan's seminar that convention planners (in contrast to the policy development efforts of 1960-61) now gave more attention to the *process* of developing policy than to the end result, a *program* for the party. In other respects, however, the convention appeared still to be transfixed by the inventions of Guttenberg and his successors. The sixty-two task force papers that awaited each delegate at Harrison weighed in at *eleven pounds*. Whether quantity served as an accurate indication of quality was, however, another question.

It was somehow very typical of the Liberal party to hold its thinkers' conference in an elegant mountain retreat, far removed from the madding crowd. The press had great fun at the party's expense by drawing attention to the luxurious setting. Actually, its very isolation made Harrison an ideal place for such a conference and the deliberations of thinkers and delegates carried on uninterrupted, even in the three hot spring-fed swimming pools.

---

[27] LPC, vol. 1134, file: "Liberal Party of Canada Through the Eyes of Dick Stanbury", February, 1969.

[28] 1966 Constitution, 9-I-1.

In his opening remarks at Harrison, Trudeau cautioned the conference against taking what he called the "Coney Island cowboy" approach—firing away at each policy issue as it came into view. In what was perhaps an unfavourable allusion to the 1966 convention's debate over the postponement of medicare, he urged them not to debate decisions which the government had just made or was about to make. Instead, he called on "thinkers" and delegates to look ahead to the future. Their time frame should not be the next year, but the next decade, because, if it was going to alter the future, a political party or a government had to plan that far ahead. "We are like the pilots of a supersonic airplane. By the time an airport comes into the pilot's field of vision, it is too late to begin the landing procedure. Such planes must be navigated by radar. A political party, in formulating policy, can act as a society's radar." One might observe, cynically, that Trudeau simply wanted to discourage public criticism of the government by its own supporters; on the other hand, one has to acknowledge that a political party is more likely to influence leadership policies if it concentrates on those areas in which the leader and his government have not already committed themselves publicly. In any case, the conference, for the most part, did not take up Trudeau's challenge and, as an exercise in futurism, the Harrison conference did not probe very far into the next decade. One is hard pressed to find much discussion of—let alone solutions to—the problems that did dominate the seventies: energy, inflation, sluggish economic growth. One of the more wildly mistaken predictions was that inflation would "average approximately 3 percent over the next decade."[29]

Even the constitution and Quebec were noticeably absent from the Harrison agenda, though this was by design rather than through oversight. When Trudeau became leader of the party in 1968, his views on the constitution were well known and clearly formulated in a series of articles which were brought together in *Federalism and the French Canadians.* Soon after he was elected as an MP in 1965, his influence could be seen in the shift of government policy away from giving Quebec special status (in taxation, for example) and towards increased support for official bilingualism; but at neither the 1966 nor the 1968 conventions did the party officially endorse the Trudeau position on the constitution. Admittedly, there were no formal policy resolutions adopted by the 1968 convention and, in electing Trudeau as leader, the party by implication accepted his principal policy positions—and his position on the constitution was one of the few areas in which Trudeau's views were clearly spelled out. Nevertheless, Harrison's avoidance of this topic made

[29] Notes for Remarks by the Prime Minister at the Harrison Liberal Conference, Harrison Hot Springs, British Columbia, November 21, 1969. C.S. Carter, "Economic Problems Facing Canada in the 1970's."

questionable the point of the whole exercise. The convention steering committee was criticized for avoiding this and other current issues such as tax reform. John Payne, an influential Montreal member of the convention organizing committee argued that it was time to take constitutional questions out of the hands of the mandarins and bureaucrats and place them in a political milieu; "maybe our convention could make a major contribution in bringing this about." But with uncharacteristic blindness to portents, he commented that "the language issue can be left dormant for the time being. It has no sex appeal, even in Quebec."[30]

The format of the conference allowed for a varied but not very thorough examination of a number of subject areas. Each session began with "task force reports" from five or six panelists and then the conference broke up into smaller discussion groups. The total time allotted to each subject area was between two and three hours, which was hardly long enough to deal with a complex problem like poverty, regional development or industrial relations. Intellectual indigestion was a perpetual hazard. (The format was in sharp contrast to a Conservative policy conference held a month before in Niagara Falls. There, delegates divided themselves into eight policy streams; each stream dealt with only one policy area for five morning and afternoon sessions of panels and papers given by experts; these were followed by two caucus sessions in which the group attempted to arrive at a consensus. With that amount of time, each group was able to cover its subject matter reasonably thoroughly and acquire a certain *esprit* and momentum of its own.) Significantly, it was not until the last evening that the Harrison conference really caught fire in discussion groups devoted to a paper by Stanbury entitled, "Why the Party?".

The paper was a thoughtful re-examination of the functions of the political party in a democratic state. It acknowledged public disenchantment with what was seen as "a sinister machine" that bought votes, dispensed patronage and engaged in an unproductive adversary system in parliament. Governments, for their part, had treated it "as a useful tool at election time and as a nuisance between elections. The elite have regarded it as being beneath contempt." Alternative ways in which people could organize themselves to put their views before the government were set out with the advantages and disadvantaes of each: protest groups, "cable-vision democracy" (an electronic adaptation of direct democracy through referenda), rule by experts, a one-party system, and a "Two-or More Party System." These alternatives were assumed to be mutually exclusive, although no explanation was given as to why that should be. Stanbury saw the "Two-or More Party System" as still preferable; but, if it

30. LPC, vol. 1166, file: LPC 1970; C.O.C. Steering Committee - Minutes and Documents, "Addendum" by Payne, 8.6.70.

was to be retained, then the Liberal party would have to be reformed. The necessary reforms reiterated familiar themes of Stanbury's. The party would have to be:

A. In continuing and effective existence
B. Open and democratic
C. Representative of the profile of the community
D. Competent in the techniques of involvement
E. Providing the mechanics for effective, two-way flow between government and the community
F. Made up of people whose motive is public service, not patronage.

In the discussions provoked by the paper, some Liberals were genuinely excited by the prospect of reaching out to ordinary people who had, in the past, been repelled or intimidated by the party. Delegates heard reports from some MPs of imaginative initiatives already being taken: monthly policy meetings attended by several hundred constituents; or referral of constituents' problems to a network of local experts. Not all were converted to Stanbury's new design. One hard-nosed MP scoffed that constituents were often just trying to get free legal aid; that open meetings would produce "badly-worded" resolutions; and that he already had *too much* communication with the public in the form of twenty-five letters and twenty-five telephone calls a day, and the expectation that he should attend every rural funeral in his constituency! That was, however, not the view of the majority. Most of the delegates were genuinely concerned about how a traditional, elitist party could transform itself into a popularly based party when it was saddled with members who were mainly interested in fighting elections. Furthermore, as the party in power, the Liberals were concerned that they had inevitably attracted people who wanted power, patronage, or preferment for themselves rather than involvement with the masses. As the Harrison conference concluded, there seemed to be a will to overcome these problems, great as they were.

A book entitled *Living in the Seventies* was published in 1970 as a collection of twenty-four of the most important papers given at Harrison. Unfortunately it did not appear soon enough to have any impact on Phases II or III although, during Phase II, the party headquarters brought out a series of short pamphlets to stimulate discussion. They included such issues as foreign ownership, inflation, pollution, bilingualism and constitutional reform, which had been passed over at Harrison. While some constituencies dutifully held their public policy meetings on the topics covered by the pamphlets, public involvement in Phase II was not all it was supposed to have been; Torrance Wylie, the national director, complained that "Phase II is almost a well kept secret." At the regional level, conventions were more faithfully carried through. There were nine in British Columbia, Western and Arctic conferences, meetings by Canadian Student Liberals, Toronto and District, the Liberal Party in Ontario, Montreal and Quebec Liberals. A Maritime conference was cancelled, however, when fall elections were called in New Brunswick and Nova Scotia.[31] None could accuse the Liberal party of putting policy ahead of electoral concerns.

Phase III, the policy convention, was held in Ottawa on 20-22 November 1970 in the sombre atmosphere that followed the October FLQ kidnappings and the invoking of the War Measures Act. The convention organizers had been genuinely anxious to develop its potential for delegate participation and to avoid the more traditional, heavily structured convention format with its lengthy speeches and procedural proprieties—all closely monitored by cabinet or an ever-watchful resolutions committee who ensured that the convention never strayed too far from the views of the party establishment. There were apparently no cabinet vetoes of the convention organization committee's work[32] and the Phase II policy pamphlets had even levelled oblique criticisms at the government by pointing to problem areas where more could be done. As originally envisaged, the convention was to be an intelligent, responsible exercise in mass decision-making. On any single policy, delegates were to be presented with a number of options, which they could discuss and alter. Then they would vote on the options by secret ballot—at the same time indicating priorities, suggesting how government funds should be reallocated, and setting long-term goals for the various policy proposals which the convention approved. In conception it was to be the most democratic policy convention ever held by a political party in Canada—perhaps anywhere!

A three-day convention of up to 2,000 delegates is, in even its most traditional format, a complex operation; it was not immediately apparent to the Convention Organization Committee just how much more complex their convention would be. Resolutions received from Phase II conventions were to be collated (without prejudice) by task forces in twelve policy areas and each task force was expected to report to the convention on one sheet of paper. The task force report would form the basis for discussion in one of the workshops or policy forums into which the delegates would be divided (four workshops would run concurrently) and

31. A.M. Linden, ed. The Peterborough Liberal Association, for example, made a serious effort to implement Phase II with half-a-dozen well-publicized policy forums. The public, however, did not apparently see this as a remarkable opportunity to participate in politics; only a few dozen attended each meeting. Stanbury estimated that "only about 25 local Liberal parties succeeded in involving the public; perhaps another 50 made a worthwhile effort." A. Westell, p. 127. LPC, vol. 1137, file: Executive Committee Meeting, 14-15.3.70; 20-21.6.70; 12-13.9.70. Liberal, June 1970.

32. Interview with Sidney Gerschberg, 18.3.70.

new resolutions or amendments would not be allowed until the workshop had spent an hour on the task force report. By way of illustration, a convention steering committee meeting estimated that there might be eight resolutions presented in a task force report, four new resolutions added by the policy forum, making a total of twelve to be forwarded to the plenary session, which would not be allowed to add any new resolutions. The time allotted to each policy area was three hours; three-quarters of an hour was given to plenary. (Voting by ballot on the various resolutions would be done in the delegates' own time.) A total of forty-five hours spent on an estimated one hundred and forty-four resolutions might just have been practicable. What actually occurred was an equatorial rainstorm of resolutions, new resolutions, amendments and ballot papers. It was a feat in itself for the convention staff to have coped with the 800,000 sheets of paper prepared in advance and the 500,000 turned out at the convention![33]

To begin with, the task force reports, containing 164 resolutions, were longer than anticipated; also, the delegates wanted to add so many new resolutions that, in the end, the ballot papers consisted of sixty-four legal-size sheets containing 398 resolutions. It is no wonder that one city delegate, when faced with fifty-eight resolutions on agriculture, ranging from the desirability of protein grading for wheat to a call for a "check off on Western grain under producer control", threw up her hands in dismay. The ballot complicated delegates' tasks further by asking them to indicate whether they strongly agreed, agreed, were not sure, disagreed or strongly disagreed with each resolution. Nor was it clear to delegates how these five categories of preferences would affect the vote tabulations. In the end, five vote totals were given for each resolution and this was all that remained of the original plan to determine priorities for the resolutions.[34] The idea of presenting options within certain resolutions was found to be unmanageable; consequently, the convention produced some confusing and often ludicrous combinations of policies. The delegates, for example, were inclined to take a fairly liberal position on the question of marijuana. But because they were not asked to choose among options, they voted in *favour* of a moratorium on prosecutions for possession of marijuana; in *favour* of making marijuana available through government outlets like liquor stores; but, at the same time, in *favour* of making possession a minor offence punishable by fine only! They *defeated* a motion which would have made possession and distribution no longer an offence. The only way to make sense out of that com-

[33] LPC, vol. 1166, file: LPC 1970, C.O.C. Steering Committee - Minutes and Documents. *Liberal,* Extra Post Convention Issue, n.d.

[34] The first mailing to the Consultative Council asked members to indicate priorities among eleven general policy areas. See the following chapter.

bination of resolutions was to conceive of the government-run marijuana stores as a game of bait and trap! On the other hand, they did vote logically on resolutions dealing with party finances. They rejected two resolutions that would have allowed political parties to be financed only by public funds and only by private funds, respectively. A resolution calling for parties to be financed by a mixture of public funds and private donations was passed.

Perhaps the most publicized innovation of the convention was the so-called "accountability session." Following the new clause in the party's constitution, Trudeau "report[ed] upon the consideration given, the decisions made and the reasoning therefore regarding resolutions passed at the previous Convention." The decisions were to be taken as ratified unless there was a contrary decision by the Convention.[35] (The constitution actually stipulated that, when the party formed the government, this accounting should be done by "a member of the Cabinet appointed by the Leader." The convention organization committee wisely decided that Trudeau would have to accept that responsibility himself. No one objected that the constitution had been violated!) As part of this accounting, delegates were asked, also for the first time at a Liberal convention, to vote by secret ballot on whether they wanted a leadership convention to be called. In 1966, when this clause had been added to the party's constitution, it had been seen as decisively confirming the authority of the extra-parliamentary party over the leader and the party's elected representatives in parliament—though such was demonstrated more dramatically by the Conservatives at their convention of the same year. During the convention planning discussions, the national director, Torrance Wylie, had suggested that the leadership review should be done "with the minimum of drama"; the prime minister would give a short fifteen-minute presentation followed by written questions from the floor and balloting on the question of calling a leadership convention could take place over the three days of the convention. In the event, Trudeau had no reason to fear a fate similar to Diefenbaker's in 1966. Among Liberals, he still continued largely to enjoy the popularity which had been christened Trudeaumania in 1968 and, in the immediate aftermath of the October crisis, Liberals, in common with most Canadians, were inclined to rally round the government and its leader—though, as we shall see later, the convention had reservations about the Public Order (Temporary Measures) Act, which replaced the War Measures Act. Trudeau gave a sober, tough speech in which he warned delegates that a society (and a party?) which created expectations that could not be fulfilled was heading for violence. It was the duty of responsible people, he said, not to let these expectations get out of hand and it was the duty of all governments

---

35. 1966 Constitution, 9-I-2.

"to show their priorities to the people so that they can choose them."[36] In the question-and-answer period, no attempt was made to take the leader to task over any failure to implement policies adopted at the 1966 convention—in spite of the constitution providing for that opportunity—and the call for a leadership convention was defeated 132 to 1064.

Ironically, one of the serious problems with the format of the convention was that the obsession with making it a grass-roots affair impeded any real dialogue between the rank and file and the parliamentary leadership, especially the cabinet. The accountability session with Trudeau was more like a Bonapartist renewal of leadership authority by the accolades of the masses—and thus typical of Canadian party meetings—than a serious accounting of stewardship. As far as the rest of the cabinet was concerned, the convention carried over from the 1966 meeting the fiction that cabinet ministers were just ordinary delegates who had to wait their turn at the microphones, if they spoke at all. An exception was the Minister of Agriculture, the Hon. H.A. Olson, who chaired the plenary session on agriculture and drew attention to several resolutions which he opposed. (They passed.) The delegates also displayed a high degree of critical independence in expressing their reservations about the government's decision to assume emergency powers following the terrorist kidnapping in October of British diplomat, James Cross, and Quebec cabinet minister, Pierre Laporte. In response to the government's temporary emergency powers act, the convention passed a resolution calling for an independent review board as "an additional safeguard to our democratic principles in the current situation." With so many other mini-debates going on, delegates went about their work oblivious to how their myriad resolutions would be greeted by those responsible for implementing them. However one incident, which did not bode well for the future, was Trudeau's offhand rejection (like the "Coney Island cowboy" he decried at Harrison) of the guaranteed annual income proposal, when he was asked about it by television reporters.

One can question whether a three-day gathering of 1,600 people who have the time and money to attend a conference in Ottawa has any moral authority, beyond what is self-declared, to determine the basic policies of any party which forms the government. There is, of course, the constitutional problem that the responsibility of elected representatives to the voters has to take priority over their responsibility to the very much smaller party membership. Trudeau made his position clear when he said in an interview that "participation doesn't mean participating in the *decisions*"[37] and when he wrote to the delegates after the convention explain-

[36] LPC, vol. 1166, file: LPC 1970, Steering Committee - Minutes and Documents, Meeting No. 1, 11.5.70. *CAR 1970*, p. 181.
[37] Radwanski, p. 126.

ing in detail why his government would not implement two of the convention's more controversial resolutions (the endorsement of a guaranteed annual income and negative income tax; the call for an independent board to review government actions taken under the authority of the Public Order (Temporary Measures) Act).

Some would go further and argue that, in any case, participation is inappropriate for a party which traditionally attempts to appeal across regional and class lines. John Roberts, a member of parliament and later a cabinet minister, wrote in the *Globe and Mail* on the opening day of the convention: "The attempt to make political parties mechanisms for effective participation in government decision-making flies in the face of history and political experience . . . it misconceives the essential function parties have played in our political system. That function is the brokerage role of political parties."[38]

The appropriateness of the brokerage model is questioned by others, however, on the grounds that Canada is a European-style, consociational democracy in which elites accommodate differences between various competing groups, while minimizing the contact which one group's rank-and-file members have with another's. In that sort of political system, it follows that a political party should not promote widespread participation in policy deliberations because the groups within the party would only fight with each other. In fact, both the 1966 and 1970 conventions struck an issue which threatened alarmingly to divide the party along regional lines. That was the issue of foreign investment. Economic nationalists, chiefly from capital-rich southern Ontario, came to both conventions hoping to get a commitment by the party to a target of "majority Canadian control of important industries." In both conventions, they ran into determined opposition from the other, capital-poor regions of the country. In 1970, their resolution was defeated and replaced with a Quebec resolution favouring restrictions on foreign investment only in key economic and cultural sectors and affirming the need for foreign investment in less developed areas. However, when taken together with the other resolutions touching on foreign investment, the convention did produce a total package of some subtlety and sophistication. An open door on foreign investment was rejected, while specific measures, which dealt with the undesirable aspects of foreign investment or which aimed at strengthening the position of Canadian capital—Canada Development Corporation, foreign investment review board, concern over the sales of two textbook publishers—were passed. Thus, the convention *was* able to perform a brokerage function more effectively than might have been expected.[39]

38. 20.11.70.

39. S.J.R. Noel, "Political Parties and Elite Accommodation: Interpretations of Canadian Federalism" in J.P. Meekison, ed., *Canadian Federalism: Myth or Reality*, 2nd ed., pp. 121-140. Report of the Task Force on the Economy, Draft Policy Resolution #9, 1970. *Liberal*: Extra post-convention issue, The Economy, #14.

The real test came after the convention. Allen Linden, who was co-chairman of the policy committee and of the convention organization committee, wanted the resolutions to form the basis of the party's manifesto for the next election. (The party's constitution, after all, declared that "The basic policies of the Party shall be established by the Party assembled in National Convention.")[40] With considerable ingenuity, they were welded together into a consistent document entitled "Liberal Charter for the Seventies", which was detailed and did not attempt to dodge controversial issues. But the cabinet were becoming increasingly unhappy. They had not liked the resolutions on abortion, the guaranteed annual income, or the independent review board. Furthermore, because there had been no parliamentarians on the policy committee, they had felt excluded from the whole process. When the Charter was presented to the cabinet, Linden and Stanbury were surprised by the barrage of criticism that it encountered. Cabinet refused to have anything to do with it and, significantly, not even the national executive put up a fight on behalf of the policy statement which had been so laboriously developed over two years by the extra-parliamentary wing of the party. It had all led to nothing. Neither Trudeau nor any of the other proponents of participation were prepared to fight for it. In retrospect, there was regret for not having taken a tough stand, "but that wasn't our style", said one of the key actors.[41]

Other attempts were made by the party office and the Prime Minister's Office to draft a party platform, but none met the approval of the cabinet.[42] When the election came in 1972, instead of the "Liberal Charter", the party went to the electorate with "The Land is Strong"—a slogan that was justly scorned as an avoidance of a program. Trudeau had to wage a campaign in the form of a Socratic dialogue, asking the voters to tell him what they wanted, because he had no party platform to give them. The theoretical argument against Linden's method of drawing up a platform is that policies adopted in a convention may be quite irrelevant by the time an election is called. In fact, the 1970 resolutions were mostly concerned with medium- to long-term goals—more so than the Harrison thinkers' papers. During the period of minority government that followed the election, a number of these ideas were embodied in legislation: election expenses, the establishment of a foreign investment review board, the end of special concessions to *Time* and *Reader's Digest* are the most obvious examples. Ironically, the public perceived that it was the pressures of minority government that had forced the government to act. No one remembered that they had been "official party policy" since 1970.

40. Clause 9-1-1.

41. LPC, vol. 1104, file: Consultative Council General - 1971, Linden to Stanbury, 3.2.71; vol. 1137, file: National Executive Meeting, 13-14.2.71; 3-4.4.71; 26-27.6.71; 18-19.9.71; 17-18.6.72. Confidential Source.

42. Interview with Senator Stanbury, 4.8.78.

Conclusion

By 1972, it was clear that the steam had gone out of the participatory experiment in its various manifestations. The public had shown little interest in using the party to gain access to government. (Indeed, some of the advocates of participation naïvely expressed surprise when the public did not respond in a rush to the announcement that, henceforth, they welcomed their views on how the country should be governed.) Participation, in the more restricted sense of providing local party elites with more influence, had been difficult to incorporate into existing party structures and had encountered opposition from the cabinet. Finally, even in the third sense of a charismatic leader mobilizing the general population, the 1972 election would show that participation had died down and that Trudeau was either reluctant or unable to revive it.

Stanbury and others within the party remained convinced that Trudeau genuinely believed in the concept. Indeed, both he and Stanbury thought it was essential if people were not to become alienated from the political process and take their protests into the streets. Several years later, however, Stanbury admitted that, as neophytes in 1968, neither he nor Trudeau had had any idea of the difficulties they would encounter and that, eventually, both of them had become frustrated with the attempt.[43]

To some observers, the whole participatory process had been a fraudulent public relations exercise to mould and manipulate public opinion.[44] Certainly the viewpoint of the PMO and most of the cabinet was that the quality of advice which they got in Ottawa was superb and that to get a lot of people with inexpert opinions involved in policy making was simply confusing and unproductive. Their one-way view of participation was well illustrated in a comment by Trudeau's principal secretary, Marc Lalonde, that, if the government found itself in disagreement with the party, then the government would simply have to do a better job of explaining its policies.[45] On the other hand, there can be no question about the commitment of key party people like Stanbury and Linden to the idea of transforming the Liberal party into a genuinely participatory and programmatic party. What the whole experiment showed was that, in a showdown, the extra-parliamentary party could not and would not overcome opposition.

[43.] Interview with Senator Stanbury, 4.8.78.

[44.] Walter Stewart, *Shrug: Trudeau in Power*, pp. 92-96. K.R.V. Lyon, "Democracy and the Canadian Political System: An analysis of the responsiveness of the political system to pressures to increase citizen participation in policy-making." Ph.D. Thesis, University of British Columbia, 1974, p. 226.

[45.] Peter Reilly, "When Trudeau's Out of the Country, Marc Lalonde Runs Things", *Saturday Night* (October 1970), 22.

It would be wrong, however, to conclude that the experiment with participation had had no impact on the party. Looking back on his time as president, Stanbury was convinced that important changes had taken place. The party was no longer run by powerful individuals in the cabinet (as had been the case before 1957) and policy conventions, as opportunities for a free and independent expression of rank-and-file opinion, were at least by now a regular occurrence.[46] Furthermore, under Stanbury and Torrance Wylie, the national office had developed the potential to play a more significant role than it had ever played before. The next few years would be crucial, if the initial disappointments of the participatory experiment were to be overcome and the party was to make the most of the reforms that had been initiated after 1968.

FINANCES—THE ATTEMPT TO MAKE THE FEDERATION FINANCIALLY RESPONSIBLE

The participatory experiments after 1968 raised more questions about the party's finances. In the first place, the expanded operations of the national office necessitated a much increased budget; secondly, in addition to efforts made during the Pearson period, further steps had to be taken to shift from the reliance on a few large corporate donors to a much broader base of individual contributors; thirdly, during the transition, the traditional funding operations had to be monitored to ensure that the public's worst suspicions were unfounded. While these goals were similar to those of the "new politics", the new context of "participatory democracy" at least gave them a new thrust.

Before 1968, financial control of party funds had rested with a shadowy group of fund raisers known as the "Treasurers" of the "Party", who were nowhere mentioned in the party's constitution and should not be confused with the Treasurer of the Federation (or Secretary-Treasurer before 1968), then a largely honorary position which *was* mentioned in the constitution. The leader appointed the chief fund raiser and he, in turn, appointed a fund raiser in each province. In theory, they were supposed to raise the amounts needed by the campaign committees for elections and by the Federation for its operations between elections. But the fund raisers had their own views on how much could be raised and they made the allocations to the campaign committees and the Federation. That is not to say that their judgments—about how much should be turned over when—were always meekly accepted. On the contrary, in the last few weeks of an election, increasingly strident demands for more funds were

---

[46] Interview with Senator Stanbury, 4.8.78.

commonplace. Nevertheless, in the final analysis, the fund raisers held the purse-strings. Ultimately, they were responsible to the leader, but ever since Beauharnois, leaders had tried—not always successfully—to keep the fund-raising operations at arm's length. In effect, these "Treasurers" of the "Party" operated on their own and this was obviously an outmoded arrangement for a party which claimed to have any control over its own operations as the Liberal Federation of Canada.

In 1968, a special party committee on finance recommended that the Federation assume control of its own finances and that the party's financial statements be published. That meant, of course, that the national executive would also get to see them and this revolutionary step (revolutionary, at least in the light of past practices) went so far as to give the national executive responsibility for setting the Federation's budget as well.

All fund raising would henceforth come within the purview of the Federation. The "Treasurers" of the "Party" would now become the "Treasury Committee of the Federation" with the same responsibility as before to collect large donations from major corporations and individual donors. The Federation's Finance Committee (which had previously filled no function whatever beyond providing its members with a vote at Liberal conventions[47]) would, for the first time, have real duties: raising money from individual party members or supporters to cover the annual budget of the Ottawa headquarters; and developing new methods for broadening the base of fund raising generally. Two co-chairmen were to head both committees and appoint the Treasury Committee themselves. The co-chairman would have to be acceptable to the party leader but, apart from that, the leader would have no direct responsibility for overseeing fund-raising activities and no information would be disclosed to him "except where deemed necessary by one of the co-chairman."[48] The two co-chairmen were Jean Ostiguy, an eminent Montreal investment dealer, and John Godfrey (later Senator), a salty but affable patrician, known for his impeccable honesty. A Toronto corporation lawyer and member of the firm of Campbell, Godfrey and Lewtes, Godfrey was in the tradition of Liberal fund raisers, inasmuch as an earlier law partner, Peter Campbell, had been party treasurer in the 1940s.

Subsequent developments were to show that it was one thing to say that the Federation was now the authority in financial matters, but to have that authority actually count for something was quite another. One of the perennial problems was how to allocate funds to the various levels of the party and how to divide fund-raising responsibilities in a country

47. Report of the Chairman of the Standing Committee on Finance and of the Treasury Committee to the Convention of the Liberal Party of Canada, September 14-16, 1973.

48. Godfrey Papers, Report of the Special Committee on Finance to the Executive Committee, 14.12.68; Godfrey to Stanbury, 27.3.75.

where decentralization is such an inherent feature of the political system. Behind the smooth facade of the various committees lay a jungle of competition for a scarce resource - money.

One has to remember, first of all, that even though the techniques of marketing a political party sometimes seem to resemble those employed for selling soap, one essential difference remains. Selling soap is a continuous operation which can be put under centralized control. If competitors are increasing their share of the market, the advertising strategy may be altered and the budget increased. A political party, however, is "marketed" only for a one-day sale. If the strategy fails, if funds are spent in the wrong way, there is no opportunity to make adjustments and no second chance for perhaps another four years. What is more, the "sale" takes place at over two hundred "branch locations" across the country and, although the success of each determines the overall success of the party, each has the primary goal of "selling" its own candidate.

The 1974 Election Expenses Act has radically altered the internal financing arrangements of all parties. As we shall see in chapter 6, local committees now find it easier to raise their own campaign funds; furthermore, all campaign committees, from the riding to the national level, are subject to limitations on expenditures. Before 1974, every committee, traditionally, was in competition with the others for a slice of the Treasury Committee's rich budgets. Admittedly, some national and provincial campaign expenditures supposedly benefited all the party's candidates, but the problem was really more complex than that. A media campaign might have more appeal for metropolitan voters than those in rural areas; the events included in the leader's tour were (and still are) chosen according to which will get the best media coverage; even the decision to take money out of a national advertising campaign and give it to ridings to spend in more traditional ways (such as paying poll workers—before the 1975 election expenses legislation prohibited such practices) discriminated against those ridings where the traditional methods had fallen out of favour. That was why it was so difficult to set party budgets and even more difficult to have them adhered to.

Even if no one in a political party actually believed that "money wins elections"[49], very few politicians were so confident of winning that they would accept a modest budget with equanimity. Between elections, money was squirreled away and private sources were tapped on an annual basis. As an election drew near, however, demands for extra funds became more urgent and pleas were heard to the effect that an extra thousand here or there would provide just that extra push or encouragement which would tip Riding A or Riding B into the party's win-

---

[49] Report of the Chairman of the Standing Committee on Finance and of the Treasury Committee to the Convention of the Liberal Party of Canada, September 14-16, 1973.

ning column. Negotiations were described as resembling those between foreign countries, where an occasional deception is the diplomat's stock-in-trade. A provincial committee would plead financial hardship, brandishing a large overdraft or bank loan, but would avoid saying anything about a more recent deposit or another account which showed a healthy balance. A cabinet minister with good connections might poach on a provincial fund raiser's territory and distribute money to his personal following among the other candidates—all of whom would be singularly vague about how much came from where.

Such goings-on were by no means confined to the Liberal party, but the party's Standing Committee on Finance attempted to come to grips with them in guidelines which were drawn up in 1968. First of all, candidates and constituency associations were encouraged to raise funds for their own local purposes, including the fighting of election campaigns. Large donors were to be the preserve of the Treasury Committee who would approach only those corporations expected to contribute at least $1,000. It was suggested that any single donation over $1,000 raised on behalf of an individual candidate should be turned over to the relevant provincial member of the Treasury Committee, who would honour a request that a portion be designated to that candidate, provided the amount was not above $5,000.[50]

Even with these guidelines, demarcation disputes arose. In one instance, the Treasury Committee were of the opinion that a certain minister's fund raisers in the Ottawa area were tapping potential national donors; they also disapproved of the way his organization, on his instructions, used surplus funds to give direct financial aid to other candidates instead of turning the money over to the party.[51] Conceivably he wanted to create a network of clients who would pay back their political debts in the next leadership campaign. Officially, there was disapproval of "the attitude so neatly expressed by one Minister that when the bell rings for an election it is every man for himself in the collection of funds"[52], but violations nevertheless occurred.

The trickiest area is the transfer of funds between provincial and federal finance committees. In general, a company is approached by the provincial Treasury member in the province where the company's "working head office" is located. Most major corporations have their head offices in either Montreal or Toronto and, historically, the lion's share of the fund raising has been done in those two cities. On the other hand, most companies have extensive operations outside Ontario and

[50.] Godfrey Papers, Report of the Special Committee on Finance to the Executive Committee, 14.12.68; Memo by Godfrey, 19.3.69.

[51.] LPC, vol. 1088, file: Finance Sub-Committee, Stanbury to Cruden, 28.3.72.

[52.] Godfrey Papers, Memo by Godfrey, 19.3.69.

Quebec, so other provincial committees—as well as the federal committee—have a claim on these funds,[53] at least to the extent that they should be relieved from contributing to the expenses of the national office in Ottawa or to the national campaign expenses. Determining the "fair share" is by no means an easy matter. The Quebec organization has always operated as a quasi-separate entity. The Ottawa office has some responsibilities in Quebec, but French-language election advertising, for instance, is done from the Montreal office. Consequently it is always larger than its counterpart in Toronto and expenses are always higher; but just how much higher they should be is a nice question. Ontario fund raisers usually felt that they had to carry the major burden of financing the national party and suspected the Quebec organization of profligacy and too great a reliance on old-style electioneering methods, such as the payment of poll workers. Quebec party people retorted that their province's distinctive political culture and practices had to be taken into account, and that in Ontario individual candidates were able to raise more money locally and were less in need of provincial committee funds than their Quebec counterparts.

When the 1968 election was over, Quebec still owed the federal campaign fund $85,000 out of what it had agreed to provide and were overdrawn $100,000 at the bank. After the election, Ontario and Quebec were supposed to share equally on a monthly basis the operating expenses of the Ottawa office, but Quebec fund raisers were slow to get started and contributed nothing in the first year. The Ontario committee, on the other hand, were in the enviable position of having come out of the election with half a million dollars in the bank and had greatly expanded their fund-raising activities after the election. Their mistake, perhaps, was in letting the fact be known. Immediately after the election Ontario sent $250,000 to the Federation to pay off its bank loan. But instead of discharging the loan, the money was placed in a different bank account and used to help pay the operating expenses for the first year. And after this ran out the chief Ontario fund raiser, John Godfrey, was asked for periodic supplements of $50,000 to cover the shortfall in the current operating expenses of the Federation, whose yearly budget had doubled from $250,000 per year to $500,000 per year after 1968 as a consequence of the new participatory programs. The party executive tended to evade the problem but, after coming to the rescue on several occasions, Godfrey decided to dig in his heels. Convinced that the party was headed for "financial disaster", he "unilaterally and without any legality whatsoever other than the fact that possession is nine-tenths of the law" told the party president, Dick Stanbury, and the national director, Tor-

---

[53.] Godfrey Papers, "Treasury Committee, Rules Re: Solicitation of Funds", 22.2.73. K.Z. Paltiel, *Political Party Financing in Canada,* chap. 2.

rance Wylie, "that I would no longer fork over the dough every time someone called from Ottawa, but would instead put the Federation on a monthly allowance equal to the amount I had been originally told should be provided from Ontario and that you (Stanbury and Wylie) would have to look elsewhere (meaning, of course, Quebec) for the balance." The result was a financial crisis which brought action. The prime minister had to be called in to put pressure on the chief Quebec fund raiser, whom he eventually replaced with two co-chairmen, Maurice Riel and Fraser Elliot, prominent Montreal lawyers, who were able to come up with more funds for the national office.[54]

In 1972, there were more problems between Ontario and Quebec. A budget drawn up before the calling of the election indicated that Ontario would contribute $830,000 to the national campaign and would pay off a $300,000 overdraft at the Ottawa office; another $240,000 from Ontario was to go towards maintenance of the Ottawa headquarters after the election. Quebec's contribution to the national campaign was set at just $375,000, while its own provincial campaign budget of $1,000,000 was two-thirds again as large as Ontario's. In the course of the campaign, Ontario agreed to contribute another $415,000, while the Quebec provincial campaign budget increased to $1,565,000 and Quebec's contribution to the national campaign remained at $375,000. In parsimonious Ontario, there were misgivings over the size of the Quebec committee's campaign budget and the wild extravagance of having seventy-two paid employees in the Montreal headquarters. Considering that Ontario was generally agreed to be the province where the election would be won or lost, it was argued that, even granting the difficulty of comparing the two provincial budgets, there was a misallocation of financial resources on a nationwide basis.[55]

In 1974, Ontario's contribution was set at $960,000—just twice the Quebec assessment of $480,000—and as the campaign began, a familiar pattern re-emerged. Quebec fell behind in its payments and, four weeks before the election, the province's fund raisers reported that no more than $1.6 million in total could be raised in Quebec even though $2.5 million had been raised in 1972. Ontario agreed to prevent cuts in the federal budget by putting another $185,000 into the federal kitty, provided that Quebec immediately came up with another $150,000 in addition to the $145,000 which had been contributed thus far, and suggested that the Quebec campaign budget be reduced from $1,550,000 to $1,300,000—a request considered not unreasonable in view of the fact

---

54. Godfrey Papers, Godfrey to Stanbury, 27.3.75.

55. LPC, vol. 1085, file: Budgeting and Financing, Godfrey to Andras, 11.2.72, 12.10.72. Godfrey Papers, National Campaign Budget, 1.5.72, Budget, 23.10.72. Godfrey to the author, 8,18.9.78.

that Ontario's provincial budget was just $750,000. In the end, the Quebec budget was not reduced and the $150,000 was not paid immediately. Relations within the Treasury Committee became strained, with Ontario accusing Quebec of acting in bad faith and the chairman demanding that the Quebec books be opened so that their true financial position be disclosed. For their part, the Quebec fund raisers had been instructed by the senior Quebec minister, Jean Marchand, not to open their books in spite of a party memo, approved by the prime minister, that required each member of the Treasury Committee to account to the chairman. Once again, the prime minister was called in by Ontario to arbitrate, in spite of the party's attempt in 1968 to divorce him from the fund-raising process.[56] The dispute between the fund raisers, however, was settled amicably in the prime minister's ante-room just a few minutes before they were to see him. It was just as admirable in theory as it had been in 1932 to make the Federation responsible for fund raising, but just as difficult in practice as it had been then. The buck (non-monetary, of course), when passed up the hierarchy of party command, can stop only when it arrives—or threatens to arrive—at the prime minister's desk. Provincial fund raisers often act like the rulers of independent fiefdoms and when they disagreed on some issue, the Federation executive simply did not have the clout to settle it nor did they really want to become involved. There were even suggestions of a return to the old system where the Treasury Committee was personally appointed by the prime minister.

Even the chief fund raiser had his doubts about how much clout he could exercise. On a few occasions, Godfrey's power to sign the cheques gave him some leverage. He was, for example, able to get $10,000 channeled through the Federation from Ontario funds to support the Nova Scotia Liberal party which was desperate for money to fight the 1970 provincial election. In 1973, he held back Ontario's monthly contribution to the national office in order to ensure that funds were made available to hire federal organizers for Ontario.[57] On other occasions Godfrey refused to make payments or pay bills because he was not satisfied that the payments had been properly authorized or that they accorded with the budget. Vigilance also had to be exercised in not allowing a campaign committee to succumb to spending temptations during elections because then there would be nothing left over to run the party between elections —a difficulty often experienced during the St. Laurent era. The special party committee on finance had recommended that the chairman of the Treasury Committee should have the responsibility to take action when any expenditures were unduly out of line with the budget. Godfrey would have gone further by allowing the Treasury Committee to say

---

[56] Confidential source.
[57] Godfrey Papers, Godfrey to Stanbury, 27.3.75.

when a budget was too high; otherwise, he was concerned that, if too much pressure were put on the fund raisers, they might be tempted to indulge in toll-gating, or other questionable practices.

The chief fund raiser, however, was no tin god and on at least two occasions, Godfrey was told, politely but firmly, that the job of the fund raisers was to supply the money and that, if they could not, then the party executive "would simply have to find someone else that could." From his own experience, Godfrey concluded, with a characteristic touch of hyperbole, that "the fund raiser, as such, rates about Z in the political pecking order and often about the same in personal popularity with senior officials of the Party, who often resent and are irritated by his efforts to keep the Party solvent by constant reminders that they shouldn't spend money they haven't got and can't realistically expect to get." His experience as chief bagman for the Liberal party, he concluded, was uncannily like the time he had been president of the National Ballet. While attempting to instil financial responsibility into an organization that was going deeper and deeper into debt, he was told by the Ballet's artistic director, Celia Franca, that his job was simply to raise whatever money she and the Ballet required. Years later, speaking on the occasion of the Ballet's twenty-fifth anniversary, Godfrey conceded that Franca had been right and courageous to stick to her vision of what the Ballet should become. In the case of the Liberal party, he was provoked to the point of resignation over not being consulted on a decision to establish a new "Leader's Finance Co-ordinating Committee" which was to be given full control over the disposition of funds without any consultation with the Ontario representative on the Treasury Committee. Past history had shown, he argued, that such a committee would "simply take the line of least resistance and tap the person who had the money in the bank (or at least admits that he has it in the bank) and that Ontario will carry a disproportionate amount of the burden. Unless Quebec agrees to unreservedly co-operate, then it just won't work." It was a battle he had fought often, but, in the end, even a chief fund raiser had to admit, laconically, to defeat.[58]

MONITORING THE TRADITIONAL METHODS

In attempting to avoid another Pacific Scandal or Beauharnois, the party executive took the approach that, if fund-raising activities were carefully insulated to eliminate, where feasible, all contact between donors and practising politicians, then such temptations to influence or be influ-

---

[58] Godfrey Papers, Godfrey to Stanbury, 27.3.75; Memo for file: Financing 1974 Federal Election, 2.12.74. *Senate Debates* (16.11.76), 145-147. Interview with Godfrey, 15.8.77.

enced would be avoided. A Special Committee on Finance laid down that

All contributions shall be solicited on the strict understanding that the name of any contributor, the source and amount of any contribution, the fact that any contribution solicited has been refused shall be disclosed by any solicitor only to his provincial representative on the Treasury Committee or to the Co-Chairmen and Director of Finance. Such information shall not, under any circumstances, be disclosed to the Leader of the Party except where deemed necessary by one of the Co-Chairmen for the sole purpose of assuring compliance with these rules or any directives approved by such Leader.

All contributions shall be simple unconditional donations and no solicitor shall either directly or by inference suggest to any donor that he may be entitled by reason of such donation to any favour, special consideration or representation of any kind with respect to proposed legislation, regulations or orders of the Government of Canada or any province thereof or to any contract transaction or other affairs of any nature or kind whatsoever in which the Government of Canada or Parliament or any province thereof, their agencies and dependencies have a direct or indirect interest.[59]

In some instances, at least, the rules were followed—almost ruthlessly. An Alberta fund raiser was told that the party could not consent to a donor's request that a Federal cabinet minister be informed of his contribution; a firm was forced to admit finally, as mere "washroom gossip", the charge by one of its executives that it would be subject to adverse rulings by the Department of National Revenue for not contributing to the Liberal party; a company being prosecuted by the government stopped its contributions but, in return, one of the chief fund raisers offered to help the company if it could demonstrate to the fund raiser that it had been treated unfairly and added that he would, under the circumstances, accept no contribution from that company even if it changed its mind—the company did not take up the offer; a donation, which was smaller than the previous year's, was returned because it was thought that the donor had chosen this way of indicating displeasure with the government and was hoping thereby to influence future government action; the Chairman of the Treasury Committee advised cabinet ministers that individual campaign contributions should not be accepted from anyone doing business with the department for which they were responsible.[60] Donors were generally told that their contributions should be regarded as support for the democratic process, not as an indication of support for the Liberal party or the Liberal government, and that they should contribute equally to both "free enterprise parties." The suggestion of an equal contribution to

---

[59] Godfrey Papers, "Report of the Special Committee on Finance" (presented to Executive Committee), 14.12.68.
[60] Confidential sources.

the Conservative party was also thought by Liberal fund raisers to be a clever way of putting at his ease a corporate executive, who presumably would be happier about contributing to the Conservative party anyway! In time, the federal Treasury Committee got such a reputation for scrupulosity that some companies began donating directly to candidates. One fund raiser complained, "the smart cookies . . . think they get more value for their money if they donate to candidates rather than to the Party, and of course they are right!" In one instance, a large company was chastized for making donations exclusively to individual candidates and told that companies who give to political parties know that they get no benefit, other than the "satisfaction of knowing that they are good corporate citizens."[61]

Critics of the "traditional methods" usually fail to ackowledge that a political party, as opposed to an individual candidate, is in a very strong tactical position when dealing with potential donors. In a political system where there are only a few parties and many donors, the party's potential for controlling the situation is similar to an economist's oligopoly: a market where there are few sellers and many buyers. The bargaining strength of a political party is neatly illustrated by a remark made by the Hon. Jack Pickersgill at a party meeting in 1961, while the party was in oppositon. A number of potential contributors had expressed unhappiness with the party's medicare policy and Pickersgill replied that fund raisers should tell them that "if the electorate wants such a plan—as our research indicated— they were bound to get it eventually. They should be convinced that what we offer is better than any plan brought in by the other two parties."[62] In other words—you may not be completely happy with our product, but your choice is very limited and what you could get from our competitors would suit you even less. Even if you choose not to contribute, there are many others who will! In fact, most fund raisers admit that fund raising from corporations is almost routine—at least it was before the law requiring disclosure came into effect. One British Columbia fund raiser for the provincial Liberal party, making his first trip to Toronto, was amazed at how quickly and how easily he was able to raise a substantial sum. He added that he hoped the word would not get around because then everyone would become a fund raiser in order to get a senatorship!

[61] Confidential sources.

[62] LPC, vol. 698, file: Public Relations and Communications, Minutes of a Meeting of the Communications Committee, 12.6.61.

BROADENING THE BASE OF FINANCIAL CONTRIBUTIONS

Logically, it would have made sense for the Liberal party to have launched a nationwide membership campaign in its attempt to broaden its financial base and to increase public participation in the party. It would, moreover, have been following the pattern of the European mass-membership parties who raise a large portion of their funds through membership fees. When that has been tried in Canada, however, the results have been meagre, except in Saskatchewan.[63] The Liberal party experimented again when the 1968 leadership campaign raised public interest in the party, but the results were discouraging. Trial advertisements were placed in the *London Free Press,* the *Kitchener-Waterloo Record* and Sherbrooke's *La Tribune* inviting people to have a part in choosing the next prime minister by returning a coupon application for party membership. Out of a total circulation of 200,000, only thirty-two were returned. A door-to-door canvass by poll captains was also discussed and a trial run in Scarborough produced a much better result. However, the decentralized nature of the Liberal party created problems for any national membership campaign. Only the riding associations have the right to confer membership and the Federation has never been able to lay down membership qualifications that would be accepted by the provincial associations, let alone the ridings. For example, some ridings charge membership fees and others do not. The only standardization attempted by the federal party is contained in clause 2-A-2 of the constitution: "the member organizations . . . shall . . . specify as thoroughly as possible the qualifications and procedures required for obtaining membership therein through the constituent Liberal associations affiliated therewith; and strive to assure the conferring of membership cards or other membership certification on successful applicants for such membership." So the only practicable solution was to leave the riding and provincial associations with exclusive use of the funds raised through membership fees.[64]

In any case, simply as a fund-raising device, the party had already found in the early 1960s, that more money could be raised with less effort by going after the $100 donation. The people who could afford to give $100 were certainly not average rank-and-file Liberal supporters, but they enabled the party to become less dependent on the $5,000- and $10,000-

[63] K.Z. Paltiel, *Political Party Financing in Canada.* J.C. Courtney & D.E. Smith, "Saskatchewan" in M. Robin, ed., *Canadian Provincial Politics,* p. 313.

[64] LPC, vol. 1028, file: Membership Recruitment Ad Material, Stanfield, Etc.; file: 1968-69 Membership Recruitment; vol. 1136, file: Membership Applications for, Stanbury to Fairclough, 8.7.68.

donors who had contributed the bulk of party funds in the past. Fund-raising dinners attended by the prime minister became annual events in Toronto, Montreal and Vancouver, and brought in net receipts of $30,000 to $100,000. The only problem was that Trudeau did not like them and the opinion was expressed at party headquarters that, in that case, he should get party finance legislation before parliament so that the party could get on with developing alternative, more broadly based methods of fund raising. In the meantime—which, exasperatingly, grew longer and longer—the party executive agreed that the prime minister would be asked to do no more than six dinners a year (far fewer than President Johnson was asked to do for the Democratic party in an election year) and that they should be sponsored by provincial rather than just local as-sociations. The party was, however, sensitive to the charge that a prime minister's dinner was a dinner for the rich and recommended that it should be accompanied, where possible, with an event for a larger num-ber of people at a modest price.[65]

Because contributions to political parties did not qualify for tax exemp-tions, Torrance Wylie and Bruce Powe had the ingenious idea of setting up an educational body called the Liberal Foundation which would take over the research and educational functions of the Federation office, in-cluding publications and the organizing of policy conferences, and thus qualify for tax-exempt status. Donors would get tax receipts like those given for charitable donations. The Foundation's capital fund, it was hoped, would eventually amount to $10 million and, to get things started, the party executive agreed to assign to it assets of the Liberal Realty Com-pany worth about $100,000 (the proceeds from the sale of the Cooper Street property). By the time the Foundation was set up in 1970, its aims had to be modified. It was felt that too broad a mandate would cut into the activities of the party office. As well, the new publicly financed re-search bureau for MPs made research a less important priority for the Foundation. Finally, the prospect of legislation under which tax credits would be given for party contributions made the Foundation less im-portant as an alternative fund-raising device. Stanbury saw this as an op-portunity for giving one more push to the participatory concept. "The unexpected difficulty of the past two years in developing effective tech-niques to convert the Party into the vehicle of public participation re-quested by our Leader" suggested to him that the Foundation's aims could be redefined to give it "the broad task of research into the re-lationship between the people and their governmental institutions and as-pirations of the people to participate in the governmental process and the means of satisfying those aspirations within the framework of our parlia-mentary democracy. More specifically, the Foundation . . . would begin

[65] LPC, vol. 1137, file: Executive Committee Meeting, 13-14.9.69.

training people . . . to use these techniques in their communities . . . with the aim of reversing the trend toward polarization in our society and promoting understanding and conciliation among various groups and regions."[66] Stanbury certainly kept trying. Once established, however, the Foundation disappeared mysteriously from view. The provincial associations showed little interest in naming representatives to the Foundation. Other vehicles for fund raising and participation eclipsed it in importance and, within a few years, it was forgotten.

A fund-raising concept of greater significance was the Red Carnation Fund. Mention has already been made of the Liberal Unions and Century Clubs which had been established in some of the provinces during the Pearson period. The Red Carnation Fund was to co-ordinate already established provincial organizations and initiate new ones in provinces where they did not already exist. The Fund would seek donations of between $100 and $500 with two-thirds going to the provincial association and one-third to the federal party for inter-election maintenance. The Fund was astutely conceived as appealing to relatively apolitical professional and business people who are over-awed by the mighty. Potential donors probably voted Liberal in federal elections, but did not see themselves as party members. "Most people in our target class yearn to support a cause and we should stress the patriotic national aspects. The general approach should come down hard on the theme—"Support the democratic two party system in this country." We should define, in a very few words, the vital role played by a political party in the *maintenance of our democratic way of life* and our political and economic independence." A prospective donor would receive from a cabinet minister or senator an "individualized" letter (produced by an automatic typing machine) to soften him up for the visit by "My friend, Sam Jones, [who] will be around to see you in the next few weeks." All contributors would receive a letter of thanks from the prime minister (signed by an ingenious automatic signature machine which uses a pen to recreate a signature exactly) and donors of $500 or more would get an annual Christmas card. When the prime minister was in town, donors would have precedence in meeting him and would be given a red carnation to wear at prime ministerial functions. Provincial fund raisers would be photographed with the prime minister for release to the press; community fund raisers qualified for a photograph with a cabinet minister. Although most of the provincial organizations agreed to join the Red Carnation Fund, it was slow in getting off the ground. The exception was Ontario, where $30,000 was raised in 1972 despite the competition for funds from an impending elec-

---

[66] LPC, vol. 1096, file: Stanbury - Corr. & Memos 1968, Wylie to Trudeau, 10.7.68; vol. 1137, file: Executive Committee Meeting, 12-13.9.70, Report by Stanbury, 2.9.70; file: Executive Committee Meeting, 23.11.70; vol. 1037, file: Ontario Campaign Committee, Powe to Davey, 15.10.63.

tion. In most provinces, the more immediate urgency to raise money for the election forced the suspension of the Red Carnation canvass until after the election.[67]

Although some progress had been made in reforming the party's financial operations, major changes could not be made until the long-awaited legislation on party finance was passed. There was no doubt as to where the party executive stood on this question. They made a strong recommendation to cabinet in December 1968. Again in 1971, a motion by Payne and Godfrey declared that "the National Executive considers it urgent, and in the public interest, that the government give a first priority to the passage of an Election Expenses Act, at this or the next session of Parliament, so that provision would be applicable to the next general election."[68] But when Parliament was dissolved almost a year later, they were still waiting for legislation to be passed.

[67] LPC, vol. 1137, file: Executive Committee Meeting, 14-15.3.70; 20-21.6.70; 13-14.2.71; 3-4.4.71; 26-27.6.71; 18-19.9.71; 27-28.11.71; 17-18.6.72. Report of the Chairman of the Standing Committee on Finance and of the Treasury Committee to the Convention of the Liberal Party of Canada, 14-16.9.73. Emphasis in the original.

[68] LPC, vol. 1138, file: National Executive Meeting, 18-19.9.71.

CHAPTER 6. SETBACK AND REASSESSMENT (1972-78)

According to the popular mythology of a few years ago, modern governments were thought to be almost invincible, fortified as they were with surveys of voter opinion and with access to the traditional levers of government propaganda and patronage, as well as the new lever of Keynesian management of the economy. An election could be called to coincide with an economic boom and a rising trend in the governing party's popularity, while a judicious reallocation of government expenditures could be applied to mop up any persisting areas of discontent. However, not only have governments in the 1970s had to cope with the intractable problem of stagflation, but public opinion is now recognized as a largely independent, fluctuating variable in the electoral equation. Rather than make quixotic attempts to alter the values and predispositions of the voters, parties and candidates are now tempted to change themselves—or, more accurately, to change the public's perception of them.[1]

The information provided by the pollsters is used, then, not to alter public opinion, but to provide the often narrow parameters within which the party will attempt to devise a winning electoral strategy. If, however, the surveys provide the bad news that the leader is disliked, that the electorate has no interest in the party's issues and that very few identify themselves as party supporters, then the predicament of the campaign strategists is difficult indeed. (Robert Nixon observed in his self-mocking way that, while he was Ontario leader, they might have spent $35,000 on a poll which told him what he already suspected: that the voters knew Bill Davis better and thought Stephen Lewis was smarter than he. "What do you do with information like that? When they gave me good news in 1975, they were wrong!"[2]) In extremis, a party may well be tempted to fire its leader and change its policies in an attempt to project a different

---

[1] Dan Nimmo, The Political Persuaders.
[2] Interview, 5.9.78.

Chart III   **LIBERAL STANDINGS IN THE GALLUP POLL (1968-80)**

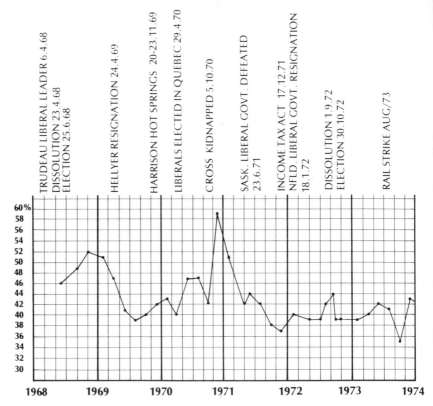

SOURCE: *Gallup Poll Report*

image. The usual election strategy, however, does not go that far; rather it attempts to respond creatively to the mood of the public as revealed in the surveys. The danger, more and more, is that a party and its leader will follow public opinion, looking to seize favourable opportunities rather than lead the electorate. (Don and Věra Murray show that, when Robert Bourassa was premier of Quebec, he paid increasingly more attention to the information provided by public opinion surveys, even though short term advantages created longer term problems.[3])

[3.] *de Bourassa à Lévesque,* see especially, pp. 121-127.

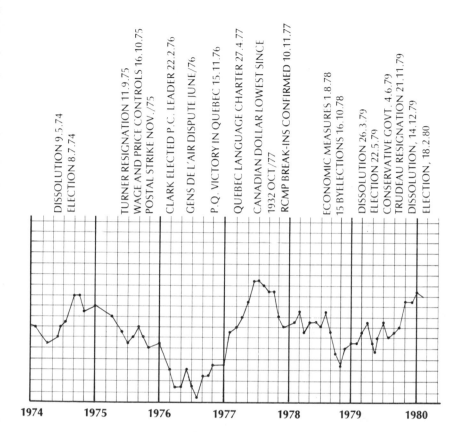

DISSOLUTION 9.5.74
ELECTION 8.7.74
TURNER RESIGNATION 11.9.75
WAGE AND PRICE CONTROLS 16.10.75
POSTAL STRIKE NOV./75
CLARK ELECTED P.C. LEADER 22.2.76
GENS DE L'AIR DISPUTE JUNE/76
P.Q. VICTORY IN QUEBEC 15.11.76
QUEBEC LANGUAGE CHARTER 27.4.77
CANADIAN DOLLAR LOWEST SINCE 1932 OCT/77
RCMP BREAK-INS CONFIRMED 10.11.77
ECONOMIC MEASURES 1.8.78
15 BY-ELECTIONS 16.10.78
DISSOLUTION 26.3.79
ELECTION 22.5.79
CONSERVATIVE GOVT. 4.6.79
TRUDEAU RESIGNATION 21.11.79
DISSOLUTION, 14.12.79
ELECTION, 18.2.80

1974   1975   1976   1977   1978   1979   1980

Even if the voters' basic values change only very gradually, their answer to the question—If a federal election were held today, which party's candidate do you think you would favour?—is as variable as the stock market. A glance at a graph of support for the Liberal party, as revealed by the monthly or bimonthly Gallup poll shown above, illustrates this point aptly. Three-quarters of the periodic changes are in the range of 0 to 3 percent, but a rise or fall of between 4 and 6 percent is not uncommon. After the October crisis of 1970, the party's popularity went up dramatically by seventeen percentage points. Furthermore a trend rarely continues for any more than six months, though one can see an *overall* trend in the decline of the party's popularity from mid-1974 to mid-1976 and from mid-1977 to the end of 1979. Two additional problems, which the stock-market speculator does not have, are that the polls allow themselves a 3 to 4 percent margin of error nineteen times out of twenty. Secondly, the data may be three weeks old by the time it is available and, since the campaign lasts at least seven or eight weeks, the decision to dissolve thus has to be made on a sampling of opinion taken at least three months before the date of the election.

THE TRUDEAU ELECTIONS

The election campaigns in which Trudeau has been leader are eloquent testimony both to the limits of party organization and to the strains that electoral considerations place on the extra-parliamentary party. In 1968 and 1972 especially, a number of campaign management problems were evident.

Trudeaumania, which had been born in the few months leading up to the 1968 convention, provided the wave of enthusiasm which Trudeau himself capitalized on by asking for a dissolution seventeen days later. Because no formal policy positions had been adopted at the convention, the party went into the election without having had the opportunity to draw up an agenda as it had done under Pearson in 1960-61. In the spring of 1968, no one seemed to care about the omission, though it had serious consequences later on.

O'Brien, who was national director at the time, recalled that the campaign was designed simply to capture the euphoria produced by the sunshine, the people and the fresh air in the spring of 1968 and to slough off the discontent of the Pearson-Diefenbaker years. An examination of the party files suggests that Liberal strategists hardly understood Trudeaumania—let alone created it. A party strategy paper acknowledged that television had something to do with it, but saw it as little more than a case of the networks having been able "to smarten up their techniques of making politics exciting" and thus making "television exposure of the new leadership . . . an important element in the Liberal campaign."[4]

As the campaign went into its latter stages, Liberal strategists even started to get defensive and apprehensive about this new electoral phenomenon. The party president, Dick Stanbury, was concerned about press criticism that "we are simply marketing a hot product." The campaign was beginning to slump in Toronto, he thought, and there was some disenchantment with Trudeau. In the early stages of the campaign, people had looked on Trudeau as being new, exciting, ready to change

---

4. Interview with O'Brien, 24.8.77. LPC, vol. 1084, file: Policy-Platform, "Strategy Notes", no author, 4.5.68.

things and the huge crowds were taken as confirmation of this. But that had "begun to pall. They are looking for him to say something new and exciting. The Press give the impression that he is saying nothing and our policy papers have indicated to those who are looking for change that he is not going to change much." Party strategists also began to worry about Trudeau's unconventional, carefree spontaneity—a quality which had first endeared him to the Canadian public. Following a television broadcast, John Nichol, national campaign co-chairman, wrote "For the Prime Minister's Eyes Only" that his jocular reply to the question of why he had wanted to become prime minister had not come across as intended. Nichol suggested that Trudeau work up a serious answer, without necessarily being pompous.[5] Throughout the campaign the medium of television was approached with caution. Because of the fear of overexposure, no advertising was done on television and one of the potentially more significant innovations of the campaign—a televised leaders' debate—turned out to be a disappointing bore because party strategists were so afraid of any uncontrolled spontaneity.

Because of complaints about the "monolithic" campaigns of the early 1960s, the 1968 campaign was less centralized, especially with respect to advertising. The Hon. Joe Greene, Minister of Agriculture, told Nichol that earlier campaigns had failed "in the rural and small towns in Canada" and the Hon. Allan MacEachen, senior minister from the Maritimes, concurred. The national campaign communications committee agreed to adopt a more regional approach to advertising and public relations than had been the case earlier. Greene recommended J.E. (Ned) Belliveau, whose experience spanned several Maritime provincial elections, as one of the few with "a real understanding of the political game as it applies to non-metropolitan Canada." His firm, Tandy Advertising, was supposed to look after the three Maritime provinces; but, when it became clear that MacLaren would still be the only agency to handle national advertising, Belliveau complained that the whole purpose of the regional campaign had been frustrated. "That, and my inability to achieve [either] an interview or instructions, left me in full confusion . . . I am leaving for the Maritimes to do what we can on our own for the provincial organizations. We are interested in electing candidates, not playing games."[6]

[5] LPC, vol. 1083, file: Campaign Committee - Ontario, Stanbury to Lalonde, 4.6.68; vol. 1084, file: Election, 1968 - General (Sen. Nichol), Nichol to Prime Minister, n.d.

[6] LPC, vol. 1084, file: Election 1968, Communications, Greene to Nichol, 29.4.68; Allan MacEachen to Stanbury, 24.4.68; Stanbury to Provincial Campaign Chairmen for provinces of Newfoundland, Ontario, Manitoba, Saskatchewan, Alberta, British Columbia, 7.5.68; Stanbury to Provincial Campaign Chairmen for P.E.I., Nova Scotia, New Brunswick; Belliveau to Stanbury, 11.5.68.

Belliveau's outburst notwithstanding, it was felt that the campaign had been in retrospect, too decentralized. Although the prime minister's tour was supposed to have operated within general guidelines established by the federal campaign committee, it was too often subject to pressures from a cabinet minister or "panicky candidate [who] . . . pressure[d] the Provincial or the National Planning Team into throwing the P.M.'s time away", according to one observer.[7]

Those who managed the Liberal campaign might differ among themselves as to what had gone well and what had not. In any case, Trudeaumania produced 155 seats for the Liberals to the opposition parties' 107 and, looking back to 1968, it is hard to imagine that changes in the campaign really could have affected the results. It was the sort of campaign which ran itself.

MAJORITY GOVERNMENT AND ELECTION ORGANIZATION

Between 1962 and 1968, there were four elections. The people who had run those campaigns—and they were mostly from the volunteer wing of the party—had had as intensive a training in fighting elections as a previous generation would have got in twelve or fifteen years. But with a majority government in office for the first time since 1962, it did not seem as important to keep the election machine idling. Indeed, the prime minister's new advisers in the PMO created the impression—at least in the eyes of the key volunteers who ran campaigns—that a party organization would not really be necessary for fighting the next election, that it could all be done with regional desks and computers. Many of those leading figures in the volunteer wing, who are already established lawyers or businessmen, are often far more susceptible to the blandishments of what is called psychological patronage than the more traditional variety. These are the little courtesies, favours, an invitation to a prestigious government function, a flattering telephone call from Ottawa to ask for the local assessment of a current issue. (Just to indicate how little things count, one of the party's chief fund raisers recalls that he used to arrange to have his fund-raising team invited to lunch at the prime minister's residence once a year. His special request to the staff of 24 Sussex was that lots of the residence's official match covers be put out because even a corporation executive liked to leave with a couple in his pocket!) The PMO neglected

---

7. LPC, vol. 1084, file: 1968 Election, A Thinking Man's Guide to Summer Travel in Canada or how i helped pierre elliott who? win the '72 election, n. name, n.d.

this psychological patronage or "ego-stroking", though in this respect they were no worse than their boss, who is notorious for being either indifferent to or disdainful of the need to recognize such niceties. One key member of the B.C. federal campaign committee recalls that he had been kept very busy with party affairs before 1968; but, between 1968 and 1972, he got only one telephone call. After 1968, many such people lost interest and drifted away from having any active involvement with the party. Time would show their enthusiasms could not be rekindled easily.

By the summer of 1971, it was clear that the government's popularity with the electorate had fallen off sharply from the incredible peak it had enjoyed following the October crisis of 1970. Mid-term opinion surveys indicated that Canadians were concerned about unemployment, about the government's tight money attack on inflation, about Trudeau's losing touch with the public. Jim Davey, the English-born computer expert who was program secretary in the PMO, wrote a strategy paper in the summer of 1971, in which he analyzed what the opinion surveys had to say about the government's problems. The major issues were the bread-and-butter ones like unemployment, he said, although, with the exception of farm problems, most people believed that the Liberals were better able to deal with these than the other parties. Although the climate of public opinion was slightly right-of-centre, Stanfield was seen as decent, honest, but dull. There was therefore no point in attacking the Conservatives. Davey say the NDP as the more serious "wild card" because of the increasingly prevalent notion that perhaps they deserved a chance: "This is the danger. At the same time, a good proportion of their present support believes that there is only a 50% chance that they will actually vote for them on election day. This is our chance." Along with stimulating the economy, the government should adopt the strategy of engaging in highly visible programs like the Hon. Bryce Mackasey's broadening of unemployment insurance benefits, and of generally convincing "the various groups of electors by present performance and future plans that this government is more capable of running the country well than any alternative." Davey very much opposed any suggestion of attempting to change Trudeau's basic style since those qualities cited in unfavourable comments by some were often the same as those that elicited strongly favourable responses from others. There was more to be gained by the PMO getting him and his ministers to spend more time putting the government's message across. Also, as a means of neutralizing the adverse publicity generated by Trudeau's frequent travels and holidays, he suggested photographs of him "in the very typical pose of shirt sleeves, tie off, working in his office." (This was to become a familiar photograph.)

Davey was generally sanguine about being able to deal with the party's problems. The Liberal Federation was better organized than ever before, caucus was causing no more problems than usual and the PMO rejoiced in being a "very professional organization."[8]

Others were more worried. Stanbury was afraid that Trudeau was losing interest in the party's programs and that the party was going to fall back into its traditional election role. Another member of the PMO, who did not share Jim Davey's confidence that political operations could be smoothly managed from the East Block of the Parliamentary Buildings, was Gordon Gibson, the charmingly ebullient young scion of a prominent British Columbian political family. Like Stanbury, he genuinely believed in the value of participation and of party input into the governmental process. That set him apart from most of the others in the PMO. Participation should have been the hallmark of Trudeau's administration, he told the prime minister in April 1971, but the government had procrastinated disgracefully. What participation there had been was more a case of having gone through the forms while the real decisions were made by "an even smaller and more rigid group." In effect, this pseudo-participation either stifled criticism or gave the government the advantage of knowing in advance where opposition was likely to arise. Not without betraying a trace of his own elitist predilections, Gibson saw Trudeau's administration as having undervalued the opinions of ordinary people and having been unsympathetic to "the intuitive, the inarticulate, the uninformed, and the uncomprehending, which on most issues constitutes almost all of the population, and most of the Caucus too. Cleverness in Government can generally in the short run direct and silence people, but it cannot convince and persuade. There are a lot of people who three years ago would almost literally have laid down their lives for this Government, and who today would scarcely walk across the street to come to its assistance."

Part of the problem, Gibson thought, was that the government's decision-making process had become ponderous and complex. Ministers were caught on a treadmill, which almost none understood; they had become exhausted, discouraged, and unable to respond to new problems with any imagination. Showing perhaps too much deference towards his boss, Gibson did not blame Trudeau for having created the treadmill; but he found it was of "such clever construction" that it could be dismantled only by Trudeau personally. Significantly, both Davey and Gibson, who had had the opportunity to observe Trudeau's handling of his cabinet more closely than most, thought that, far from being the autocrat of his public image, Trudeau really needed to give more leadership to his cabinet. Occasionally he should use his prime ministerial prerogative arbitrarily to set

---

8. LPC, vol. 1083, file: Election Timing and Other Polical [sic] Memos 1971-1972, J.M. Davey, Towards a Strategy for 1971-72, 29.7.71. *The Gallup Report*, 16.5.70; 8.7.70; 7.11.70; 17.11.71.

priorities and assign personnel; both men considered a cabinet shuffle essential. Gibson also urged Trudeau to create an expanded "and less comfortable" circle of advisers, further recommending a co-ordinated effort to get ministers to do "*a great deal less administration* and a *great deal more travelling and communication.*" Jim Davey's prescription was not all bitter medicine, however. The government's main asset, he told Trudeau, was "your own personal popularity and the separation that people make between you and the rest of the government. Apart from Messrs. Jamieson, Olson, Andras, Pépin, Turner and Mackasey, and possibly [Jack] Davis, Chrétien and Marchand at the outside, your Ministers may contribute much to the internal workings of government, but publicly they are a 'drag'."[9]

Gibson thought that the most effective way of reinvigorating the administration was to call an early election in the summer of 1971. The possibility of a confrontation with the Quebec government over social policy and communications at the Victoria Conference on the Constitution, as well as the need to get electoral confirmation of the government's bilingual policies, justified an early election in Gibson's mind. By the late 1970s, many observers saw the Liberal party's use of the "national unity" issue as a cynical and desperate electoral ploy when all else had failed; but in 1971, Gibson's concerns were genuine. For him, the communications issue was especially crucial. "Today's society *is* communications, and the product of communications. There is no other thing of a substantial nature (except traditional ties) binding this unusual country together . . . in today's world, what is required is the cement of shared experience via a Canadian communications system, and that in turn means regulatory control over mass communications delivery mechanisms." The platform for an early election should include constitutional changes to strengthen federal powers and to entrench a Bill of Rights in the constitution; the commitment to a guaranteed annual income; policies to stimulate competition in business and to break up the monopoly power wielded by professional associations and unions; and moves to facilitate real participation by outsiders in the executive process by means of advisory groups, for example. Gibson feared that the alternative was the sort of "charismatic leader" campaign, which, if unavoidable to some extent, could not be relied upon totally and certainly not in the longer term.[10]

Some ministers such as Marchand, Mackasey, Greene and Jamieson were attracted to the idea of an election in the fall of 1971, but Jim Davey

---

9. LPC, vol. 1083, file: Election Timing etc. Davey to Trudeau, 16.7.71; vol. 1087, file: Campaign Plan, Davey to Lalonde, 11.12.71.

10. LPC, vol. 1083, file: Election Timing etc., Gibson to Trudeau, 22.4.71, 11.8.71. Emphasis in the original.

advised Trudeau that the public would see through the cynicism of an early election called simply in order to avoid the necessity of dealing with the worsening economic conditions that some predicted. "What we would be doing, in fact, would be to seek a political (electoral) solution (clearing the air) to what are principally internal managerial problems of maintaining Cabinet and Caucus harmony."[11] In any case, the party's private polls indicated that, with growing doubts about the government having overreacted in the October crisis, its popularity had fallen off sharply. It would win only 120 seats in an election—about a dozen short of a majority. An internal problem that could not easily be ignored was that MPs who had been elected in November 1965 would become eligible for pensions in November 1971 and would greatly resent a dissolution before that date.[12]

The election was not called in 1971, but the government and the party continued to drift. The federal campaign committee also called for a cabinet shuffle, but no real prime ministerial housecleaning took place. Trudeau did shift some ministers in the spring of 1971 and early in 1972, though these moves were largely prompted by two key ministers, Benson and Greene, requesting lighter responsibilities. Overall, the cabinet remained virtually unchanged. We have already noted in chapter 5, that the party's draft election program got nowhere and Gibson's met the same fate, even though (or perhaps, because) both overlapped with positions the party had already adopted in convention. There was little indication that Gibson's warnings had been taken seriously.

As the possibility of an early election receded, the fifth year of the government's mandate turned the optional into the inevitable. A government which had got increasingly caught up with its decision-making processes in Ottawa now had to call on its volunteer wing to man the hundreds of campaign committees across the country. And it soon became apparent that there were problems. Many new people had come into the party in 1968, but these new recruits had not been put to use in the organization. Senator Royce Frith recalled that, when he had been active in the Ontario volunteer wing in the early 1960s, he always travelled with his black book, noting the "good guys"—the sympathetic, dependable ones that Cell 13 could count on. He fully expected that, after 1968, a Trudeau-era equivalent of Cell 13 would scour the country with their own black books; but that never happened.[13] An election was coming, but the party workers were not in place. The alternative was to call back the old Pearson stalwarts, though that, for the most part, meant people who had sup-

---

[11] LPC, vol. 1083, file: Election Timing and Other Polical [sic] memos 1971-1972, Davey to Trudeau, 2.3.71; 27.5.71.

[12] LPC, file: Election Timing etc., Gibson to Trudeau 22.4.71, Marginal Notes on covering memo, 29.4.71.

[13] Interview with Senator Frith, 24.8.78.

ported Winters, Turner or Hellyer in 1968. The party was not so easy to revive when it was needed. The first choice as federal co-chairman of the national campaign committee was Senator John Nichol, who had headed it in 1968. But he too had been on the sidelines since then and, not having developed the sort of loyalty to Trudeau that Pearson had been able to inspire, he turned down the job.

Astonishingly, in view of later recriminations against the PMO, Torrance Wylie suggested that one of the co-chairmen be Marc Lalonde who was principal secretary in charge of the PMO. Wylie recognized that Lalonde was the sort who really took charge of any operation he had responsibility for. "The greatest reservation one can have about Marc's appointment" he wrote to Trudeau, "centers on the question of whether this is an indication of the P.M.O. super group reaching out again to control an area of activity. I want to emphasize that in my view, this will be an issue only with certain elements of the media (e.g. Fisher, Stewart, etc.) and not be a serious factor in the party or in the caucus . . . . In fact a case can be made that Marc's appointment would represent a dismantling of the P.M.O. as seen by its critics . . . . Marc's ultimate withdrawal from the P.M.O. would undermine this argument at least at the personality level and his responsibility as campaign chairman would legitimize his political role." In the end, two cabinet ministers became co-chairmen, the Hon. Jean Marchand and the Hon. Robert Andras. Although this might be taken as evidence that the parliamentary wing had become supreme, it also showed the extent to which the extra-parliamentary wing had atrophied.[14]

The choice of two cabinet ministers turned out not to be a particularly happy arrangement. Partly because of their departmental responsibilities and concerns for their own re-election campaigns, effective co-ordination was missing, especially in the post-writ period. One member of the 1972 campaign committee summed it all up. "The bottom line of the 1972 election was that no one called the shots." The only real strategy was to run a low-key, reassuring campaign. That would have been appropriate for a party in power which was on the way to being re-elected; but such was not the case in 1972. Both Wylie and Linden felt the country was yearning for a quiet time. "Let us avoid stirring things up too much," was Linden's advice, "for this will only anger the voters." Wylie thought they should conduct a "confident, optimistic, future-oriented campaign because voters feel confident." The campaign slogan produced by MacLaren—"The Land is Strong"—was intended to reinforce the basic message that "Problems, frustrations and anxieties remain but we have the will, the energy, the ability to deal with them." At least some members of

14. LPC, vol. 1089, file: National Advisory Committee, Wylie to Prime Minister, 30.9.71. Interview with Wylie, 22.2.80.

the party recognized that such a message of effulgent optimism was more a case of whistling in the dark; but none voiced objections.[15] They had already given up the fight.

In contrast to the campaigns of the 1960s which had been criticized for being ill-attuned to regional sensitivities, this one, according to internal party assessments, went too far in the other direction. In Quebec, a television commercial showed the province's ministers talking about the power and influence francophones had in Ottawa. Such a regional appeal produced a regional reaction. "French power" became an issue, not least because no significant campaign emerged to fill the gap in Ontario or nationally. Even within the province of Quebec, advertising was decentralized to such an extent that eight agencies handled what had formerly been done by MacLaren alone.[16]

A serious misjudgment of the campaign was that the NDP would be ignored by the electorate. But when David Lewis seized the initiative early in the campaign, charging that business—"corporate welfare bums"—was raking in huge government handouts, he threw the Liberal campaign, such as it was, into disarray and, in the last weeks of the campaign, Trudeau was reduced to indiscriminate promises of "candy" and "goodies" like the waterfront park in Toronto. Such old-style electioneering marked a sad decline from the high idealism of 1970.

Another last-minute development of longer-term significance was the re-entry into the campaign of Toronto party stalwarts who had been entreated to salvage whatever they could from a threatened rout by the Tories. Their most noticeable feat was a quickly organized rally in Nathan Phillips Square, which was described as the biggest political rally in Canadian history. Their immodest claim to have saved the Rosedale seat of cabinet minister Donald Macdonald (whose majority fell from over 9,000 in 1968 to just over 1,000 in 1972) gave them considerable leverage when the election post-mortems began.[17]

[15] LPC, vol. 1138, file: National Executive Meeting, 10.11.72; vol. 1083, file: Election Timing etc., J. Davey to Andras, 29.2.72; vol. 1088, file: Communication Committee meetings, Notes of the Meeting of the Campaign Communications Committee, 8.2.72; vol. 1119, file Voting Statistics and Surveys, A.M. Linden, "Secret Document Operation Increase: The Ontario Liberal Strategy 1972", 10.8.72; vol. 1087, file: Campaign Plan, Memo from Wylie to Andras, Marchand and Stanbury. Confidential Source.

[16] LPC, vol. 1133, file: National Campaign Committee, S. Callary to Stanbury, 16.11.72. Walter Stewart gives a transcript of the television ad in *Divide & Con*, pp. 147-149. *Le Devoir*, 7.7.72.

[17] Interview with Jerry Grafstein, 24.8.78.

THE FALLOUT FROM THE 1972 ELECTION

Even if Rosedale was saved, the party sustained heavy losses elsewhere, especially in B.C. and south-central Ontario, including Toronto. It lost its overall majority and ended up with just two seats more than the Conservatives. (Standings were Liberals 109; Progressive Conservatives 107; NDP 31; Social Credit 15; Others 2.) The near defeat inevitably produced recriminations within the party. (Surprisingly, a national executive meeting following the election agreed that anti-Trudeau feelings had not been a significant factor in the results, even though many Liberal candidates thought so and surveys by Gallup and Radio Canada indicated that an anti-Trudeau vote was the most commonly held reason for Liberal losses.[18])

In the party's private deliberations, it was conceded that a lack of overall direction had been one of the main problems with the campaign. The public scapegoat, however, was the PMO which was accused of having been unrealistic and overly intellectual. In the previous chapter (pp. 155-157), we mentioned the resentment which the Liberal Federation felt toward the PMO in the first year or two of the Trudeau administration. However the party's election records provide no evidence of any serious friction between the two groups; and the fact that Wylie could recommend Lalonde as federal campaign co-chairman suggests that tensions had subsided in the months before the election.

The charge against the PMO was led by a group of Toronto Liberals (who might well have been called Cell 13—phase II, but were not). They began to hold regular Monday evening meetings and sought to reactivate the party from its Toronto base as Cell 13 had done in the fifties. They were determined to see a housecleaning of PMO personnel followed by the installation there of some seasoned Toronto Liberals, specifically two defeated Toronto MPs, Martin O'Connell and John Roberts, as PMO advisers and Keith Davey as federal campaign chairman. The first two suggestions were acted on quickly. O'Connell was made principal secretary, replacing Marc Lalonde, who had already left the PMO to run in the election; John Roberts became program secretary, taking over from Jim Davey, who was shunted off to the Department of Transport. (Two years later, he was tragically killed in an accidental fall at his home.) The third recommendation took much longer to materialize. Although Trudeau had agreed to appoint Davey, he prevaricated. According to one version of the incident, it was only the Toronto Liberals' persistent pressure

---

[18] LPC, vol. 1138, file: National Executive Meeting, 10.11.72; vol. 1090, file: Post-Election letters to and from candidates. *CAR, 1972*, p. 77. *The Gallup Report*, 17.2.73.

which led Trudeau to contact Davey and make the announcement six months later.[19]

With the return of a minority government in 1972, electoral considerations remained in the forefront and the extra-parliamentary party enjoyed a return to the limelight. There were several reasons for this.

Firstly, election post-mortems within the government and the party judged that the government's near defeat had not been due to bad policies, but to the government's failure to communicate to the electorate how wise and constructive its policies were. There was more than a little self-delusion in such an assessment and the Trudeau government was by no means the first to think that, if only the electorate had better understood what the government was doing, it would not have been so thoughtlessly cruel on election day! In any case, shortly after the election a communications committee—similar to the one that had existed before the 1962 election (see page 32)—was set up with responsibility for vetting government actions from the perspective of how they would be seen by the electorate. Trudeau was convinced of the value of this sort of communications/public relations exercise and gave strong support to the committee if, for example, it was critical of a minister's proposal to cabinet. The committee had a membership of about fifteen and included ministers, PMO officials, caucus representatives, the party president and the national director. Significantly, it provided a central platform for the party's viewpoint, since it included a number of people with solid party credentials: Don Jamieson, Jean Chrétien, Martin O'Connell, Pierre O'Neil, Jim Fleming, Gil Molgat and Blair Williams.[20]

Secondly, the Liberals decided to take a radically different approach to advertising in the upcoming campaign. In the past, the party had maintained a client relationship with various advertising agencies which it used and, for almost the last twenty years, the principal agency had been MacLaren. But MacLaren and MacLaren's George Elliott were held responsible (probably unfairly) for having saddled the party with its 1972 slogan, "The Land is Strong." But according to Jerry Grafstein, the root of the problem was that MacLaren had become both "judge and jury" of the entire media campaign. The party felt it had not participated enough in advertising decisions that were being made by admen who spent most of their time selling soap. The decision to set up their own "in-house" agency, christened Red Leaf, followed a similar move by the Conservative party prior to the 1972 election and may also have been inspired by the Nixon campaign in the United States which established its own agency to ensure "loyalty, secrecy and greater control of its opera-

---

[19.] Interview with Jerry Grafstein, 24.8.78.
[20.] Interview with Williams, 29.9.78.

tions."[21] The agency employed paid professionals from a variety of firms and they were chosen on the basis of both their expertise and their Liberal loyalties. Grafstein, by profession a lawyer and by temperament a man whose words can barely keep up to a mind that races ahead with boundless enthusiasm, was the self-described "political commissar" of the agency—working with the admen through all the stages of copy, design, layout, and ensuring that the party's advertising adhered closely to the campaign committee's strategy of emphasizing the prime minister, the Liberal party label and the issue of wage and price controls.

Another idea freely borrowed from the Conservatives' 1972 campaign was the use of uniform graphics, such as the red "L" and maple leaf logo. However, Grafstein was forced to acknowledge the persisting federalist nature of the Liberal party: the graphic designs had to be approved by each provincial communications representative and, although Red Leaf did all the national advertising, provincial campaign committees did not employ it exclusively for their regional spots.

Thirdly, the 1972 election had been a sharp reminder that, even in the days of sophisticated polling and advertising, a party's volunteer wing was of great value. A brilliantly conceived advertising campaign is no more than an artillery attack on the positions that have to be taken in hand-to-hand combat by an army of volunteers whose enthusiasm is built upon a self-reinforcing esprit de corps. Colin Kenny, who worked as a party organizer in Ontario before he went with the PMO, has a theory that, in order to win an election, the party has to have 80 to 90 percent of Liberals voting for it. To get that loyalty, the party leadership has to keep in touch with the party core, by whatever means, and carry that core with it on every major issue or the party's support disintegrates.[22] Party strategists concluded that the Liberals who had sat on the sidelines after 1968 had to have their interest in the party reawakened. It was essentially a return to Stanbury's approach of using participation as the key to waging an election campaign—with one important difference. From 1968 to 1971, and even before, participation had had its own rationale. Party democracy had been considered a good in itself, though, in theory, also useful for winning elections. From near-defeat in 1972 to victory in 1974, participation came to be seen almost exclusively in terms of electoral considerations. The 1973 policy convention was aimed primarily at giving a solid show of support for the leader and, in particular, getting a massive rejection of the constitutionally required motion for a leadership convention; the standing committees of LPC lapsed into dormancy; the pol-

[21] *Wall Street Journal*, 6.3.72. LPO Conference, 18.8.74. Interview with Grafstein, 24.8.78. *Marketing* 11.2.74; 15.7.74.
[22] Interview with Kenny, 29.9.78.

icy and research department in the national office disappeared. This rearrangement of priorities encountered no real objection from within the party. It does not take much to convince Liberals that power has to have first priority, and it was somewhat glibly assumed that more experimentation with the practicalities of participatory democracy would resume once the period of minority government was over.

THE 1974 ELECTION

Within Liberal mythology, there are two conflicting theories about why the party was able to regain its majority in 1974.[23] Firstly, the party rebuilders argue that, from the leader to the parliamentary caucus and the PMO down to the riding level, the "party" (that amorphous, undefinable ganglion) brought political concerns and political realities to bear on government. Organizers from the national office renewed contacts with Liberals throughout the country, got them involved in the party and convinced them again that politics was exciting. In Ottawa, attention was focused on the parliamentary battle in order to win legislative support from NDP members during the minority parliament and election-day support from NDP voters, especially in Ontario and B.C. When the opposition finally obliged by uniting to defeat the government's budget in May 1974, the Liberal party had already won the election, according to the first version. The campaign was little more than a formality.

The other theory of how the election was won holds that a campaign strategy, based on the imaginative interpretation of surveys, was crucial. At first glance, the surveys provided little consolation: inflation was considered to be the country's major problem, an issue that aroused more concern than any since the war. Furthermore, a majority of the electorate thought that the answer lay in wage and price controls as proposed by the Conservatives. Inflation was the Tories' issue and it could not be ignored. Party strategists decided, however, that nothing would be gained by being defensive. The Liberals had to make inflation *their* issue. The surveys did reveal a hole in the Conservative attack: everyone wanted prices frozen, but there was less enthusiasm for freezing wages. Furthermore, voters who had supported the NDP in 1972 were wavering. For labour, free collective bargaining is almost like a religious dogma and Liberal strategists calculated that a strong stand against wage controls would strike a sympathetic chord in that sector. The early surveys also showed that, while inflation overshadowed the question of who was best suited to lead the country, voters, when asked about the qualities they looked

---

[23.] For a full account of the election, see Howard R. Penniman, ed., *Canada at the Polls: The General Election of 1974.*

for in a leader, admitted that they admired Trudeau for his intelligence and his toughness. Thus, if the Liberals could make leadership a campaign issue, they would be in a good position to take advantage of it. So one of the constant themes of Trudeau's aggressive campaign was to insist that leadership *was* an issue. One can imagine the delight within the Liberal camp when, by the middle of the campaign, surveys at last indicated that, indeed, the voters had begun to say that leadership really was an issue![24]

The 1974 strategy was thus carefully conceived to deal with a potentially dangerous situation in which the party's weaknesses might easily have become exposed. Accordingly, the campaign was tightly run and tightly controlled by a much smaller group than had run the amorphous campaign of 1972. It was also oriented much more toward the leader. Whereas in 1972, each cabinet minister was required to donate three days to the national campaign, in 1974, only the two ministers with high national profiles, John Turner and Mitchell Sharp, were used nationally. The campaign committee was anxious to keep everything focused on the issues of leadership and wage controls. Their theory was that only a very few ideas can be put across in a campaign. Both the leader and the media get terribly bored with the same few points repeated over and over again; but, if frequent press conferences are allowed, there is a danger that the message will become fragmented and the voters will become confused. Accordingly, Trudeau was allowed to do only two interviews (with Betty Kennedy and John Bassett), there were no hot-line shows, and daily announcements were issued under the maxim, "An announcement a day keeps the press conference away."

The actual campaign followed the strategy very closely. It was tightly controlled by Keith Davey and, once the campaign was underway, he and Jim Coutts became the only people who advised Trudeau. Such a campaign was not without its tensions, however; the campaign committee was reportedly upset with the overwhelming emphasis on the leader and, according to one assessment, "the whole campaign would have come apart if it had gone on for another week."[25]

It is impossible to state categorically that the election was won by either the polls or the party. (The results—Liberals 141, Conservatives 95, NDP 16, Socred 11, Independent 1—gave the government a smaller majority than that of 1968, but still a comfortable 32-seat margin.) However, the principal survey-research study of the election does shed some light

[24] Liberal Party in Ontario Conference, 18.8.74.
[25] LPO Conference, 18.8.74. Interviews with Grafstein, 24.8.78; Blair Williams, 28.7.76; 29.9.78.

on the two conflicting interpretations.[26] While inflation was indeed the major concern of voters, it produced little vote switching—mainly because no one party was seen as having the answer to the problem. But the authors did not attempt to discover whether the voters had become less convinced by the Conservatives' wage and price controls policy as the campaign went on. In other words, it could be that the Liberal strategy *was* successful in defusing the issue by the time the vote took place. Furthermore, the Gallup poll indicates that the 1974 campaign was unique in that, for the first time in twenty years, Liberal support did not fall off between the writ and the election.

On the leadership question, the article provides the surprising revelation that, although Trudeau was more popular than the other three leaders, his popularity barely exceeded that of his own party, leading the authors to conclude that negative feelings towards Stanfield may have worked to the Liberals' advantage as much as positive feelings towards Trudeau. The study also refutes Liberal claims after the election that three-quarters of the Liberals' increased vote had come from the NDP. The net shift from that source was just 0.7 percent of the electorate; in fact, the net switches from all the other parties were much less than the Liberal gains made among those who did not or could not vote in 1972. If anything, this evidence suggests that the effort between elections to rekindle the enthusiasm of the rank and file may have been one of the most significant factors in the outcome.

AFTERMATH OF THE 1974 ELECTION

For the moment, the party seemed to have been vindicated: the PMO had been put in its place and the old hands who had come to the aid of the party had demonstrated their effectiveness. There were, nevertheless, a number of disturbing hostages to fortune which had been given during the course of the election and the two years of minority government. The extra-parliamentary party had willingly acquiesced in having itself turned into an electoral machine after 1972. The party had merely gone through the motions of democratic participation at the 1973 convention when, in reality, it had been the disciplined participation of electoral warfare. Furthermore, Trudeau's campaign, instead of committing the government to a program which had been developed by the party, was based on rejecting a policy—selected price and income controls—which the party had already endorsed on several occasions. Moreover the two elections of 1972 and 1974 had led Trudeau to several conclusions: firstly, that the

---

[26] J.H. Pammett *et al.*, "The Perception and Impact of Issues in the 1974 Federal Election", *CJPS* (1977), 93-126.

party organization had let him down in 1972 (instead of the other way around, as many party people saw it); secondly, that in Keith Davey he had found a political "boss" who could reactivate on demand this party organization which, by his own admission, he had trouble understanding; thirdly, that in Jim Coutts, he had found a political tactician on whom he could rely completely; fourthly, that the party could be put into neutral for the time being; and fifthly, that the surveys provided the clue to winning the next election at the end of the current parliamentary term.

Soon after the election, important changes in personnel indicated how party-government relations would evolve in the second Trudeau majority government. Under minority government, the trio of party president Senator Molgat, national director Blair Williams, and PMO principal secretary Martin O'Connell had worked well together and had done a great deal to rebuild the party operation. After October 1974, O'Connell was back in the House of Commons; Williams was anxious to leave the post which he had accepted on only a short-term basis; and both he and Molgat had become increasingly frustrated in their attempts to arrange meetings with Trudeau. None of the three ever seemed able to win Trudeau's confidence as Wylie and Lalonde had done before or as Davey and Coutts did later. Trudeau does not work well with "soft-edged" politicians like Williams, Molgat and O'Connell who are described as being practitioners of the "touchy-feely" approach to politics. Whenever they met with Trudeau, the conversation would go along these lines: "We *think* there could be a problem developing with such-and-such and we want to talk about it, to toss some ideas around." Trudeau, even more addicted to the well-written memorandum than his ministers, would become more and more exasperated. By contrast, Keith Davey's mode of operation appealed to him much more: "Here's the problem, here's the solution—and, furthermore, I'll look after it for you."

In any case, key personnel changes after the 1974 election suggested that the "hard-edged" people were again taking over from the "soft-edged" variety. The more heavy-handed, supremely self-confident Jack Austin replaced the affable Martin O'Connell as principal secretary; the brilliant Michael Pitfield replaced the lower-key Gordon Robertson as secretary to the cabinet. The next step was to give official recognition to Keith Davey's *de facto* position by having him elected party president. Indeed, this was seen by some in party circles as legitimizing the influential role that Davey had played since his return in 1973. Besides, there was nothing unusual, as we have seen, in the federal leader picking his own party president. Others, however, feared that the sort of tight control which had worked well for Davey in an election campaign would be bad for the party over the longer term. And when Trudeau, on Davey's advice, appointed Gerry Robinson as national director without consulting the party president or the national executive, "all hell threatened to break loose." A flurry of behind-the-scenes activity, particularly by Liberal senators, who had never been keen on Trudeau, produced a challenger. Senator Alasdair Graham, a genial, ruddy-faced Nova Scotian, may have been an unlikely casting for the role of David; in any case, when the fight became public, Goliath backed off. Graham was not nearly as well known within the party as Davey, nor did he have anything like Davey's credentials. A contest between the two men, as well as being unprecedented, might have clarified the nebulous position of party president; but Graham became president by default and Davey, who had been virtually Mr. Liberal of the 1960s, receded further into the shadows behind Trudeau's throne.

Over the next few years, policy conventions, the national office and the national executive continued to function ostensibly as before; but the aspirations which had given a thrust to the extra-parliamentary party in the 1960s were now largely a thing of the past. A few voices in the party called for a renewed initiative to make it more than just an election machine. Rosalind Mellander, a vice-president of the Youth Commission from British Columbia, in the Autumn 1975 issue of a new party magazine called "*Dialogue*", urged the grass roots of the party to "play a real role in policy formulation." By and large, she said, the mechanisms were in place, but not functioning. "We have a policy committee at the national executive level but it exists in name only; we have had a policy director working out of the national office but this position has been vacant since the last convention . . . . Since these mechanisms are not effective, the government is formulating policy and making legislative decisions that neither have the advice nor reflect the views of the Party. The ridings feel alienated both from caucus and the Party hierarchy." She urged that a policy secretariat be established in the national office and that the policy committee follow up the resolutions passed at conventions by making specific recommendations for action, that the finance committee take over the functions of the treasury committee, and that the national executive meet with the cabinet once a year. But her plea fell on deaf ears.[27]

POLICY CONVENTIONS OF THE SEVENTIES

Many in the party had become disillusioned with the whole policy process after Trudeau's rejection of two of the most important resolutions emanating from the 1970 convention (the guaranteed annual income and the emergency powers review board) and the cabinet's rejection of the whole Liberal Charter. Not to be daunted, Allen Linden, the co-chairman

[27] Vol. 1, No. 2, 6-7.

of the policy committee, kept advancing the case for a real policy role for the party. The cabinet, he thought, should have to account to the national executive and the policy committee at least once a year; furthermore, the government should not "announce any major policy decisions or introduce any major legislation without some consultation with the party." As planning for the 1973 convention began, Linden again urged that convention resolutions be used to develop a platform which would be ratified by both the parliamentary and the extra-parliamentary wings of the party. If the government was not prepared to commit itself to a platform, he said, then there was no point in having a convention.[28]

Linden's urgings, however, were to no avail and, until 1980, no real attempt was made to draw up an election platform based on convention resolutions. Nevertheless, policy conventions have become a regular, if disconnected, feature of Liberal party operations. None has been as ambitious in concept as that of 1970, but attendance is consistently well over 2,000, with each riding sending about three-quarters of the delegates to which it is entitled (the riding president and seven elected delegates).

There have been some improvements in format. The 1973 convention began the practice of presenting delegates with a report that showed what action had been taken by the government on the previous convention's resolutions. Stanbury, in a covering letter to the report, drew attention to some of the government's sins of omission, but, ever the optimist, he went on, "in huge areas of policy the government has been almost slavish in its pursuit of the decisions of the Convention." For example, fifty-three out of fifty-eight agricultural resolutions, he said, had been acted upon. He was decidedly premature, though, in declaring that the guaranteed annual income resolution was well on its way to implementation.[29]

Subsequent reports have occasionally taken advantage of vaguely worded resolutions in order to interpret the government's record more generously than circumstances warranted. For example, two resolutions in 1975 urged "that Canada carry a fair share in the NATO alliance" and "that the government investigate the inflationary impact of various government agencies and regulations." The Report to the 1978 National Convention was pleased to confirm that both had been "implemented in full or in part"! Positive action by the government was interpreted even more loosely when claiming, for example, that MPs had got "access to all information not necessary for national security" or that "reinstat[ing] the position of policy director in the national office" and the setting up of a "policy secretariat . . . with sufficient funds and staff" had been acted upon. More wishful thinking than positive action.

[28.] LPC, vol. 1104, file: Consultative Council General - 1971, Linden to Stanbury, 3.2.71; vol. 1138, file: National Executive Meeting, 10.11.72.

[29.] LPC, vol. 1115, file: 1970 Liberal Policy Convention: What Action has been Taken?

These reports are supposed to provide ammunition for the delegates to exercise the accountability provisions in the party's constitution. In the leader's accountability sessions, however, delegates have tended to be as deferential as in 1970 and there have been very few occasions when a questioner has referred to a resolution passed at a previous convention. A more significant innovation in 1973 was the "ministerial session" where questions have usually been much more direct and specific. These sessions are well attended and often livelier than the workshops. The accounting, nevertheless, could be further developed, since delegates, if they are interested in doing so, must search through scattered resolutions to find those which pertain to a particular minister. The accounting would be more to the point if, for example, a member of the party's policy committee led off each session with a detailed assessment of how that minister's department had responded to party recommendations as set out at the last convention.

Ironically, the accounting to the convention by the party's own executive is the least satisfactory of all. In 1970 and in 1973, Stanbury, as president, wrote full reports which frankly acknowledged certain problem areas. Godfrey likewise gave a detailed financial report to the 1973 convention when he was chairman of both the treasury committee and the finance committee. But apart from the occasional short statement from a committee chairman, complaining of the difficulty in getting his committee together, no other written reports have been made to party members. Even the party's financial statements are no longer made public apart from the global totals which appear in the return to the chief electoral officer.

A useful innovation, that of priority resolutions, was introduced in 1978. The number of resolutions coming in from riding associations, regional meetings, provincial policy committees, youth's and women's commissions and provincial executives is truly staggering, even after similar resolutions are combined: 450 in 1973, 355 in 1975 and 775 in 1978. In 1970, delegates attempted to debate and vote on everything. In 1973, a new rule was introduced whereby a resolution had to be introduced by a delegate in a convention workshop, even if it had been properly submitted in advance and appeared in the booklet of resolutions. That reduced the number of resolutions to less than a third of the original total, simply because there was not enough time for all the delegates with resolutions in hand to get to the microphones before the time for a given workshop expired.

In 1978, the convention policy committee decided that, instead of the agenda being thus fortuitously determined by the delegates' places in the microphone queue at the beginning of a workshop, three resolutions would be given priority in each of the fourteen workshops. To be avoided, however, was the paternalistic sort of resolutions committee which used to keep a watchful eye over pre-1960s Liberal proceedings and which still operates as an important control mechanism at NDP conventions. The priority resolutions were chosen in an ingenious manner. The convention policy organization committee met with provincial representatives over a period of three days before the convention. The fifty people were divided into five groups. After each group bargained and battled over which resolutions should be given priority, half of the group moved on to another group, while the other half stayed put and were joined by five new members. Then the drawing up of an agenda started all over again.[30] (A procedure of ingenious complexity, vaguely resembling the shifting of opponents in duplicate bridge, it could only have been invented by Quebeckers!) This was a worthwhile innovation because it ensured that some of the more important and controversial items were assured of consideration.

The committee did manage to avoid having the priority resolutions become simply a platform for the government's viewpoint. Several either conflicted with or exceeded government policy, such as worker participation in the management of Crown corporations (248), constitutional human rights guarantees prohibiting discrimination on the grounds of age, mental and physical disability, and sexual orientation (556), the perennial guaranteed annual income based on a negative income tax (688), and a ceiling on the indexing of public service pensions (including MPs') comparable to the private sector (731). All these passed. On the other hand, thirteen of the forty-one priority resolutions failed, including those calling for a limitation on the right to strike in the public service (249), the direct election of senators (400), mortgage interest deductibility from income tax (733), and a fanciful resolution to admit the Turks and Caicos Islands into Confederation (662). But the convention was concerned with more than the government's sins of omission and commission. It endorsed the thrust of the Liberal government's language policies in calling for federal funds to be provided to the provinces for second language instruction (511) and constitutional guarantees for the minority official language in Quebec and outside Quebec (512).

Even with the device of the priority resolutions, the impact of the resolutions is still weakened by the fact that so many are passed without the party having made much of a conscious commitment. Instead of the mammoth ballots of 1970, procedures have been simplified so that, in a plenary session, a resolution automatically passes without debate unless twenty-five delegates request a debate and vote. The assumption is that workshops can be considered representative of the convention as a whole and that the scarce time of the plenary should be used only to debate genuinely controversial items. The assumption is not always justi-

---

[30] Interviews with Michel Rochon, 8.9.78; Céline Hervieux-Payette, 2.11.78.

fied. In 1975, a number of technical resolutions on fishing and agriculture were being passed in plenary without debate. Finally, the fourteenth resolution—to put all agencies and government departments directly related to agriculture under the minister of agriculture—prompted Toronto lawyer, Joe Potts, to leap to his feet saying that he wanted to slow down the automatic acceptance of resolutions which he did not understand. Number fourteen was at least one he understood and he wanted some explanation. As it turned out, the resolution had almost no support and it was defeated!

That incident illustrates how little significance can be attached to many of the resolutions which theoretically become party policy. This was precisely the conclusion of gay rights spokesmen when the 1978 convention adopted their position on amending the Canadian constitution to prohibit discrimination on various grounds, including sexual preference. The resolution had been passed with no debate in the plenary and therefore, they concluded, little real commitment had been made by the party. The national executive attempted to make Liberal cabinets more aware of the party's official stands by getting a statement put on every cabinet policy document indicating how the proposal in question related to policies adopted by the party's most recent convention. But at least one minister did not recall any occasion on which this had influenced cabinet in arriving at a decision—with the exception of the still well remembered debate on the postponement of medicare in 1966.[31] In other words, a convention resolution on a particular issue which is passed after a highly publicized major debate is remembered and not easily ignored; the others are forgotten.

There have been complaints that none of the recent conventions has been as truly participatory as that of 1970; that they have been manipulated by caucus, ministers, the PMO, and have been planned primarily to look good to the media. It is certainly true that, since 1970, parliamentarians have held the key convention positions. In 1970, the party's policy co-chairman, Allen Linden, was also the convention co-chairman; but since then the co-chairmen have always been MPs or senators, except in 1975 when B.C. president, Doreen Braverman, was named co-chairman. A special convention policy committee is formed for each convention, taking over responsibilities one would have expected to be carried out by the party's standing committee on policy—which has always had difficulty finding a role for itself.

It has also been suggested that the presence of ministers actively promoting resolutions that bolster their pet projects in cabinet is another example of parliamentary dominance. We have already referred to the

---

[31.] *The Body Politic* (April 1978), 7. Confidential Source.

Hon. Otto Lang's prairie rail rehabilitation motion in 1978 (see chapter 4). The Hon. Monique Bégin was convinced that that convention's renewed commitment to the guaranteed annual income was an important factor in overcoming opposition which her department's child tax credit scheme had encountered from the Department of Finance.[32] In these two instances, whose ox was being gored? It is just as easy to argue that it was cabinet, rather than the convention, that was being manipulated. At the very least, the examples suggest that ministers themselves consider a demonstration of party support to be important.

The real problem with the convention is less one of caucus or cabinet domination—as we saw in chapter 5, the *exclusion* of cabinet from the 1970 deliberations caused serious problems afterwards—but rather, the lack of any real follow-up apart from the formal, though unpublicized, printing of resolutions which are sent to every convention delegate. Resolutions serve different purposes. There are those that reaffirm existing policy (the language resolutions of 1978) or express the mood of the party on big issues of the day (the postponement of medicare in 1966, capital punishment in 1975). Others are an expression of concern (such as that expressed over the growth of the federal public service in 1978), while some make very specific recommendations, such as making possession of small amounts of marijuana no longer a criminal offence. Finally, conventions may reject possible options (universal wage and price controls in 1973; allowing interest payments on mortgages to be tax deductible in 1975). Unfortunately these are all relegated to the same sort of post-convention limbo. Those that require further development ought ideally to be referred to the party's policy committee or to a party task force or to a caucus committee; but the original grass-roots idea—perhaps not fully developed, but prompted by a real problem—goes nowhere as far as the initiator of the resolution knows.

This gap is supposedly filled, at least to a certain extent, by the consultative council, which was created in 1970. It consists of the delegates to the previous convention (unless replaced as a result of new elections or appointments) and, in the words of the party constitution, is supposed "to serve as a forum for the examination of important political issues, to serve as a mechanism for consultation and to guide the National Executive of the Liberal Party of Canada in expressing the views of the Liberal Party of Canada on these issues." Regular consultations with the con-

---

[32] Interview with Bégin, 13.10.79. A few weeks after cabinet started looking at the proposal, opposition developed again, so she kept it from going before full cabinet for fear that it would be defeated. For the next several months, she spoke to various interested organizations across the country and, in August, when she saw the chance of getting the proposal moving again—everyone was feeling so guilty about the August spending cuts, she said—she was able to make a quick call for telegrams of support from the various Liberal organizations with which she had kept in close contact.

sultative council were intended to make it into a kind of continuing convention. Al Linden saw "fantastic" possibilities for thus breathing life into the party between conventions. "We will be able eventually to hold simultaneous meetings in different parts of the country, if we so choose. We will be able to consult our party via television or radio on any matter that we put to them."[33]

The council seems to have been taken seriously, at least to begin with. It was directed by a co-ordinating committee of influential Liberals, chaired by L.C. Jolivet, and given a budget of $5,500.

Originally conceived as a means of getting a regular updating of opinion on current issues and of resubmitting resolutions for reconsideration after analysis had been done on them, the first consultation with the council was somewhat mundane and got it off to an uncertain start. Following the 1970 convention, delegates were asked to indicate the relative priority that they attached to the various policy areas which the convention had dealt with: the economy, pollution, poverty, international relations, etc. (This somewhat meaningless exercise replaced the original idea of asking delegates to attach a priority to each of the 396 resolutions —plainly an impossible task). The council members were also asked to vote on forty-nine resolutions which had not been considered at the convention because of time constraints. These tag-end resolutions were not well received. Vaguely worded sentiments, while perhaps acceptable amidst the bustle of a convention, did not stand up to close examination in the quiet of a delegate's study. The idea of a continuing convention was nevertheless enthusiastically received—as evidenced by the phenomenally high return of 43 percent or 917 replies.[34]

The consultative council's co-ordinating committee decided after that simply to poll the council on two issues four times a year and to include with the ballot a brief statement on the various sides to the question. The next mailing was originally going to be on the desirability of some form of wage and price control and on safeguarding minority language rights. After discussions with the federal and Quebec governments, the latter idea was dropped; but the co-ordinating committee was allowed to go ahead with the ballot on wage and price controls, which was then not as controversial as it was later to become. The ballot was accompanied by a brief, but balanced, analysis of the various alternatives and replies from over five hundred delegates indicating that a substantial majority favoured controls. (40 percent favoured selected controls, while 26 percent

[33] LPC Constitution, Clause 6-A, B. LPC, vol. 1137, file: National Executive Meeting, 13-14.2.71.

[34] LPC, vol. 1104, file: First Mailing to the Consultative Council March, 1971, *passim*; file: Consultative Council; General - 1971, National Executive Meeting, 13-14.2.71; Stanbury to Consultative Council, 31.8.71.

wanted full controls. 13 percent thought no additional interventions in the market were necessary and 21 percent preferred voluntary guidelines.)[35]

Following the report of the Royal Commission on the Status of Women in 1970, a three-woman party task force was set up to make recommendations on behalf of LPC. In conjunction with the task force, the consultative council was sent a questionnaire which elicited over 750 replies. A substantial majority favoured government-financed daycare centres and the giving of Canadian Pension Plan benefits to the spouse who stays at home. A small majority favoured the removal of abortion from the criminal code—only 18 percent favoured the existing law—and thus put the party in opposition to the government on a highly contentious issue.[36]

During the period of minority government from 1972 to 1974 the consultative council was deliberately ignored. Gordon Floyd, the director of policy research, made suggestions for submitting questions to the consultative council, but the national executive decided that policy concerns were a luxury and that all available resources had to be channeled into electoral preparedness.[37]

Although the consultative council was revived in 1974, the sense of adventure had gone out of the idea. Members of the council were asked to consider various suggestions for reform of the Senate. The response—just over 250—was the lowest to date. They were also asked for their views on gun control; but, since then, the council has been reduced to playing a largely formal role as the body to which reports are made on the fate of the last convention's resolutions. In amendments made to the party's constitution at the last two conventions, party members have attempted to breathe some life back into the council. In 1975, the policy chairman was made responsible for the functioning of the consultative council and was required to report to each meeting of the national executive. When that did not work, an amendment was passed in 1978 requiring the national executive to activate the council at least twice yearly, but still the council lies fallow. The original vision of a continuing convention has been abandoned. If members of the consultative council were really determined to turn it into an active body, they could call on a provision in the constitution according to which specific questions can be referred to the council on the request of one hundred members, no more than fifty of

[35] LPC, vol. 1104, file: Consultative Council; General - 1971, Minutes of Co-ordinating Committee, 11.3.71; Press Release, 22.11.71; file: Second Mailing to the Consultative Council July/71; vol. 1137, file: National Executive Meeting, 3-4.4.71; vol. 1138, file: National Executive Meeting, 18-19.9.71; 27-28.11.71.

[36] LPC, vol. 1138, file: National Executive Meeting, 11.3.72.

[37] Blair Williams to the author, 3.8.76. Interview with Gordon Floyd, 29.10.79.

whom can come from one province. (It was lowered to twenty-five in 1975 and then raised back to fifty in 1978.)[38] Conceivably, the council could even be activated to force the national executive into calling a convention, if the latter were reluctant to do so (as it was in 1979); but so far, the rank-and-file members of the council have refrained from demonstrating any such plucky independence.

NATIONAL OFFICE

After 1968, as we saw in chapter 5, the responsibilities of the national office were expanded and its budget doubled to over $300,000.[39] The office flowered for a short period in the 1970s and began to look like the modest equivalent of a European party office, but then it went into a period of relative decline, partly because of inadequate funding and partly because of inadequate direction by the national executive. The office has always had to overcome a kind of Cinderella problem within the party. Its duties, chiefly those of keeping the party alive between elections, are mundane; the leader tends to see it as being less responsive to his own needs than his personal staff on Parliament Hill; the fund raisers see it as a drain on election funds; the parliamentary caucus want to use it as an MPs' re-election office; and the provincial organizations see it as yet another manifestation of distant, insensitive Ottawa. One might have expected the national executive to be the party office's fairy godmother, but through most of the 1970s, they seemed unconcerned about the possibility of it turning into a pumpkin.

In 1979, the national office had an annual budget of $600,000, an increase of just 60 percent over the last ten years and barely more than two-and-a-half times what it was in 1957. During the last decade, the PMO doubled its staff from forty-four to over ninety, while the party office shrank by about half to its present eighteen. Many of those staff members held lower level positions than their predecessors and only two were paid, for example, a salary equivalent to a minister's executive assistant. Even taking into account the Montreal office of LPC(Q), which is about the same size as the Ottawa office, the smaller Toronto office of LPC(O), and the very modest offices in the other provinces, the Liberal Party of Canada is dwarfed beside the party offices in England. The Con-

---

38. Report of the Consultative Council, Response to Senate Questionnaire, n.d. [c. 1975] Constitution of the Liberal Party of Canada, 1975, 1978, Clause No. 6.

39. Besides the documentary sources to which specific reference is made, much of the material for this section is based on interviews with Torrance Wylie, 8.9.71; Blair Williams, 29.9.78; Roger Hébert, 2.11.78; Colin Kenny, 29.9.78; Gerry Robinson, 4.2.77; Micheline Côté, 3.11.78; Gordon Ashworth, 4.10.79; Audrey Gill, 24.10.79. Blair Williams to the author, 3.8.76.

servative party there has a headquarters staff of almost one hundred, excluding clerical and ancillary staff, and an additional four hundred in regional and constituency offices. The Labour party, with about half the staff, is still much larger than LPC.[40]

The office reached a high point in the early 1970s. Torrance Wylie, formerly an executive assistant to Senator Connolly and the prime minister, L.B. Pearson, was national director from 1969 to 1972. He has an ever-fresh, young man's enthusiasm combined with a lucid, penetrating mind which Trudeau respects. On the other hand, his whole-hearted commitment to participation meant that he could work well with the party president, Richard Stanbury. In spite of struggles with the PMO over respective areas of jurisdiction, Wylie's national office developed a broader capability than it had before or has had since.

Blair Williams was national director (1973-75) mostly during the period of minority government. An Albertan and a political scientist by training, Williams has a low-key manner that, on first meeting, conveys the image of an easy-going, relaxed westerner. And while this first impression is not inaccurate,one is less immediately aware of his flinty confidence, conviction, and ability to inspire devotion from those who work with him. With a staff that included such talented people as Bob Foulkes, Gordon Floyd and Roger Hébert, the national office happily immersed itself in the job of reactivating the Liberal party and, as long as Martin O'Connell was principal secretary, maintained a good relationship with the PMO.

Gerry Robinson, the national director from 1975 to 1978, reflected the less ambitious perspective of the national office in the seventies. A sleek, good-looking, thirtyish lawyer from Vancouver, Robinson is a cautious man, who, as director of organization under Torrance Wylie, gave close, dogged attention to the minutiae of party organization. As national director, he was more a Bob Kidd than a Keith Davey. It is inconceivable, for example, that he would have given Trudeau blunt assessments of his ministers' performances as Davey and O'Brien had occasionally given Pearson. At the national office, there was a return to the sort of attention that Kidd used to give to the mailing list, except that in the mid-seventies this took the form of a streamlined, computerized list of 500,000 names and addresses. Partly because his staff was smaller, Robinson spent more time than his predecessors filling an administrative role in Ottawa, rather than engaging in high-profile fraternizing activities across the country.

The several postponements of an election in 1978 put the national office into a state of flux for over a year. Robinson was unable to stay on in his post when the election was finally put off to 1979. His successor, Gor-

---

[40]. Richard Rose, *The Problem of Party Government*, p. 169.

don Gibson, having strong policy concerns and sufficient prestige within the party, would have restored the post of national director to the visibility it had had in previous years. But he resigned a few months later to run, unsuccessfully, for a seat in B.C. Gordon Ashworth, who was acting national director during the campaign, had served a kind of apprenticeship as director of organization and finance, as had Gerry Robinson before him. In late 1979, he was appointed permanently to the position. Ashworth is an engaging, unassuming young man with a good understanding of the role of a party bureaucracy. It remains to be seen whether he can be a tenacious, forceful defender of the party's interests or whether he will permit the drift in the party organization to continue.

The six departments into which the national office was re-organized in 1968 have not met all their original expectations. Policy research disappeared, as we have seen; organization is an area where the national party's effectiveness has always been somewhat limited by the fact that field organizers are employed by the provincial organizations. At times in the early 1970s, there was no director of fund raising, although more recently the whole fund-raising operation, including the separate Liberal Agency under Torrance Wylie, has become a more important sector. Programs and communications will be discussed in more detail.

Women's and Youth Commissions

The program department's broad mandate to promote participation generally within the party was, in reality, restricted to women and youth. Today that part of the national office's activity is handled by one co-ordinator who assists the Youth Commission, the Women's Commission, and the Speaker's Bureau.

Before the 1950s, the Liberal party was effectively a men's organization; women and young people were hived off into three separate organizations, which were affiliated with the senior party: the Women's Liberal Federation of Canada (WLFC), the Young Liberal Federation, and the Canadian University Liberal Federation (CULF). Although women performed much of the donkey work in the ridings, they were effectively barred from taking a significant part in the National Liberal Federation. There were only ten women delegates at the 1919 leadership convention, for example, and in 1948, just twenty-seven. The Young Liberals and CULF were supposedly training ground for future leaders of the party; but instead of providing an appropriate avenue for channeling their talents into the mainstream of the party, all three affiliated organizations were actually a backwater for "the young who might talk too much and the women who might also talk too much."[41]

[41.] Reginald Whitaker, *The Government Party*, pp. 78-79, 194-195. Women's Liberal Commission, *Contact*, June 1975. LPC, vol. 1137, file: Executive Committee Meeting, 14-15.3.70.

The WLFC was formed in 1928 and, in its early years, was reasonably successful in providing political involvement for that half of the population which had only recently acquired the vote. But by the early 1960s, it had clearly outlived its usefulness. Keith Davey described it as an organization which had been spawned by Mackenzie King and whose members had grown old with him. "The resultant inbred organization is far more concerned about who is going to be Queen Bee on this or that executive than the building of an effective organization." Far from attracting young, intelligent women into the party, it repelled them.[42]

CULF was the most effective of the three because the university was a logical base for organizing students who were living away from home and had no contacts with the local riding associations. The Young Liberal Federation, on the other hand, was in bad shape. Years before, when young people had not been readily accepted in the senior party, it had served a purpose. But by the 1960s, young people were frequently recruited directly into the senior organization with the result that no Young Liberal clubs existed in over two-thirds of the ridings. Where they continued to function, the upper age limit of thirty-five had created a bizarre membership composed of high school students and late-twenties executives who were former members of CULF. Any organization runs the risk of being turned into a vehicle for simply serving the members' own interests and losing sight of the original stated aims, but the Young Liberals were accused of having carried this to extremes. The clubs in Edmonton and Calgary were described as "essentially junior bar societies, attracting young lawyers hoping to acquire background to power and patronage, and nurses, secretaries, etc. hoping to acquire young lawyers." [43]

In the late 1960s, there was a growing consensus within the party that the three affiliates should be disbanded. The official position was that women and young people should be integrated into the main organization as a way of furthering the "new politics" of an open party, but

[42] LPC, vol. 728, file: Federal Organization Confidential, Davey to Nichol, 31.3.66; vol. 744, file: PMO - L.B. Pearson 1964, Davey to Pearson, 3.12.64; vol. 738, file: National Federation of Liberal Women, Personal Commentary of the Recent Discussion on Aims of the Liberal Women of Canada, Paul Goulet, 5.3.64.

[43] LPC, vol. 1033, file: Youth - Canadian Student Liberals, Report to the Executive of the Liberal Party in Alberta concerning the Alberta Young Liberal Association; file: Youth Organizer - Sheppard, Patrick 1966-67, Sheppard to Molgat et al., 14.7.67; vol. 1032, file: Young Liberal Federation, The Youth Wing of the Liberal Party, 15.1.66; Report to Young Liberal National Executive and Provincial Presidents, Pat Sheppard, 22.6.67; vol. 687, file: Correspondence & Memoranda Oct. - Dec. 1961, President's Report to the Young Liberal Federation of Canada, 21.12.61; vol. 738, file: National Liberal Federation - Employees, A Brief: On the desirability of Splitting the Job of Executive Director of CULF and the Young Liberals, David Smith, 10.5.65; vol. 1092, file: Liberal Party in Manitoba June 1966 - October 1968, Tom Bernes to Russ Hunt, 2.11.67.

it also provided ample justification for getting rid of three white elephants. In 1969, Ontario led the way by integrating its women's and youth groups at the provincial level and the national Young Liberals voted themselves out of existence. Women at the national level first balked at the idea of integration, allegedly because the elderly members were afraid of losing their right to attend national meetings as women's delegates. In a final paternalistic *coup de grace*, the national executive cut off their funding and in 1973 the women at last accepted the wisdom of disbanding the organization.[44]

Not all was lost however to the larger cause of integration. Local women's Liberal clubs and post-secondary student Liberal clubs still have separate representation at party conventions, and the constitution provides minimum guarantees of the number of party positions that must be held by women and young people. Even the original 1932 constitution stipulated that certain executive positions be held by women or young Liberals. In 1961, the constitution was amended to provide that, when ridings elected their six delegates to national meetings, at least one had to be a Liberal woman and one a Young Liberal. In 1973, the number of delegates was increased to seven per riding at least two of whom had to be women and two youths. In 1975, a group of women, apparently moved by the plight of the middle-aged man, attempted to introduce male guarantees, but their amendment was defeated.

In place of the former women's and youth organizations a Women's Liberal Commission and a National Youth Commission, each with its own executive, were established in 1973. In some respects they carry on the functions of the previous organizations, except that they are responsible to caucuses of women or youth delegates respectively at national meetings, instead of being separate, affiliated units.

The Women's Commission has been active in helping women candidates to get nominations in good ridings and in developing policy positions on issues which particularly affect women, although members of the commission admit to its having had limited impact. The problem is that many women who join women's organizations are used to being protected and do not change. The exceptional ones either go directly into active politics or use the women's organization simply as a training ground. Still, that is no doubt an improvement on being in a ghetto as the old Women's Federation was. The Youth Commission has also been active on the policy front. The youth caucus, for example, was the best organized group at the 1978 convention. They got the party to adopt a position on legalizing marijuana and combated a backlash on social policies.

---

[44] LPC, vol. 1137, file: National Executive Meeting, 13-14.2.71.

Communications

As other departments have either disappeared or declined in significance, the communications department has once again become the largest, relatively, in the national office. But even it has had to conform to reduced expectations. From 1975 to 1978, the department produced a stylish magazine of party news and opinion called "*Dialogue*" which appeared from four to seven times a year and replaced the federal-provincial tabloid, *The Canadian Liberal.* It was imaginatively edited by a former Ottawa bureau writer for the *Financial Post,* Audrey Gill, who found, particularly at the beginning, that she had complete freedom in producing the magazine. Early issues rose to the challenge of John deB. Payne, former chairman of the party's communications committee, who urged the magazine to "open the windows", to become "a respository for new ideas" and avoid being simply a "vehicle for apologia of the government."

But as possible election dates drew nearer, members of the parliamentary caucus argued that the more immediate need was for a short newsletter purveying Tory-bashing ammunition for the party faithful to use on their cocktail circuits. In contrast to earlier thought-provoking articles on abortion, the constitution, the status of women, and international terrorism, later issues attempted to "explain" government policies by claiming, for example, that Trudeau's economic program of August 1978 was "neither a radical departure from existing policy nor did it suddenly emerge full-fledged in August." (Why then was even the cabinet taken by surprise?) Or it sought to stir up party enthusiasm with the startlingly immodest claim that, among 163 contemporary world leaders, Trudeau was "without question . . . the most capable, national political leader in the world."[45]

One of the reasons why "*Dialogue*" could be diverted from its founding conception and made to serve more immediate propaganda needs, before being dropped completely, was that the party's communications committee failed to take responsibility for defining the basic goals of the party's publications. The "standing committee on communications and publicity," whose membership is set out in the constitution (clause 8.A.3), makes provision for provincial representatives but only one member of caucus. It followed the fate of most party committees and failed to function effectively. The other communications committee, which was created after the 1972 election, had broader responsibilities and, as we have seen, included a sizable PMO/cabinet/caucus contingent. It was quite unofficial, as far as the party's constitution was concerned, but with

45. Quotations from vol. 1, no. 2, p. 2; vol. 3, no. 7, p. 9; vol. 4, no. 3, p. 3.

the inactivity of the party's standing committee, it became the only body to which the national office communications staff reported.

After the election, a new political communications committee was formed under the chairmanship of James Fleming, MP, and it included only the elected chairman of the LPC standing committee as the somewhat infrequent spokesman for the volunteer wing of the party. It was this new committee that made the decision to publish a party news and propaganda tabloid, called *Ad Lib* which is sent to about 35,000 readers every six weeks. This has been another clear instance of the extent to which the resources of the national office have come under the control of the party's parliamentary-leadership wing. The fact that few Liberals would quarrel with maintaining the party's communications on an election footing only demonstrates how much the volunteer wing has been willing to sacrifice the long-term health of the party to short-run electoral purposes. While *Ad Lib* undoubtedly fills a need, there is also a need for a publication which is primarily the vehicle of the extra-parliamentary party, one that seeks to stimulate policy discussion. Indeed, Audrey Gill recalls that she received a surprising number of requests for the magazine from school libraries. Unfortunately, the party is now less interested in the important public contribution that a magazine like *"Dialogue"* could make.

NATIONAL EXECUTIVE

We have seen a number of instances in which the extra-parliamentary party was treated in cavalier fashion by the parliamentary party. The authority to fight back rests with the convention in its accountability sessions and, between conventions, with the executive and table officers.[46] For the most part, they have tended to be quite docile tigers. The accountability clauses may yet provide the convention with occasion to bare its teeth, but conventions are in session for just three days every two or three years at dates set by the national executive.

According to the constitution, the national executive is mandated "to carry out the aims and purposes of the Liberal Party of Canada" and, more specifically, to make appointments and to refer matters to the Consultative Council.[47] If it wanted to be assertive, the national executive might be inclined to interpret these powers broadly, but in practice it has

[46] *LPC Constitution*, Clause No. 9 H, I.
[47] Clause No. 5B; No. 6 C; No. 7 B; No. 8 A-2, A-4, B, D; No. 9 C, D-9.

not done so, partly for structural reasons.[48] Firstly, it meets just four or five times a year, usually for two days. This obviously militates against its riding herd on a cabinet or caucus which meets every week. Secondly, the federal character of the party works against its sense of cohesion. The national executive includes the presidents of the twelve member associations, whose annual meetings can be held at any time during the year. Consequently, since every national executive meeting includes some new presidents, continuity is difficult to establish. Furthermore, nine of the presidents head organizations which have both federal and provincial responsibilities. Even if they accept the indivisibility of the Liberal party as an article of faith, they inevitably have to give priority to either one level or the other at various times, depending on forthcoming elections, conventions, fund-raising drives, etc. A recurring complaint by other members of the national executive, whose responsibilities are solely federal, is that provincial presidents too often put provincial matters first.

Of the remaining twenty-six members of the national executive, all but five are elected by the biennial convention. (The three financial chairmen—of the Standing Committee on Finance, of the Federal Liberal Agency, and of the National Treasury Committee—are appointed. The leader, of course, is elected at a separate leadership convention. Separate caucuses of youth and women delegates to the convention elect their respective presidents, four regional representatives of the Women's Commission and five vice-presidents of the Youth Commission, all of whom are on the national executive.) In spite of this, they do not feel that they have a strong mandate from the extra-parliamentary party. One of the vice-presidents becomes the chairman of the standing committee on organization and constitution, but apart from that, a literal reading of the constitution would suggest that their primary function is simply to be either male or female, English-speaking or French-speaking in the four possible combinations. (So much for bilinguals and other bi-possibilities!)

The table officers have the advantage over the full executive of meeting once a month and could theoretically provide the cohesion which it lacks. However, they are given no formal authority to act between national executive meetings and, because no minutes are kept on their own meetings, the president has considerable discretion to interpret the sense of these meetings as he sees fit.

Even granting structural problems, the effectiveness of the national executive depends very much on the people involved, especially the presi-

<hr>

[48] Much of the material for this section is based on interviews with Colin Kenny, 29.9.78; David Collenette, 18.8.78; Senator Stanbury, 4.8.78; Senator Frith, 24.8.78; Blair Williams, 3.8.76; Gordon Ashworth, 4.10.79; Lorna Marsden, 13.10.79; Bernard Deschenes, 31.10.78; Micheline Côté, 3.11.78; Confidential Sources.

dent. Because there has rarely been an actual contest for the office, his election is really a formality and so he is without the authority to act on his own as was Dalton Camp, for example, when he won re-election as Progressive Conservative party president in 1966 on the issue of leadership review. The Liberal president's effectiveness consequently depends on the nature of his relationship with the leader. John Nichol and John Connolly were close to Pearson and occasionally gave him pointed advice.[49] None of the three presidents since 1968, however, have been very close to Trudeau. Stanbury speaks of him as having always been cooperative and cordial, but even an irrepressible optimist like Stanbury got so frustrated after a couple of years as president that he spent more time speaking at meetings across the country than he did in Ottawa. Generally, party presidents have been shunted aside by governmental and party bureaucrats. Graham became part of Trudeau's election entourage in 1979 and 1980, but he was singularly disinclined to press the party's point of view on the leader. Apart from Connolly, no party president has also been a member of the cabinet.

The president's counterpart in the British Conservative party is always in a Conservative ministry; no doubt the Liberal party's voice would be strengthened if that practice were followed here. As we saw earlier (pp. 49-51), the standing committees of LPC were originally conceived as a vital part of the party's national structures, but their performance has been very mixed. From 1972 to 1975 they were defunct, the casualties of minority government. The rest of the time, they have been left to define their own objectives without much guidance from the constitution, the national executive or the past performance (when there was any) of their predecessors. The vastness of the country makes it physically difficult to get a committee together on any kind of regular basis. Correspondence has proved to be a poor second best. Frequently committee chairmen have complained at national executive meetings about not having heard from their members in spite of proddings. These problems could be alleviated if the party office were to provide a proper secretariat for the committees; but, because the Bank Street Office has decreased generally in size since 1968 and lacks specifically a policy research department, such support is beyond its present resources.

The only committee which has met steadily over the last few years is the finance committee. Though it does no fund raising itself, it has over-

---

[49]. After a meeting of the party executive in 1964, Nichol, for example, told Pearson that "I would be doing less than my responsibility to yourself and to our Party if I did not write this to you." Diefenbaker was using the flag debate in order to destroy Pearson's reputation, Nichol said. If the government did not stand firm and introduce a motion to limit debate, Diefenbaker would be seen by the public as having routed the Liberals. The government introduced closure three months later. LPC, vol. 739, file: Nichol, John, President - LFC, Nichol to Pearson, 9.9.64.

all responsibility to see that the various systems are in place. The many changes that have come about as a result of the Election Expenses Act have given it a timely function which the other committees lack. By contrast, the chairman of the committee on organization and constitution reported in 1973 that its duties were not defined in the constitution, that very few of its recommendations to the national executive and the national campaign committee had been acted on, and that the national and provincial party offices were better able to do the ongoing work of party organization. He recommended that the committee be abolished, but even that recommendation was ignored. It continues in suspended inactivity along with most of the others. On the other hand, *ad hoc* committees—such as the one on communications—and caucus committees, which exist outside the LPC structures, have been much more active than the party's own standing committees.[50]

With no strong direction coming from within, national executive meetings have been taken up more with routine operations than with fresh initiatives, though in the last few years, considerable time has been spent dealing with the many new demands made on the party by the new Election Expenses legislation. The rest of the time has largely been given to hearing provincial reports, planning future conventions, and wrestling with financial stringencies. Occasionally, the executive has instituted useful studies, such as the 1971 Task Force on the Status of Women in Canada or the 1976 Western Commission to study the party's problems in the West. The latter, however, has been a victim of the caution and secrecy which have recently afflicted the party, for it has yet to be made public. On those comparatively rare occasions when there was a strong consensus within it, the national executive appears to have had some impact. For example, some party strategists favoured an election in the fall of 1977 to take advantage of the party's high standing in the polls. The national executive, however, were sure that the public would see through the sheer opportunism of a premature dissolution and advised against it.

The national executive, its table officers, and its committees ought to perform a key function in acting on behalf of the extra-parliamentary party between conventions, in providing liaison with the parliamentary party and in directing the activities of the national office. Mostly, however, it operates in a kind of vacuum, while the other segments of the party go their own way. When an election approaches and the federal

50. LPC, vol. 1115, file: Al Linden, 1968-69; Gershberg to Linden, 16.10.68; vol. 1137, files: National Executive Meeting, 13-14.2.71, Linden to Stanbury, 3.2.71; National Executive Meeting, 3-4.4.71; vol. 1138, files: National Executive Meeting, 18-19.9.71; National Executive Meeting, 11.3.72; vol. 1140, file: Standing Committee on Organization & Constitution, Memo for National Executive Meeting, 3-4.4.71, Agenda Item 7: Report Re LPC Standing, Special and Ad Hoc Committees.

campaign committee is appointed, the national executive's role is more nebulous than ever.

The extra-parliamentary party has always been scrupulous about keeping the parliamentary wing at arm's length and, consequently, it is represented on the national executive by only a member of caucus and the party leader. That may very well work against the national executive. Because its decisions do not represent a consensus within the party, other co-ordinating bodies then have to be invented. If the parliamentary contingent on the national executive were increased, there would certainly be more arguments, but also more legitimacy for the eventual decisions reached by the national executive. One could see it then as having the credibility to issue formal policy statements on behalf of the entire party and even to issue the party's manifesto. In recent years, as we have seen, the volunteer wing of the party has abdicated its policy role, except when a policy convention is in session. It can be argued, however, that the election manifesto, in particular, is too important for the long-run health of the party and for the government's sense of overall direction (if the party wins the election) to be left to the short-term, expedient uses of the campaign committee.

The other factor that works against the national executive is its practice of holding meetings in closed session, since it thereby denies itself a platform. The parallel is not really with the cabinet and the rule of cabinet secrecy, because each minister already has a political base which counts for far more than that of any member of the executive. Instead, the meetings of the national executive should be seen as the only occasions between conventions when the extra-parliamentary party has a forum for public discussion of party business. If no one listens to the national executive, it is because they have muzzled themselves.

FINANCES AND FUND RAISING

The Election Expenses Act,[51] which came into effect just after the 1974 election, has had a profound impact on all parties. So far, campaign spending practices have been affected much less than fund raising because the spending limits operate primarily as a gentle curb on existing practices with a few extra provisions that the parties are happy to see — such as the ban on media advertising until twenty-nine days before the

---

[51] The Act with its subsequent amendments are 21-22 Elizabeth, ch. 51; 23-24 Elizabeth, ch. 66; 26-27 Elizabeth, ch. 8. 26 Elizabeth, ch. 3.

polling day and the requirement that the media cannot charge political parties higher rates than other buyers.[52]

On the income side, the Act gives public subsidies for the campaign expenses of both individual candidates and national campaigns, and it provides tax credits for political donations of up to $500. The tax credits have lent an air of respectability to what was once regarded as a somewhat shady and suspect operation; indeed, from the taxpayer's point of view, a political contribution is now more attractive than a charitable donation for which one receives only a deduction from taxable income. On the other hand, the disclosure requirement for donations over $100 forced some corporations to reconsider their policies on political contributions, at least initially. Respectability, it would seem, was fine so long as it was only the taxman who knew for sure.

As we noted in chapter 5, fund raising is carried out at three levels: the Treasury Committee collects the big donations from the corporate head offices; sector committees at the provincial level collect smaller amounts from medium-sized companies and individuals, while the constituencies go after the small donors. Before the Act, the Treasury Committee used to collect the big money which, after complex negotiations between the three levels, was distributed to the national and provincial campaign committees, who in turn made allocations to the ridings. While the Treasury Committee was not always able to call the shots, it was pivotal to the whole funding operation.

The new Act has had the effect of markedly altering the financial balance of power within the party. On the one hand, the Treasury Committee does not raise as much money as it used to do during campaigns. On the other hand, the provincial and riding levels find it much easier to get more modest donations from a relatively large number of contributors and have been told not to expect help from Treasury Committee funds.

Soon after the Act came into force, each party made its own internal arrangements about allocating funds to the various levels. The Liberals were anxious to encourage the ridings to become more active in fund raising than they had been in the past, so it was agreed that 50 percent of the money raised locally would be held in trust for the riding's election expenses, 25 percent would go to the riding association for inter-election expenses, and 25 percent would go to the provincial office for its ongoing maintenance. The national level agreed to make no claim on these funds,

52. Much of the material for this section is based on interviews with Senator John Godfrey, 5.11.79; 11.1.80; Torrance Wylie, 25.10.79; Gordon Dryden, 24.10.79. See also, K.Z. Paltiel, "Campaign Financing in Canada and its Reform" in H.R. Penniman, ed., Canada at the Polls: The General Election of 1974, pp. 181-208.

but to rely solely on the Treasury Committee and the national campaign subsidies.

While disclosure has certainly reduced the fund-raising potential of the Treasury Committee, it is difficult to say by how much. In the first reporting year, only seventeen corporations gave $10,000 or more. Old friends, such as Canadian Pacific and Inco at first refused to give anything and the fund raisers of both the older parties feared an organized boycott by some of the big corporations.[53] Over the next few years, however, the number of large corporate donations increased. CP and Inco renewed their traditional generosity and, by 1978, forty-one corporations were making contributions of $10,000 or more. A number of companies still hold out. Chief among these are the foreign-owned corporations, (see Table 1, pp. 227-231), including those such as IBM and Swifts, which used to make substantial contributions. It is not just the disclosure requirement that has stopped them; even more, it has been the criticism levelled at American multinational corporations during the Watergate investigations. Because corporate donations are illegal in the United States and often indistinguishable from outright bribery in many other parts of the world, many multinationals have simply adopted a blanket policy against making political contributions anywhere. Canadian fund raisers are, for the most part, unable to convince them that in Canada good corporate citizens ought to support the democratic process by contributing to political parties. One of the major exceptions is Gulf Canada, which contributes commensurately with its status as a major Canadian company, in spite of complaints in the United States. Ford of Canada took the position that the party should raise money from individuals. It gradually scaled down its contributions so that by 1979 it had joined the other car manufacturers in making no political donations.

Even among Canadian-owned firms, there are some anomalies. Power Corporation, a large holding company, and the companies it controls, such as Consolidated Bathurst and Investors Group, give considerable support between elections, whereas its rival, Argus, and its companies (Dominion Stores, Massey-Ferguson), do not. Bell Canada is sensitive about being a government-regulated utility and contributes only through its subsidiary, Northern Telecom. Abitibi and its score of companies each give $500; collectively, they get a much larger tax credit than would a parent company giving a straight $10,000. Most companies are careful to give the same amount to both the Liberal and Conservative parties. (Occasionally an administrative slip-up gives the impression that a company has favoured one party over the other. In 1978, for instance, Steel Company of Canada was recorded as having given twice as much to the Liber-

[53] *Registered Party Fiscal Period Returns,* 1974-75, 1975-76, 1977, 1978. Whitaker, p. 200.

Table 1 **CONTRIBUTIONS TO LPC BY CANADA'S TOP 100 COMPANIES (1978)**

Wholly Owned by Foreign Parent

Rank	Company	Parent	Donation
1	General Motors of Canada	US	—
9	Chrysler Canada	US	—
19	Canada Safeway	US	—
31	F.W. Woolworth	US	—
37	IBM Canada	US	—
42	Alberta and Southern Gas	US	—
43	International Harvester Co. of Canada	US	—
44	Ensite	US	—
45	Mitsubishi Canada	Japanese	—
48	Canadian International Paper	US	$15,124
64	Kmart Canada	US	—
65	Amoco Canada Petroleum	US	—
66	Mobil Oil Canada	US	—
73	Maple Leaf Mills	US	3,000
74	Canadian Bechtel	US	2,480
81	Sun Oil	US	1,200
82	ITT Canada	US	—
83	Dow Chemical of Canada	US	1,200
90	Swift Canadian	US	—
			($996 in 1977)
91	General Foods	US	—
92	Golden Eagle Canada	UK	450 (2 companies)
95	Mitsui & Co. (Canada)	Japanese	—
97	Marubeni Canada	Japanese	—

Financial Institutions

15	General Motors Acceptance Corp. of Canada	US	—
25	Ford Credit Canada	US	—

SOURCES: Registered Party Fiscal Period Returns to the Chief Electoral Officer, Liberal Party of Canada, 1978. *Canadian Business,* July 1979. *The Financial Post Survey of Industrials,* 1979.

— indicates that a donation was not reported; a donation of $100 or less would not be reported.

w.h. ownership widely held.

CANADA'S TOP 100 COMPANIES (2)
Majority Ownership by Foreign Parent

Rank	Company	Parent	Donation
2	Ford Motor Co. of Canada	US	$10,000
4	Imperial Oil	US	—
10	Shell Canada	Neth/UK	—
12	Gulf Canada	US	27,200
21	Texaco Canada	US	—
39	Canadian General Electric	US	—
51	BP Canada	UK	4,500
58	Canadian Industries Ltd.	UK	240
60	Imasco	UK	10,839
67	Total Petroleum (North America)	French	—
68	Cargill Grain	US	2,500
69	Du Pont of Canada	US	1,000
71	Anglo-Canadian Telephone	US	—
75	Petrofina Canada	Belgian	—
79	Canadian Utilities	US	—
80	British Columbia Telephone	US	—
84	Canada Cement Lafarge	French	10,600
86	Union Carbide Canada	US	2,500
89	Crown Zellerbach Canada	US	5,000
94	The Great Atlantic & Pacific Co. of Canada	US	—
96	Weldwood of Canada	US	4,000

Financial Institutions

10	The Mercantile Bank of Canada	US	400

Canadian Owned or Widely Held

Rank	Company	Ownership	Donation
3	Canadian Pacific	w.h.	$25,000
5	George Weston	54% by Wittington Investments	6,198
6	Alcan Aluminum	w.h.	15,000 from subsidiary
7	Bell Canada	w.h.	—
8	Massey-Ferguson	16% by Argus (Can)	— (5,000 in 1977)
11	The Seagram Co.	34% by Bronfman family trusts	9,500 from subsidiaries
13	Simpsons-Sears	Sears (US)/ Hudson's Bay (Can)	14,900

CANADA'S TOP 100 COMPANIES (3)
Canadian Owned or Widely Held

Rank	Company	Ownership	Donation
14	Inco	w.h.	$ 15,000
15	Dominion Stores	26% by Argus	—
16	TransCanada Pipelines	23% by Dome Petroleum	16,690
17	Provigo	23% by Caisse de dépôt du Québec (Crown corporation)	—
18	MacMillan Bloedel	13% by CPI	13,460
20	Steinberg Inc.	100% by Steinberg family	7,761
22	Hudson's Bay	w.h.	16,798 (6 companies)
23	Canada Packers	21% by W.F. McLean and associates	7,500
24	The Steel Co. of Canada	w.h.	51,200
25	Noranda Mines	w.h.	15,500
26	Moore Corp.	w.h.	5,000
27	Northern Telecom	69% by Bell Canada	27,000
28	International Thomson Organisation	% owned by Thomson family not available	—
29	The Oshawa Group	20% by Ray D. Wolfe	1,200
30	M. Loeb	80% by Provigo	—
32	Abitibi Paper	w.h.	3,500 (6 companies)
33	Canada Development Corp.	68% by Government of Canada	—
34	Domtar	18% by MacMillan-Bloedel	4,000

Canadian Owned or Widely Held

Rank	Company	Ownership	Donation
35	Kelly, Douglas & Co.	66% by Loblaw	— (1,000 in 1977)
36	Genstar	10% by Associated International Cement (UK)	8,734 (7 companies)
38	Dominion Foundries and Steel	w.h.	30,000
40	Consolidated-Bathurst	37% by Power Corp.	14,200
41	Dominion Bridge	43% by Algoma Steel	6,181
46	Burns Food	100% by WCB holdings	2,940
47	Cominco	54% by CPI	—
49	Algoma Steel	54% by CPI	—
50	Westcoast Transmission	32% by PetroCanada	7,500

CANADA'S TOP 100 COMPANIES (4)
Canadian Owned or Widely Held

Rank	Company	Ownership	Donation
52	John Labatt	26% by Brascan	$13,240 (3 companies)
53	The Molson Companies	20% by Malsham Corp.	9,095
54	Canadian Tire	60% by National Trust voting trustee	1,350
55	Woodward Stores	39% by CNW Woodward	—
56	Norcen Energy Resources	w.h.	6,190
57	Hiram Walker Gooderham & Worts	w.h.	—
59	Simpsons	88% by Hudson's Bay	11,200 (4 companies)
61	Consumer's Gas	w.h.	10,790
62	British Columbia Forest Products	28% by Noranda	— ($10,000 in 1977)
63	Husky Oil	49% by Alberta Gas Trunk	5,800
70	Zeller's	57% by Hudson's Bay	1,000
72	Dome Petroleum	25% by Dome Mines	650
77	Dominion Textile	w.h.	8,000
78	Union Gas	w.h.	2,360
88	Falconbridge	37% by McIntyre Mines	— (1,000 in 1977)
93	Westburne International Industries	18% by J.A. Scrymgeour 21% by W.H. Atkinson estate	2,000
98	Alberta Gas Trunk Line	w.h.	15,800
99	Hudson Bay Mining and Smelting	44% by Anglo American Corp. of Canada	5,000
100	Price	99% by Abitibi	—

Financial Institutions

Rank	Company	Ownership	Donation
1	The Royal Bank of Canada	w.h.	$25,000
2	Canadian Imperial Bank of Commerce	w.h.	25,000
3	Bank of Montreal	w.h.	25,000
4	The Bank of Nova Scotia	w.h.	20,000
5	The Toronto-Dominion Bank	w.h.	20,000

CANADA'S TOP 100 COMPANIES (5)

Canadian Owned or Widely Held

Financial Institutions

Rank	Company	Ownership	Donation
6	Banque Canadienne Nationale	w.h.	$6,240
7	Royal Trustco	w.h.	7,240
8	Canada Trustco Mortgage	w.h.	680
9	The Provincial Bank of Canada	w.h.	5,000
10	Canada Permanent Mortgage	w.h.	4,198
11	IAC	w.h.	8,700
13	Victoria and Grey Trust	98% by VGM Trust Co.	4,700
14	National Trust	w.h.	1,400
16	Guaranty Trust Co. of Canada	99% by Traders Group	— (199 in 1977)
17	Bank of British Columbia	w.h.	—
18	Credit Foncier Franco-Canadien	Montreal City & District % not available	—
19	Central & Eastern Trust	26% by H.R. Cohen 24% by L. Ellen	1,000
20	The Montreal City & District Savings Bank	w.h.	—
21	Traders Group	81% by Canadian General Securities	440
22	Montreal Trust	50% by Investors	2,000
23	Investors Group	99% by Power Corp.	1,500 by subsidiary
24	Wood Gundy	w.h.	5,440

als as to the Conservatives; but its total contributions to each party, since reporting became mandatory, have been almost equal.) Only a few private companies do not feel the same obligation to give equal treatment to both. A. Janin, a private Quebec construction company, has given $40,644 to the Liberal party since 1974 and only $2,399 to the Conservatives. Conversely, it cannot be coincidental that Eaton's has supported the Conservatives, but not the Liberals since 1975. John Craig Eaton is an active fund raiser for the Conservative party.

Another reason why it is difficult to tell how much the Act has affected the Treasury Committee's fund-raising ability is that companies now tend to spread their donations more evenly between election and non-election years. Before 1974, the Treasury Committee raised most of its money during election years—exercising a self-imposed limit of $100,000 per company—and was usually able to end up with a surplus which paid the running expenses of the party for a year or two. When the money ran out, twelve to fifteen companies were asked for contributions of between one-quarter and one-fifth of what they had given during the election. After the Act, Liberal and Conservative fund raisers agreed that the limit would be lowered to $50,000 for elections and set at $25,000 between elections. Although fund raising was higher between the 1974 and 1979 elections than it used to be in non-election years, the Treasury Committee did not do nearly as well in the second election: in Ontario, in 1974 they raised $2,250,000 but only $1,150,000 five years later.

In the four and a half years after the Act came into effect, the party collected almost $17 million from all sources. Over the same period, $4.3 million was transferred to the ridings according to the 50/25/25-percent formula and so we can deduce that they were able to raise $5.7 million on their own. $2.4 million was transferred to provincial organizations, including the 25 percent share of constituency fund raising as well as the money coming from the efforts of sector committees. In other words, $6.7 million was raised at the provincial and riding levels, while the balance, or $11.3 million, was raised nationally.

An examination of types of donors also makes clear that the party's fund-raising base has broadened considerably. The number of individual contributors has increased from 9,882 in 1974/75 to 22,350 in 1978 and Table II (see page 000) indicates that the Liberals' most important fund-raising source is individual donors in the $100 to $1,000 range. Next are individuals who give $100 or less and third are the corporate donors of $10,000 or more.

The constituencies raised far more money than they had ever raised before, but not all put forth the same effort. The national office does not list constituency fund-raising totals by province, but it is clear that Quebec has done best, even though grass-roots fund raising was not part of that province's tradition. According to one estimate, by the time the writs were issued in 1979, three-quarters of the Quebec ridings had raised

Table II **CONTRIBUTIONS TO LPC BY CLASS OF CONTRIBUTOR (1978)**

Class of Contributor — **Total Value of Contributions (Number of Contributors)**

Class of Contributor	Less than $100	$100-999	$1,000-4,999	$5,000-9,999	$10,000 †	Total
1. Individuals	$853,146	$1,049,447	$199,123	—	—	$2,101,716
	(18,228)	(3,957)	(165)			(22,350)
2. Public Corporations	34,866	33,966	197,954	$203,568	$584,484	1,054,838
	(172)	(85)	(113)	(33)	(32)	(435)
3. Private Corporations	198,706	460,696	450,292	213,182	110,300	1,433,176
	(3,541)	(696)	(304)	(36)	(9)	(4,586)
4. Governments	—	—	—	—	—	—
5. Trade Unions	—	400	—	—	—	400
		(1)				(1)
6. Corporations without Share Capital	234	325	—	—	—	559
	(3)	(2)				(5)
7. Unincorporated Organizations	11,099	65,576	70,210	5,486	36,634	189,005
	(480)	(188)	(41)	(1)	(3)	(713)
Totals	$1,098,051	$1,610,410	$917,579	$422,236	$731,418	$4,779,694
	(22,424)	(4,929)	(623)	(70)	(44)	(28,090)

SOURCE: Registered Party Fiscal Period Returns to the Chief Electoral Officer, Liberal Party of Canada, 1978.

233

more money than they could spend under the new limits on campaign expenditures. A number of ridings, especially in western Canada, did not begin their fund raising until the campaign had started because then, according to the party formula, they could keep everything that they raised. Also under the new Act, candidates received reimbursement from public funds for part of their campaign expenses. Consequently, the ridings were far more financially independent than they had ever been before and none of the ridings received any money from the Treasury Committee.

While the ridings and the provincial offices are experiencing a quite unaccustomed munificence, the national level has become a poor stepchild. In an attempt to correct some of the imbalance, candidates were asked to give the national party one-third of the rebate they received from public funds for election expenses in 1979. The basic problem, however, is that the national executive has not yet acquired the control over party finances that it was supposed to have been given in 1968. The Treasury Committee, still appointed by the prime minister, continues to hold the purse-strings and the annual budget of LPC is still subject to negotiation with them. If they do not approve of what the national executive wants to do, they will not give it the money. The national executive could be forgiven for despairing of real change ever happening!

CHAPTER 7. POSTSCRIPT: REFORM PRE-EMPTED (1979-80) CONCLUSION

Looking at the history of the Liberal party in perspective, one can clearly see a cyclical pattern of decay and renewal; the decay coming after a number of years in power and the renewal prompted by electoral defeat, either threatened or actual. During the periods of decline, the parliamentary party and the leader have become progressively more isolated from opinion in the party and in the country at large, while the volunteer or extra-parliamentary wing have grown disillusioned and uninterested. The sobering reality of electoral losses has then prompted the parliamentary leadership to take the volunteer wing more seriously, as King did after 1930 and 1943, as Pearson did after 1958 and as Trudeau did after 1972. The extra-parliamentary wing has subsequently become the source of new ideas and fresh faces; but, with the party safely back in power, the whole cycle starts again within a few years.

The other constant theme in Liberal history is the interplay between two *leitmotivs:* an idealistic one that seeks to make the Liberal party into a democratic, reformist, broadly based organization, and a cynical one in which the party is controlled autocratically by an ever-diminishing coterie around the leader; the volunteer wing is then used only for whatever it may contribute to the winning of elections.

This chapter will not attempt to examine in detail the Liberal party's performance in the two elections of 1979 and 1980, but will look at recent developments in light of the questions they raise about the party's future and, particularly, the role of the volunteer wing.

A number of the party's problems are directly attributable to Trudeau's difficulties in adapting to the role of party leader. More specifically, he has often been insensitive or inconsiderate of the needs of people in the party. Several years after having won the leadership, he admitted that, at first, he had regarded the party as a "mechanical thing", as "a powerful lever." Subsequently, he came to recognize that it was also a very fragile, complex organization of human beings that could not be programmed.[1] But his effectiveness as a party leader has suffered from his inaptitude in managing people. He is naturally solitary, in contrast to the gregarious Pearson. ("Pearson was a groupie, Trudeau is a loner", in the words of one man who knew them both.)

In any party, there are informal networks of people who like and respect each other. Being able to rely on such a network often determines a person's influence more than the formal position he or she holds in the party. When Trudeau first became prime minister, a high-ranking party official suggested that he regularly spend five minutes a day on the telephone systematically keeping in touch with one hundred key Liberals throughout the country. This would have provided Trudeau with an informal opinion network similar to that of Mackenzie King—who was much more of a recluse than Trudeau—but the recommendation was never acted upon. (See page 11.) In the face of other competing elites within the party—most notably that of the Hon. John Turner, whose supporters became a kind of opposition from within the party after Turner's resignation from the cabinet—Trudeau retreated into the PMO and came to regard his staff there as the only group whose loyalty was unquestioned.

Trudeau's other major problem as party leader was that of infusing new blood into the party and into the cabinet. Here too, Trudeau has been reluctant to emulate King, who used all his wiles in appealing to a sense of duty in those whom he wished to draft into his service. Both King and Pearson, moreover, often looked to the provincial legislatures, the bureaucracy, and the private sphere for ministerial recruits, whereas Trudeau has mostly restricted himself to a more obvious source, the parliamentary caucus. As the years passed, Trudeau, like Laurier before him, lost his outstanding ministers one by one. While their successors may often have been just as capable in cabinet and in their departments, they were mostly unable to catch the public imagination; nor could they establish political bases in their respective regions or appeal to particular constituencies of opinion within the country or the party. According to one minister, they either spent too much time in Ottawa deciding policy or filled a kind of "royal function"—which they mostly did not know how to exploit politically—at *pro forma* occasions away from Ottawa.

Geographically, the government's base became too narrow. The Atlantic provinces and Quebec were represented in cabinet by effective regional lieutenants, but there were serious gaps in Ontario and the western provinces. Alberta had elected no Liberal MPs in 1974; Manitoba had only nominal representation in the cabinet after the Hon. James Rich-

---

[1]. "Interview with Prime Minister Pierre Elliott Trudeau," *Maclean's* (10.1.77), 4.

ardson resigned; the Hon. Otto Lang worked hard at building up a base in Saskatchewan, but was ultimately unsuccessful; metropolitan Toronto, whose volatile electorate has made and unmade governments in recent years, lacked a potent political voice in cabinet after the Hon. Donald Macdonald's resignation.

Attempts to correct these regional weaknesses in the cabinet were not entirely successful. Three "star" candidates were persuaded to run in Toronto ridings—University of Toronto president, John Evans; Petro-Canada chairman, Maurice Strong; and United Church moderator, Bruce McLeod—but with the delay in calling an election, all three found that they could not keep open the option of entering public life and had to withdraw as candidates.

The other major addition to Liberal ranks was Jack Horner, the blustering Alberta Tory MP, who was enticed into crossing the floor by the promise of becoming the only Alberta minister in the cabinet. Horner had been a most outspoken opponent of one of the government's central pieces of legislation, the Official Languages Act, and many Liberals regarded him as a caricature of an old-line Diefenbaker Tory. According to one of the former members of Cell 13, the Horner affair revealed a profoundly disturbing cynicism in the party: "That was *it* as far as I was concerned."

1979 ELECTION

As the Liberals began to face the possibility of an election, in 1978 or 1979, they encountered a number of problems. The first was a direct fall-out from the successful campaign against the Conservatives' call for a wage and price freeze in 1974. When the Liberal government found it necessary to introduce its own wage and price controls fifteen months later, there were economists who defended its apparent *volte face* on the grounds that the controls, which had been unnecessary in 1974, had become essential in the fall of 1975 in order to break a wage-price spiral psychology. During the 1974 campaign, the Liberals had claimed to have their own contingency plans if controls ever became necessary, but because Trudeau unwisely had gone too far in ridiculing the Conservative plan as a disaster looking for another place to happen, he found it harder than it need have been to justify his government's own control measures fifteen months later. For the first time Trudeau's credibility was called into question and the problem continued to plague him.

The party's second problem was the public's perception of what its concerns were, as revealed by the surveys. In the wake of the Parti Québécois victory in November 1976, national unity became the electorate's principal concern even in the face of declining disposable incomes in late 1976 and early 1977. The Liberals were seen as the party who could best deal with the Quebec problem and, as a result, its standing in the Gallup poll reached heights comparable only to those it achieved after the October Crisis of 1970. The following year, people became much more concerned about their declining purchasing power, even though disposable incomes actually went up steadily through late 1977/78. The problem was psychological or perceptual and left Liberal strategists in a quandary as to how to deal with it.[2]

The third problem was simply that the electorate had got tired of the Liberals and especially Trudeau. In December 1978, a poll published by the *Toronto Star* revealed that, with John Turner as leader of the party, the Conservatives' eight-point lead over the Liberals would be turned into a Liberal four-point lead.[3] This news produced a flurry of speculation about the possibilities of a leadership convention before the election, but Turner's alleged disloyalty had aroused strong opposition to him within the parliamentary party and that option was quickly discarded.

When the polls indicated that the prospects for an election in the spring of 1978 were inauspicious, Trudeau and his closest advisers continued to probe public opinion in search of an issue that would turn the polls around to the party's advantage. The most dramatic was the announcement of harsh economic measures and spending cuts in August 1978 in response to a rightward shift by a public that was concerned about the rapid growth in public expenditure under Trudeau. The announcement took the cabinet and even the minister of finance by surprise. Trudeau and his PMO advisers had apparently become exasperated with the slow and inconclusive way in which the wheels of government decision making turned, but the incident was a startling revelation of how tempting it was to resort to autocratic methods in order to solve political problems. Walter Gordon, discussing Pearson's 1963 reversal of the party's nuclear arms policy, had commented that a prime minister had to be free to change established policies in the light of changed circumstances, but, a prime minister, he said, would not be "likely to announce or to advocate a change in an important policy unless he is reasonably certain his colleagues will support him. Except in extraordinary circumstances, this means discussing this with them in advance. Any alternative to this procedure could lead to dictatorship."[4] Trudeau's ministers did support him —some even pretended that they had been informed in advance—but Gordon's comments were very *à propos*.

When the party's standing in the polls dropped even further, an unprecedented number of by-elections (fifteen) were called for the same

---

[2] Interview with Jerry Grafstein, 24.8.78. Department of Finance, *Economic Review* (April 1979), 135.

[3] 9.12.78.

[4] *A Political Memoir*, p. 117.

day in October 1978. According to the game plan, this mini-election was to act as a catharsis to the profound discontent that the public felt towards the government and Trudeau, much as the 1972 election had done. After venting its anger, the electorate would return to its wonted ways and put a Liberal government in power with another majority. As later events were to show, the strategy made a great deal of sense, except that the electorate were not to be appeased with six by-election losses or even a Liberal minority government. Its appetite had grown since 1972 and it would be satisfied with nothing less than the prime minister's head. For that, it had to wait for a general election.

When the election finally came in 1979, the familiar Davey-Coutts hallmarks were even more pronounced than in 1974. The campaign was tightly controlled by a handful of men and there was no opportunity for countervailing opinions. In response to surveys showing that there had been a dramatic increase in the percentage of the population who were dissatisfied with the direction in which the country was going,[5] Liberal strategists attempted again to revive the leadership issue, but with the variant theme that tough, experienced leadership was needed to deal with the uncertainties of the future.[6]

Trudeau himself played on the public's general malaise by attempting to revive its flagging interest in Quebec separatism. Thus, Liberal strategy described the election as "the lull before Canada's most intense political storm begins: the fight for the very survival of our Canadian confederation."[7] Trudeau's abiding concern about Quebec was genuine, but the national unity issue was perceived by many as a last desperate ploy whose rallying cry had been used once too often. Even Liberals began to suspect that their party thrived more on national *dis*unity.

While the motives behind raising the national unity issue again *may* have been suspect, party strategists played with two other possible issues for reasons that were unquestionably cynical. The surveys showed that the public had an abiding respect for the RCMP even in the face of alleged wrongdoings, so the RCMP was protected and the issue defused by the creation of the McDonald Commission. The surveys also showed that the vast majority of Canadians were unhappy that capital punishment had been abolished, so Otto Lang flew a kite hinting that the government's proposal to introduce the referendum into the Canadian political system gave some hope to the capital punishment lobby. This was in spite of the consistent opposition to capital punishment that Liberal policy conventions and the majority of Liberal MPs had shown for the previous decade and a half.

5. *The Gallup Report*, 4.4.79.
6. See, for example, the advertisement in the *Globe and Mail*, 19.5.79.
7. Jerry Grafstein in the *Toronto Star*, 1.4.79.

The final partisan thrust came when several opposition members were offered senatorships and other government posts, because Liberal candidates were thought to have a good chance of winning the vacated seats once the incumbents were out of the way.[8] It was a sad commentary on the Liberal party that the "new politics" of the 1960s had come to this. The only consolation—and it could hardly console the electorate who mostly voted for one or the other—was that the Conservatives were at least as opportunistic with their promises to sell Petro-Canada, to introduce mortgage deductibility, and to move the Canadian embassy in Israel —the last specifically for the purpose of cracking the Liberals' hold on the Jewish vote in several of Toronto's swing ridings.

When the election came, nothing could overcome the public's overriding desire for change. Not for the first time, the electorate rejected the party whose leader it still regarded as the best man for prime minister. The weakness of the leadership strategy was no less evident than it had been in 1963, when the public preferred Diefenbaker as prime minister, but nevertheless put a Liberal government in power. What the survey-watchers forgot was that even rank-and-file Liberals were far from convinced that the Liberal government's term of office should be renewed. The flirtation with the issue of capital punishment made them even less convinced, and the low state of party morale was evident in reports that the Ontario poll organization, for example, was in worse shape than it had been for almost twenty years.

Although the Liberals sustained minimal losses in the Atlantic provinces and actually gained seats in Quebec, the party lost twenty-three seats in the crucial province of Ontario. The West, where the party's standings fell from thirteen to three, was little short of a disaster.

REBUILDING BEGUN

With defeat, the party's rebuilding cycle began again, although the national executive, true to form, hesitated to take any initiatives itself. For several months, it even procrastinated about setting the date for the policy convention which was due in 1980, because that would inevitably mean a vote on whether to call a leadership convention. Trudeau finally

---

8. *Globe and Mail*, 17.4.79. The party's explanation for the appointment of a Conservative MP to the Senate is that Trudeau had promised not to let the Senate become even more top-heavy with Liberals and would appoint a Conservative to fill a senatorship formerly held by a Conservative. Interview with Gordon Ashworth, 6.3.80.

grasped that nettle himself when, in November, he announced his resignation.

Other initiatives were being taken by others in the party. The caucus, after so many years of having to accede to Liberal cabinets, was moved into a central policy-making role when Trudeau established twenty-one caucus committees to re-examine the party's position in a whole range of policy fields. There were some mutterings from the volunteer wing that caucus ought not to presume that it could establish party policy, but the caucus committees at least filled a void left by the formal structures of LPC.

The most interesting challenge to the party establishment came as a result of the independent initiative of a group who met in Winnipeg in October, 1979. Apart from the ever-diminishing circle of Trudeau's closest advisers and the John Turner loyalists, the meeting brought together the leading activists from the volunteer wing and a number of the reform-minded members of caucus. The press made much of the implicit challenge to Trudeau's leadership, but the meeting was more interesting for what it revealed about the broader concerns of active Liberals.

For Keith Davey and Jim Coutts, the point of winning is as self-evident as it is for the Montreal Expos or the Toronto Maple Leafs; but the Liberals gathered at Winnipeg greeted defeat almost with relief because of the chance it gave the party to redefine its goals. Concern was expressed about the power of the bureaucracy, the weakness of Parliament, and the diminishing relevance of political parties. Several participants argued that it was absolutely necessary for the party to decide on new directions *before* ministers again became the captives of their bureaucracies.

Some of the discussion was a hodge-podge of well-informed comments mixed with the ill-informed—the sort of meeting which tended to confirm cabinet ministers' worst fears of such party meetings, admitted one former PMO official—but the conference provided a forum for a variety of viewpoints to be heard. In the Liberal party, it is *only* at such meetings that East and West can engage in a dialogue, which, on this occasion, was described by Nick Taylor, the Alberta Liberal leader, as the best he had seen in the party for fifteen years. As the meeting concluded, one had the sense that the renewal had begun, that an agenda for the future was beginning to take shape in areas such as individual rights, freedom of information, negative income tax, and proportional representation.

When a leadership convention was called for March, the Winnipeg group initiated a movement of unaligned Liberals who hoped the convention would give serious consideration to policy and would not degenerate into just a media event. All of that was pre-empted, however, with the extraordinary turn of events that culminated in the defeat of the Conservative government on its budget in mid-December.

1980 ELECTION

It is beyond the scope of this book to attempt to uncover all the motives and private deliberations which brought about the defeat. The other parties played their part in what *Globe and Mail* columnist Geoffrey Stevens aptly described as a game of "chicken"—the Conservatives by frustrating MacEachen in his dealings with them as house leader, by not attempting to strike a bargain with the Créditistes, and by not getting all their members to Ottawa in time for the vote; the Créditistes, by abstaining in a fit of pique against the Conservatives whom they had supported until then; the NDP, by being as determined as the Liberals to have all their members present.

It seems clear, however, that the crucial decision to have the Liberal caucus turn out in force to vote for the NDP non-confidence sub-amendment was made by a very small group of people. It was probably Davey, Coutts, MacEachen, Lalonde and Trudeau who decided that the opportunity to force a snap election—which, according to the polls, the Liberals would win—might not come again in that Parliament. There was no consultation with the party's national executive nor with key Liberals throughout the country. In fact, most of those who attempted to call and counsel restraint did not get through. When the Liberal caucus met on the morning of the day before the critical vote, they were genuinely angered by the socially regressive features of the budget, but they did not even discuss what would happen if the government was defeated. They seem to have assumed that, since an election without a Liberal leader was clearly an impossibility, MacEachen, as house leader, would "pull a rabbit out of his hat" (in the words of one member of caucus) and save the government at the last moment. The best opportunity for sober reassessment of a supposedly unplanned headlong plunge into an election would have occurred at the shadow cabinet meeting that was scheduled for Wednesday afternoon. Its cancellation lends credence to the theory that second thoughts were not wanted. The plotters, if indeed they were plotters, were playing a potentially dangerous game because the electorate was in no mood for a mid-winter election. Accordingly, the public's perception of the entire House of Commons rushing off like so many Gadarene swine was a useful one to maintain.

After the defeat, the party had to decide whether to hold a quick leadership convention or to entreat Trudeau to lead the party through one more election campaign. There are a number of indications that the decision had already been made for them. Indeed, the course that these deliberations followed provides a very revealing insight into the balance of forces within the Liberal party. On Friday, the day after the defeat, the caucus met in regional groupings. The West was unanimous in its assessment that the party would get nowhere unless it had a new leader; Ontario was two to one in favour of a convention and even in loyalist

Quebec, twelve to fifteen wanted one. At 11:15, the full caucus met. The only item of business was a speech by Trudeau in which he said, "If I decide to run, I'll really fight, but if you don't want me, I'll understand." According to one report, he was subtly but persuasively preaching for a call. His speech had a dramatic effect on the Ontario caucus which, in its afternoon session, swung sixty-forty in favour of Trudeau. When the full caucus resumed, the parliamentarians decided to ask Trudeau to lead them again.

The national executive, meeting on the weekend, were incensed that caucus had, in effect, left them with no choice but to fall into line. Still, they were determined to register some serious objections about the way in which the last campaign had been conducted. Their invitation to Trudeau was accompanied by several strong recommendations: that the campaign co-chairmen be chosen by the leader in consultation with the national executive; that the provincial executives be allowed to name five regional representatives to the national campaign committee; that the key personnel used to direct the party's advertising in the 1979 campaign (i.e., Jerry Grafstein) be changed; that the leader appoint two policy directors to the campaign committee; that the youth and women's commissions each be asked to recommend a representative for the campaign committee; and that the campaign chairman in each province be appointed with the approval of the provincial executive. When the party president, Senator Graham, presented Trudeau with these recommendations, Torrance Wylie outlined alternative plans for holding a quick leadership convention by means of a series of regional meetings across the country. Trudeau is reported to have been annoyed that the alternative was being seriously considered. (Technically, a convention has to be called at least ninety days prior to its taking place, in order to meet minimum notice requirements for election of delegates as set out in the constitutions of LPC and the provincial organizations. The party's lawyers were of the opinion that, if a leadership convention were called, then the constitutional requirements had to be followed. It would be quite possible, however, for the national executive to call a different sort of meeting other than that outlined in the constitution. One hesitates to ask these Liberal lawyers, though, if the leader thus elected could really have been called a leader or would it have been necessary, in addition, to have come up with another name for the position!)

The national executive's uncharacteristic determination did produce changes from the 1979 campaign, the two most important being the creation of a strategy committee and a platform committee.

The platform committee had forty members, half from the parliamentary wing and half from the extra-parliamentary wing of the party. It was originally expected to publish, in pamphlet form, a comprehensive program drawn from the position papers of the caucus committees and the resolutions of the last policy convention. However, the strategy committee was afraid that the more complex proposals, such as a partial mortgage interest subsidy, would blur the major focus of the campaign, that of attacking the Conservative budget. One news columnist concluded that the platform committee had been a fraud,[9] but an extra-parliamentary representative on the committee claims that it was one of the best things to have happened to the party. For the first time, the extra-parliamentary people had participated in the development of policy for a campaign. Not all their material was used, but, according to Lorna Marsden, LPC vice-president, all of Trudeau's policy announcements on energy, foreign ownership and western agriculture, for example, originated with the platform committee and none conflicted with resolutions passed at the 1978 convention.[10] Ironically, in the peculiar circumstances of the 1980 election, this impromptu creation had more impact than all the elaborate policy deliberations of 1969-70.

The significance of the strategy committee is more difficult to judge at this point. In setting up the strategy committee, with its five regional representatives, Trudeau wanted to show that he had taken seriously the spirit of the national executive's recommendations and was not relying on the same old closed circle. The renaming of campaign positions and the rearrangement of personnel (which was positively Teutonic in the hierarchical complexity of titles) carried the same message. Whereas Lalonde and Davey had been national campaign co-chairman in 1979, this time Trudeau was chairman of both the campaign and the strategy committees; party president, Al Graham, and caucus chairman, Jacques Guilbault, were co-vice-chairmen of the strategy committee; Lalonde and Davey were campaign co-directors; and the party's national director, Gordon Ashworth, was named executive director of the campaign.

In past campaigns, the national campaign committee had been primarily an operational committee and strategy had been developed by the leader and his closest advisers. With the creation of the strategy committee, the key campaign decisions were purportedly made by a larger number of people than had been the case with Keith Davey's previous campaigns. Besides the various chairmen, directors, and regional representatives, the strategy committee also included the president of Red Leaf, Jerry Grafstein (pace the national executive), the platform committee chairman, Allan MacEachen, and youth and women's representatives. The committee met only once by itself and, because other meetings included the ten provincial campaign chairmen, in practice the distinction between it and the national campaign committee was blurred. The strategy committee apparently made some of the key decisions such

9. Geoffrey Stevens, *Globe and Mail*, 11.2.80.
10. Interview, 23.2.80.

as the plan to have the leader lie low throughout the campaign and so minimize the risk of reviving the anti-Trudeau emotions which had been such a feature of the 1979 campaign. They also planned the leader's tour and the timing of major policy announcements. It is debatable whether the patently calculated decision to kill the leaders' debate on television was really taken by Trudeau, his closest advisers, or the whole committee. But the strategy committee at the very least gave the opportunity for contrary views to be expressed, as indeed they were on the debate decision. Furthermore, it had to accept responsibility for the whole tenor of the campaign and that could set a valuable precedent for future campaigns.

Trudeau's astonishing comeback after the party's defeat in 1979 was one of the most extraordinary feats in Canadian political history, even more than Sir John A. Macdonald's return to power in 1878 or Mackenzie King's victory in 1926. But the strategic decision to run negative television attacks on Clark and to bore the electorate in order to avoid anything that might disturb the Liberals' eighteen- to twenty-point lead over the Conservatives in December created a disturbing malaise among many Liberals, the media and the electorate. Liberal strategists, in defence of their campaign, argue that Conservative experience had shown how unwise it was to make specific, highly visible promises that were not part of a comprehensive, well-planned program. Accordingly, the Liberal platform committee adopted the rule that it would not announce any policies unless it could also give an indication of the financing. Inevitably too, because the government had been defeated on its budget, the Liberal campaign had to dwell on the budget's alleged faults.

The longer term danger, however, is that the lessons of 1979/80 will determine the stance for the future—both eyes glued to the polls and both hands carefully covering the party's backside. But, at the same time, both the electorate and the party rank and file may well become increasingly disillusioned with what they regard as the cynical competition of the political parties.

American parties, it is said, currently face a viability crisis. They no longer perform many of the functions classically ascribed to them. 1) Candidates are no longer nominated by those who have worked for the party and have a sense of what it is to be a Democrat or a Republican, but by everyone who chooses to vote in Democratic or Republican primaries. (For many years, the presidential nominating convention was the last holdout for the party power-brokers, but with almost two-thirds of the states now holding some form of primary, the convention has become a largely pro forma gathering to add up the results in the various states.) 2) Proliferating single-issue interest groups are using the referendum process to bypass elected party legislators and officials, while the quadrennial policy pronouncements of the national party platform committees are usually forgotten the day after their convention. 3) The voter's loyalty to a political party and his identification with it have declined steadily in recent years, while in Congress party lines have never counted for much. 4) The most striking loss of function is the electoral one. Almost all statewide races now employ the services of professional campaign management firms which use all the latest marketing and fund-raising skills to run a candidate's entire campaign from the primary through to the general election. The party, as such, does little more than confer a label, either Democrat or Republican.[11]

In Canada, the parliamentary system has given more scope for party government than the Congressional model, though bureaucracies, interest groups and provincial governments have made great inroads into the parties' governing function. Dalton Camp has gone so far as to conclude that, apart from its parliamentary role, the only essential job of a party is to choose the leader. "Anyone who wants to change anything [else] these days, whether it's foreign policy or the status of women, will avoid political parties as a means of doing it."[12] But Canadian parties still play an important role in elections, not only by giving points of reference (even if ambiguous) to the voters, but also in running campaigns and, under the new legislation, in collecting money for candidates. Since an individual candidate's fate is largely determined by national or provincial trends, there is little scope in Canada for the services of a campaign management firm. The federal and provincial party organizations certainly use the specialized skills of advertisers and survey researchers, but, as we saw in the previous chapter, the purpose of setting up Red Leaf was to give the party *increased* control over its campaign advertising.

Canadian parties, however, do face a more subtle challenge which arises out of the realities of contemporary electoral technology. As election campaigns have become more sophisticated, the parties, while attempting to exploit the possibilities offered by television, opinion surveys and jet-age transportation, have become the captives of the very technologies which they seek to control. The accepted wisdom is that the only campaign which sinks into the public consciousness is one that endlessly reiterates a few points, allowing no room for detail or complexity. Television with its thirty-second clips accentuates the need to give a narrow, personalized focus to a campaign and makes the negative, personal attack more effective than the positive, broad program, which simply cannot be dealt with on television. These maxims for campaigners have always had their place in election campaigns, but technology has pushed

---

[11]. R.K. Scott and R.J. Hrebenar, *Parties in Crisis: Party Politics in America*, chap. 1.

[12]. "Are political parties obsolete?", *Saturday Night* (May 1969), 24-25. See also John Meisel, "The Decline of Party in Canada" in H.G. Thorburn, ed., *Party Politics in Canada*, 4th ed., pp. 119-135.

the parties ever further in that direction. In 1980, for example, the Liberals conducted elaborate market research to test their television ads. The studies showed that the undecided, marginally interested voter liked the hard-hitting attacks on Joe Clark best. When people within the party were shown the same set of advertisements, they preferred the softer, more positive ones. But it was the undecided vote that counted, so the negative ads were run.

The danger is that the battle may be won at the cost of losing the war. Many voters, including many Liberals, were disgusted with the 1980 campaign and that was probably reflected in the lower turnout on election day. The fault lay not only with the Liberals. The early Conservative ads featured unflattering portrayals of Trudeau in an attempt to revive the public's 1978-79 antipathy to him.

THE FUTURE

A superficial conclusion to be drawn from the 1980 election is that the traditional party organization has become expendable, that it can all be done with surveys and mirrors that transmogrify the leader's style from one election to another. Indeed, early in the campaign, one of the key Ontario organizers admitted that improvements in campaign organization over 1979 were probably not going to have any bearing on the outcome, that they were going to win anyway. When the election was over, however, he was relieved to note that his job still had some validity after all. According to the admittedly impressionistic and subjective estimate of LPC(O), eight Ontario ridings were lost through poor local organization and inferior candidates. On the other hand, an equal number were won through good local organization and help which came from the provincial level. In the larger perspective, it is surely no coincidence that the Liberals benefited from Conservative losses in the eastern half of the country where the volunteer wing really exists at the riding level. In the two most western provinces, where it does not, the Conservative decline was accompanied by a rise in the NDP vote or in the level of abstentions.

Secondly, a governing party (or "ministerialist party", to use Whitaker's term) that lacks a strong volunteer wing becomes extremely vulnerable when it loses office. After May 1979, many of those who, at least nominally, worked full-time for the Liberal party—ministers, MPs and their assistants—had to concentrate on rebuilding their own careers and left to the volunteer wing the job of rebuilding the party. However, even the volunteer wing runs the risk of becoming just a party of notables who represent no one apart from themselves, if the party lacks a strong base in the ridings. (One has only to note the number of key Ontario Liberals who have offices in the one-quarter square kilometre of downtown Toronto bounded by Yonge, Wellington, York and Richmond Streets to realize how narrow the apex of the party is.)

Thirdly, a strong volunteer wing *should* act both as a brake on those who are tempted to go after the short-term gains and as a reference point in the midst of opportunism. The alternative, that of changing the party's course with every shift in the merry little breezes of public opinion, means that, over the longer term, the party comes to stand for nothing in the public mind. This, we argued in chapter 4, is already the fate of the Liberals in the West. As one long-term Liberal activist has said, "Our society is now too complex to be governed by a small, isolated impervious clique." The only corrective mechanism is "a party with an active, imaginative and broadly based non-parliamentary wing."

But people have to *believe* in a party if they are going to give it their time and energy, particularly at the riding level. The "new politics" of the 1960s was surely correct in arguing that a party cannot be built solely on patronage and the vicarious delights of being a member of the party in power. Or, as Trudeau himself said in 1976, "You can't organize without fire in your bellies, without faith in something, and the reason we are not growing stronger in organization and drawing new sections of the population into our party may be a more worrisome sign of the fact that the Liberals don't have a sense of mission and a sense of desire to guide the destinies of this country in the next quarter of a century."[13]

That is why it is so vital for the health of the Liberal party and of the Canadian body politic in general that the Liberal reform movement, born of defeat, continue through victory.

The obstacles are considerable. The election showed that the cynical, autocratic *leitmotiv* was the dominant one. Furthermore the party is blessed with a leader who has, in the past, shown only sporadic interest in the extra-parliamentary wing of the party; a cabinet whose members have more confidence in their bureaucracies than the party (if past experience is any guide); the "kneebusters" in the PMO (as one Liberal describes them) who are positively hostile to an active volunteer wing; a national office which has inadequate resources to service the party; a rank and file that has so often been no more than lukewarm about its own role. Michels' Iron Law of Oligarchy is as powerful a force as ever!

The problems revealed by the 1979 election, however, remain as pressing as ever. The government still needs an agenda and an influx of fresh

---

13. *Globe and Mail,* 4.10.76.

ideas if it is to avoid the drift it experienced after winning majorities in 1968 and 1974. Secondly, the appalling weakness of the party in western Canada has become even graver.

Experience has shown conclusively that the West cannot be seduced with the promise of a slice of power if only western voters would deign to elect Liberal MPs; nor does the record from Hazen Argue to Jack Horner prove that there is much to be gained by dangling similar enticements before the MPs of other parties. The Liberal party will revive in the West only when westerners come to see it as a genuine vehicle for western aspirations, not just something to be manipulated to suit the designs of Ottawa lever-pullers. A noisy and rebellious western Liberal wing that sent the party establishment running for cover would probably be a reassuring (if unlikely) sign of health in the party.

If the party is to break the cycle of renewal in opposition and decline in government, it might begin by electing a strong, activist executive. Because the president is paid a salary and is virtually guaranteed a senatorship when the party is in power, he is the only full-time member of the executive. Consequently, his leadership is critical if LPC is to have a strong voice. The party also has to gain genuine control over its own inter-election finances, as is the case with the Ontario Liberal Party. Otherwise, it continues to run the risk of seeing its longer term interests sacrificed to short-term campaign needs.

The new platform committee, if it remains in operation, promises to be a more practical vehicle for developing policy than anything the party has had so far. Without abrogating anything from the biennial policy conventions, it could provide the continuity in policy development that has been so lacking in the past. To this end, it might well consider reactivating the consultative council according to its original purposes. By giving equal representation to the parliamentary and extra-parliamentary wings of the party, the platform committee avoids the earlier pitfall of LPC policy deliberations being carried out in splendid, but ineffectual isolation. It may also enable reformers from the volunteer wing to find useful allies within caucus. But if it is to have a serious role, the volunteer members must have expense allowances to attend meetings in Ottawa; otherwise the committee will most certainly go the way of all the similar good intentions of the past. The Liberal parliamentary research office was integrated with the national office after the 1979 election. (In physical terms, the communications department moved into the parliamentary research office across the street from the national office.) That could be a significant development in terms of giving LPC access to a much better funded research staff than it could ever hope to set up itself, or, on the other hand, it could be one more step in the direction of caucus control of LPC.

CONCLUSION

Historians may well conclude that, through the unsettling and dramatic events of 1979/80, the Liberal party did not survive with its soul intact, that the Valhalla of Liberal idealism had finally been engulfed. On the other hand, the opportunity to break the cycle of reform and decay is there. The party has to make its choice.

INTERVIEWS

Al Abraham, 28.6.78
John Aird, 6.9.78
David Anderson, 12.6.75
Gordon Anton, 7.6.75
Gordon Ashworth, 4.10.79, 14.10.79,
  6.3.80
Hon. Monique Bégin, 13.10.79
Harvey Bliss, 14.9.78
Doreen Braverman, 9.6.75
Hon. Norman Cafik, 31.7.70
Charles Campbell, 10.6.75
Colin Campbell, 14.6.74
David Collenette, 23.3.74, 18.8.74
Senator John Connolly, 4.2.75
Sean Conway, 5.9.78
Micheline Côté, 3.11.78
Senator Keith Davey, 15.1.72, 4.2.75,
  12.3.80
John Patrick Day, 2.6.74
Grant Deachman, 11.6.70
Bernard Deschenes, 31.10.78
Gordon Dryden, 3.4.74, 18.9.79,
  4.10.79, 24.10.79
Gordon Edick, 13.6.74
Hon. Hugh Faulkner, 11.6.70, 5.10.79
Gordon Floyd, 29.10.79, 22.2.80
Jean Fortier, 29.10.79
Bob Fowkes, 14.10.79
Claude Frenette, 3.10.79
Senator Royce Frith, 24.8.78
Sydney Gerschberg, 18.3.70, 26.8.77
Audrey Gill, 24.10.79
Senator John Godfrey, 15.8.77, 30.9.77,
  5.11.79
Eddie Goldenberg, 2.9.79
Jerry Grafstein, 24.8.78
Roger Hébert, 2.11.78
Céline Hervieux-Payette, 2.11.78
Lawrence Jolivet, 11.6.75
Colin Kenny, 29.9.78

H.E. Kidd, 14.1.72
Jeff King, 7.9.78
Paul Klie, 18.8.78, 5.5.79, 6.11.79,
  29.2.80
Senator Paul Lafond, 26.8.77
Bruce Laird, 18.8.78
Senator Daniel Lang, 16.3.79
Mr. Justice Linden, 6.9.78
Hon. Donald Macdonald, 12.6.70,
  19.2.80
Lorna Marsden, 13.10.79, 23.2.80
Frank Matheson, 28.6.78
Cameron Millikin, 6.6.75
Senator Gildas Molgat, 1.3.79
John Nichol, 9.6.75
Senator Joan Nieman, 7.9.78
Robert Nixon, 5.9.78
Allan O'Brien, 24.8.77
Geoffrey O'Brien, 14.10.79
John deB Payne, 13.1.72, 3.10.79
Hon. Jack Pickersgill, 13.1.72
Michel Rochon, 8.9.78
Robert Reed, 10.6.74
Hon. John Roberts, 12.6.70, 4.11.77
Gerry Robinson, 4.2.77
Kathy Robinson, 6.9.78, 2.3.80
James Robson, 30.6.78
Robert Russell, 5.6.74
J.R. Scott, 2.9.72
Bill Simpson, 29.6.78
Senator Richard Stanbury, 6.4.70, 4.8.78
Nick Taylor, 6.6.75
Dale Thomson, 3.11.78
Boyd Upper, 19.6.74
Michel Vennat, 11.6.70
Alan Williams, 12.6.75
Blair Williams, 15.7.75, 28.7.76, 29.9.78
Senator Dalia Wood, 1.11.78
Torrance Wylie, 5.8.70, 8.9.71, 21.7.78,
  25.10.79, 22.2.80

INDEX

A. Janin, 232
Abitibi Paper, 226
Accountability
  (see Leadership accountability)
Ad Lib, 220
Advertising, 37-40, 42-43, 57-58, 69, 191, 198, 200-201, 246-247
  (See also Cockfield Brown Inc.; MacLaren Advertising; Walsh Advertising)
Advisory Council, 8-9, 21-22
Advisory groups
  (see Troikas/advisory groups)
Aird, John, 58, 62-64, 113
American political parties, 119, 245-246
Anderson, David (B.C.), 122, 124-125
Anderson, David (Ont.), 24
Andras, Robert, 195, 197
Aquin, François, 98
Argue, Hazen, 43, 72, 123, 249
Argus, 226
Ashworth, Gordon, 216, 244
Asper, I.H. (Izzy), 124, 128-129
Austin, Jack, 205
Axworthy, Lloyd, 128, 135

Balcolm, Eric, 93
Baldwin, Robert, 3
Barbeau Report
  (Report of the Committee on Election Expenses), 62-63
Basford, Ronald, 137-138
Bassett, John, 203
Beauharnois scandal, 7, 59, 174, 181
Bégin, Monique, 103, 211
Bell, Richard, 14
Bell Canada, 226
Belliveau, J.E. (Ned), 92, 191
Bend, Robert, 124, 128
Bennett, R.B., 37
Bennett, W.A.C., 124-125, 131
Bennett, William R., 125, 134
Benson, Edgar, 196
Berry, Adrian, 122, 124
Beveridge, Lord, 4
Bilingualism, 44, 195, 209, 211-212
Blake, Edward, 4
Blakeney, Allan, 131
Boss, Bill, 116
Bouchard, Jacques, 104
Bourassa, Robert, 108, 188
Braverman, Doreen, 125, 210
British political parties, 130, 214-215
  Conservative party, 119
  Labour party, 119, 150
Brokerage politics, 170
Brown, George, 4
Buchanan, Judd, 153
Buckwold, Sidney, 43

Cabinet ministers, 9-12, 18, 21, 45, 50-51, 54-59, 64-67, 71-73, 78-79, 97, 99-100, 103, 135-139, 148-155, 169, 171-173, 176, 181-182, 194-196, 203, 207-211, 248
Cairns, Alan C., 139
Camp, Dalton, 92, 222, 246
Campbell, Douglas, 1, 128
Campbell, Peter, 59, 174
Campney, Ralph, 16, 120
Canadian Liberal, 219
Canadian Pacific, 226
Canadian University Liberal Federation (CULF)
  (see Liberal Youth)
Caouette, Réal, 39
Capital punishment, 239-240
Caucus, 143-144, 148-152, 194, 196, 207, 210, 219-220, 241-243
Cell 13, 24-26, 47, 77, 99, 196
Central Information Office, 7
Chevrier, Lionel, 31, 42, 99
Chrétien, Jean, 100, 195, 200
Clark, Joe, 245
Clark, Joseph, 33
Claxton, Brooke, 9, 10, 12
Clear Grits, 5, 36
Coalition, 124-125, 133
Coates, Daniel, 51
Cockfield Brown Inc., 11-12, 20, 57-58
Collenette, David, 114
Communications committees, 32, 57, 200, 219-220
Connolly, John, 18, 23-24, 31, 55, 61, 66, 222
Consociational democracy, 170
Consolidated-Bathurst, 226
Constitution, 20-22, 49, 74-76, 157-161, 213-214, 218
Consultative Council, 159, 211-214
Conventions:
  1893, 7
  1919, 7, 216
  1948, 74-75, 216
  1961, 19, 75, 79
  1966, 73-76, 139
  1968, 76-80, 141, 144, 183
  1970, 157-172
  1973, 139, 201, 206-208, 211
  1975, 207-210
  1978, 136, 207-211
  1980, 140
Côté, Jean-Pierre, 104
Côté, Micheline, 106
Coutts, James, 203-205, 239-242
Créditistes
  (see Social Credit/Créditistes)
Crerar, T.A., 10
Croll, David, 108
Crosbie, John, 87

Cross, James, 169
Cruickshank, Jack, 93

Daigle, Joseph, 90
Danson, Barney, 151
Davey, James, 142, 193-196, 199
Davey, Keith, 215, 241
  and federal campaign committees, 30-32,
    52-56, 68-73, 92-93, 121-123
  federal campaign committee chairman,
    199-200
  and Liberal party: provincial level, 92-93,
    109, 121-123
  and Liberal Women, 217
  and the "new politics", 46-64, 141
  and 1962 federal election, 30-40
  and 1963 federal election, 42-44
  and 1965 federal election, 64-68
  and 1968 leadership convention, 77
  and 1974 federal election, 203-206
  and 1979 federal election, 239
  and 1980 federal election, 242-244
  and organizational revival, 23-29
  and patronage, 150, 152
Davis, Jack, 69, 137, 195
Davis, William, 111, 187
Demers, Yves, 103
Denis, Azellus, 99
DesBrisay, L.G., 90
Deschatelets, Jean-Paul, 99
Desjardins, Laurent (Larry), 129
Desrochers, Paul, 102
"Dialogue", 206, 219
Dickie, William, 126
Diefenbaker, John, 14, 33-36, 40-44, 64-65,
    72, 240
Dominion Stores, 226
Dryden, Gordon, 16-17, 24-26, 142, 157
Dunning, Charles, 10
Dupuis, Yvon, 99
Duverger, Maurice, 6

Eaton, John Craig, 232
Eaton's, 232
Election expenses
  (see Finances)
Election Expenses Act, 175, 184, 186, 223-234
Electoral system, 2, 120, 139
Elliot, Fraser, 178
Elliott, George, 32-33, 142-143, 200
Embury, John, 136
Evans, John, 237
Everett, Douglas, 135

Favreau, Guy, 42, 98
Federal campaign committees, 30-32, 44-45,
    52-56, 68-73, 92-93, 121-123, 134, 137,
    196-197, 203, 223-224, 243-244
Federal elections, 82-86
  1917, 1

1921, 7
1925, 7
1935, 2, 37
1957, 12-16
1958, 1, 18
1962, 30-40
1963, 40-45
1965, 26, 64-68
1968, 79, 87, 123, 177, 190-192
1972, 178, 196-199
1974, 178-179, 202-205
1979, 1, 235, 237-238
1980, 140, 235, 242-245
Federalism and the French Canadians, 163
Fielding, W.S., 10
Finances, 7, 60, 133-134, 147-148, 173-180,
    208, 214, 224, 232-234
Fisher, Douglas, 197
Fleming, James, 200, 220
Floyd, Gordon, 213, 215
Fogo, Gordon, 9, 11
Ford, Arthur, 37
Ford of Canada, 226
Foreign ownership, 170
Forget, Victor, 103
Fortier, Jean, 102-104
Foulkes, Robert, 215
Franca, Celia, 180
Frenette, Claude, 78, 101-102
Frith, Royce, 24, 33, 196
Fund raising, 11, 23, 51, 57-64, 107, 113-115,
    133-134, 176, 181-186, 224-234
  (See also Treasury Committee)

Gallup poll, 40-43, 188-189, 199
Gardiner, J.G. (Jimmy), 1, 10, 12, 55, 59, 72,
    123, 135
Garson, Graeme, 132
Garson, Stuart, 16, 120
Gay rights, 209-210.
Gibson, Gordon, 122, 124, 130, 134, 194-195,
    216
Giguère, L.G. (Bob), 33, 42, 67, 77
Gill, Audrey, 219-220
Gladstone, W.E., 4
Godfrey, John, 59, 63, 174-186, 208
Gordon, Walter, 19-20, 22-26, 29-35, 40-41,
    46, 60, 64-69, 73-74, 77, 109-110, 122,
    238
Goulet, Paul, 58
Gourd, Robert, 32
Goyer, Jean-Pierre, 78, 103
Grafstein, Jerry, 77, 200-201, 243
Graham, Alasdair, 206, 222, 243-244
Greene, J.J., 66, 191, 195-196
Greene, T.H., 4
Greenspan, David, 36
Guay, Joseph, 135
Guilbault, Jacques, 244
Gulf Canada, 226

Hamilton, Alvin, 72
Harris, Louis, 33, 35
Harris, Walter, 24, 109
Harrison Liberal Conference (1969), 162-165
Haydon, Andrew, 8
Hays, Harry, 43, 126, 137
Hébert, Roger, 105, 215
Hellyer, Paul, 61, 77-78, 197
Hepburn, Mitch, 108
Hervieux-Payette, Céline, 106
Higgins, Robert, 91-92
Hobhouse, L.T., 4
Horler, Hugh, 32
Horner, Jack, 137, 237, 249
Howe, C.D., 10, 12, 16, 24, 32, 59, 109
Huband, Charles, 124, 129
Hunter, David, 124
Hurtig, Mel, 126

IBM Canada, 226
Ilsley, J.L., 10
Inco, 226
Investors Group, 226

Jamieson, Donald, 6, 33, 88-89, 195, 200
Jewett, Pauline, 69, 77
Johnson, Lyndon B., 184
Jolivet, L.C., 65, 122, 137, 212

Kennedy, Betty, 203
Kennedy, Jacqueline, 34
Kennedy, John F., 33-34, 48, 88
Kenny, Colin, 201
Kent, Tom, 33, 40-41
Kidd, H.E. (Bob), 11, 18, 57-58, 215
Kierans, Eric, 78-79
King, W.L.M.:
    and cabinet ministers, 10, 68, 71-72, 135,
        236
    and conventions, 74-75
    and fund raising, 8, 63
    and Liberal party: provincial level, 81, 108
    and Liberalism, 4
    and National Liberal Federation, 10, 235
    and national office, 7, 12
    and patronage, 11
Kingston Study Conference on National Prob-
    lems (1960), 19

Labelle, Maurice, 104
Lafond, Paul, 33
Laing, Arthur, 29, 122, 137, 152-153
Lalonde, Marc, 104, 142, 155, 172, 197, 199,
    205, 242, 244
LaMarsh, Judy, 24, 66, 77, 98
Lambert, Norman, 9, 10-11, 25, 51, 57, 59-60,
    63, 150
Lamontagne, Maurice, 67, 99
Lang, Daniel, 24, 35

Lang, Otto, 28, 43, 72, 123, 133, 136, 211,
    237, 239
Lapointe, Ernest, 10
Laporte, Pierre, 169
Laurier, Sir Wilfrid, 4, 236
Leader
    (see King, W.L.M.; Laurier, Sir Wilfrid;
        Leadership accountability; Pearson,
        L.B. (Mike); St. Laurent, Louis; Tru-
        deau, P.-E.)
Leader's Advisory Committee/ Political Advi-
    sory Committee, 23, 31, 66
Leader's Finance Co-ordinating Committee,
    180
Leadership accountability, 74-75, 95-96, 168-
    169, 208, 220
Lefebvre, Jean-Paul, 102-104
Lesage, Jean, 98, 108
Levasseur, Pierre, 78, 101, 142, 156
Lévesque, René, 98, 100
Lewis, David, 198
Lewis, Stephen, 187
Liberal Agency, 216
"Liberal Charter for the Seventies", 171-172
Liberal Federation of Canada
    (see Liberal Party of Canada)
Liberal Foundation, 184-185
Liberal party:
    provincial level, 13, 16-17, 23, 32, 52, 70-
        72, 81, 221
    Alberta, 29, 43, 120-140
    British Columbia, 29-30, 43, 120-140,
        182-183
    Manitoba, 28, 120-140
    New Brunswick, 1, 26, 89-92, 95
    Newfoundland, 1-2, 26, 87-89
    Nova Scotia, 1, 26, 52, 71, 90, 93-96,
        179
    Ontario, 2, 16-17, 24-25, 70, 108-119,
        130, 132, 177-180, 186, 218
    Prince Edward Island, 1, 26, 90-91, 95
    Quebec, 1-2, 26-28, 32, 39, 42, 70-71,
        96-108, 119, 177-180, 232-234
    Saskatchewan, 1, 28-29, 42-43, 71-72,
        120-140
    separation, 107-108, 111-113, 126, 132-
        139
    riding level, 23-24, 36-40, 56, 67, 92, 101-
        108, 116-119, 225, 232-234, 247
    (See also Advisory Council; Cabinet minis-
        ters; Caucus; Communications com-
        mittees; Consultative Council;
        Conventions; Federal campaign com-
        mittees; Finances; Fund raising; Liberal
        Agency; Liberal Foundation; Liberal
        Union; Liberal Women; Liberal Youth;
        Membership; National executive; Na-
        tional office; Policy; Standing commit-
        tees; Strategy committee; Treasury
        Committee; Troikas/advisory groups)

Liberal Party of Canada/Liberal
    Federation of Canada/National Liberal
    Federation, 8, 31-32, 47, 56, 60-61, 81,
    97, 144, 157-158, 174-186, 193, 199
Liberal Union, 62
Liberal Women, 147, 161, 216-218, 221
Liberal Youth, 147, 161, 216-218, 221
Liberalism, 3-6, 160-161
    British, 3, 4
    European, 4
Linden, Allen, 144, 171, 197, 206-207, 210,
    212
Living in the Seventies, 165
Lougheed, Peter, 120
Lowery, Jack, 124, 126
Lyon, Sterling, 129

McCabe, Michael, 32
Maccagno, Mike, 124
McDonald, David, 122, 239
Macdonald, Donald, 142, 198, 237
Macdonald, Sir John A., 4
Macdonald, Mary, 18
MacEachen, Allan, 31, 94-95, 153-154, 191,
    242, 244
MacEwan, Grant, 124
McGeer, Patrick, 67, 122, 124-125
Mackasey, Bryce, 193, 195
MacLaren Advertising, 32-33, 58, 191, 197-
    198, 200
McLean, Allan, 11
McLeod, Bruce, 237
McLuhan, Marshall, 142-143, 162
McNish, J.D., 109
MacRae, A.D., 37
Mahoney, Pat, 126
Malone, E.C. (Ted), 124, 127-128, 133
Marchand, Jean, 42, 67, 77, 100-105, 179,
    195, 197
Marsden, Lorna, 244
Marsh Report, 4
Martin, Paul, 10, 23, 31, 78, 142
Massey, Vincent, 8-9
Massey-Ferguson, 226
Matthews, A.Bruce, 31, 61, 63
Medicare, 44, 73-74, 163, 182, 210-211
Meerburg, Peter, 95
Meisel, John, 12
Mellander, Rosalind, 206
MPs (see Caucus)
Membership, 105, 117-118, 149, 183
    (See also Liberal Party: riding level)
Merchant, E.F.A. (Tony), 133
Mercier, Honoré, 5
Michels, R., 103
Mill, John Stuart, 4
Ministers (see Cabinet ministers)
Molgat, Gildas, 28-29, 123-124, 131, 200, 205
Mongeau, Jean-Pierre, 104
Mowat, Oliver, 5

Munro, John, 69, 153
Murphy, Charles, 10
Murray, Don and Věra, 188

National Director/National Or-
    ganizer/General Secretary, 21, 23-26, 44
    (See also Ashworth, Gordon; Davey, Keith;
    Fogo, Gordon; Gibson, Gordon; Kidd,
    H.E. (Bob); Lambert, Norman;
    McLean, Allan; O'Brien, Allan; Rob-
    inson, Gerry; Scott, James; Williams,
    Blair; Wylie, Torrance)
National executive, 8, 171, 177, 181, 186,
    199, 205-207, 210, 213-214, 218, 220-224,
    240, 242-243
National Liberal Federation
    (see Liberal Party of Canada)
National Liberal Organization Committee, 7
National Office, 11, 144-148, 154-156, 202,
    206-207, 214-220, 222, 249-250
National Unity, 195, 237-238
National Youth Commission
    (see Liberal Youth)
NDP/CCF 5, 37, 63, 109, 113-115, 125, 128-
    129, 131, 193, 198, 202, 242
"New Politics", 26, 46-64, 76, 141, 240
Nichol, John, 65-66, 78-79, 137, 191, 197, 222
Nicholson, John, 137
Nixon, Robert, 70, 110-112, 187
Northern Telecom, 226
Nuclear arms, 40-45, 238

O'Brien, Allan, 29, 95, 133, 136, 142-143,
    148, 190, 215
O'Connell, Martin, 199-200, 205, 215
October crisis, 166, 168-170, 193, 196
O'Hagan, Richard, 31-32, 58
Oliver, Farquhar, 109
Oliver Quayle, 64
Olson, H.A. (Bud), 126, 137, 169, 195
O'Neil, Pierre, 200
Ostiguy, Jean, 174

Parisien, Yves, 116-117
"Participatory democracy," 141-145, 157-
    173, 183-186, 194, 201-202, 210
Patronage, 10-11, 51-58, 90-94, 99, 101, 122-
    123, 132, 149, 152-154, 156, 240
Pattullo, T.D., 1
Payette, Céline
    (see Hervieux-Payette, Céline)
Payne, John deB., 27, 32, 39, 42, 65, 99, 163-
    164, 186, 219
Pearson, L.B. (Mike):
    and cabinet ministers, 236
    and Liberal party: provincial level, 27-28,
    91, 100, 137
    and Liberalism, 4
    and National Liberal Federation, 23-26,
    215, 235-236

and the "new politics", 46-64, 141
and 1957-58 federal elections, 16-18
and 1961 policy convention, 19-20
and 1962 federal election, 30-40
and 1963 federal election, 41-45
and 1965 federal election, 64-68
and 1966 policy convention, 75
Pearson, Maryon, 34
Pelletier, Gérard, 67, 100
Pépin, Jean-Luc, 42, 100, 195
Pépin-Roberts Report
 (Report of The Task Force on Canadian
  Unity), 139
Perrault, Raymond, 29, 58, 122, 124, 137
Pickersgill, J., 1, 12, 26, 31, 33, 182
Pitfield, Michael, 205
Plant, Paul, 137
Polarization, 1, 16, 124-131
Policy, 64-65, 75, 78-79, 106, 115-116, 127-
  128, 147, 190, 195-196,
  206-214, 224, 241-245, 249
 (See also Bilingualism; Capital pun-
  ishment; Foreign ownership; Harrison
  Liberal Conference; Kingston Study
  Conference on National Problems;
  Medicare; National unity; Nuclear
  arms; Port Hope summer conference;
  Wage and price controls)
Political Cabinet, 139, 149, 154-155
Political Planning Committee, 155
Polls and surveys, 35-36, 42-43, 67, 187-190,
  193, 196, 199, 202-205, 238-240, 242,
  245-246
Port Hope summer conference (1933), 8
Potts, Joseph, 210
Powe, Bruce, 184
Power, C.G. (Chubby), 10, 18, 76
Power Corp., 226
President, 44
 (See also Connolly, John; Fogo, Gordon;
  Graham, Alasdair; Lambert, Norman;
  Massey, Vincent; Matthews, A.Bruce;
  Molgat, Gildas; Nichol, John; Robe-
  rtson, Wishart; Stanbury, Richard)
Prime Minister's Office, 89, 148, 153, 155-
  157, 171, 192-194, 197-200, 204-205, 210,
  214-215
Progressive Conservative party, 6, 13-15, 33-
  36, 40-41, 63-65, 70, 81, 115, 121, 125,
  127-129, 131, 164, 182, 200-202, 226,
  232, 242
Progressives, 5, 7
Provincial associations
 (see Liberal party: provincial level)
Provincial elections, 82-86
Prowse, Harper, 29, 53, 120, 124, 134
Prudham, George, 120, 134
Publications, Liberal party
 (see Ad Lib, Canadian Liberal, "Dialogue")
Pugsley, William, 27

Ralston, J.L., 10
Rattenbury, Nelson, 92
Red Carnation Fund, 185-186
Red Leaf, 200-201, 244, 246
Reform party, 6
Regan, Gerald, 71, 90, 93-94
Ricard, Théogène, 101
Richard, Jean, 116-117
Richardson, Claude, 27
Richardson, James, 129, 135, 237
Rideout, Margaret, 90
Riel, Maurice, 178
Roberts, Edward, 88-89
Roberts, John, 160, 170, 199
Robertson, Gordon, 205
Robertson, Wishart, 12
Robichaud, Louis, 90, 95
Robinson, Gerry, 205, 215
Roblin, Dufferin, 131
Rogers, MacLeod, 52, 93
Rouges, 4
Rouleau, Guy, 99
Rowe, William, 88
RCMP, 239
Russell, Robert, 124, 126, 134

St.Laurent, Louis, 12
Sauvé, Maurice, 27, 100-101
Schreyer, Edward, 1, 128, 131
Scott, Alan, 37
Scott, James, 23-24, 32-33, 35
Scott, Walter, 132
Service, James, 24
Sharp, Mitchell, 74, 77-78, 203
Sinclair, George, 32
Sinclair, James, 120
Smallwood, Joey, 6, 26, 87-89, 95
Smiley, D.V., 138
Smith, G.I. (Ike), 94
Smith, Stuart, 112
Social Credit/Créditistes, 29-30, 39, 42-43,
  124, 126, 130-131, 134, 242
Stanbury, Richard, 24-25, 50, 59, 76, 79, 143-
  157, 164-165, 171-173, 178, 184-185, 190-
  191, 194, 207-208, 215, 222
Stanbury, Robert, 24
Standing committees, 49-51, 201, 210-211,
  219-220, 222-223
Stanfield, Robert, 94, 193, 204
The Steel Co. of Canada, 226
Steuart, David, 124, 127
Stevens, Geoffrey, 242
Stewart, Walter, 197
Strategy committee, 244-245
Strong, Maurice, 237
Swift Canadian, 226

Tandy Advertising, 191
Taylor, Nick, 122, 124, 126, 138, 241
Teillet, Roger-Joseph, 135

Television, 190-191
Thatcher, Colin, 127
Thatcher, Ross, 1, 28-29, 42-43, 72, 74, 121, 123, 127, 131-132, 136
Thompson, Andrew, 70, 74, 109
Thompson, Walter, 109
Tothill, Jev, 124
Treasury Committee, 59, 173-183, 225-234
Troikas/advisory groups, 101-102, 110, 135, 149-153
Trudeau, P.-E.:
  and cabinet ministers, 102, 137-138, 196, 236, 238
  and fund raising, 64, 184-186
  and Liberal party: provincial level, 100-104, 111, 114, 139
  and Liberal party of Canada, 194, 205, 215, 222, 235-236, 248
  and Liberalism, 4
  and 1963 federal election, 42
  and 1965 federal election, 67-68
  and 1968 federal election, 190-192
  and 1968 leadership convention, 77-80
  and 1972 federal election, 198-200
  and 1974 federal election, 203-205
  and 1979 federal election, 239
  and 1980 federal election, 242-245
  and participatory democracy, 141-142, 162-163, 168-169, 171-172, 194
  and party finances, 179
  and patronage, 153
  and P.M.O., 155
  resignation as party leader, 240-241
  resignation as prime minister, 1
  (*See also* Federalism and the French Canadians)
Truth Squad, 44

Turner, John, 27-28, 69, 77-78, 111, 144, 195, 197, 203, 236, 238

Union Nationale, 97
United Farmers of Alberta, 5
Upper, Boyd, 16, 24
Urquhart, Earl, 93

Van Roggen, George, 122, 137
Varley, John, 157-159

Wage and price controls, 202-204, 211-213, 237
Walsh Advertising, 58
Walters, Linda, 51

Walton, Alex, 137
Weber, Max, 141
Whitaker, Reginald, 60, 247
White, T.H., 33
Williams, Allan, 130
Williams, Blair, 200, 205, 215
Winnipeg Meeting (1979), 241
Wintermeyer, John, 25, 109
Winters, Robert, 67, 69, 77-78, 197
Women's Liberal Commission
  (*see* Liberal Women)
Women's Liberal Federation of Canada (WLFC)
  (*see* Liberal Women)
Wood, Dalia, 104-105
Wylie, Torrance, 132, 139, 144, 165, 168, 173, 178, 184, 197, 199, 205, 215-216, 243

Young Liberals
  (*see* Liberal Youth)